JAMES MADISON

The Theory and Practice of
Republican Government

SOCIAL SCIENCE HISTORY

Edited by Stephen Haber and David Brady

Noel Maurer, *The Power and the Money*

David W. Brady and Mathew D. McCubbins, *Party, Process, and Political Change in Congress*

Jeffrey Bortz and Stephen Haber, *The Mexican Economy, 1870–1930*

Edward Beatty, *Institutions and Investment*

Jeremy Baskes, *Indians, Merchants, and Markets*

JAMES MADISON

The Theory and Practice of Republican Government

Edited by

SAMUEL KERNELL

STANFORD UNIVERSITY PRESS

Stanford, California 2003

Stanford University Press
Stanford, California

Printed in the United States of America
on acid-free, archival-quality paper

Library of Congress Cataloging-in-Publication Data

James Madison : the theory and practice of republican
government / edited by Samuel Kernell.
      p. cm.—(Social science history)
   Includes bibliographical references and index.
   ISBN 0-8047-4495-5 (alk. paper)
      1. Madison, James, 1751-1836—Political and social views.
2. United States—Politics and government—1783-1809.
3. United States—Politics and government—Philosophy.
4. Republicanism—United States—History—18th century.
5. Federal government—United States—History—18th
century. 6. Political leadership—United States—History—
18th century. 7. Political science—United States—
History—18th century. I. Kernell, Samuel. II. Series.

E342 .J37 2003
320.97′01 DC21   2003010774

Original Printing 2003

Last figure below indicates year of this printing:
12   11   10   09   08   07   06   05   04   03

Typeset at Stanford University Press in 10.5/13 Bembo

CONTENTS

Jenna Bednar is an assistant professor in the Department of Political Science at the University of Michigan and is an associated faculty member with the Olin Center for Law and Economics at the University of Michigan Law School. Her work has been published in the *Southern California Law Review* and the *International Review of Law and Economics*. She is currently writing a book about the relationship between federalism and democratic theory.

Keith L. Dougherty is an assistant professor of political science at the University of Georgia, with research interests in American political development, federalism, and social choice. His previous publications on the American Founding include: *Collective Action under the Articles of Confederation* (Cambridge University Press, 2001); "Defending the Articles of Confederation," *Public Choice* (2001); "Suppressing Shays' Rebellion" (with Michael Cain), *Journal of Theoretical Politics* (1999); as well as several chapters in edited volumes.

John Ferejohn is the Carolyn S. G. Munro Professor of Political Science and senior fellow of the Hoover Institution at Stanford University. He is coauthor or coeditor of *Pork Barrel Politics; The Personal Vote; Federalism: Can the States Be Trusted; and Constitutional Culture and Democratic Rule*. He has written variously about American politics and political institutions, comparative politics, political theory and mathematical models in politics. He is currently working on issues of comparative constitutional law and jurisprudence as well as on topics of American politics.

Samuel Kernell is a professor of political science at the University of California, San Diego. He is the author of numerous books and articles, including *Going Public: New Strategies of Presidential Leadership* 3d ed. (CQ Press, 1997); and (with Gary C. Jacobson) *Strategy and Choice in Congressional Elections* (Yale, 1983) as well as *The Logic of American Politics* (CQ Press, 2000). His current research concerns the institutional determinants of elections and political career development during the nineteenth and early twentieth centuries.

D. Roderick Kiewiet is Professor of Political Science at the California Institute of Technology. He is the author of *Macroeconomics and Micropolitics: The Electoral Ef-*

fects of Economic Issues (Chicago, 1983); coauthor of *The Logic of Delegation: Congressional Parties and the Appropriations Process* (Chicago, 1991); and *Stealing the Initiative: How State Government Responds to Direct Democracy* (Prentice-Hall, 2000). His recent journal articles and continuing research interests center on American policy and politics, Russian politics, and the history of the early American republic.

Iain McLean is Professor of Politics, Oxford University, and a fellow of Nuffield College. Recent books and papers include *Rational Choice & British Politics: An Analysis of Rhetoric and Manipulation from Peel to Blair* (Oxford University Press, 2001); *International Trade and Political Institutions* (with three coauthors) (Elgar, 2001); and "William H. Riker and the Invention of Heresthetics," *British Journal of Political Science* (July 2002). Current research interests include: heresthetics in political history and public policy.

David Brian Robertson is Professor of Political Science and a fellow in the Public Policy Research Center, University of Missouri—St. Louis. He is the author of *The Development of American Public Policy: The Structure of Policy Restraint* (with Dennis R. Judd); and *Capital, Labor, and State: The Battle for American Labor Markets from the Civil War to the New Deal*; as well as numerous articles and chapters on American political development. He currently is working on two books: *Constituting American Politics: The Framers and America's Political Destiny;* and *Capital, Environment, and State.*

Norman Schofield is the William Taussig Professor of Political Economy at Washington University. His numerous articles and books include *Social Choice and Democracy* (Springer 1985); and *Multiparty Government* (with Michael Laver) (Oxford University Press, 1990, and University of Michigan Press, 1995). He has recently been engaged in attempts to apply these theories to the origins of American political economy.

Randall Strahan is Associate Professor of Political Science at Emory University. He is author of "The Clay Speakership Revisited," *Polity* 32 (summer 2000): 561–93 (with Vincent Moscardelli, Moshe Haspel, and Richard Wike); and "Leadership and Institutional Change in the Nineteenth-Century House," in *Party, Process, and Political Change: New Perspectives on the History of Congress,* ed. David W. Brady and Mathew D. McCubbins (Stanford, 2002). He is currently completing a study of leadership and institutional development in the U.S. House from the early nineteenth century to the present.

Rick K. Wilson is Professor of Political Science at Rice University. His interests focus on institutional analysis and design, decision-making, and political history.

Among his publications, *Congressional Dynamics: Structure, Coordination and Choice in the First American Congress, 1774–1789* (with Calvin Jillson) first identified the collective action problems endemic in America's first Constitution. His current research has taken him to Siberia, where he has conducted experiments relating to trust, fairness, and reciprocity among different ethnic groups.

Daniel Wirls is Associate Professor of Politics at the University of California, Santa Cruz. He is the author of *Buildup: The Politics of Defense in the Reagan Era*; articles and chapters on Congress, American political history, and political behavior; and coauthor of *The Invention of the United States Senate* (Johns Hopkins University Press, forthcoming 2003).

JAMES MADISON

The Theory and Practice of
Republican Government

Chapter 1

Introduction:
James Madison and Political Science

SAMUEL KERNELL

To his apparent discomfort, James Madison came to be celebrated during his lifetime as the "father of the Constitution." Modern-day students of American politics appreciate his contribution somewhat differently, more for the quality of his political science than for his stamp on the Constitution that the above moniker implies. In other words, modern political scientists view James Madison as one of them—another, arguably America's first, political scientist. It is this interest in Madison that motivates the contributors to this volume. Even those essays that examine his politics depict Madison, as one delegate to the Philadelphia Convention summed him up as "a profound politician" combined with a "scholar" (Adair 1974d, 193). We begin, then, with an overview of Madison's scholarship and contributions to political science.

Early in his education, Madison's personal habits and intellectual tastes revealed an individual inclined to scholarship. After graduating from Princeton, Madison stayed another year to continue his studies, during which time he read Adam Smith, David Hume, and other Enlightenment theorists. The next year, Madison returned to Virginia and began studying law to prepare for a career for which he had apparently little enthusiasm. In correspondence, he explained to a college friend that what most interested him was political science: "[T]he principles and modes of government [which] are too important to be disregarded by an inquisitive mind" (*The Papers of James Madison* [hereafter MP] I, 100–101). He then advised his friend to begin his

1

studies by examining "principles of Legislation" and, where necessary, consulting with lawyers and politicians. Years later, Madison followed his own advice by preparing for the Philadelphia Convention through an intensive investigation of the histories of past confederations extending back into antiquity. For this, Madison sent Jefferson a list of nearly two hundred books needed for his research. Jefferson scoured Paris bookstores and shipped to Madison a "literary cargo" that provided the basis for his essay "Of Ancient and Modern Confederacies."

At the Constitutional Convention the scholarly Madison reappears vividly in the accounts of fellow delegates. While others headed straight to a tavern after their long and exhausting daily sessions, Madison returned to his boarding house, where he spent the evening transcribing and filling in his notes on the day's proceedings. He complained privately that this grueling routine was ruining his health (a familiar scholarly complaint) but he persevered. As he explained in the preface to *Notes of the Debates to the Federal Convention of 1787* (Madison 1966), his purpose in this exercise was essentially academic—namely, to provide a record for future generations of scholars on the motivation behind and expectations for the performance of the Constitution's plan of government. In his study of ancient governments, Madison had repeatedly found himself frustrated by the dearth of information on what the constitutional framers of antiquity had in mind as they designed what in some instances struck Madison as peculiar institutional arrangements.

As he approached the political science literature of his day, Madison conveyed the confident, independent judgment of a scholar who had his bearings. Writing as Publius in Number 51 of *The Federalist*, he enlists Montesquieu as the "oracle who is always consulted," but privately he was more reserved, concluding that Montesquieu "lifted the veil from the venerable errors which enslaved opinion, and pointed the way to those luminous truths of which he had but a glimpse himself" (MP 14, 233–34). The constitutional concoctions of Hume and Condorcet were summarily dismissed as the fanciful mind games of those who had no responsibility for designing real governments. Many more vignettes of a mind devoted to dispassionate inquiry into the organization of the civic life in a republic abound in Madison's letters and other writings and in the reports of those who knew him. "All his life," sums up biographer Jack N. Rakove (1990a, 178), Madison "approached political problems with a quizzical intelligence that preferred careful distinctions to simple formulations."

Scholars evaluate one another by the quality of their writing. Madison stands up well to such scrutiny. Easily the most important and famous of his writings are his essays in *The Federalist*, especially Numbers 10 and 51 (both reprinted in the appendix). Although published in newspapers to promote ratification of the Constitution, these essays' deductive arguments, abstract reasoning, and reliance on general principles stand them apart from the campaign rhetoric of scare tactics and sloganeering (Riker 1991) that flowed from both sides of the ratification debate. In contrast, Madison's *Federalist* essays reflect their source origins. Most contained arguments that were developed earlier in more dispassionate contexts more suitable for scholarship. These include a lengthy and deeply comparative essay, "Of Ancient and Modern Confederacies" (1786), and, a year later, "Vices of the Political System of the United States" (1787, see appendix), which examines the different governmental arrangements adopted in the states and by the national government.

The first was written after months of study. Madison compiled his notes into a forty-one-page, pocket-size booklet, perhaps designed to be readily available for floor debates in the legislature or some future constitutional reform convention (Ketcham 1990). Passages from this essay later appear in *Federalist* 14 through 18. "Vices" is briefer and written as a kind of executive summary for fellow nationalists. It highlights the problems of confederation and the kinds of reforms appropriate for strengthening the national government. In addition, it notably introduces a rudimentary version of the factional competition argument that would receive refinement in floor addresses at the Constitutional Convention and assume its canonical form in *Federalist* 10. Finally, published posthumously (intentionally so, in part to provide for his wife's financial security) are Madison's *Notes of Debates in the Federal Convention of 1787* (Madison 1966), which analyzes as well as reports arguments and issues that would receive their initial public airing in *The Federalist*.

One of these writings stands apart from the others and assures Madison a place in the bibliography of essential republican theory. *Federalist* 10 has at times been chided (Epstein 1993) for failing to defend the Constitution's actual provisions and, hence, being largely parenthetic to the ratification debate. Yet over the years a consensus has emerged that it is the most important theoretical statement to come out of this era. In part, this essay's durability can be found in the logic of its argument. Precise yet broadly applicable definitions enter syllogisms from which he deduces the counterintuitive conclusion that the solution to factional tyranny lies in the profusion of factions. Substantively, this conclusion served the ratification's cause by answering critics that republican institutions could survive only in compact, homogeneous settings. For the modern reader, this conclusion provides the theoretical rationale for pluralism.

Within several years Madison's intellectual contribution to the Founding

appeared well established. Thomas Jefferson had assigned it as required reading (the only book of political science on the list) for students at the University of Virginia. Professors were dedicating their early American government textbooks to him (see, for example, Duer 1833). Before embarking on
his trip through America, Alexis de Tocqueville had consulted *The Federalist*
closely (Jardin 1988) and had even planned to end his journey by visiting the
"last of the founders" at his home in Montpelier, but he fell behind sched-
ule and had to return to France. During this half-century, *The Federalist* had
been published dozens of times in America and abroad. Given this early
recognition, one might reasonably assume that the enthusiasm with which
modern students of American politics approach Madison's scholarship reflects his unflagging fame from then until now. The history, however, is actually quite different. Madison's impact on political science is in reality comparatively recent.

From the Civil War until the early twentieth century, Madison's scholarship steadily sank into obscurity, even disrepute. Indeed, the most widely
read biography on Madison of that era "treated him with contempt and
scorn" (Adair 1974c, 112–13). Several editions of *The Federalist* published toward the end of the century "stole twelve of the essays written by Madison
and attributed them to Hamilton, who all . . . the editors agreed was the
greatest of the Founding Fathers" (Adair 1974c, 112–13). The *coup de grace*
came in a 1904 article in the *American Historical Review* (Ford 1904, 97), in
which, when compared with Hamilton, Madison cut a second-rate figure:
"[T]he colorless attitude of the mind, in which his learning threatened to
neutralize his energy" left Madison playing a "small" part at the Convention,
"in spite of the many times that he took part in the debates." About the only
compliment the author managed for this erstwhile "father of the Constitution," was that "this [scholarly] attitude made him the best possible recorder
of the debates as he was in a receptive frame of mind . . . ready to study what
others had to propose."

By the 1880s a recognizable political science literature began emerging
from American universities and so, too, one might think, would interest in
Madison and *The Federalist.* As important as the institutional arrangements of
America's separation of powers were to Woodrow Wilson in *Congressional
Government* in 1885 and Henry Jones Ford (1898) in *The Rise and Growth of
American Politics,* neither examined the theoretical rationale Madison offers
for the institutions they critique. Rather these and the other contemporary
progressives dismissed him as an anachronism. Questioning "whether the
Constitution is still adapted to serve the purposes for which it was intended,"
Wilson (1885, 27 and 215) called for reforms "to make government among

us a straight-forward thing of simple method, single, unstinted power and clear responsibility." As Mahoney (1987, 257) has observed, it was the Framers' success in thwarting tyranny of the majority that allowed this era's scholarly reformers to view popular majorities as safe and deserving control of the levers of a responsive national government. With the publication of two other books a decade later, Madison was brought to the dock to account for the reactionary constitutional system he and his interested co-conspirators had foisted onto the nation. These are J. Allen Smith's *The Spirit of American Government* in 1907 and Charles Beard's classic *An Economic Interpretation of the Constitution of the United States* in 1913. Beard had far greater impact on subsequent scholarship, but both books help explain why even after Madison's rediscovery in these prominent sources, the next generation of political scientists still failed to embrace his political science.

Smith and Beard reflect their era's distinct but related intellectual currents of populism and progressivism, respectively. Both movements sprang from deep dissatisfaction with the state of the nation's civic life and its seeming intractability to reform. For Smith and Beard, the Constitution was the product of a conspiracy of a landed aristocracy intent on limiting the prerogatives of states while hamstringing national action. With Madison they discover the behind-the-scenes ringleader to sustain their conspiracy theory. In *Federalist* 10, which had virtually disappeared along with its author, each found a frank discussion of society's competing interests that must be contained. After heavily excerpting *Federalist* 10, the populist Smith railed against the anti-majoritarian institutions in Washington and their preemption of more responsive state governments. Much of his argument has the coloration and urgency of a polemicist, but Smith strikes home with the theoretical sensibilities that reveal him to be a genuine political scientist working his way through Madison's arguments. One example: where most reformers of the era were antipartisan, Smith berates Madison for setting up a governmental system that spawned irresponsible political parties and hence stripped majorities of a vehicle for controlling national policy. "The fact that under the American form of government the party can not be held accountable for failure to carry out its ante-election pledges has had the natural and inevitable result" (Smith 1907, 210) of allowing parties to issue promises, "recklessly and extravagantly." Party platforms are merely means to winning election rather than a statement of obligations. Smith is working the same distinction between strong and weak political parties as would his contemporary, Ostrogorski (1964), but Smith is more directly locating it in Madison's political science.

Beard offers a progressive, even Marxian slant to the conspiracy. He begins with the same basic aristocratic origins of a constitution designed to im-

pede majority control, and he even quotes the same passages from *Federalist*
10 on the relevance of economic cleavages for factional conflict. But Beard's
real target lies beyond majority rule and is instead a governmental system that
appears incapable of the kinds of regulation of the economy that a modern
industrial nation requires. For Beard *Federalist* 51's separation of powers reinforced by checks and balances constitutes the real problem for twentieth century American politics. Beard does not hesitate to tie Numbers 10 and 51 together by declaring their author to be James Madison, the ringleader. In
fairness, Beard's reading offers Madison certain compensations that eluded
Smith, and contributed to Madison's elevation by future scholars. For one,
Beard acknowledges the brilliance of Number 10 and describes it as the foremost theoretical statement of American politics. While, like Smith, he ignores all but the economic cleavages in that essay, the prominence he gives it
led others to the essay, such as Lippman (1922), who were inclined to read it
more objectively and even appreciatively. Equally important, in associating
factional competition in 10 with constitutional separation of powers in 51—
which, frankly, was easy to do since 51 concludes by reprising much of 10—
Beard presents for the first time the Madisonian model that has over the years
come to encapsulate Madison's theory of governance (Dahl 1956).

From a cursory inspection, the next generation of scholarship appears as
though it turned *Federalist* 10 into a research agenda. Interest groups became
the main topic of investigation, whether in the formation of national, state,
or local policy. And yet, these scholars failed to cite, much less draw upon, the
fundamental rationale for their work—namely, that by design majorities in
America are composed of coalitions among factions. Rice (1924), Merriam
(1931), Odegard (1928), Bentley (1908), Herring (1929), and toward the end,
Latham (1952) all fail to recognize Madison as their intellectual godfather.

This introduces a striking irony about Madison's political science. All recognize the singular quality of *Federalist* 10. Yet this rigorous and elegant syl-
logistic argument on a topic that everyone seems to acknowledge lies at the
foundation of America's pluralism failed to serve as more than a lightning
rod. Rediscovery of Madison's political science came much later, arguably as
late as the 1950s and 1960s, when political scientists turned their analytical
sites from groups to institutions. Apparently *Federalist* 51 and its related essays
(47–50) provided more hypotheses and insights relevant to the research
agenda of this generation's scholars than did Number 10 for those of preceding generations who studied the group basis of politics.

David Truman's 1951 classic, *The Governmental Process*, offers a good
benchmark for Madison's resurgence. Truman opens by directly addressing
the limitations of the literature that fails to take government adequately into

account. Ironically, he frames this literature in Madison's vernacular, "The Alleged Mischiefs of Faction" (chapter 1), which, as noted, the literature itself fails to do. Truman praises Bentley's work as "a well developed argument for concentration on political behavior and the proper object of political research. It develops and elaborates some of the leading ideas found in James Madison's essay Number 10 of *The Federalist*." And yet, Bentley never acknowledges Madison.

To quantify the profession's emerging interest in locating contemporary political science with that of Madison, during the 1950s fifteen articles published in the *American Political Science Review* cited Madison, which is just one short of the total number of such citations in the journal's previous forty-four-year history. And in the next four decades, the *Review*'s citations of Madison have averaged fourteen per year.

If the shift from groups to institutions as the central concern of political science research accounts for Madison's restoration, then the more recent emergence of the "new institutionalism," or the application of microeconomics to institutions, should only serve to burnish Madison's relevance and fame even further. Indeed, during the 1990s twenty *Review* articles, or one every other issue, cited Madison, which is more than in any other decade. Where Madison's political science shared substantive interests with the previous research agendas of twentieth century political science, his attraction to the new institutionalism extends well beyond their common terrain. For one, they share common antecedents. We know that Madison read and invoked Adam Smith and David Hume, both of whom couch their arguments either explicitly or implicitly in utility theory conceptions of individual behavior. And with "interest," whether for groups in society (i.e., factions) or politicians in office, comes attention to incentives. Moreover, McLean (this volume) offers intriguing evidence that Madison's political science was to a degree also informed by the highly analytic and choice theoretic ideas of Condorcet, particularly familiarity with a couple of his counterintuitive principles of interest aggregation (most notably, the jury theorem and cycling). Similarly, Dougherty (this volume) finds numerous instances of Madison in varying contexts sounding remarkably close to Mancur Olson (1965). One does not need to read much into Madison to find him grappling with many of the same issues for which modern scholars rely on choice theory.

One does not, however, need to have Madison reading choice theory to understand how he came to practice it. From his early adulthood, before he became politically active, Madison appears to have been interested in analysis of political institutions. And from his early experiences in public office (see Wilson, this volume), he was thinking about how institutions could be

configured differently to produce different outcomes. As he deliberated reforms, he necessarily thought about their results. And given his inclination
to concentrate on interest and incentives, it was quite natural to work
through these dynamics by addressing how an institutional feature would
lead a politician, a citizen, or a faction to act in a particular way. That is to
say, Madison's political science always generated statements about "balance,"
stability, and durability. In the vernacular of choice theory, Madison's arguments—especially during the productive years from 1785 to 1788—always
conclude with a description of the equilibrium properties of his proposals
(Schwartz 1989). And as a republican theorist, he was interested in "delegation" of authority from citizens to officeholders and in the "agency" responsibilities of representatives, two important concepts in modern research
on institutions. In sum, current scholarship is more indebted to and comfortable with James Madison's political science than was any previous generation. This volume is a natural tribute of scholars acknowledging their debt.

The Essays

None of the authors of the essays here is a "Madison scholar" per se, and only
a couple have written elsewhere about the nation's constitutional development. Yet, as is commonplace these days, all in the course of their research
had encountered something about Madison's ideas or politics that intrigued
or puzzled them. This project afforded all the occasion to turn their research
toward topics that for some were quite distant from their specialty in order
to satisfy their curiosity.

In "Before and after Publius: The Sources and Influence of Madison's Political Thought," Iain McLean explores the intellectual origins of Madison's
ideas on republican theory and constitutional design, as stated in his core
writings beginning with "Notes on Ancient and Modern Confederations"
and ending with *The Federalist*. In light of Madison's influence on modern
political science, McLean pays particular attention to the arguments from in-
cipient game theory—particularly Condorcet—as well as from the congenial arguments of the Scottish Enlightenment. McLean then turns from the
roots of Madison's original ideas to their branches—that is, their effects on
subsequent constitutional development in Europe and the British Empire.
The pre- and post-Publius domains, McLean demonstrates, are not really
separate topics, for this was an era of fervently developing theory and rapidly
democratizing institutions.

In the next chapter, "Madison's Theory of Public Goods," Keith
Dougherty continues McLean's consideration of the choice theoretic con-

tent of Madison's ideas. James Madison had a clear understanding of the logic of collective action, which he developed while observing state behavior during the Revolutionary War. As the war progressed, Madison joined in a movement to end the collective action problem among states, using selective incentives and joint products. This chapter compares Madison's theory of public goods with that of Mancur Olson, investigates the origins of Madison's thinking on the subject, and shows how Madison applied collective action theory to his more famous works on pluralism and republican government.

In "Personal Motives, Constitutional Forms, and the Public Good: Madison on Political Leadership," Randall Strahan portrays Madison's political science as more complex than it is typically represented as being. While Madison sought republican institutions capable of checking or controlling self-interested behavior by both citizens and their leaders, he also aspired to design institutions, Strahan argues, that would motivate political leaders to advance the public good. Staying close to his writings and other statements during the years surrounding the Constitutional Convention, Strahan examines Madison's understanding of the personal motives that lie behind political action, paying particular attention to the respects in which these motivations will differ between officeholders and ordinary citizens. This requires that he consider Madison's arguments about the basic objectives or ends of republican constitutions and what he meant by "the public good." These fundamental ideas, Strahan shows, informed Madison's analysis of constitutional forms in which a republican constitution could be designed both to channel and control the lower or most common motivations of political officeholders and to encourage them to advance the public good. Strahan concludes by comparing Madison's approach with current research on political leadership.

In *Federalist* Numbers 10 and 51, James Madison addressed the problem of configuring republican institutions to thwart tyranny. The first essay grapples with the tyrannical impulses of society's factions and the second, with self-interested politicians who might be tempted to usurp their authority. Each finds a solution in a principle—the first, in factional competition and the second, in separation of powers. These two principles have been universally accepted as representing the theoretical pillars of the Constitution and of Madison's political science, but in the next essay, "'The True Principles of Republican Government': Reassessing James Madison's Political Science," Samuel Kernell concludes that these principles have proven far less compatible than generally assumed, and Madison's reputation as a theorist has suffered for it. In this paper he tests the proposition that in these campaign essays, Madison intentionally conflated his sincere views on republican

governance with campaign rhetoric designed to rebut Anti-Federalist claims
that the Constitution would lead the nation to tyranny. Kernell arrives at this
conclusion after examining the essays' internal consistency, novelty, and
rhetorical value. By these criteria critical arguments within Number 51, but
not Number 10, appear to have been fashioned for the ratification debate and
have little place in Madison's theory of republican institutions. He concludes
that James Madison was less attracted to separation of powers and more willing to rely on pluralism to regulate democracy than is generally assumed.

Whatever Madison's private preferences and motivation for tendering the
particular variant of separation of powers that appears in *Federalist* 51, it remains a compelling conjecture about the likely equilibrium properties of the
institutional arrangements implanted in the new Constitution. John Ferejohn in "Madisonian Separation of Powers" assesses the rationale of Madison's proposition that the legislature is the chief threat to liberty in republican government. All of his prescriptions for checking powers amounted to
separating and checking the power of the legislature. The other branches of
government were thought to have too little natural authority in a republican
scheme, and to be too simple and limited in their powers, to pose any real
threat to liberty. The early experience of the new government showed Madison that these assumptions were incorrect and that the president and his ministers had resources for usurping power that had not been imagined. As a result, over the first decade of the American republic, Madison and his allies
were forced to develop new means of checking and separating powers. This
new project—developing a Madisonian separation of powers—remains as
urgent today as it was in those early tumultuous years.

Whatever the value of the Senate in protecting the constitutional order
against an aggrandizing House of Representatives, at the Convention Madison was preoccupied by the downside of the particular upper chamber promulgated by the small states' delegates and embedded in the compromise.
Daniel Wirls, in "Madison's Dilemma: Revisiting the Relationship between
the Senate and the 'Great Compromise' at the Constitutional Convention,"
re-examines the Great Compromise from Madison's perspective. A properly
constructed Senate and proportional representation were the keystones of
Madison's institutional architecture for a national republic. The deliberations
of the Constitutional Convention quickly showed, however, that these two
keystones could not fit in the same edifice. Madison and some of his fellow
delegates were vexed by the dilemma he helped create, a dilemma that ultimately led to the decision in favor of equal representation for the Senate.
While it would be stretching the truth to argue that representational compromise came into existence because of the Senate, or more precisely, be-

cause of the near consensus on the need for an upper house, Wirls identifies significant ways in which the widespread agreement on the need for a republican Senate in a stronger national system helped define the alternatives from which a compromise would be fashioned. A Senate was crucial to the new system, regardless of any struggles for political power. The Convention made sure that there would be a Senate, even if it were not precisely the one Madison had sought.

In "Constituting a National Interest: Madison against the States' Autonomy," David Brian Robertson returns us to the collective action issues identified by Dougherty. The Constitutional Convention primarily aimed to correct the path of American economic policy. Endowed with varied economic assets, the thirteen new states were pursuing different, often rivalrous and self-defeating economic policies. James Madison proposed to remedy American economic governance by investing national policy-makers with the means and the motive to pursue national economic interests, completely independent of the interests of individual states or coalitions of states. Madison aimed to make a reconstituted national government the sovereign economic authority in the United States. He proposed national policy-making processes that would motivate national policy-makers to pursue national economic interests rather than state interests, including a national veto of state policies that diverged from the national interest. Commercially vulnerable states in the middle of the Confederation resisted Madison's plan, seeking national authority over a more limited set of public goods, protection for the remaining economic prerogatives of the states, and a national economic policy process controlled by a supermajority of the states. Madison's opponents largely won. The Constitution expanded some national economic authority, but it also protected state officials' control over their economic endowments, including slavery, the regulation of domestic markets, resource use, economic development, and the encouragement of enterprise. This understanding of Constitutional design helps explain several unique aspects of American political development, including policy fragmentation, the mixed record of the states in mitigating the effects of capitalist development, the business corporation as a distinct feature of American capitalism, and the absence of a programmatic labor party.

Madison set out to cure state mischief by strengthening the national government, a solution Jenna Bednar argues in the next essay, "The Madisonian Scheme to Control the National Government," that begs the question of how one controls this new power. Madison had a two-pronged approach: interinstitutional conflict and elections. This essay assesses the weaknesses of both approaches. First, the federal structure creates a national power whose members will at times find it attractive to put aside its internal disagreements and to dominate policy in the states. Second, electoral control may fail because voters have no way to articulate their general vision of the federation. The consequence of oversubscription to Madison's political science is that we undervalue judicial review's stabilizing potential.

In the last three essays we turn from Madison's ideas and role in shaping the Constitution to his performance in the political arena. The first surveys Madison's experiences under the Articles of Confederation, and the next two his early efforts under the new republic to influence its subsequent development.

Surveying Madison's unhappy experiences in the Confederation Congress, Rick Wilson, in "Madison at the First Congress: Institutional Design and Lessons from the Continental Congress, 1780–1783," shows clearly that both the purposes and institutional provisions for reform followed as much from his experience as from political theory. Indeed, comparing the state of the literature (a familiar phrase of Madison's) with his reactions to the dilemmas posed by the Confederation, one finds experience providing the clearer lessons about the collective action problems inherent in civic life. This essay examines Madison's experiences in the Continental Congress and links them to his later efforts to change the institutional infrastructure of the federal system. Wilson reveals Madison to have been well aware of several important problems of institutional design that concern contemporary political science. He learned of these problems from firsthand experience, and they in turn influenced the way he thought about institutional change. The hodgepodge institutional arrangements of the Continental Congress were a breeding ground for a variety of collective action problems. It is no wonder that Madison would concentrate his energies on analyzing and repairing the deleterious effects of "private passions" on collective action.

In his diaries, Thomas Jefferson notes that in June of 1790 he helped broker a deal between Secretary of the Treasury Alexander Hamilton and Virginia congressman James Madison that settled two issues that had vexed the First Federal Congress—determining the location of the new nation's capital and the assumption by the federal government of state war debts. The historiography of the Compromise, as well as certain theoretical difficulties, raises serious questions about aspects of Jefferson's account. In his essay "Vote Trading in the First Federal Congress? James Madison and the Compromise of 1790," D. Roderick Kiewiet offers a clearer and more compelling account of what actually happened. Adopting a rational choice framework, he specifies the legislative goals that Madison sought to achieve, the obstacles that stood in his path, and the strategies that he pursued to overcome them. The results portray a Madison mastering the game of bicameral legislative politics that he had been so instrumental in devising.

James Madison and Alexander Hamilton were allies during the ratification campaign but soon came to oppose each other during the formation of the two-party system. In "Madison and the Founding of the Two-Party System," Norman Schofield argues that Hamilton intended to construct a version of what he refers to as the Walpole Equilibrium in the United States. The Walpole Equilibrium in Britain, formed in the 1720s, allowed Britain to stabilize its fiscal system and increase both agricultural and manufacturing output dramatically. Because of the differences between the British and U.S. economies, Hamilton's version would have benefited manufacturing over agriculture, and in response, it drove Madison and Jefferson to create an agrarian, Republican coalition. Hence the appearance of a two-party system. This partisan cleavage remained stable until the slavery crisis of the 1850s. In recounting this partisan history, Schofield has Madison and Jefferson enlisting principles akin to social choice theory in strategically "designing" the political economy of the United States.

Acknowledgment

This volume began as a conference held at UC San Diego on March 16 and 17, 2001, to celebrate James Madison's 250th birthday. The conference and production of this book have been generously supported by UCSD's American Political Institutions Project and the Office of the Dean of Graduate Studies. In addition to the contributors to this volume, the following discussants offered keen stimulation: Gary C. Cox, Elisabeth Gerber, Alan Houston, Gary C. Jacobson, Mathew McCubbins, and Thomas Schwartz. Erik J. Engstrom, Chris den Hartog, and Georgia Kernell generously volunteered their time, their patience, and their cars.

Chapter 2

Before and after Publius: The Sources and Influence of Madison's Political Thought

IAIN MCLEAN

> The important distinction so well understood in America between a
> constitution established by the people, and unalterable by the govern-
> ment; and a law established by the government, and alterable by the
> government, seems to have been little understood and less observed in
> any other country.... Even in Great Britain, where the principles of
> political and civil liberty have been most discussed, and where we hear
> most of the rights of the constitution, it is maintained that the author-
> ity of the parliament is transcendent and uncontrolable, as well with
> regard to the constitution, as the ordinary objects of legislative provi-
> sion.
>> Publius (James Madison), *The Federalist* Number 53, quoted in part by
>> Fabbrini (1999)

The Search for the Real Madison

This chapter aims to establish the sources of Madison's thought, including
the context of the striking but inconsistent claims he makes in *Federalist*
Numbers 10 and 51 (on which see Kernell, this volume); to trace its influence on constitution-making in the Anglophone world; and to explain
why the modern Madison is such a recent discovery. The chapter is organized as follows: This section explains the current fascination with Madison's
thought. Section 2 explores its Scottish, and Section 3 its French, roots. Sections 4 and 5 examine Madison's sincere and strategic arguments for federalism in the light of these roots. Sections 6 and 7 examine why Madisonian
federalism found no echoes in the British Empire nor in France, even though
Madison's best friend helped to write the French constitution. Section 8
concludes.

Madison is the most modern of the ancients. His rise in political science
since the 1950s is surely because we like the way he argues. He thinks like an
economist and reasons like a game theorist (Rakove 2000; see also
Dougherty; Strahan; this volume). So it is with two other political theorists

whose stock has risen rapidly: Hobbes and Hume. Hobbes has been rebadged in the last thirty years as the first game theorist. Hume's writings on politics used to be seen as a very minor footnote to his philosophy, but his *Essays* are now quarried for game-theoretical insights.

Here are some typical pieces of Madisonian economics and game theory:

[T]he most common and durable source of faction has been the various and unequal distribution of property. Those who hold and those who are without property have ever formed distinct interests in society. (*Federalist* Number 10)

In the compound republic of America, the power surrendered by the people is first divided between two distinct governments, and then the portion allotted to each subdivided among distinct and separate departments. Hence a double security arises to the rights of the people. The different governments will control each other, at the same time that each will be controlled by itself. (*Federalist* Number 51)

Mr MADISON considered it as a primary object [of the article dealing with the Electoral College] to render an eventual[1] resort to any part of the Legislature improbable. He was apprehensive that the proposed alteration [viz., throwing the choice of a president, if no candidate had a majority in the Electoral College, into the House rather than the Senate] would turn the attention of the large States too much to the appointment of candidates, instead of aiming at an effectual appointment of the officer [i.e., the president], as the large States would predominate in the Legislature which would have the final choice out of the Candidates. (Speech at the Convention, Sept. 5, 1787, in Madison's own report, Farrand 1966, 2, 513)[2]

He [Benjamin Franklin] then moved that the Constitution be signed by the members and offered the following as a convenient form viz. "Done in Convention by the unanimous consent of *the States* present the 17th of Sept. etc—In Witness whereof we have hereunto subscribed our names."

This ambiguous form had been drawn up by Mr G[ouverneur] M[orris] in order to gain the dissenting members, and put in the hands of Doc.r Franklin that it might have the better chance of success. (From Madison's notes of proceedings on the last day of the Convention. Ibid., 2, 643. Madison was not a heresthetician, but he recognized one when he saw one.)

Of course, this is a tempting but dangerous way to do intellectual history. We read Madison and Jefferson because we find them intellectually congenial. In this regard, we are little different from earlier generations of scholars, who at various times, from their particular vantages, read Madison and his contribution to the founding quite differently than we do today. In fact, as noted in the Introduction Madison's standing as a theorist has ranged from the invisible man whose important *Federalist* essays were attributed to others (i.e. Alexander Hamilton) to the intellectual leader and political strategist of a class conspiracy. But the past is another country; they do things differently there. If we read Madison without paying attention to context, we misread him. Context includes not only the history of how his thought was formed, but also attention to his shifting audiences and the shifting institutions he defended.

Before Publius: Scotsmen and Country Whigs

Until Adair (1943, 1974, 2000), the genealogy of American revolutionary thought seemed perfectly clear. Locke's *Second Treatise of Government* was the seed. By Locke's formula:

> *Reason*, which is that Law [of Nature], teaches all Mankind, who will but consult it, that being all equal and independent, no one ought to harm another in his Life, Health, Liberty, or Possessions. (2d Treatise, §6)

From this Locke derives his propositions that government depends on the consent of the governed, who may withdraw it. The Lockean ancestry of the Declaration of Independence could hardly be clearer.

Montesquieu amplified Locke's remarks on the separation of powers. As Locke repeatedly seeks authority in "the judicious Hooker," even as he sets out an argument that undercuts Hooker, so did all sides in the American revolutionary debate appeal to Montesquieu's doctrine of separation of powers. Therefore the colonists' rebellion against George III fitted comfortably into an extant constitutional doctrine.

Adair (himself of Ulster-Scot origins) pointed out that it was not so simple. American thinkers' knowledge of Locke was filtered through the Scottish Enlightenment, channeled by the Scots professors of Jefferson (William Small at William & Mary) and Madison (John Witherspoon at Princeton). Witherspoon's lectures on moral philosophy, which we may assume that Madison attended, have been transcribed from student notes. Witherspoon expounded the Scottish "moral sense" or "common sense" philosophy thus:

> A sense of moral good and evil, is as really a principle of our nature, as either the gross external or reflex senses, and as truly distinct from both as they are from each other. This moral sense is precisely the same thing with what, in Scripture and common language, we call conscience. (Witherspoon 1982, 78)

Witherspoon was a religious conservative but a political radical (see esp. Witherspoon 1778). However, it was possible to divorce conscience from Scripture.

Himself a student of the Glasgow professor Francis Hutcheson (see Hutcheson 1993), Witherspoon seems to have transmitted the Scots' secular moral thought, and failed to transmit his (or anyone else's) Puritan fervor, to his star student, Madison.

The dominant figures of the Scottish Enlightenment, the close friends David Hume and Adam Smith, dethroned both Locke's social contract and his Protestant theology. Hume shows that social contract reasoning is unsustainable. Both Hume and Smith offer the alternative account of an invisible hand—spontaneous social coordination. Although the phrase and the idea are always attributed to Smith, they are there in Hume as well. Although Witherspoon correctly described Hume as an "infidel writer," Madison may have known Hume's game-theoretic argument that although two neighbors sharing a boggy meadow may be in an assurance game such that they police each other's efforts to drain it, "it is very difficult, and indeed impossible, that a thousand persons should agree in any such action" (Hume 1978 II, iii, 2, vii, "Of the origin of government"; Dougherty, this volume). Adair has pointed to telling echoes of Hume in Madison.[3]

The Scots also secularized Locke. Locke's egalitarianism derives from his Protestant theology, as §6 of the *Second Treatise* immediately goes on to make clear. The reason men are equal is that they are "all the Workmanship of one Omnipotent, and infinitely wise Maker. . . . [T]hey are his Property, whose Workmanship they are, made to last during his, not one anothers Pleasure." Remove that theology and the edifice risks collapse (a probably fatal problem for Nozick's [1974] rights-based Lockean theory). The moral sense philosopher Hutcheson and the infidel Hume offered alternative underpinnings. Hume must have been more congenial than Locke to Madison and Jefferson, struggling against the claims of the established Anglican church in the Virginia legislature. For both of them, the removal of theology from politics was essential to protect rights:

> All the powers of government, legislative, executive, and judiciary, result to the legislative body. The concentrating these in the same hands is precisely the definition of despotic government. It will be no alleviation that these powers will be exercised by a plurality of hands, and not by a single one. 173 despots would surely be as oppressive as one. . . . An *elective despotism* was not the government we fought for. (Jefferson 1781, Query XIII, quoted by Madison in *Federalist* 48, 8; Rakove 1999, 283)

> The Rulers who are guilty of such an encroachment, exceed the commission from which they derive their authority, and are Tyrants. The People who submit to it are governed by laws made neither by themselves nor by an authority derived from them, and are slaves. . . . Who does not see that the same authority which can establish Christianity, in exclusion of all other Religions, may establish with the same ease any particular sect of Christians, in exclusion of all other Sects?

(Madison, "Memorial and Remonstrance against Religious Assessments," 1785,
The Papers of James Madison [hereafter MP] 8, 299–300)

That America is constitutionally barred from an established religion is
probably Madison's and Jefferson's greatest contribution—from Jefferson's
"nature's God" (who or whatever that might be) in the Declaration of Independence, to their jointly authored religious section of the First Amendment.

All the Scots moralists except Hume were "country Whigs." Whig politics had been forged in seventeenth-century Britain, culminating in Locke's
doctrine of the right to resist, and the deposition of King James II, to be replaced by William III, invited to the thrones of England and Scotland by Parliament. Most eighteenth-century British governments professed to support
Whig principles. In the natural way, their opponents might all have claimed
to be Tories. But after the Jacobite rebellions of 1715 and 1745, it was dangerous to proclaim oneself a Tory. Therefore, politicians identified themselves
as "Court" (supporters of the executive) or "Country" (opponents of the executive). We might now, in the shadow of Lipset and Rokkan (1967), prefer
the terms "center" and "periphery." Eighteenth-century British politics were
the politics of a nation-building core and a peripheral resistance. Scotland
and the American colonies were both part of the peripheral resistance. Even
loyal supporters of the union in both countries sometimes resented the way
that unionists treated them. That, essentially, is why the American revolutionaries loved the Scots Enlightenment, and why even a fundamentalist di-
vine like Witherspoon, who hated Hutcheson's liberal religion and Hume's
atheism, nevertheless transmitted their political theory to his star pupil.

Opposition Whig ideology created a myth of the independent yeoman
farmer of Saxon England, crushed by the Norman yoke in 1066, who fought
to regain his ancestral liberties in the English rebellion against Charles I. This
myth fascinated Jefferson—it resonates through his rosy evening correspondence with John Adams and others, up to his very last letter, to Mayor Roger
C. Weightman of Washington, DC, in June 1826 (Adair 2000; Cappon 1959;
Peterson 1984, 1516–17). It made no impact on the more down-to-earth
Madison. What he did draw from country ideology was an appreciation of
politics as faction and of the likelihood that the core would exploit the periphery in its own interest. Hume, no country Whig but the most acute observer of contemporary Scottish politics, sharpened Madison's insights.

The Scots had been more or less coerced into parliamentary union with
England in 1707. The union was nominally voluntary, but the Scottish leaders saw no hope of resistance to the economic and military power of England. The leading opponent of union, Andrew Fletcher of Saltoun, drew

heavily on country Whig ideology (and not at all on what we would now call Scottish nationalism) to justify his positions (Fletcher 1997). No sooner was union achieved than the new British government broke one of the articles of the Treaty of Union—as it seemed to the Scots—by introducing patronage to the Church of Scotland in 1712. This was probably in Hutcheson's mind when he penned a remarkable defense of the right of colonies to rebel in his *System of Moral Philosophy* (1755; see Robbins 1954). Hutcheson answered his own question, "When [is it] that Colonies may rebel?" by answering: when the executive makes oppressive laws. The Americans had obvious reason to turn to the Scots for a lesson in resisting oppressive laws.

The French and American Enlightenments

The American Enlightenment has a French accent too (although it is said that Madison spoke French with a Scottish accent he picked up at Princeton). The American and French revolutions intertwined. The French Revolution was brought on by yet another threat of bankruptcy of the old regime. It was unable to raise enough tax revenue to pay for its military operations in support of the American revolutionaries. It has been suggested (Schofield, this volume) that the American revolutionaries must have received a signal before July 4, 1776, that they would get French help, otherwise the Declaration of Independence would have been inexplicably costly to them.

Two of the American rebels, Franklin and Jefferson, had close and affectionate contacts in the salons of Enlightenment Paris; John Adams also sat there but did not enjoy them. Jefferson succeeded Franklin as American minister to France. Both of them, as natural and social scientists, met the Marquis de Condorcet and empathized with him (an empathy that he returned: see the *Eloge de Franklin* that he wrote upon the death of his fellow academician—Arago and O'Connor 1847, III, 377–423—and his letters to Jefferson in *The Papers of Thomas Jefferson* [hereafter JP]). Condorcet, perpetual secretary of the French Academy of Sciences, was a key figure in the transmission belt between France and America. His good friend Jefferson was another.[4]

Franklin, Jefferson, and Condorcet all shared the wish of David Hume, that politics might be reduced to a science. Condorcet was probably the first person to use the phrase *science politique* (as one of the *sciences morales et politiques),* and Jefferson the first to use it in English as *political science.* As is (only) now well known, Condorcet's *Essai sur l'application de l'analyse* ... (Condorcet 1785) contains two startling innovations. One is the suggestion that both choices and choice procedures may be evaluated according to the probability that they produce the correct outcome. The probability that a decision is correct is an increasing function of two numbers, in Condorcet's notation v and $h - k$. The letter v (for *vérité*) denotes the average probability that a juror is correct; h denotes the number of votes cast on the majority side, and k denotes the number of votes cast on the minority side. So long as v is greater than 0.5, the opinion of the majority is more reliable than that of any one juror. If we know v, we need only set $h - k$ at such a level that the probability of the majority arriving at the wrong decision is held to an acceptably low level. Or we may intensively educate the population to increase their average enlightenment, something about which Condorcet wrote extensively. His efforts to design a secular science-based education system in France finally bore fruit under the Third Republic (1871–1940).

Condorcet's first innovation is now known as the Condorcet jury theorem. His second—more problematic for him but better understood now than the jury theorem—was his discovery of majority-rule cycles and some possible ways out. This is at the heart of Arrow's theorem and the whole discipline of social choice, including the concepts of Condorcet winner and Condorcet efficiency. Jefferson and Madison understood the jury theorem, but they probably did not understand the problem of cycles.

Jefferson not only spent time in Condorcet's company but also bought many of the books of Condorcet and other figures of the Enlightenment, shipping them out to Virginia either for himself or his friends. One such batch reached Madison in 1786, as he was preparing the memoranda on "Notes on Ancient and Modern Confederacies" and "Vices of the Political System of the United States," which were the seed of *Federalist* Numbers 18–20 and 10, respectively, and which informed Madison's thoughts and strategies during the Constitutional Convention. In turn, Jefferson proselytized among French intellectuals in behalf of the American Revolution, sponsoring the production of pro-American books and pamphlets. One of the pro-American propagandists was Condorcet.

In a challenging thesis, McGrath (1983) argues that Madison was a bicameralist because he understood the problem of cyclical majorities. If that were so, Condorcet could be shown to have had enduring influence on the design of institutions—not only in the United States but also anywhere that Madison was read. More cautiously, Schofield (this volume) infers that Madison may have learned of Condorcet's jury theorem through Franklin upon Franklin's return from Paris to Philadelphia in 1785 or 1786, and that might account for Madison's jury-theoretic argument in Number 10, 15–16.

Unfortunately, no such influence can be proven (see also Dougherty, this volume). Elsewhere (McLean and Urken 1992; McLean and Hewitt 1994) we have traced the routes by which Madison may have encountered Condorcet's thought:

1. Jefferson's letter to Madison, anthologized as "The earth belongs in usufruct to the living" (Jefferson 1789), derives both its formulae and its modes of reasoning from Condorcet, not (as the editors of the *Jefferson Papers* believed—JP 15, 390ff) from Richard Gem;

2. Jefferson sent Madison a copy of the *Essai* (Condorcet 1785) to pass on to Edmund Randolph, governor of Virginia. Madison had it for nine days before passing it on. It strains belief that even Madison can have taken in its lessons (from a book that was not even intended for him to read) in that time.

3. Another intermediary between Condorcet and Madison was Philip (Filippo) Mazzei, a disreputable Italian-Virginian who wrote frequently to Madison and Jefferson (usually asking for money or to help settle suits against him; see JP passim; MP passim; Marchione 1975). Jefferson commissioned Mazzei to write a four-volume *Recherches Historiques . . . sur les Etats-Unis* in order to counter anti-American propaganda in Paris (much the same motive as for his own *Notes on . . . Virginia*). Mazzei (or Jefferson) inserted four chapters by Condorcet into this book, which Mazzei sent to Madison, unsuccessfully asking Madison to arrange a translation.

4. Condorcet's four chapters were called *Lettres d'un bourgeois de New Haven à un citoyen de Virginie*. Condorcet was indeed a *bourgeois de New Haven*— he was one of ten distinguished Frenchmen made a freeman of New Haven at a town meeting in 1785. The *citoyen de Virginie* was Mazzei.

5. These New Haven Letters argue for a unicameral national legislature, with representatives selected by a very complicated Condorcet-efficient procedure.

6. Madison refused Mazzei's request to get them translated, saying, "I could not spare the time [and] . . . I did not approve the tendency of it. . . . If your plan of a single Legislature etc. as in Pena. were adopted, I sincerly [*sic*] believe that it would prove the most deadly blow ever given to republicanism" (JM to F. Mazzei, Dec. 10, 1788, MP 11, 388–89; see also JM to Mazzei, Oct. 8, 1788, MP 11, 278–79).

Thus we have found no convincing evidence for the McGrath hypothesis. But Madison may have understood the Condorcet jury theorem. By the jury theorem, the probability of a correct decision is a positive monotonic function of two things, the margin of victory and the "enlightenment" of each juror (McLean and Hewitt 1994, 35–40). Therefore, to improve the quality of decision-making, the writers of constitutions should do two things, not mutually exclusive. They should raise the qualified-majority threshold required before constitutional decisions are ratified. And they should increase the enlightenment of the voters.

One way of doing the latter was to extend the republic. Toward the end of *Federalist* Number 10, Madison notes that in an extended republic the legislature will constitute a smaller proportion of the population than in a state. As is well known, Madison and Jefferson both thought that the state legislatures tended to consist of selfish legislators ("173 despots") who passed destructive legislation. If we compare the texts of "Vices" and *Federalist* 10, both Madison's deletions and his additions tell us about the progress of his thought between April and November 1787. He deletes from "Vices" some pointed examples of the irresponsibility of particular state legislatures, such as his comment that an assemblyman of Rhode Island might not consider the effect of repudiating debts on England or Holland. He also deletes a fierce section on curbing religious passions, no doubt because it would not have helped in the task of *The Federalist*—namely, in persuading the New York convention to ratify the Constitution.

"Vices," which is incomplete, tails off with the statement that

> [an] auxiliary desideratum for the melioration of the Republican form is such a process of elections as will most certainly extract from the mass of the Society the purest and noblest characters which it contains.

Over the following six months,[5] Madison completed the argument: an extended republic was more likely to elect "fit characters" to office than a State, just because, the legislature being smaller in proportion to population, it would fish less deeply in the pool of qualified characters (*Federalist* 10, para. 15 and 16; Schofield, this volume).

It fell to Hamilton to make an equally Condorcetian argument in favor of the Electoral College. In the New Haven Letters, citizens would elect electors, who would be people of superior discernment. These electors would then elect executives. Condorcet produced many such schemes, of baroque elaboration. And so did the Framers. They spent many days in September 1787 on the Electoral College. Madison had severe doubts as to whether the Electoral College as finally designed would work in a Condorcetian way (see his notes on Sept. 5, 1787, quoted above). As we all know, it did not. But Hamilton's defense of the Electoral College in *Federalist* 68 is probabilistic:

> This process of election affords a moral certainty that the office of President will seldom fall to the lot of any man who is not in an eminent degree endowed with the requisite qualifications. (*Federalist* 68, 8)

"Moral certainty" (*certitude morale*) is pure Condorcet (McLean and Hewitt 1994, 36). Did Hamilton get the justification of the Electoral College as a filter from Hume's "Idea of a Perfect Commonwealth," or from Condorcet?[6] Likewise, are paragraphs 15 and 16 of Madison's Number 10 an application of Condorcetian probabilism? Or is it an independent invention of the American Enlightenment?

Federalist 10—"The Same Subject Continued"

Madison was not Hamilton's first choice for coauthor of *The Federalist*. Hamilton first "warmly pressed" Gouverneur Morris, a Pennsylvania delegate but New York resident (MP 10, 259; Adair 1974, 59–60). Morris would have been a more appropriate choice. He was an extreme nationalist, much closer to Hamilton's views than was Madison. However, he declined, and at his third attempt, on or around November 17, 1787, Hamilton brought Madison in as coauthor of the letters of Publius, which had already reached Number 7. There was no time for Madison to present any new material. So he reworked one he had done earlier—namely, "Vices," a note he had prepared and circulated to his fellow Virginia delegates in the spring of 1787. This duly appeared as *Federalist* Number 10 under the singularly uninformative title "The same subject continued." These contextual facts make the neglect of Number 10 as a distinct text until the twentieth century less surprising than it appears at first sight.

By contrast, Madison had until late January 1788 to prepare Numbers 45–51, in which he takes a different line on tyranny and its prevention. Whereas in Number 10 the solution to tyranny is an extensive republic, by Number 51 it has become the separation of powers (see Kernell, this volume). It is the latter that we normally term "Madisonian,"[7] but the former is probably Madison's sincere doctrine. Those scholars since Schattschneider who have noticed the tension have divided into three camps:

1. Madison contradicted himself (e.g., Dahl 1956);
2. Madison changed his mind while writing his numbers of *The Federalist* (Banning 1995);
3. Madison changed his mind, but not until after writing his numbers of *The Federalist* (Kernell, this volume; Schofield 2000a).

Response 1 is correct, but it does not take us very far. In particular, if that was all there was to say, it would be hard to explain why Madison studies, and citations of *The Federalist*,[8] are burgeoning as never before. Response 2 faces an evidence problem. Madison was a third-choice collaborator. Although he and Hamilton were closer than at any other time in their lives, they were not particularly close. The numbers were coming off the press so fast that they did not have time to review each other's contributions before they appeared. The tone of Hamilton's numbers is clearly more nationalistic than that of Madison's. The change from Number 10 to Number 51 cannot be put down to Hamilton. The two numbers differ in that Number 51 appeals to separation of powers, both vertical and horizontal. Hamilton, as his scheme presented at the Convention on June 18 (Farrand 1966, 1, 283–301) and his con-

temptuous dismissal of Montesquieu both show, was even less a friend of separation of powers than was Madison. Occasional attempts to show that
Madison was a states-righter before and after Philadelphia, and a nationalist
only there because he came under Hamilton's "enchantment" (e.g., Oliver
1906), have no support in the record.

Therefore I follow in particular Kernell (this volume) and Schofield
(2000a) in believing that Madison's apparent change of mind while writing
The Federalist was strategic, and his real change of mind came during the
Washington administration, when Hamilton's extreme nationalism and the
disappearance of what seemed in 1787 an urgent foreign threat (cf. *Federalist*
Number 4, 8) turned Madison into a states-righter.

The Strategic Doctrine: *Federalist* 51

The examples of improper or wicked projects in Number 51 are the same as
those in Number 10; only the remedy differs. One example, the one that excited Beard and the Populists, is the states' issuance of paper money and other
measures that privileged debtors against creditors. Madison discusses this at
length in "Vices of the Political Systems of the United States" and in his October 24, 1787, letter to Jefferson, as well as in the two most famous numbers
of *The Federalist*. The other form of tyranny is religious tyranny. That was the
form that Madison and Jefferson had combined to defeat in Virginia. The 173
despots had tried to privilege one religious faction, not one economic faction. Madison had built a coalition of all the non-Episcopalian sects and persuaded them to put aside their normal mutual hatreds (Kernell, this volume;
Rakove 1990a, 34–35).

How did Madison's obsessions fare at the Constitutional Convention?
(Wirls, this volume.) The article reserving the currency to the federal government (Article I, Sect. 10) passed the Convention on August 28 with ease
(Farrand 1966, 2, 439). Religion was not discussed on the floor of the Convention. The provision that no religious test should be required for any federal office (Article VI, sect. 3) was proposed by Charles Pinckney (S.C.) on
August 30 and agreed nem. con. The First Amendment was inserted to meet
the vociferous objections of Jefferson and of Anti-Federalists that the Constitution contained too little protection of rights. Before he changed his
mind on this matter, Madison presumably believed that the mechanism of
Federalist 10—the inability of any sect to dominate the extended republic—
would suffice.

As is well known, *The Federalist* soon became a canonical text of U.S. government. Jefferson told his son-in-law: "Descending from theory to practice

there is no better book than the Federalist." Later he assigned it for the first students of the University of Virginia. (Jefferson to Thomas Mann Randolph, May 30, 1790, JP 16, 449; Minutes of the Board of Visitors, University of Virginia, Mar. 4, 1825, in Peterson 1984, 479). Its canonical status in the United States has never been in doubt since. Too much so, indeed: the habit of some judges of quoting *The Federalist* as if it were part of the Constitution muddies the already turbid waters of original intent still more (Rakove 1990b, passim).

If designers of constitutions since 1787 had read Madison as carefully as political scientists read him now, what would they have drawn from him? From *Federalist* 10 they would have drawn the inference that it is easier to protect liberty, and to ensure enlightened government, in a large state than in a small one. From *Federalist* 45–53, especially Number 51, they would have learned that some antimajoritarian devices might protect liberty. One set of devices was vertical separation of powers between two houses of the legislature and the executive, all three popularly elected in a fashion (one of them directly, two indirectly). Some actions require more than a simple majority in each of the three, for instance amending the Constitution, or overriding a presidential veto. Another set of devices was horizontal separation of powers between lower (state) and higher (federal) levels of government, each with its constitutionally protected sphere of authority. A third, expounded in *The Federalist* not by Madison (who by then was back in Virginia persuading his home state to ratify) but by Hamilton, was the duty of a supreme court to interpret the Constitution. In the next section of this chapter we examine the impact of these lessons in the two countries from which Madison had drawn his ideas: Britain—and hence, the British Empire—and France. Britain, France, and the British colonies in Canada, Australia, and India were all large countries in population, in area, or both. In principle, they were favorable places in which to try out the political prescriptions of *Federalist* 10.

Federalism in the British Empire

British writers took a long time to forgive Americans for winning their war of independence. British Enlightenment thinkers (Tom Paine, Richard Price, Joseph Priestley) supported the American and French revolutions, and therefore were regarded as all but traitors in their home country. The utilitarian revival of political thought in Britain under Bentham and the Mills seems to have owed nothing to American thought. The rights-based approach of Madison and Jefferson was anathema to Jeremy Bentham, who called talk of natural rights nonsense, and imprescriptible natural rights nonsense on stilts. Madisonian political thought, whatever it is, is not utilitarian.

J. S. Mill, it is true, was a less thoroughgoing utilitarian, and as a left-wing liberal, he was quite sympathetic to the U.S. Constitution. He was aware of the
reasons for the failure of government under the Articles of Confederation,
and called *The Federalist* "even now the most instructive treatise we possess
on federal government" (Mill 1972, 369). He was obviously well-read on
American constitutional matters, but his thought was in no way derived from
Madison's.

Alexis de Tocqueville was widely read in Britain, and the first serious British attempt to examine U.S. politics after the Civil War (Gladstone 1878)
opens by citing him. Some Americans were impressed that W. E. Gladstone
no less, the (supposedly) retired leader of the British Liberal Party, should call
the U.S. Constitution "the most wonderful work ever struck off at a given
time by the brain and purpose of man" (ibid., 185). Those who praise Gladstone for his insight into American government may have cited him but cannot have read him. Gladstone's article contains some wise words about the
predictable rise of the United States to an economic superpower, and on the
resilience of the Constitution after the end of the Civil War. He introduces
his American readers to Bagehot's description of British cabinet government. But he reveals no detailed knowledge of the "most wonderful work"
at all. His paper, published in a U.S. review, introduces the British constitution to Americans, not the U.S. Constitution to Britons. His Government of
Ireland ("Home Rule") bills of 1886 and 1893 tackled the most difficult
problem in United Kingdom politics. Gladstone had declared in 1869: "My
mission is to pacify Ireland." For the rest of his life, he devoted more attention to the Irish constitutional problem than to any other, to the fury and
frustration of his own party colleagues. If he had absorbed anything from
Madison or from the study of the U.S. Constitution, one would expect to
find it embodied in either of his two Irish bills. But these bills reveal no
knowledge of federalism, having neither a defensible arrangement for parliamentary representation nor one for finance. As Madison had observed in
Federalist Number 53 (see the epigraph to this chapter), British constitutional
thought was wedded to parliamentary sovereignty. This made it impossible
either for Gladstone or for the designers of constitutions for the British Empire to create a true federation.

The British Empire

Suppose indeed that a diligent British colonial administrator in Gladstone's
generation had wanted to learn about American federalism. What would he
have found in the library? Freeman (1863) announced a four-volume study

of the four cases that "perfectly, or nearly perfectly, realized the Federal idea"—namely, the Achaean League (281–146 B.C.); Switzerland since 1291; the Netherlands from 1579 to 1795; and the United States since 1778. But only the first volume was published. It repeats in huge detail and erudition what Madison had already found out in his "Notes on Ancient and Modern Confederacies" of 1786. It chides Madison (pp. 124–26) for relying on minor authorities instead of "the emphatic silence of Thucydides." Madison therefore misrepresented the Amphyctionic League as a political federation when, according to Freeman, it was a religious organization. Judging by the condition of the Oxford University copies, Freeman (ibid.) was an assigned text for many decades. But only by analogy with ancient Greece would it have helped our reader to govern New South Wales.

On American politics, the authoritative texts were Tocqueville and Bryce (1888). Bryce wrote at the height of post–Civil War Hamiltonianism. For Bryce, Alexander Hamilton was the real hero of the Founding period. He refers to Hamilton twice as often as to Madison, and in more laudatory terms ("this brilliant figure, to Europeans the most interesting in the earlier history of the Republic . . . his less famous coadjutors, Madison and Jay" [ibid., i, 29, ii.8]). Most of his references to *The Federalist* are either to Hamilton's numbers or to Madison numbers that he mistakenly attributed to Hamilton. The copy of Bryce in Nuffield College Library, in which I checked these citations, originally belonged to "W. S. Lamont, H[is] B[ritannic] M[ajesty's] C[onsul], Congo." Consul Lamont would have learned nothing from Bryce about how to create a working federation in the Congo, or anywhere else.

If disappointed by Bryce, one might have consulted the authoritative 11th edition of the *Encyclopaedia Britannica* (Cambridge University Press, 1911). This contains an insightful, but unsigned, article on Madison and a longer enthusiastic one on Hamilton by F. S. Philbrick of Harvard (but with the encyclopedia's editor appearing as coauthor). The entry on the Federalist Party is a counterweight, written by one who did not love Hamilton. A long entry on Federal Government reduces the United States, Canada, and Australia to a mediocre paragraph each at the end. *The Federalist Papers* do not warrant an entry.

In the same year appeared the first British edition of *The Federalist Papers,* edited by W. J. Ashley in the Everyman series. Ashley was an economic historian from Birmingham who was a keen supporter of Joseph Chamberlain's campaigns to revive the British Empire and to introduce protective tariffs there. His earlier *The Tariff Problem* (Ashley 1903) was written to order, at Chamberlain's request, to supply his political campaign with appropriate economic arguments. His brief introduction to *The Federalist* is less obviously propagandist. He makes his ulterior purpose clear, though:

> Any grant of self-government to Ireland will necessarily involve a definition of
> powers, in a document which (like the Acts establishing the Canadian and Aus-
> tralian federations) will be an ordinary statute, and will need a court for its inter-
> pretation. . . . [T]he general English public has hitherto been but little interested
> in questions of federal government. But that lack of interest, in all probability, will
> no longer characterise us. (Ashley 1911, xiii–xiv)

Although Ashley's brief comments on Madison are correct as far as they go,
he follows the custom of the time in attributing *The Federalist* almost entirely
to Hamilton. He ascribes Numbers 18–20 and 49–58 to "Hamilton or Madison."

   Imagine yourself as a British lecturer in constitutional law at the turn of
the twentieth century, when Australia and then South Africa were devising
their governments, and the British government was tentatively experiment-
ing in India also. What would you have used to teach those who were going
out to govern the federal domains of this confederal empire? They lay under
the long shadow of A.V. Dicey. Under the guise of Vinerian professor of English law at Oxford University and leading constitutional theorist, Dicey was
a unionist ideologue. Unionism in his generation meant retaining Ireland in
the United Kingdom and refusing it even a devolved government, let alone
the status of a U.S. state or Canadian province.

The Long Shadow of Albert Venn Dicey

Dicey's fundamental doctrine is this:

> Parliament . . . has, under the English constitution, the right to make or unmake
> any law whatever; and further, that no person or body is recognised by the law of
> England as having a right to override or set aside the legislation of Parliament.
> (Dicey 1885, 3–4)

"No person or body" means no person or body, anywhere in the world. In
his discussion of the powers of the parliaments of the colonies and dominions of the British Empire, Dicey again and again stresses that they are no different from those of British railway companies. The Commonwealth of Australia and the London and North Western Railway are equally liable to have
their laws ruled ultra vires if they conflict with their enabling statute. The
constitutions of Canada, Australia, South Africa, and New Zealand—the first
two of these being federal states—were all statutes of the Imperial (i.e., UK)
Parliament, as were the acts empowering railway companies to fine people
forty shillings for failing to shut field gates. In an exercise of remarkable men-

tal agility, Dicey manages to view the U.S. Constitution in the same light:

> Their [the Framers'] true merit was that they applied with extraordinary skill the notions which they had inherited from English law to the novel circumstances of the new republic.... [T]he fathers of the republic treated Acts of Congress as English Courts treat by-laws.

Used as (Dicey says) they were to having the vires of Colonial laws tested and sometimes rejected by the Privy Council, they merely transferred the powers of the Privy Council to the Supreme Court, thus putting every legislature in the United States, state and federal, in the analogous position to the London & North Western Railway (ibid., 92–93). Dicey shows no awareness of *Federalist* 53.

Such a reading of the U.S. Constitution and the intentions of the Framers might be thought eccentric even for 1885, but it persisted throughout the period that the lawmakers of the British Empire and Commonwealth were being trained at British universities. Dicey's text went through ten editions between 1885 and 1960. The eighth edition, the last one revised by him, was current from 1915 to 1939, and was republished in 1982, curiously as a "Liberty Classic." Thus fully three generations of imperial administrators, educated mostly at Oxford, Cambridge, and London universities, learned their constitutional law from Dicey. Although as an intellectual he stands no comparison to Madison or Hamilton, as a practical ideologue he was for almost a century as important as them. All the Anglophone democracies, except the United States and Australia, have Diceyan, not Madisonian, constitutions. By headcount, Dicey rules over more than a billion people (in India, the UK, Canada, South Africa, New Zealand, and the former British colonies that have achieved democracy) to Madison's 300 million or so.

Dicey had a visceral hatred of Irish Home Rule, as some of his book titles reveal: *England's Case against Home Rule* (1886); *Unionist Delusions* (1887; these were the delusions of Liberal unionists who thought some compromise on Home Rule was possible); *A Leap in the Dark* (1893; an attack on the second Irish Home Rule bill); *A Fool's Paradise, a Constitutionalist's Criticism on the Home Rule Bill of 1912*. Even devolution to Ireland, let alone federalism, was anathema to the Vinerian professor of English law. These attitudes led him into self-contradiction during the constitutional crisis of 1909–14, when he suddenly discovered that parliamentary sovereignty might not after all apply to the Government of Ireland Bill. The eighth edition contains a long preface, dropped by the editor of the ninth and tenth editions, but now reinstated thanks to Liberty Classics. In it, Dicey maintains that "the Parliament Act [of 1911] enables the majority of the House of Commons to resist or overrule the will of the electors or, in other words, of the nation." Therefore he advocated a referendum "in England" on Home Rule. He is silent on whether a referendum on Ireland, or in the United Kingdom including Ireland, would be a good idea (Dicey 1885, lxxi, xcvii–ci).

In the words of the editor of the ninth and tenth editions, Dicey "impresses the reader as one convinced of the truth of his assertions, which accordingly tend to be adopted by succeeding generations as axiomatic" (ibid., xxvii). This may help to explain the strange combination of arrogance and neglect with which the Imperial Parliament enacted the constitutions of Canada, Australia, and South Africa, and drafted one for India.[9] As Dicey himself reports, the Colonial Laws Validity Act 1865 "seems (oddly enough) to have passed through Parliament without discussion" (ibid., 49). The British North America Act 1867, which remained, with later amendments, the Constitution of Canada until 1982, slid through almost as silently. It was bipartisan. It was enacted on the watch of Benjamin Disraeli, often seen as the prophet and ideologue of empire par excellence; but the six-volume biography of Disraeli by Monypenny and Buckle (1910–20, iv, 556) hardly mentions it at all.

The 1865 act provided that any colonial law "repugnant" to the provisions of any act of Parliament applying to that colony "shall, to the extent of such repugnancy, but not otherwise, be and remain absolutely void and inoperative" (s.2). If that was the mindset of Victorian legislators toward the federal parliament of Canada (let alone toward what became the provincial legislatures), it is unsurprising that they did not read Madison into the 1867 act.

The 1867 act originated in Canadian, not in British, politics. Like the British, the Canadians did not regard the United States as a model. Federation in Canada was largely a defensive reaction to the Union victory in the U.S. Civil War. Flushed with success, some Union politicians were demanding the annexation of Canada. As Madison and Hamilton had done at Annapolis in 1786, so did the Canadian federalists in 1864. They hijacked a conference at Charlottetown that had been called to discuss unity among the Maritime colonies only. Turning up uninvited, they put a federation of the whole of Canada on the agenda. Within a few weeks, a further conference in Quebec had produced seventy-two resolutions for a federation of all the then-existing Canadian colonies. Resolution Number 3 stated:

> In framing a Constitution for the General Government, the Conference, with a view to the perpetuation of our connection with the Mother Country, and to the promotion of the best interests of the people of these Provinces, desire to follow the model of the British Constitution, so far as our circumstances will permit.

Now supported, for strategic reasons, by the British government, this federation was enacted with little elite dissent in either Canada or the UK in 1867.

Contemporary Canadian leaders knew that it would be unpopular in some provinces at least (the federalist administration of New Brunswick was unseated in the next general election there). Perhaps for this reason, perhaps also because Madisonian ideas had no roots in Canada, it was not submitted to the people for ratification. An act of the UK Parliament could not have been submitted to the Canadian people for ratification without destroying the ruling constitutional doctrine in both countries. The Anti-Federalists—the Rhode Islands of Canada—were Prince Edward Island (PEI) and Newfoundland. PEI joined Canada in 1873. Newfoundland remained outside and became a separate dominion, but the state went bankrupt in the 1930s and it was absorbed in Canada in 1949 (Jackson and Jackson 1998, 30–38, 204–7; *http://www.nlc-bnc.ca/confed/e–1867.htm* [accessed Sept.–Oct. 2000]).

Canadian federalism remained more Diceyan (if that is not a contradiction in terms) than Madisonian. This is exemplified by the role of the Judicial Committee of the Privy Council (JCPC) as the locus for settling disputes between the federal and provincial governments. The Privy Council, that is, of the king of Canada. Dicey's idea that the U.S. Framers saw the Supreme Court as a simple successor to the Privy Council is a fantasy; but it fits Canadian reality much better. Appeal to the JCPC disappeared in Canada only in 1949 (it still exists for New Zealand and some Caribbean states). The Canadian cabinet office is still called the Privy Council Office.

The Australian founding was more American than was the Canadian. Indeed, in Galligan's (1995) persuasive account it was federalist all along, but for much of Australia's Commonwealth history the centralist ideologies of the national parties, especially Labor, have hidden that fact. Galligan, who wrote a Ph.D. thesis in Canada on the Australian constitution, maintains (p. viii) that "the Australian people, in contrast to the Canadians, did constitute themselves as a sovereign people in adopting the Australian Constitution in 1901."

The Australian constitution, like the Canadian, was embodied in an act of the Imperial Parliament, promulgated by Britain's highest imperialist, Joseph Chamberlain. Chamberlain forced a provision for a wider range of appeals to the JCPC on the reluctant Australians (Australian Constitution sec. 74; McLean 2001, 119). According to a long-serving Australian chief justice (Latham 1952, 7–8, 26–27), the Privy Council delivered such ignorant judgments in the early days, showing no understanding of federalism, that the High Court simply "refused to follow the decision of the Privy Council and held that the Constitution and the Judiciary Act had effectively made the High Court the final arbiter" on Australian constitutional cases. The Privy Council did not fight back.

According to the preamble to the Australian constitution:

[T]he people of New South Wales, Victoria, South Australia, Queensland, and Tasmania [Western Australia was the Rhode Island of Australia] . . . have agreed to unite in one indissoluble Federal Commonwealth under the Crown of the United Kingdom of Great Britain and Ireland, and under the Constitution hereby established.

The Constitutional Convention of 1897–98 was popularly elected, and the constitution was ratified by popular referendum (not by a ratifying convention) in all five participating colonies before enactment at Westminster (Quick and Garran 1901, 144–54, 225–42; Galligan 1995, 25–29). Note too the subtle phrase "under the Crown of the United Kingdom of Great Britain and Ireland." The Australians were choosing a monarch who happened to be the monarch of somewhere else. As they choose, however, so may they reject. The constitutional crisis of 1975 brought that rejection closer, although the referendum of 1999 managed to choose the unpopular option of the continuation of the monarchy (List et al. 2000).

The amendment procedure for the Australian Constitution is closer to the people than that of the U.S. Constitution. Under Section 128, a majority of the electors voting in a majority of the states, and a majority of all electors voting, must approve changes in the constitution. This has stymied the large class of amendments that politicians would have liked but the qualified majority of the people did not. More than one hundred amendments have been proposed; forty-two have gone to referendum; only eight have carried (*http://fed.gov.au/constit.htm*, accessed October 2000; *http://www.founding-docs.gov.au/places/cth/cth1.htm*, accessed May 2002).

These features show that Australian federalism is truly Madisonian in some respects. Why then have Australian politicians and scholars for a century either ignored or denied this? Those who have studied the record of the Australian framing report that the framers "found the American instrument of government an incomparable model. They could not escape from its fascination. Its contemplation damped the smouldering fire of their originality" (O. Dixon quoted by Galligan 1995, 47).

As Charles Beard might have pointed out, the class background of the Australian constitutional convention was vastly different from that of the Philadelphia Convention. Active interventionist governments, some of them containing socialists, ran the Australian states. The Australian framers, who unlike their American counterparts represented the governing factions in their state governments, saw state intervention in society as a benefit, not as an improper or wicked project. So they were much less concerned than their American forebears about factionalism or minority rights. After federation, governments of both parties continued the welfarist theme. Australia was one of the first countries to have a Labor government, and one of the first to develop a welfare state. A welfare state involves extensive redistribution of tax receipts, and social spending in accordance with perceived needs, regardless of the geography of federalism. It is not surprising that only recently have scholars started to stress that the constitution has been federal all along. To do so they had to contend against a long political and legal tradition (see especially Latham 1952).

Not all British Unionists were as extreme as Dicey. Alfred Milner, the prophet of empire in South Africa, founded a network of unionist administrators ("Milner's kindergarten"; later the Round Table) to be a think-tank advising the governors of the empire. One leading member was F. S. Oliver, who characteristically wrote a biography of Alexander Hamilton. Like W. J. Ashley in his introduction to *The Federalist*, he draws parallels between the union of the United States in 1787 and the British Empire in 1906. His relative valuation of Hamilton and Madison is of its time. He believes that Madison was under Hamilton's "enchantment" at Philadelphia, and that the reason Hamilton left the Convention after his speech of June 18 praising the British constitution was that "the power of his ideas was secure enough in the minds of his party for it to be left without his presence to work out the details of the constitution" (Oliver 1906, 148, 213). This interpretation of the Convention receives no support from any contemporary document, but it fits the Hamiltonian temper of the times.

The Round Table group sought to influence the constitutions of the most difficult parts of the empire—Ireland and India. On Ireland, Oliver (1914) took a more moderate line than Dicey (1885). He wanted Ireland to have the same powers as the Canadian or South African provinces, or the Australian states. He explained that federalism comprises "a central government . . . and . . . subordinate authorities," and warned that, compared with Canada, Australia had reverted to the old, undesirable American version because of "old jealousies between the individual states" (Oliver 1914, 38, 39, 50). To us, this seems like an astonishing failure to grasp what federalism is about. But it was a persistent mind-set among British imperial administrators. The model federal constitution was the Canadian, not the Australian; and Ireland and India would be given institutions analogous to those of the provinces, not the dominions.

Ireland and India were troublesome because it was common knowledge that their citizens, if consulted, might reject the empire altogether. Therefore, if the builders of empire were to design constitutions for them, they must avoid the dangerous idea of popular ratification. In the imperialist ideology of the times, Catholic Irish and colored Indian people were not at as high a stage of mental development as the white Protestant people of Canada and South Africa. But that ideology became harder to defend as the twentieth century wore on. Re-enacting the Canadian constitution was a less controversial, and less flagrantly racialist, way of ensuring that the constitutions of Ireland and India would not be put to their voters for ratification.

The constitution of Ireland was determined at the British-Irish Treaty negotiations of October–December 1921. Lionel Curtis, the principal knight of the Round Table, was assistant secretary to the British team. Elsewhere (McLean 2001, ch. 7), I have analysed the surprising process by which the British prime minister Lloyd George got the whole Irish delegation, including two uncompromising republicans, to sign, and recommend to their principals, a treaty that retained the Irish Free State within the empire. Curtis insisted that Ireland's position would parallel Canada's (Jones 1971, 123, 162), a formula that finds its way into clauses 2 and 3 of the treaty.[10] Curtis was asked to show his arguments to one of his Irish counterparts, the republican Erskine Childers. Childers's cutting riposte, "Law and Fact in Canada" (Childers MSS, Trinity College, Dublin MSS 7814), claimed that the supposed analogies between Canada and Ireland broke down over the fact that Canada was thousands of miles away and Ireland was on Britain's doorstep. But Childers was in a minority in his own deputation. The treaty was signed. It was ratified by both parliaments but not submitted to the people of either country, and the Irish Free State came into being in 1922.

The Simon Committee of 1930 proposed a new constitution for India. Comprising a leading constitutional lawyer and an all-party group of MPs (two of them Labour, including the future Labour leader Clement Attlee), it expressed alarm about the unstable state of India, where the Congress Party under Gandhi and Nehru was demanding independence, and there seemed to be ever-present threats of inter-religious rioting and of invasion via the north-west frontier. India was a patchwork, most of it ruled directly from Britain, but patches of varying size—some of them huge—comprised princely states not ruled (directly) by the British. Simon said that the "ultimate constitution of India must be federal," because of the sheer size of India and the problem of the princely states. To begin with, it would comprise British India, divided into provinces, which the princely states would be invited to join if they wished. There would have to be special provision for the north-west frontier, "and the so-called Backward Tracts," which were not yet ready for responsible government. The constitution must embed protection for minorities, but "Declarations of Rights are useless, unless there exist the will and the means to make them effective." Nehru's proposal for adult suffrage, which would add 100 million voters to the existing 6.5 million, was for the time being "quite impracticable." It would not be possible to subject the Indian Army, officered by Britons and responsible for the protection of the empire (although paid for out of Indian tax revenues), to the control of the Indian government. The federal government was to consist of a federal assembly chosen by provincial councils; the existing partly nominated council of state should be retained, as it "has been a steadying influence.... There is an analogy of some value [to the proposals for a federation that other territories could later join] to be found in the development of the Dominion of Canada" (Brock 1930, part II, quoted at 83, 84, 88, 98, 103, 110, 129).

There was equally an analogy to be found in the development of the Commonwealth of Australia. Both the Canadian and the Australian constitutions provided for territories not among the founders to join later; in both cases, this had happened by 1930. But as with Ireland, the Australian analogy was not found to be of equal value to the Canadian.

Although enormous changes took place between 1930 and Indian independence in 1947, the constitutional framework laid out by Simon is visible in the constitution of India. Because of India's diversity and vast size (even after partition carved the present Pakistan, Bangladesh, and Burma (Myanmar) out of the India of 1930), it could not be a unitary state. But it is not a federal state either. The government of India may create and abolish states, and suspend state governments, at will. Not much Madisonian theorizing there.

The One and Indivisible French Republic

"Every body here is trying their hands at forming declarations of rights. As something of that kind is going on with you also, I send you two specimens from hence," wrote Jefferson in Paris to Madison on January 12, 1789 (JP 14, 437). Jefferson's first "specimen" was nominally by Lafayette, but he himself had had a considerable hand in it. It was less radical than Jefferson's efforts in the Declaration of Independence or the Virginia Declaration of Religious Freedom, because Jefferson believed that France, an old country with entrenched privileges, was not yet ready for a Virginian declaration. (It is only fair to add that, although Jefferson started to translate one of Condorcet's main works on human rights, the *Réflexions sur l'esclavage des Nègres* of 1781, he completed only a few paragraphs—JP 14, 494–98.)

Jefferson's letter formed part of his campaign to persuade Madison that the U.S. Constitution must be augmented by a bill of rights. Madison was initially reluctant, but in 1789 he became the floor manager in the House for the proposed rights amendments, the ten survivors of which became the Bill of Rights. Thus Jefferson's and Madison's efforts began with religious freedom in Virginia and ended with rights embedded in the constitutions of both the United States and France.

Lafayette presented his (and Jefferson's) efforts to the National Assembly of 1789, which revised them and promulgated them as the Declaration of the Rights of Man and the Citizen. This remains a definitive statement of the revolutionary values of 1789. Not all of its phrases derive from Madison or Jefferson. Two that do not are:

> 4. The basis of all sovereignty lies essentially in the Nation. No corporation or individual may exercise any authority that is not expressly derived therefrom....
>
> 6. Legislation is the expression of the general will. (Translated by Finer 1997, 1539)

Often, in the trite phrase, the general will turns out to be the will of a general. In the Terror of 1793, these articles in the Declaration turned out to be convenient covers for the bloody suppression of the individual rights enumerated elsewhere in the document. And unlike the Bill of Rights, it could not be used to press individual claims against the state until very recently. One central feature of postrevolutionary French constitutionalism, which remains in place today, is the prohibition of judicial review of legislation (the general will can never be wrong). Despite the recital of the 1789 Declaration and the preamble to the 1946 constitution in that of 1958, only in 1971 did the French Constitutional Council first decide that these texts conferred judicial rights. In the most important such case to date, the council partly invalidated the Socialist government's nationalization laws of 1981. In so doing, they had to rule among three incompatible texts. They decided that the "inviolable and sacred right" (1789) for property not to be taken except with "just and previously determined compensation" overrode an apparent duty to nationalize every "public national service or . . . monopoly" (1946) and a power for the legislature to "establish rules concerning . . . the nationalization of enterprises" (1958) (Stone Sweet 2000, 66–68). That these three contradictory texts nestled together in the French constitution for twenty-three years eloquently addresses the difference between French and American constitutionalism. Individual litigants have no access to the Constitutional Council, and therefore the 1789 (and 1946) Declarations have no direct effect in the judicial order, although the Declaration is gradually permeating the work of the civil and administrative courts also.

Having started with a partly Madisonian text, the French Revolution marched off in a thoroughly non-Madisonian direction. Education has always been an instrument of state in the one and indivisible French Republic. This derives from Condorcet. That fiercely antireligious rationalist believed that an essential step to enlightened government was an enlightened people. The probability that a Condorcet jury gets the right answer is a positive monotonic function of the enlightenment of the average juror. Condorcet was interested in education at all levels from primary to university, and he wrote a plan for national education shortly before his fall in 1793 (Coutel 1988). Condorcet's plan has inspired all subsequent republican plans, which have produced a nationally uniform educational system, designed to increase enlightenment, to turn peasants into Frenchmen and Frenchwomen, and to banish religious superstition. The aim is similar to Madison's and Hamilton's: improve the enlightenment of decisions by improving the enlightenment of the deciders. But the methods could not be more different. France has the most centralized, and the United States the most decentralized, school system in the world.

Of course, if Madison's first thoughts on liberty in an extended republic were correct, his and Condorcet's visions need not have diverged. In *Federalist* 10 the solution to faction and tyranny is an extended republic. Madison's second thoughts (*Federalist* 45–51) justified bicameralism, federalism, and separation of powers. Condorcet's *New Haven Letters* show how totally he rejected those ideas, and Madison's eloquent refusal to translate them into English show that he understood the difference between their positions. Madison's third thoughts came as he changed his mind, under pressure from Jefferson, on the need for a bill of rights. The French state has not followed either his prescriptions or his thinking. As a rough and unreliable test of this, I searched the website of the leading French teaching and research institution in political science, Sciences Po in Paris. The string "Madison" generated four hits, three of which referred to Madison, Wisconsin. Only one web document at Sciences Po cites James Madison (http://www.sciences-po.fr/formation/cours_en_ligne/archives/2ndcycle/gedpes/planmanin.htm, accessed May 2002).[11]

Conclusion: The Elusiveness of Publius

Madison derived some of his political concerns from the Scots, and some of his methodology from both the Scots and the French. From the Scottish "country Whigs" he saw that one function of a constitution was to curb the executive. From Hume he learned the importance of faction; from Hume and others, the undesirability of establishing religion. Montesquieu contributed the separation of powers. But in 1786–88, Madison was a separation of powers advocate only tactically (compare "Vices" and the Virginia Plan

with *Federalist* Number 51). The Americans worked out for themselves, with
no great help from Montesquieu, that parliamentary sovereignty was incompatible with federalism. Madison says so in *Federalist* Number 53. Either from
the French Enlightenment or from his own head Madison drew his game-
theoretic mode of reasoning. But the political conclusions that Madison
drew using these methodological tools were not followed in Scotland, nor
anywhere else in the British Empire, with the partial exception of Australia,
nor in France. How can this be?

The main reason is that for so much of the time since 1787, the ideological climate in France, the British Empire, and even the United States itself
was so hostile to Madison and his thought that it was neither studied nor understood. After the Civil War, Madison the states-righter (as he had become
by 1798) and slaveholder (as he was all his life) was under a cloud. Hamilton
the nationalist was intellectually triumphant. Even some of Madison's most
important numbers of *The Federalist* were mostly ascribed to Hamilton. The
earliest discussion of Madisonian federalism by a British academic I have discovered is as recent as Vile (1967). Until then, British scholars, and through
them the administrators of empire, paid little attention to Madison's thought
and conflated it with Hamilton's. Specifically, they failed to understand from
Federalist Number 53 that federalism and parliamentary sovereignty are incompatible.

Therefore I return to my first point. Madison thrives because he is congenial to us. In a way, that is as nakedly contextual, and therefore subject to
the same sort of distortion, as the neglect of Madison for most of the intervening years. On the other hand, it is Madison's *intellectual* position, not the
political causes he advanced, that attracts intellectual historians, political scientists, and economists today.

How much does he owe directly to Condorcet's social mathematics—the
ultimate ancestor of much of modern social science? I cannot disprove
Schofield's conjecture that Madison understood Condorcet's deep work
through the intermediation of Franklin. But I think that independent discovery is a more likely story. Madison (like Lewis Carroll a century later) had
a game-theoretic cast of mind, which he managed to express two centuries
before game theory provided the tools for expressing it as we now would.
Ultimately, that is why Madison is the most modern of the ancients.

Notes

1. "Eventual" carries its eighteenth-century sense of "possible," not the modern sense. Cf. French *éventuel*.

2. The Convention accepted Madison's argument and modified the article further to introduce the unit voting rule for states in the House when they are selecting a president.

3. For example, Madison's and Hume's use of the unusual word *aliment* (Adair might have added that it is a technical term in Scots law, where it means the same as *alimony* in common-law systems); and Madison's obscure reference, in *Federalist* Number 10, paragraph 7, to "attachment to . . . persons . . . whose fortunes have been interesting to the human passions." Adair (1974b, 104) sees this as an echo of the final paragraph of Hume's Essay Number 7, "Of Parties in General," where it is a disguised reference to the Jacobites, whose rebellion of 1745 was very recent when Hume wrote. See Hume 1994, 39.

4. Some (especially Sloan 1995; O'Brien 1996) have denied that Jefferson and Condorcet were close. However they do not cite earlier papers in which the link has been demonstrated (McLean and Urken 1992; McLean and Hewitt 1994).

5. Probably in the last month before the publication of *Federalist* Number 10. The most important intermediate text, Madison's letter to Jefferson of Oct. 24, 1787, recapitulates "Vices" but does not have the probabilistic argument for an extended republic. That letter acknowledges receipt of Jefferson's box of books sent on August 2. The box included Condorcet's *Vie de M. Turgot* (a source for Condorcet's economics) and some volumes of the new *Encyclopédie* (a source for the whole range of French Enlightenment thought). See invoice accompanying TJ to JM, Aug. 2, 1787, MP 10, 128–29.

6. Note: the *justification* of the Electoral College, not the idea of it. The way that the Convention wandered back and forth among possible ways of electing the president, before finally settling on the form of the Electoral College on September 6, precludes any claim that it was Madison's invention. Hamilton had already left the Convention. See in particular Riker 1987, 37.

7. "Of or pertaining to President Madison or his political doctrines, esp. his federalist views on democracy"—*Oxford English Dictionary* online edition. One of the defining citations is: *Economist* 32, no. 2 (Oct. 25, 1975). America's multi-consensus Madisonian system is now causing the money spent on government to soar and yet be insufficient at the same time.

8. A rough search in the on-line *Social Sciences Citation Index* from 1981 through Sept. 2000 yielded 2,634 hits, some of them covering multiple citations.

9. Although the constitution of India sets down the relationship between the government of India and state governments, it is not a federal constitution. The government of India can (and does) suspend state governments, alter state boundaries, and so on, without needing to seek any other party's consent. The Union of South Africa (1910), enacted eight years after the British defeat of the Boer republics in the South African War (1899–1902), created a unitary, not a federal, state out of the two former British colonies and the two former Boer republics. New Zealand has never been a federal state.

10. "[T]he position of the Irish Free State in relation to the Imperial Parlia-

ment and Government and otherwise shall be that of the Dominion of Canada." Articles of Agreement for a Treaty between Great Britain and Ireland, Dec. 6, 1921, cl. 2.

11. And of the two hits on "Jefferson" one relates to William Jefferson Clinton.

Chapter 3

Madison's Theory of Public Goods

KEITH L. DOUGHERTY

Introduction

It is well known that Americans faced a collective action problem under the Articles of Confederation.[1] The Confederation raised resources through a system of requisition that worked like unenforced taxes on the states. States took advantage of the system's voluntary nature and free-rode on their contributions. What is less well known is that James Madison, and other early Americans, understood the problem. They developed comprehensive theories of free-riding behavior and used these theories to address several problems in the American Confederation.

Although Madison was not the first American to understand the problem of acting collectively, nor the first to put his ideas in print, he was certainly at the forefront of early American intellectuals who wrestled with the idea. By 1788, Madison had developed a theory that surpassed anything written by his contemporaries. Comprehensive understanding of a problem was Madison's hallmark. He applied it to his theory of pluralism and to his framework for the Constitution.

This chapter compares Madison's version of collective action theory with that of Mancur Olson. It describes the development of Madison's thinking on the subject from his college graduation in 1771 to the ratification debates in 1788. And it shows how Madison applied his understanding of public goods to his more familiar works on republican government and pluralism.

Madison and Olson

In comparing the theories of James Madison and Mancur Olson, it is clear that Olson had the upper hand. Olson (1965) described the logic of collective action much more fully than Madison and showed how his ideas applied to a variety of settings.[2] He worked out the rational response to nonexcludable and nonrival goods using costs and benefits, then created general postulates about group size and group asymmetries. Olson showed that under certain assumptions one individual would contribute to a collective good while others would free-ride.[3] Such an approach allowed Olson to show why rational actors would not contribute to their collective needs.

Madison, on the other hand, was not a mathematical economist. He did not use costs and benefits nor did he clearly distinguish public goods from other types of goods.[4] He started from specific examples and created generalized theories based on these examples. He worked with archetypes, as did Olson, but his archetypes were not deduced from formal assumptions. Instead, Madison determined the most reasonable response to a particular situation, then applied the same response to other situations. Madison wrote statements like: "[T]he requisitions of Congress will continue to be mere calls for voluntary contributions, which every State will be tempted to evade, by the uniform experience that those States have come off best which have done so most." This mixture of theory and observation led him to a loose understanding of free-riding behavior, which he related to individuals, districts, and states. He claimed: "States will be governed by the motives that actuate individuals," similar to the unitary actor assumption in international relations. Such simplifications allowed him to think about specific aspects of politics while setting other, confounding aspects aside.[5]

FREE-RIDING

Both theorists recognized the conflict between voluntary contribution and unilateral interests. Olson learned this by studying unions, interest groups, and the Marxist state. Madison learned this by studying state responses to requisitions. Requisitions were an appropriation of state monies, soldiers, or supplies by the Confederation—similar to an unenforced tax upon the states.

When Congress requisitioned the states, it first determined the amount of money (or soldiers) needed for the ensuing year, then asked each state to contribute a fixed proportion of the total by a particular date. Article VIII and Article IX provided Congress with the clear constitutional authority to requisition the states, but these articles did not provide Congress with an enforcement mechanism. Since Congress typically used its resources to provide public goods,[6] the states frequently did not comply. This gave Madison, and other early Americans, the perfect laboratory in which to study collective action.

Unlike most laboratories, however, Madison could not control for extraneous factors. As a result, Madison's public goods argument is sometimes muddied by a multiplicity of other factors. In a letter to Pendleton, for example, Madison described the problem as one of tedious collection and transportation. His friend, Joseph Jones, told Madison that the problem stemmed from lack of resources. These other factors clearly affected state behavior and made it difficult for Madison to develop a clear theory of collective action. Eventually, however, Madison came to view free-riding as the central vice of the Confederation.[7]

When Madison was clear, he almost always described a decision that hinged on the behavior of others. For example, he wrote: "[O]ne reason to prevent the concurrent exertions of all the States will arise from the suspicion, in some States, of delinquency in others" (June 11, 1788, DH 9, 1144).[8] In many ways, his descriptions were similar to an assurance game (Sandler 1992). If everyone else cooperated, then Madison's archetype would cooperate as well. If some states defected—because of inability, tedious collection, or some other problem—Madison's archetype would withhold its contribution. In his mind, anticipating the behavior of others was critical to the decision. One or two defections would cause Madison's archetype to defect as well.

Characterizing Madison's descriptions as an assurance game is supported by his perception that the severity of threat encouraged contributions. John Marshall wrote: "We are told that the Confederation carried us through the war. Had not the enthusiasm of liberty inspired us with unanimity, that system would never have carried us through it." Madison made similar remarks. In "Vices of the Political System of the United States" (hereafter "Vices"), he wrote: "[E]xternal danger supplied in some degree the defect of legal & coercive sanctions." In other words, he believed that the size of the benefits that everyone gained would affect compliance with requisitions.[9]

If Madison saw the problem as a prisoners' dilemma, then the size of the nonexcludable benefit would not affect state behavior. States would free-ride regardless of the size of the nonexcludable benefits. If they were playing more of an assurance game, large benefits from mutual cooperation could signal a focal point and encourage mutual cooperation. Such claims support the idea that Madison's thoughts on the matter were better characterized by assurance games than by prisoners' dilemmas.

Olson would have characterized the problem differently. Olson usually described collective action problems as quasi–prisoners' dilemmas. Olson wrote: "Though all of the members of the group therefore have a common interest in obtaining this collective benefit, they have no common interest in paying the cost of providing that collective good. Each would prefer that the others pay the entire cost" (Olson 1965, 21). For Olson, actors did not anticipate the actions of others. They defected whether other actors cooperated or not. Alexander Hamilton concurred.[10] Which characterization was more accurate is a separate issue.

In making such a distinction between Madison and Olson, it is important to note that Madison was not a formal theorist. He frequently made claims that appeared *like* assurance games, but he clearly did not conceptualize the problem *as* an assurance game. Such developments were too precise for his time.

SELECTIVE INCENTIVES

In addition to explaining why individuals would free-ride, Madison and Olson both recognized the importance of selective incentives. Selective incentives were rewards or punishments for cooperative and noncooperative behavior, respectively.

Olson, on the one hand, showed how selective incentives fit into his cost-benefit framework and introduced a variety of examples in which selective incentives were used to elicit contribution. Among the most important were social sanctions that could be used to embarrass noncontributors. "It is in the nature of social incentive that they can distinguish among individuals," Olson wrote. "[T]he recalcitrant individual can be ostracized, and the cooperative individual can be invited into the center of the charmed circle" (ibid., 61).

Madison, on the other hand, put selective incentives to use. He was well aware of how punishing noncontributors and rewarding contributors could be used to solve the free-rider problem, though he rarely elaborated on the idea in theoretical terms. In the early 1780s, he, Alexander Hamilton, Robert Morris, and other nationalists joined in a movement to solve the collective action problem among states using selective incentives.

Their first attempt was to propose an amendment to the Articles of Confederation that allowed Congress to coerce delinquent states. In the spring of 1781, Madison led a congressional committee that proposed to give the union the power to march the army into a delinquent state or to blockade its harbors with military ships. In Madison's mind, "[t]he situation of most states is such that two or three vessels of force employed against their trade will make it their interest to yield prompt obedience to all just requisitions

on them." Applying such coercion selectively would encourage state legislatures to pass taxes, raise soldiers, and transfer these resources to the Confederation. If they did not, soldiers would march on a state legislature and force
them to pay in a Hobbesian way. Such a proposal was a clear application of
selective incentives.[11]

Madison's committee soon realized, however, that the states would never
ratify such an amendment. "If they should refuse," Madison wrote Jefferson,
"Congress will be in a worse situation than at present; for as the confederation now stands ... there is an implied right of coer[c]io[n] against the delinquent party" (*The Papers of James Madison* [hereafter MP] 3, 72). Article XIII
required that every state abide by the resolutions of Congress. Madison believed that this article also gave Congress the implicit power to enforce its
requisitions. He was ready to try the idea, but other members of Congress
were not. Congress never passed the coercive powers amendment and never
asserted an implied right of coercion.

Punishing the states for noncompliance was a selective incentive that
would encourage cooperation, but it would infringe upon state sovereignty
and remove a powerful protection against congressional tyranny. As time progressed, many early Americans eventually concluded that coercing the states
had two big defects. Unlike Hobbes' description of an all-powerful
Leviathan, Congress did not have an independent military to force compliance from its members. If Congress tried to coerce noncomplying states to
pay their requisitions, it would have to depend upon complying states to apply the force. Pitting complying states against noncomplying states in open
battle would produce what Hamilton described as a "civil war."[12]

In addition, early American elites realized that coercion could never be
applied against states as distinct entities. It would always be applied against
individuals within a state and cause harm to those who paid their taxes as
well as those who were delinquent. In other words, those who paid their
taxes would be punished just as much as those who did not, when Congress
acted on states rather than on individuals. After hearing these objections at
the Constitutional Convention, Madison slowly backed off the idea. There
he declared that "the more he reflected on the use of force, the more he
doubted the practicability, the justice and the efficacy of it when applied to
people collectively and not individually." Although coercing the states was
given serious consideration, it was not an acceptable selective incentive and
it never passed Congress.[13]

Shortly after considering the coercive powers amendment, members of
Congress attempted to apply a milder selective incentive that was within
their means. Rather than coerce noncomplying states, Madison and other

members of Congress attempted to apply social sanctions—similar to the ones described by Olson. Morris, Madison, and other members of Congress sent circulars to the states clearly marking which states were behind in their quotas. They arranged for the receivers of the Continental tax to publish the arrears of their state in local newspapers.[14] And they wrote letters that attributed patriotism to the act of contributing and shame to the act of withholding contributions.

Some of these attempts may have been more effective than others. For example, sending circulars to state governments might have reminded state politicians of their common duty and allowed complying states to ostracize those who did not comply. But publishing a state's arrears in local newspapers should have been less effective. If voters fully understood the collective action problem, they would reward politicians for protecting their unilateral interests, not ostracize them. In other words, self-interested voters would support free-riding. Only civically minded individuals, who thought it would be better to sacrifice the immediate interests of their state for the good of the union, would scorn their politicians for not contributing.[15]

In either case, social sanctions proved too weak for government. A more permanent answer to the collective action problem required a revision of the Articles of Confederation. Ultimately, early Americans found a solution in the Constitution, which sidestepped the collective action problem among the states by acting directly upon the people.

JOINT PRODUCTS

Finally, Olson postulated theories about privileged, intermediate, and latent groups and distinguished inclusive groups from exclusive ones. Madison did not theorize about any of these things, but he did have some loose notion of joint products, which Olson never mentioned.

Joint products are collective goods with multiple aspects of publicness—in this context, goods that produce both public benefits and private benefits (Sandler 1992). For example, the confederative government created nonexcludable, public benefits for the states when it reduced debts commonly owed by all states. It created private, excludable benefits for the states when these payments went to bond-holders living within a particular state (Dougherty 2001). The latter injected money into a state's economy and paid off important constituents. Although states would not have an incentive to contribute to the production of the public aspects of a joint product (since every state receives public benefits whether they contribute or not), states could have an incentive to contribute to the production of the private aspects of a joint product (since only contributing states obtain private benefits).[16]

Madison recognized these distinctions and was part of a group who put joint products to use. He worked on the special requisition of 1782 and was subsequently exposed to the system of indents. Both required a knowledge of joint products to engineer.[17]

In creating the special requisition of September 10, 1782, Madison and other members of Congress showed that they understood the difference between excludable and nonexcludable benefits. The special requisition was designed for the explicit purpose of paying the interest due on the loan office debt (public bonds). Rather than asking the states to pool their monies in the usual fashion, Congress directed the receivers of the Continental tax to pay bond-holders within their states directly, "before any part thereof shall be paid into the public treasury" (JCC, 23, 545–46). In other words, monies received from each state would go directly to the bond-holders within their state. They would not go to bond-holders in other states until local creditors were paid in full. Congress made the distinction in an attempt to tie the private benefit of paying local citizens directly to the act of paying requisitions. Had Congress pooled receipts from requisitions in the usual way, states would not have the same motivation to contribute. Monies would be used to pay bond-holders in all states, producing the same collective action problem as before. Not surprisingly, states whose citizens were owed greater amounts of the federal debt contributed more to the special requisition than states who were owed less (Dougherty 1999; Dougherty 2001, 97–98).

The care used in crafting this plan demonstrated that members of Congress were at least partially aware of the distinction between excludable and nonexcludable benefits. Madison's role in this machination gave him exposure to joint products well before he described how they worked at the Virginia ratifying convention. Then he described them in a theoretical tone. He said, "In cases of imminent danger, the States more immediately exposed to it, would only exert themselves—Those remote from it, would be too supine to interest themselves warmly in the fate of those whose distresses they did not immediately perceive." According to Madison, states exposed to the enemy had unique reasons to contribute—namely the desire to avoid damage inflicted on their own state.[18] Those that were less exposed did not gain those benefits and did not have the same incentive to contribute.

The Development of Madison's Thought

But if Madison had such a well-developed theory of collective action, then where did he get it from? And how did it affect his political philosophy? The answer to the first question appears to be his exposure to the system of requisitions and his communications with contemporaries.

ORIGINS

Madison entered the College of New Jersey at Princeton in 1769, when he was eighteen years old. There he took several classes from John Witherspoon, who was a preacher and the president of the college. Witherspoon had great influence on Madison's early thinking. Although he was never dogmatic, Witherspoon generally disagreed with the rational philosophers of the Scottish Enlightenment. He assigned Adam Smith, Lord Kames, and David Hume, but he argued against them, calling Hume an "infidel writer." Witherspoon preferred Montesquieu and Francis Hutcheson. He believed that the purpose of government was to encourage a life of virtue and that democracy needed virtue to function. Virtue, good faith, and noble character were among the greatest qualities of men. Creating a society that cultivated these qualities was a cardinal goal.[19]

Witherspoon's teachings, as well as the patriotic fervor swelling on the eve of the Revolution, affected Madison's writings. In 1774, three years after graduating from college, Madison wrote: "A spirit of Liberty and Patriotism animates all degrees and denominations of men. Many publickly declare themselves ready to join the Bostonians as soon as violence is offered." A year later he claimed: "I am persuaded that the Union, Virtue & Love of Liberty at present prevailing thro[ugh]out the Colonies" is enough to prevent the British from putting "the yoke upon us." These passages suggest that young James Madison did not yet understand the problem of free-riding. He believed that patriotism and civic virtue would stimulate men to their collective needs much in accord with Witherspoon's teachings.[20]

Madison's experiences on the Executive Council of Virginia, which he joined on January 14, 1778, soon changed his view. In this position, he read war correspondences, worked on the logistics of supply, and aided Governor Patrick Henry in the affairs of the state. The position exposed him to the details of the army's condition at Valley Forge and state responses to requisitions in 1778 and 1779.[21] Letters from the army, Congress, and other states were data that Madison could use to develop a theory of collective action. But free-riding was not the only explanation for why the states did not fully support the army. Inadequate resources within the states and problems shipping materials between enemy lines were equally plausible explanations. Just because Madison was exposed to problems with requisitions does not mean that he immediately developed a theory of collective action.

And it does not appear that he received the theory from someone in the field. Even though some war correspondences hinted at the free-riding component of the problem, they did not provide enough pieces of the theory to be considered a developed theory. For example, in one of the clearest letters

George Washington wrote, "the States, separately, are too much engaged in their local concerns, and have too many of their ablest men withdrawn from the general council for the good of the common weal."[22] Such tidbits were too short and too oblique to be considered a theory of collective action. Since they were buried among a variety of confounding explanations, Madison would have to piece together the theory from some other source.

Clearly his experiences in the government of Virginia affected his thinking. They were enough to encourage him to reflect critically on the nature of the union and to develop a theory of free-riding behavior on his own. But they were not the whole story.

In December 1779, the legislature picked Madison as a delegate to Congress. Upon hearing the news, Madison quickly resigned his post and laid plans for Philadelphia. He arrived at Congress in the early spring and officially took his seat on March 20, 1780.

Madison's first description of free-riding behavior came one week after his arrival, four months after he left the Executive Council of Virginia, and shortly after he appeared to be entirely unaware of the problem.[23] In a letter to Jefferson (March 20, 1780) Madison noted that the Continental Army was on the verge of disbanding, the Confederation treasury was empty, and the public credit was exhausted. Congress was "recommending plans to the several states for execution" and the states were "separately rejudging the expediency of such plans" (MP 2, 5–7). After rejudgment, they were not contributing. Why? Because "the same distrust of concurrent exertions that has damped the ardor of patriotic individuals, must produce the same effect among the States themselves."[24]

This short passage offers three insights. First, Madison now believed that individuals were not as patriotic as he had described on the eve of the Revolution. Second, he realized that the distrust of "concurrent exertions," a key component to the assurance game, could discourage cooperation. And third, he knew that the problem applied both to individuals and to states. In other words, Madison had seen both the cause of free-riding behavior and applied it to more than one setting at an early stage of his career.

The timing of the letter suggests that Madison either acquired the theory while serving on the Executive Council of Virginia or heard it from other members of Congress during his first week in Philadelphia. The former gave Madison ample opportunity to observe state responses to the war effort and to develop a good understanding of how states acted collectively.

The latter was consistent with his claim in the same letter that a disbanded army, an empty treasury, and exhausted credit were "*our* great apprehensions" (emphasis added). In other words, other members of Congress recognized these problems. From the style of his writing it is not clear whether the "distrust of concurrent exertions," the explanation for these problems, should be attributed to a common view of Congress or whether it was Madison's own insight.

What we do know, however, is that Madison was not the first member of Congress to advance a theory of free-riding behavior. Joseph Galloway clearly described the problem in 1774—years before Madison or Hamilton. Galloway was a prominent Philadelphian, a member of the First Continental Congress, and a well-reasoned loyalist. When a handful of Americans were calling for independence, Galloway was calmly noticing that Britain had helped them with collective action problems in the past. In a speech before the First Continental Congress, Galloway claimed that the states had acted unilaterally during the French and Indian War, rather than contribute to their common cause:

> You all know [that] there were Colonies which at some times granted liberal aids, and at others nothing; other Colonies gave nothing during the war; none gave equitably in proportion to their wealth, and all that did give were actuated by partial and self-interested motives, and gave only in proportion to the approach or remoteness of the danger. These delinquencies were occasioned by the want of the exercise of some supreme power to ascertain, with equity, their proportions of aids, and to over-rule the particular passions, prejudices, and interests, of the several Colonies.[25]

Although this passage was not the final word on public goods theory in North America, and may not have been the first, it clearly shows that Madison was not the source of the free-riding concept among early American intellectuals. Madison was still extolling the powers of civic virtue when Galloway was explaining free-riding to Congress. Furthermore, the passage also shows that the theory of free-riding had been presented to Congress before Madison arrived, making it possible for Madison to acquire the idea there.[26]

We also know that Madison was not the first to put his ideas in print. Galloway published his theory in 1780,[27] and Hamilton beat Madison to the press in a series of papers called "The Continentalist." The latter focused on the problems of the American Confederation and confederations in general. In "The Continentalist" Number VI, Hamilton pointed out that if the states were asked to regulate trade independently, then each state would be afraid to impose duties of its own, "lest the other states, not doing the same should enjoy greater advantages." Hamilton further noted that "a mere regard to the interests of the confederacy will never be a principle sufficiently active to curb the ambitions and intrigues of different members."[28] Although he did not describe the collective action problem with the same clarity that Madison later would, both were clearly developing similar ideas with almost no direct contact from the other.[29]

Madison wrote several descriptions of the problem along the way,[30] but his culminating description came at the Virginia ratifying convention in 1788. In response to Patrick Henry's claim that requisitions were sufficient for general revenue, Madison declared that requisitions would always "disappoint those who put their trust in them" (June 11, 1788, DH 9, 1144). For Patrick Henry, deliberation was good. It allowed states to question the requisitions of Congress and to prevent the national government from abusing its powers. For Madison, deliberation was partially bad. It inspired state legislators to think about their unilateral interests, which would "cause delays." Delays would incite doubts about whether states would contribute, which in turn would "make failures everywhere else." This incentive to pursue local interests was "the principal cause of the inefficacy of requisitions" (ibid., 1145).

As Madison put it:

> When a tax law is in operation in a particular State, every citizen, if he knows the energy of the laws to enforce payment, and that every other citizen is performing his duty, will cheerfully discharge his duty; but were it known that the citizens of one district were not performing their duty, and it was left to the policy of the Government to make them come up with [their own payment], the citizens of other districts would be quite supine and careless in making provisions for payment (Ibid., 1144)

Madison clearly saw the heart of the collective action problem. Even when states mutually gain from collective action, there is no reason to believe that state politicians would act collectively. Politicians would reflect on the interests of their states, and interpret shortfalls from other states as a reason to withhold their contributions.

As Madison was describing the collective action problem to other members of the Virginia convention, a whole flock of Federalists joined in chorus. At the state ratifying convention of Connecticut, Oliver Ellsworth declared, "Since the close of the war, some of the states have done nothing towards complying with the requisitions of Congress; others, who did something at first, seeing that they were left to bear the whole burden, have become equally remiss" (DH 3, 549). Charles Pinckney told the South Carolinian convention that "the national union must ever be destroyed by selfish views and private interests" (South Carolina, House of Representatives 1788, 8). And Edmund Randolph, who initially opposed the Constitution, rose at the Virginia convention to observe: "Not a shilling has been put into the Continental Treasury, but by the utmost reluctance. The probable delinquency of other States has been the pretext for non-compliance with every State" (DH 9, 1017). Although Madison had become a thorough thinker on the subject, several prominent Americans had caught onto the idea.

But clearly others did not understand. Luther Martin still insisted that inability alone explained why states did not comply with requisitions. And James Monroe believed that a well-designed national government would encourage compliance with requisitions—regardless of the enforcement mechanism. Monroe wanted the national government to have the power to regulate trade, the power to raise the militia, and three separate branches of government. "When the United States became in effect a national government," he wrote, "I cannot but believe that their constitutional demands, or requisitions, would be complied with." Although an effective national government would give the states something worthy of their contributions, Monroe's idea would do nothing to resolve the collective action problem among states. Apparently, he did not see the potential conflict between unilateral and collective interests.[31]

A NEW REPUBLIC

Madison, however, did. And he realized the importance of his insight. The theory of collective action helped him to see the problems within the Confederation, where honor and civic virtue were supposed to make individuals, and states, adhere to mutual decisions (Wood 1969). It also helped him develop a better form of government.

Among his most familiar works, the collective action problem first showed up in "Vices." Here, Madison lists a number of problems, or vices, in the Confederation, then attempts to explain why those vices occurred. The first half of "Vices" focuses on collective action problems in the Confederation. Requisitions topped the list. Combining the section head with the first sentence, Madison writes:

> Failure of the States to comply with the Constitutional requisitions . . . has been so fully experienced both during the war and since the peace, results so naturally from the number and independent authority of the States and has been so uniformly exemplified in every similar Confederacy, that it may be considered as not less radically and permanently inherent in than it is fatal to the object of the present system. (MP 9, 348)

According to Madison, the requisition system was the primary defect of the American Confederation (see n. 7). But it also illustrated more general collective action problems in the union, some of which were less concrete.

Madison described vices such as the encroachment of states on the federal authority, unilateral violations of Confederation treaties, and trespasses of states on each other (see Wilson in this volume for additional examples not cited in "Vices"). All of these vices were directly or indirectly collective action problems. To prove that such problems were institutional, and not unique to the thirteen states, Madison investigated other confederations in an earlier work called "Ancient and Modern Confederacies" (MP 9, 3–24). He found similar problems there.[32]

After listing a series of problems under this rubric, Madison offered two reasons for why they occurred. First, he noted that the Confederation government did not have the power to enforce laws, because the authors of the Confederation assumed that state politicians would comply with acts of the Confederation out of civic duty. Taking the direct opposite stance of his claim in 1774, Madison wrote: "It is no longer doubted that a unanimous and punctual obedience of 13 independent bodies, to the acts of the federal Government ought *not* to be calculated on" ("Vices," MP 9, 351, emphasis added). In other words, they should not expect civic duty to engender cooperation. Second, Madison argued that without civic virtue states would free-ride. He explained this in three steps:

> In the first place, Every general act of the Union must necessarily bear unequally hard on some particular member or members of it. Secondly the partiality of the members to their own interests and rights, a partiality which will be fostered by the Courtiers of popularity, will naturally exaggerate the inequality where it exists, and even suspect it where it has no existence. Thirdly a distrust of the voluntary compliance of each other may prevent the compliance of any, although it should be the latent disposition of all. (Ibid., 351–52)

The first two reasons explain why the states would not cooperate in a uniform fashion. For every Confederation act, there always would be some state that believed the act was unfair. Such a state would justify its noncompliance based on principle, which would be reinforced by "the Couriers of popularity." Such lobbyists would remind politicians of their local interests. The third reason explains why the noncompliance of some states would cause the failure of other states. As in an assurance game, anticipating the noncompliance of others would discourage compliance of all. Combined, these passages clearly illustrate that the collective action problem was a major source of Madison's frustration with the Confederation. The first half of "Vices" was devoted to it. The second half dealt with the problem of tyrannical majorities, the inconsistencies of laws between states, and other vices that were unrelated to collective action problems.

Madison used "Vices" to write the Virginia Plan and to prepare for the federal convention. Some of his *Federalist Papers* were also influenced by these notes. In *Federalist* 51, Madison wrote: "In framing a government which is to be administered by men over men, the great difficulty lies in this: you must first enable the government to control the governed: and in the next place oblige it to control itself" (Hamilton et al. 1961a, 322). The first problem, of allowing the government to control the governed, stemmed from the collective action problem. The Articles of Confederation did not give Congress the power to enforce its decisions. As long as unilateral interests conflicted with collective decisions, voluntary compliance could not be expected. Instead, punishments for noncompliance would have to be enacted. In "Vices," Madison wrote: "A sanction is essential to the idea of law, as coercion is to that of Government. The federal system being destitute of both, wants the great vital principles of a Political Constitution" (MP 9, 351).

Madison first thought that Americans could revise the Articles of Confederation and apply the principle of coercion to the states. But as previously mentioned, he eventually realized that punishing the states for noncompliance would punish both disobedient and obedient individuals within a state (Dougherty 2001, 147–49, 171). For this reason, the national government could never apply punishment to states as entities. It had to reach around the states and act directly upon the people. This was the idea behind the Virginia Plan, which Madison primarily authored. The plan gave the central government the authority to coerce individuals, which solved the collective action problem among the states and avoided a new one among the people. A popularly elected government also allowed the national government to enforce its edicts consistent with the principle of taxation by consent (ibid., 18–25). Adopting such a plan allowed the governors to control the governed.

The second problem was to find a way for the government to control itself. Madison wrote: "A dependence on the people is no doubt, the primary control on the government; but experience has taught mankind the necessity of auxiliary precautions" (*Federalist* 51, Hamilton et al. 1961a, 322). The Constitution contained a variety of auxiliary precautions, such as the separation of powers between Congress and the presidency. Congress could create new laws only with the consent of the president. The president could appoint administrative officials only with the consent of the Senate. And a two-house legislature would dull the capricious acts of a single legislative body. These, and other mechanisms, helped control the government. The one-two punch of creating a government that acted directly on the people and creating a series of checks and balances to control the government required wholesale reform, not a few alterations of the Confederation. This may have been part of the reason that Madison pushed to replace the government rather than to repair the old one.[33]

In reflecting on the primary control of the new government (direct dependence on the people), Madison realized that factions of the people might threaten democracy. To make his theory more complete, he had to work out a mechanism that would explain why factions would not be worrisome. As he thought about it, Madison created his theory of pluralism,[34] which drew again from his theory of collective action. This time the free-rider problem would not be bad. It would be good. It would prevent large factions from forming and reduce the probability of tyrannical majorities.

"Extend the sphere," Madison wrote in *Federalist* 10, "and you take in a greater variety of parties and interests; you make it less probable that a majority of the whole will have a common motive to invade the rights of citizens; or if such a common motive exists, it will be more difficult for all who feel it to discover their own strength and to act in unison with each other" (Hamilton et al. 1961a, 83). Many scholars have pointed out that extending the sphere would bring in a greater diversity of interests and reduce the relative size of any single interest (Miller 1992; Banning 1995). Debtors, for example, would be less able to suppress creditors through legal-tender laws as they had in Rhode Island. And majorities in Virginia would have less of an effect on national politics than on politics within their state. This was Madison's primary argument. But what scholars have left relatively unnoticed is that the same passage contains an auxiliary argument. Madison claimed that extending the sphere made it more difficult for individuals to act in "unison" even when a "common motive exists." Increasing the size of the sphere increased the size of the factions, and that made it more difficult for individuals to act in unison. In other words, Madison was making a claim similar to Olson's size thesis: larger groups were more likely to fail than smaller ones (Olson 1965, 48–49).

The idea was simple, and Madison used it to bolster his theory of pluralism. An extended republic required very large factions in order for any single faction to constitute the majority. Therefore, majority factions were less capable of forming in larger republics than they were in smaller ones. One of the reasons why Madison believed larger factions would be less likely to form was that "communication is always checked by distrust in proportion to the number whose concurrence is necessary" (*Federalist* 10, Hamilton et al. 1961a, 83). In other words, distrust among members could prevent cooperation. In smaller factions, distrust would be overcome by signaling the desire to cooperate. In larger factions, communication would be ineffective, and distrust would reign free.

In addition, Madison argued that "respect for character," or wanting to maintain a good public image, is less effective in larger groups than it is in smaller ones. Respect for character "loses its efficacy in proportion to the number which is to divide the pain or burden," he wrote (October 24, 1787, MP 10, 213). Everything else being equal, individual behavior was more difficult to monitor in larger groups than in smaller ones. In small groups, individuals might contribute to avoid tarnishing their images. In large groups, shirkers would go unnoticed and public image would not encourage cooperation.

By extending the republic, Madison hoped to divide factions. He used his size thesis to argue against the possibility of any one faction's obtaining control over government. Not only did this give rise to his theory of pluralism but it also helped him abate concern about the size of the republic framed by the Constitution. Clearly, Madison's theory of collective action affected some of his more popular works.

It would be tempting to find a few scattered passages like these and conclude that Madison really based his theory of pluralism on theories of collective action. But that would be selective reading. The heart of Madison's argument clearly rests with the notion that larger republics contain a greater diversity of interests, not with a size thesis (see "Vices" or *Federalist* 52, for example). The idea that larger groups are less likely to be successful for collective action reasons played only a secondary role.

Moreover, Madison did not have a crisp notion about the relationship between group size and group success. In the same *Federalist* where he argued that increasing the size of a faction would make it less effective, he also argued that larger groups would prevail over smaller ones. In his words, "[T]he most numerous party, or in other words, the most powerful faction must be expected to prevail" (*Federalist* 10, Hamilton et al. 1961a, 80). How could larger factions be expected to prevail when they were more likely to founder in larger sizes? It was an irony that Madison left unanswered. Just as he had used his ideas about the collective action problem to his advantage, he had also failed to see how his idea contradicted pluralism. Ironically, later generations used the size thesis against him (Olson 1965, 141–67; Moe 1981; Brand 1983).

Madison's conception of democracy was new because it did not depend on noble character. Madison recognized that individuals could always fall back on their personal interests and that personal interests could unravel a republic like the American Confederation.

Conclusion

Several scholars have treated Madison as if he were a public choice scholar. They have claimed that he was aware of technical issues, such as the paradox of voting, and knew the importance of creating institutions to address that problem.[35] Although strong versions of such claims cannot be substantiated, this chapter shows that Madison had a handle on the preliminaries of one aspect of public choice—public goods theory. The observations, theoretical descriptions, and implementation of these ideas clearly showed that the Framers not only understood collective action problems but also could engineer institutions based on their conceptions.

Madison was at the forefront of collective action theorists in early America. He had a careful explanation for free-riding behavior, a clear notion of selective incentives, and some idea of joint products. Although his conclusions were not deduced, hence cannot be considered "rational choice," he clearly thought in terms of abstract actors and expected behaviors.

Combining Madison's reasoning with the topic of collective action produces some remarkable similarities between Madison and modern public goods theorists, such as Mancur Olson. Although Madison certainly did not have the problem completely worked out, he had a fairly comprehensive understanding of collective behavior that predates twentieth-century economics. Just as it is inaccurate to attribute the theory of collective action solely to Olson, it is equally inaccurate to attribute it solely to Samuelson, Wicksell, or any other nineteenth- or twentieth-century economist.

Even though Madison had considerable hands-on experience with a prominent collective action problem and was able to develop a better form of government based on his experiences, he did not write a treatise on the idea. Madison devoted no more than a few paragraphs to the free rider problem in any speech or writing. He only wrote sentences about joint products and even less about selective incentives and the relationship between group size and group success. More important, none of his ideas were published until after his death. They appeared in his notes, personal letters, and speeches. This may have been Madison's shortcoming. By failing to devote an essay to the subject, Madison was unable to fully convince his opponents of the collective action problem, and he was left without a legacy associated with the idea. Although Madison is remembered for his theories of pluralism and separation of powers, a theory of collective action was equally central to his thought.

Notes

My gratitude to Sam Kernell for recognizing the link between Madison's theory of public goods and his well-known theories of republican government, to Lui Hebron for editorial comments and suggestions, and to two anonymous referees for careful insights—particularly with respect to assurance games and prisoners' dilemmas.

1. Although many scholars seem to recognize the collective action problem among states under the Articles of Confederation, such descriptions have been published only recently. See, for example, Dougherty 2001; Cain and Dougherty 1999; Dougherty and Cain 1997; and Jillson and Wilson 1994. Wilson's chapter in this book, "Madison at the First Congress," carefully describes the problem as well.

2. I use the term "collective action problem" broadly. Following Sandler (1992), the term captures a variety of game theoretic structures (prisoner dilemmas, assurance, chicken, etc.) that apply to various collective goods (public goods, club goods, common pool resources, etc.).

3. Olson (1965) seemed to confuse the privileged individual with the privileged group. Contrast his statements on pp. 28–29, which describe the response of a single actor, with his statements on pp. 35–36, which describe the rational response of actors in plural. In honor of Olson, I attempted to sort out what followed from his framework in the appendix of Dougherty 2001, 183–92. Using the framework of his cost and benefit analysis, it is rational for a single actor to contribute or for no actor to contribute—regardless of group size. The single actor would be the one who benefits the most from the good, given their endowment. Actors, in plural, would contribute only when more than one of them gain the same benefits, and these same benefits are the largest obtainable benefits for the group. Such results apply to public goods with summation technology and no income effects. They would not apply to public goods with weakest link aggregation, negative income elasticities, some specialized leader-follower behaviors, and other strategic assumptions.

4. Public goods are goods that are both nonexcludable and nonrival. A nonexcludable good cannot be feasibly excluded from an actor if it is provided for other actors. A nonrival good does not reduce in quantity when an actor consumes it. For example, deterrence is a public good because adjacent actors receive the benefits of deterrence and consuming deterrence does not reduce the amount available for others. Private goods, in contrast, are both excludable and rival.

5. The first quotation comes from James Madison to Thomas Jefferson, Oct. 3, 1785, MP 8, 373–74; the second comes from the speech of James Madison, Virginia Convention Debates, June 11, 1788, in Jensen 1976, *The Documentary History of the Ratification of the Constitution* [hereafter DH], 9, 1144.

6. Roughly 95 percent of congressional expenditures were spent on the Continental Army during the Revolution, and 88 percent of the congressional budget was directed toward the reduction of war debts after the war. Both of these goods are typically considered public goods (Dougherty 2001, 10).

7. To Edmund Pendelton, November 7, 1780, MP 2, 165–68; from Joseph Jones, May 21, 1782, MP 4, 259–61; Brown 1993. In the preface to his notes on the federal convention, Madison wrote: "[T]he radical infirmity of the art[icles] of Confederation was the dependence of Congress on the voluntary and simultaneous compliance with its Requisitions, each consulting more or less its par-

ticular interests & convenience and distrusting the compliance of others" (Far-rand 1966, 3, 542–43). In the Virginia ratifying convention he described the col-lective action problem as "the principal inefficacy of requisitions" (June 11, 1788, DH 9, 1144–46). Madison's concerns with tyrannical majorities appeared sec-ondary (Dougherty 2001). For a contrasting view, see Banning (1995).

8. See also: To Jefferson, Oct. 3, 1785, MP 8, 373–74.

9. John Marshall, Virginia Convention Debates, June 10, 1788, DH 9, 1120; "Vices," MP 9, 351.

10. Alexander Hamilton, in contrast, described the problem more often like a prisoners' dilemma. Although he wrote passages in which free-riding results from the deficiencies of other states, he more frequently claimed that states had an incentive to free-ride whether others contributed or not (see Alexander Hamilton to James Duane, Sept. 3, 1780, *The Papers of Alexander Hamilton* [here-after HP] 2, 406; New York Convention, June 28, 1788, Bailyn 1993, 2, 830; Hamilton et al. 1961a, *Federalist* 15, 111, and *Federalist* 16, 114).

11. James Madison to Thomas Jefferson, April 16, 1781, MP 3, 72. Although Madison headed the congressional committee that proposed coercion, it is im-portant to note that he did not initiate the idea (Banning 1995, 20–23; Dough-erty 2001, 68–69, 133–37).

12. "The Continentalist" Number VI, July 4, 1782, HP 3, 105; and speech of Oliver Ellsworth, Connecticut Convention Debates, Jan. 7, 1788, DH 3, 553–54.

13. For Madison's quotation, see Notes on Debates, May 31, 1787, Farrand 1966, 1, 54. For a more careful explanation of why Madison became averse to coercing the states, see Dougherty 2001, 147–49, 171; Ostrom 1987, 38–41; and Virginia Convention Debates, June 12, 1788, DH 10, 1202–5. Ostrom attributes the problem of applying force against the states to Hamilton, but it is more ac-curately attributed to George Mason (Dougherty 2001, 147 n. 37).

14. For example, the receiver of the continental tax for the state of Virginia published the following excerpt in the Virginia Gazette: "I do hereby Certify, that I have not received any payment from the State of Virginia, on account of the United States for the first of October to the first of November, 1782" (quoted in MP 5, 287, n. 17).

15. On Nov. 26, 1782, Madison wrote Randolph that chiding Virginia into compliance has not worked and that Pennsylvania is reacting by assuming the debts owed by Congress to its citizens (MP 5, 328–33; also see To Edmund Ran-dolph, Dec. 10, 1782, ibid., 394–96). For examples of letters to the states, see JCC, Mar. 15, 1782, 22, 132–36; and Circular to the States, June 8, 1783, *The Writings of George Washington,* ed. John Fitzpatrick (1938) [hereafter WP], 26, 488–96.

16. One clear exception was the positive externalities produced by neigh-boring states. For example, if Pennsylvania paid its requisitions, and part of its payment went to federal creditors in the state of New York, then New York would be receiving private benefits from Pennsylvania's payment. Separating the private incentives from the public ones was part of Congress' strategy.

17. Indents were paper notes that tied the payment of a requisition directly

to the payment of bond-holders within each state. Although the system provides another example of how joint products were put to use, it only weakly represents Madison's understanding of the phenomena because Madison left Congress before they were proposed in 1784. Undoubtedly, however, he was well aware of the system and what Congress was trying to achieve by enacting it (Dougherty 2001, 77–82; Ferguson 1961, 223).

18. Virginia Convention Debates, June 7, 1788, DH 9, 1031. Perhaps Hamilton made this point clearer when he wrote: "The States near the seat of war, influenced by motives of self-preservation, made efforts to furnish their quotas, which even exceeded their abilities; while those at a distance from danger were for the most part as remiss as the others were diligent in their exertions" (Hamilton et al. 1961a, Federalist 22, 145–46). See also James Madison, June 11, 1788, DH 9, 1145; and Joseph Jones to Thomas Jefferson in James Madison to Thomas Jefferson, Apr. 16, 1781, Smith et al. 1976 [hereafter LOD] 17, 159.

19. Quoted in Ketcham (1990, 42). For more on Witherspoon's classes at Princeton and the books he exposed students to, see ibid., 41–44, and Miller (1992, 50–53). One should note that Hume described part of the free-rider problem by writing: "Two neighbors may agree to drain a meadow, which they posses in common; because 'tis easy for them to know each other's mind; and each must perceive, that the immediate consequence of his failing his part, is, the abandoning the whole project. But 'tis very difficult, and indeed impossible, that a thousand persons shou'd agree in any such action; it being difficult for them to concert so complicated a design, and still more difficult for them to execute it; while each seeks a pretext to free himself of the trouble and expence, and wou'd lay the whole burden on others" (Hume (1739–40) 1978, bk. III, pt. 2, sect. 7, p. 538; Olson 1965, 33–34, n. 53). This passage depicts the problem similar to an assurance game and contains somewhat of a size thesis. Madison may have read these passages while at the College of New Jersey, or later, but his letters in the mid-1770s suggest that he did not understand the collective action problem until years after he graduated from college.

20. James Madison to William Bradford, June 19, 1775, MP 1, 151–53; James Madison to William Bradford, Nov. 26, 1774, MP 1, 129.

21. For a sample of the relevant letters, see The Marquis de La Fayette to Patrick Henry, Jan. 3, 1778, Patrick Henry: Life Correspondence and Speeches [hereafter HP] 3, 139; An Address to the inhabitants of New Jersey, Pennsylvania, Delaware, Maryland, and Virginia, Feb. 18, 1778, WP 10, 480–81; George Washington to Patrick Henry, Feb. 19, 1778, HP 3, 148–50; and George Washington to George Mason, March 27, 1779, HP 2, 45–46.

22. To Benjamin Harrison, Speaker of the House of Delegates of Virginia, Dec. 18, 1778, The Writings of George Washington, ed. Jared Sparks (1833–37), 6, 142. Washington's most eloquent description of the problem was five years later in his infamous address to the states (Mar. 15, 1783, DH 13, 69).

23. On Dec. 8, 1779, Madison wrote his father that Virginia should zealously

support Congress in the prosecution of the war (MP 1, 315–18). This *may* suggest that Madison did not recognize the advantages of free-riding, though the passage could easily be interpreted as Madison's hope that the state contribute despite these advantages.

24. James Madison to Thomas Jefferson, Mar. 27, 1780, MP 2, 5–7.

25. JCC 1, 45. This speech was reprinted in Galloway 1972, 70–81.

26. Madison's first exposure to Galloway was at the University of New Jersey in 1769. Galloway gave one of the keynote speeches at commencement that year, which Madison described to his father (To James Madison Sr., Sept. 30, 1769, MP 1, 45). However, it is unlikely that Galloway spoke about collective action problems at that time.

27. Galloway 1972, 8–11, 74–77. It is unlikely that Madison read the published version of Galloway's work before he wrote Jefferson on Mar. 27, 1780, because Galloway moved to London in 1778 and published his *Historical and Political Reflections* there in 1780.

28. The first of six issues of "The Continentalist" was published July 12, 1781. Hamilton does not fully express his notion of the collective action problem until the final issue ("The Continentalist" Number VI, July 4, 1782, HP 3, 99–106), and then he writes no more than a few sentences. For more hands-on observations from Hamilton, see his letters as Receiver of the Continental Tax for the state of New York (Dougherty 2001, 65) and *Federalist* 15–16, 21–22, and 30.

29. Hamilton developed an almost equally compelling explanation for free-riding behavior in a letter to James Duane (Sept. 3, 1780, HP 2, 400–403). This letter was written six months after Madison wrote Jefferson and well before Hamilton and Madison met. Ralph Ketcham, a modern historian, claims that the first contact between Madison and Hamilton was when Duane read the above-mentioned letter from Hamilton to Madison in Philadelphia (1990, 113). Madison must have been surprised to find such similarity in their ideas.

30. See, for example, To Thomas Jefferson, June 2, 1780, MP 2, 37; From James Madison, April 16, 1781, *The Papers of Thomas Jefferson* [hereafter JP] 5, 473–74; Notes on Debates, Jan. 28, 1783, MP 6, 144–45; To Thomas Jefferson, Oct. 3, 1785, MP 8, 373–74; and "Vices," MP 9, 345–58.

31. Luther Martin, Madison's Notes on Debates, June 27, 1787, Farrand 1966, 1, 437; Some Observations on the Constitution, *Writings of James Monroe* 1989, 1, 307–43 (quoted on p. 323). Monroe prepared his pamphlet prior to Virginia's ratifying convention and continued to claim that a strong government would elicit requisition payments there (June 10, 1788, DH 9, 1109–10). For the latter, see William Grayson, Virginia Convention Debates, June 12, 1788, DH 10, 1186.

32. After studying ancient and modern confederations, Madison concluded that the voluntary design was a flaw not easily repaired. In a letter to Jefferson he wrote: "The authority of a Stadtholder, the influence of a Standing Army, the common interest in the conquered possessions, the pressure of surrounding danger, the guarantee of foreign powers, are not sufficient to secure the authority

and interest of the generality ag[ain]st the anti-federal tendency of the provincial sovereignties" (Oct. 24, 1787, MP 10, 210). For evidence that collective action problems were the primary motivation behind "Ancient and Modern Confederation," see DH 9, 1029–33.

33. It was also easier to reconstitute the government than to amend the Articles of Confederation. This affected Madison's decision to push for a new constitution as well (Dougherty 2001, 153–60).

34. Bourke (1975) argues that the theory of pluralism was more of a twentieth-century interpretation of Madison than a description of Madison's thinking. Although Bourke's thesis is worthy of further investigation, I will presume that the traditional interpretation is correct for the remainder of this chapter.

35. For claims that Madison used methods similar to rational choice, see several of the works within Grofman and Wittman 1989, particularly the chapter by Thomas Schwartz. For claims that Madison understood the paradox of voting, see McGrath 1983. For convincing evidence that Madison did not understand this paradox, see McLean and Urken 1992.

Chapter 4

Personal Motives, Constitutional Forms, and the Public Good: Madison on Political Leadership

RANDALL STRAHAN

Of all men, that distinguish themselves by memorable achievements, the first place of honour seems due to LEGISLATORS and founders of states, who transmit a system of laws and institutions to secure the peace, happiness, and liberty of future generations.

David Hume, 1741[1]

James Madison stands out in American history for having achieved eminence both as a politician and as a political scientist. First entering politics in his native Virginia during the American Revolution, he steadily ascended from state legislature, to the Continental and Confederation Congresses, to the new House of Representatives, to the office of Secretary of State, and finally to the highest political office in the new American republic, the presidency. But Madison's visibility today is probably due more to his achievements as a political scientist than as a politician. Madison's ideas helped define the terms of the debate in the Constitutional Convention of 1787 and, though drafted in the heat of debates over ratification of the proposed Constitution, his contributions to *The Federalist* are now widely regarded to be among the highest achievements not only of American but also of modern political thought. The focus of this chapter is on Madison the political scientist. However, my purpose is to consider an aspect of Madison's political science that may also shed some light on Madison the politician: his analysis of political leadership in modern constitutional republics.

Most political scientists probably consider Madison's major contributions to the discipline to have been his hard-headed realism about the importance of self-interest in politics, and the clarity and force with which he explained how properly designed institutions can control and channel that self-interest.[2] His treatment of factions, and of how ambitious officeholders check one another's power in a separation of powers system, is usually considered his most important contribution to the systematic study of politics.[3] While his coauthor on *The Federalist*, Alexander Hamilton, is known for his views on the importance of energetic political leadership, this subject has received less attention in discussions of Madison's ideas on the design of republican constitutions. In his most familiar writings Madison seems to place much greater emphasis on institutions than on leaders or officeholders. According to his best-known contributions to *The Federalist*, the principal solution to the problem of factions is not "enlightened statesmen" but "the extent and proper structure of the union"; likewise, the solution to tyrannical concentrations of power in the hands of government officials is to be found not in the "better motives" of officeholders, but in "contriving the interior structure of the government, as that its several constituent parts may, by their mutual relations, be the means of keeping each other in their proper places" (*Federalist* 10, *The Papers of James Madison* [hereafter MP] 10, 266, 269; *Federalist* 51, MP 10, 477, 476).

Where Madison does refer directly to political leaders, the term usually takes on a pejorative cast.[4] An "attachment to different leaders ambitiously contending for pre-eminence and power" is cited as one of the major causes of factions (*Federalist* 10, MP 10, 265). Legislative assemblies are said to be prone to being "seduced by factious leaders, into intemperate and pernicious resolutions" (*Federalist* 62, MP 10, 538). "How frequently," Madison asks himself at one point in his private notes, will those engaged in politics "be the dupe of a favorite leader, veiling his selfish views under the professions of public good, and varnishing his sophistical arguments with the glowing colours of popular eloquence" (MP 9, 354). In these and other passages, Madison seems to view political leadership more as a problem to be controlled than a capacity to be encouraged in the design of constitutions.

Yet throughout *The Federalist* and elsewhere in his writings and correspondence, Madison also speaks repeatedly of the importance of having political offices filled by "fit characters," "individuals of extended views," or persons of "generous principles," and of the need to design institutions that can select and sustain "virtuous" officeholders and "such as will feel most strongly the proper motives." Writing to Thomas Jefferson in 1780, Madison lamented the "defect of adequate statesmen" in the Continental Congress, which made it "more likely to fall into wrong measures and of less weight to enforce right ones" (MP 3, 6). What are we to make of these statements which seem to indicate that the presence of certain types of leaders would be important in determining the performance of republican institutions? Did Madison truly believe that the presence or absence of certain personal qualities in political officeholders would be an important causal factor in the politics of republican constitutional forms? How could this be the case if the fundamental principles of his political science are that most political action is motivated by personal self-interest, and that effective republican constitutions work by channeling that self-interest?

One possibility is that Madison's references to virtue and public-spiritedness on the part of political leaders are mere rhetorical or literary devices intended to take some of the edge off the unflattering realism about the motives of citizens and politicians that truly undergirds his political science.[5] In most of his writings and speeches, Madison was addressing political controversies that were very much alive. He wrote not simply to communicate his latest findings but also in the attempt to persuade those of his day who were active in those controversies. It would hardly be surprising if an author in this situation wrote in such a way as to avoid unnecessarily offending the sensibilities of his main audience. However, it may also be true that Madison's political science is simply more complex than it is sometimes portrayed, and that his analysis of the design of constitutional forms takes into account a variety of political motivations beyond narrow self-interest. In fact, as I will attempt to show in this chapter, such a broader view of the personal motives behind political action is a central feature of Madison's political science, as is the view that republican constitutions can work not only to control and channel self-interest but also to select out and encourage public-spirited officeholders. While Madison sought to design republican constitutions capable of checking or controlling certain modes of political leadership through institutional incentives and constraints, he also devoted serious attention to the question of how constitutional forms could be designed to attract and develop political leaders who would be inclined to use public office to advance the public good.

Because Madison's importance as a political scientist is tied primarily to events surrounding the 1787 Constitutional Convention, I focus on his writings from the late 1780s that reveal the state of his thinking during those years: his 1787 notes on "Vices of the Political System of the United States" and his contributions to *The Federalist*. Speeches Madison delivered at the Constitutional Convention and his personal correspondence provide additional evidence about how he understood the politics of political leadership. Staying close to what he wrote and said during these years, I first take up Madison's understanding of the personal motives that lie behind political action, paying particular attention to his views on the motivations of officeholders and how they may differ from those of ordinary citizens. Second, I examine Madison's arguments about the basic objectives or ends of republican constitutions and what he meant by "the public good." Next, I turn to Madison's analysis of constitutional forms, showing that he believed a republican constitution could be designed both to channel and control the lower or most common motivations of political officeholders, *and* to encourage and reinforce certain higher motivations that cause some leaders to seek out and advance the public good.

In the final section of the chapter I consider how Madison's approach compares with more recent political science scholarship on political leadership, and why his writings continue to remain of interest to political scientists. Quite a few scholars in recent years have noted affinities between Madison's political science and the rational choice approaches that underlie much recent work in the political science field. Iain McLean's contribution to this volume characterizes him as among the earliest to employ an economic or game theoretic approach to politics. Affinities between Madison and contemporary rational choice scholarship are clearly visible when Madison's analysis of political leadership is considered alongside recent leadership studies that employ principal-agent theories. However, when these approaches are compared with some care, equally important differences become apparent as well.

Contemporary rational choice scholarship has now advanced well beyond Madison's political science in terms of the precision and technical rigor with which it can produce generalizations about the pursuit of individual self-interest within different institutional settings. These developments within political science raise a final question to be addressed in the chapter: whether Madison's thought remains of interest to political scientists because of its contributions to American political history and to the intellectual history of political science or because it continues to supply guidance about how to study and explain politics. Taking nothing away from the importance of understanding Madison for understanding the past, I argue that as political scientists we should remain interested in Madison because his theory of politics continues to provide valuable guidance about how to understand the politics of modern constitutional republics, and particularly the politics of political leadership within these regimes.

Madison's Political Science

James Madison's most important contributions to political science were occasioned by a specific political problem: the need to establish a new constitution to remedy the weaknesses of the Articles of Confederation. Unlike some ancient founders and lawgivers who claimed to have received guidance from gods and oracles, Madison took a more systematic approach.[6] In preparing for the 1787 Constitutional Convention, he conducted comparative research of two types: he read widely in the political histories of federal and confederal regimes that had existed in both ancient and modern times; and he engaged in reflection on the political problems that had developed within existing American governments. In the latter case, his method included extensive observation at close range, having had ample opportunity to "soak and poke" as a member of the Virginia state legislature (1776–77, 1784–87), the Virginia Council of State (1777–79), and the Continental Congress (1780–83, 1787–88). The conclusions Madison drew from these empirical investigations were grounded theoretically in ideas from a number of leading European political thinkers of his day. These included John Locke's on the origins and ends of government, and David Hume's on some aspects of institutional design, and moral and political psychology.[7] Madison viewed government primarily as a compact individuals enter into to protect their rights, with the ends of establishing greater security and prosperity. His investigations of the 1780s addressed two central questions: first, why had the national and the state governments that Americans established upon gaining their independence been doing such a poor job of securing these ends, and second, how a republican constitution could be structured to secure these ends for Americans and for others in the future.

While the most extensive presentation of Madison's views on these questions is found in *The Federalist*, his 1787 notes on "Vices of the Political System of the United States" also merit close attention. "Vices" is the earliest statement of Madison's analysis of the causes and cure for the diseases of republican government that he observed in the American political situation of the 1780s. It provides a useful benchmark from which to judge the development of different elements of his thought during and after the Constitutional Convention. In addition it is the one broad statement of Madison's political science *not* intended for public consumption.[8] The later statements, during the Constitutional Convention, in *The Federalist*, and during the debates on ratification, all appear in political settings where we might not be too surprised to find some strategic or rhetorical arguments interwoven with Madison's sincere views. Despite its rough and occasionally elliptical form, "Vices" is therefore especially important for understanding what Madison the political scientist actually thought. To understand Madison's analysis of political leadership in constitutional republics, it is necessary to begin by considering his theory of the individual motivations that lie behind political action.

Personal Motives

In "Vices," Madison identifies two fundamental problems with the existing political system of the United States: the weakness of the federal government under the Articles of Confederation, and the injustice and instability of laws being enacted by the state governments. He traces the causes of both to a mismatch between political institutions and political motives. Regarding the failure of the states to meet their obligations to the federal government under the Articles of Confederation, Madison notes that the designers of the Articles neglected to provide adequate sanctions to ensure that the states would fulfill their obligations, thereby failing to take into account the "ordinary motives by which the laws secure the obedience of individuals" (MP 9, 351). Addressing next the malady of injustice in state laws, Madison asks: "To what causes is this evil to be ascribed?" His answer indicates that he believed the analysis of this problem needed to be undertaken at two levels: "The causes lie 1. in the Representative bodies. 2. In the people themselves" (MP 9, 354). Devoting separate treatment to elected officeholders and ordinary citizens, Madison traces the problem again to motivations behind political action and the inadequacy of political institutions (in this case at the state level) in relation to those motivations.

Madison's investigation of how ordinary citizens ("the people themselves") contributed to the misgovernment of the states leads him to set forth in outline the theory of majority factions that would become the central theme of some of his most important speeches at the Constitutional Convention and his best-known contribution to *The Federalist*. For our purposes what is most important in this initial statement of the theory of factions is Madison's treatment of the motivations behind political action, and the relative strength of those motivations.[9] "Interest" and "passion" are singled out as the most important motives that lie behind popular factions. Interests involve primarily the pursuit of material or economic concerns ("as they happen to be creditors or debtors—rich or poor—husbandmen, merchants or manufacturers ... inhabitants of different districts—owners of different kinds of property &c &c"), while passions may arise from a variety of nonmaterial causes ("members of different religious sects—followers of different political leaders") (MP 9, 355).

"Whenever therefore an apparent interest or common passion unites a majority," Madison asks, "what is to restrain them from unjust violations of the rights and interests of the minority, or of individuals?" (ibid.). Here, three additional political motives of ordinary citizens are identified. The first is what might be termed enlightened self-interest: "A prudent regard to their own good as involved in the general and permanent good of the community." But this motive is "found by experience to be too often unheeded" (ibid.). The second motivation is "respect for character," by which Madison means concern for one's reputation.[10] But reputational motives are also unlikely to be sufficiently strong or reliable to restrain individuals from participating in factional majorities. Probably drawing on Hume, Madison de-

scribes what he considered to be one of the most powerful regularities in political life—the tendency of individual moral responsibility and judgment to
be weakened when individuals act in concert with others.[11] "However
strong this motive [reputation] may be in individuals, it is considered as very
insufficient to restrain them from injustice. In a multitude, its efficacy is diminished in proportion to the number which is to share in the praise or
blame. Besides, as it has reference to public opinion, which within a particular Society is the opinion of the majority, the standard is fixed by those
whose conduct is to be measured by it"(ibid.). Nor is "Religion," the third
motive cited, sufficient to restrain the narrower forms of interest, or passions.
Religious scruples also lose efficacy when considering individuals "in an aggregate view," and religion itself has sometimes been "a motive to oppression" (MP 9, 356). This theory of motivations, in which public-regarding
motives exist, but are less strong than the motives of immediate interests or
passions when citizens act collectively, is restated in very similar terms in
Madison's June 6, 1787, speech to the Constitutional Convention (Farrand
1966, 1, 134–36).

Madison elaborated on his views of the political motives of citizens in his
correspondence with Thomas Jefferson. In an October 1787 letter reviewing
the outcome of the Constitutional Convention, Madison included what he
conceded was "an immoderate digression." In the course of defending to a
skeptical Jefferson his position in favor of a national veto over state laws,
Madison restates his conclusions about how factions arise from the motives
of ordinary citizens, and the inadequacy of the state governments for controlling this problem.[12] However, in the Jefferson letter Madison draws a
sharper distinction between interest and passion as motives for political action and offers an even less sanguine view of the influence of religious motives. Interests are said to arise primarily from "a distinction of property."
These distinctions are "various and unavoidable" in developed societies (MP
10, 212–13). In contrast, the political behavior motivated by passion is less
predictable and less rational:

> In addition to these natural [i.e., economic] distinctions, artificial ones will be
> founded, on accidental differences in political, religious or other opinions, or an
> attachment to the persons of leading individuals. However erroneous or ridicu-
> lous these grounds of dissention and faction may appear to the enlightened States-
> man, or the benevolent philosopher, the bulk of mankind who are neither
> Statesmen nor Philosophers, will continue to view them in a different light. (MP
> 10, 213)

Writing to his trusted ally, Madison also goes into more detail in explaining why other motives could not be relied upon to counteract the interests

or passions that animate majority factions. Of enlightened self-interest—"a
prudent regard to private or partial good, as essentially involved in the general and permanent good"—Madison observes: "Experience shews that it
has little effect on individuals, and perhaps still less on collections of individuals, and least of all on a majority with the public authority in their hands"
(ibid.). Regarding concern for reputation, Madison restates his earlier conclusion that this motive "loses its efficacy in proportion to the number which
is to divide the praise or the blame" (ibid.). But the treatment of religion as
a political motive again goes beyond what Madison would say publicly in
The Federalist and elsewhere:

> The inefficacy of this restraint on individuals is well known. The conduct of every
> popular assembly, acting on oath, the strongest of religious ties, shews that indi-
> viduals join without remorse in acts agst. which their consciences would revolt,
> if proposed to them separately in their closets. When Indeed Religion is kindled
> into enthusiasm, its force like that of other passions is increased by the sympathy
> of a multitude. But enthusiasm is only a temporary state of Religion, and whilst
> it lasts will hardly be seen with pleasure at the helm. Even in its coolest state, it
> has been much oftener a motive to oppression than a restraint from it. (MP 10,
> 213–14)[13]

This same theory of political motives appears in Madison's better known
contributions to *The Federalist*, although with some important refinements.
In Number 10, interest and passion are cited as the principal motives that
give rise to factions that pursue objectives "adverse to the rights of other citizens, or to the permanent and aggregate interests of the community" (MP
10, 264). The other, less selfish personal motives are given briefer treatment
than in the earlier writings, but are similarly noted to be less strong or reliable than immediate interest or passion, especially when citizens act in large
groups. "If the impulse and the opportunity be suffered to coincide, we well
know that neither moral nor religious motives can be relied on as an adequate control. They are not found to be such on the injustice and violence
of individuals, and lose their efficacy in proportion to the number combined
together, that is, in proportion as their efficacy becomes needful" (*Federalist*
10, MP 10, 267). The most "common and durable" of the motivations that
lie behind factions is economic interest, specifically "the various and unequal
distribution of property" (*Federalist* 10, MP 10, 265). Political action motivated by passion ("zeal for different opinions concerning religion, concerning government, and many other points, as well of speculation as of practice;
an attachment to different leaders ambitiously contending for pre-eminence
and power") is less common but also more disruptive and difficult to control
(ibid.; see also Epstein 1984, 76–78, 107–8; Matthews 1995, 74–81).

The most important refinement in the treatment of political motives in *The Federalist* is the discussion of reason as a guide or motive for political action. Reason is understood as the human faculty through which citizens recognize and pursue their collective, long-term interests—what Madison calls "the public good." (Precisely what Madison meant by the public good is addressed below.) This understanding of reason appears to be an important point where Madison diverges from Hume on human motivations; where Hume considered reason always subservient to human passions, Madison's theory allows at least the possibility for reason to prevail over passion as well as "partial" or "immediate" interests.[14] As Daniel W. Howe (1987, 491) has pointed out, a "hierarchy of motives" is presented in *The Federalist*: "first reason, then prudence (or self interest), then passion."

Drawing on this view of reason, Madison proposes in *The Federalist* that a well-designed republican constitution should give rise to officeholders who would be responsive to majorities based on citizens' reason, but not to a popular will arising from passion, or narrow or partial interests.[15] In evaluating various means of redressing imbalances in the powers of a republican constitution in *The Federalist* 49, he rejects the idea of allowing an appeal to the people during a conflict between branches for precisely this reason: "The *passions* . . . not the *reason*, of the people would sit in judgment. But it is the reason, alone, of the public that ought to control and regulate the government. The passions ought to be controlled and regulated by the government" (MP 10, 463; emphasis in original).

However, Madison also explains in *The Federalist* that a reasoned concern for the public good is normally a less powerful motive than passion or interest. Reason is fallible and almost always distorted by selfish passions or interests:

> As long as the reason of man continues fallible, and he is at liberty to exercise it, different opinions will be formed. As long as the connection subsists between his reason and his self-love, his opinions and his passions will have a reciprocal influence on each other; and the former will be the objects to which the latter will attach themselves. (*Federalist* 10, MP 10, 265)

> [T]he mild voice of reason, pleading the cause of an enlarged and permanent interest, is but too often drowned, before public bodies as well as individuals, by the clamors of an impatient avidity for immediate and immoderate gain. (*Federalist* 42, MP 10, 406)

We see, then, that among "the people themselves," Madison considered the pursuit of immediate self-interest (primarily economic interest) to be the most common and powerful political motive. Provided adequate institutions are in place, political action arising from the pursuit of economic interests can be regulated and adjusted within "the necessary and ordinary operations of government" (*Federalist* 10, MP 10, 265–66). Equally powerful, if less common, are motives that arise from the less rational passions. Madison seems less optimistic that behavior motivated by religion, ideology, personal attachments to leaders, and other passions can be adjusted within institutions, given that these motivations can create intense conflict over "the most frivolous and fanciful distinctions" and render individuals "more disposed to vex and oppress each other, than to co-operate for their common good" (*Federalist* 10, MP 10, 265).

It is clear, then, that Madison recognized public-regarding political motives to exist among ordinary citizens—including reason, an enlightened understanding of self-interest, and concern for reputation—but that he also considered these motives weaker than those of immediate interest or passion, particularly when individuals act in groups. For this reason, in small, relatively homogeneous republics such as the American states, the public-regarding motives could not be relied on to restrain popular majorities from coalescing into factions that undermined the public good or the rights of other citizens. A more extensive republic with a properly designed constitution, on the other hand, *could* control the effects of the narrower political motives while increasing the probability that popular majorities would be based on the broader motives. "In the extended republic of the United States, and among the great variety of interests, parties, and sects which it embraces, a coalition of a majority of the whole society could seldom take place on any other principles than those of justice and the general good" (*Federalist* 51, MP 10, 479).

Motives of Officeholders

The investigation of the causes of misgovernment of the states in "Vices of the Political System of the United States" considers not only causes originating in the motives of ordinary citizens but also those originating in the motives of their elected officials. The analysis here is as succinct as it is pessimistic:

> Representative appointments are sought from 3 motives. 1 ambition. 2. personal interest. 3. public good. Unhappily the two first are proved by experience to be most prevalent. Hence the candidates who feel them, particularly the second, are most industrious, and most successful in pursuing their object: and forming often a majority in the legislative Councils, with interested views, contrary to the interest and views of their Constituents, join in a perfidious sacrifice of the latter to the former. A succeeding election it might be supposed, would displace the of-

fenders, and repair the mischief. But how easily are base and selfish measures, masked by the pretexts of public good and apparent expediency? (MP 9, 354)

Madison's own political experience and reading of history had led him to conclude that some political leaders are motivated by the public good. But he did not consider this motivation sufficiently prevalent among leaders in the state governments to have had much effect. Nor does he elaborate on the underlying motives for public-spirited leadership, other than to note in the more general treatment of political motivations that actions in support of the public good could arise from an enlightened form of self-interest, or from concern for one's reputation. Political leaders are similar to ordinary citizens in being motivated by interest, but are distinctive in being also motivated by ambition, the pursuit of power for its own sake.

Given that Madison found ambition and personal interest to be the most prevalent motives among state-level officeholders, it is striking to find him concluding the analysis in "Vices" with an affirmation of the importance of designing institutions capable of selecting leaders animated by "proper" motives:

> The great desideratum in Government is such a modification of the sovereignty as will render it sufficiently neutral between the different interests and factions . . . and at the same time sufficiently controuled itself, from setting up an interest adverse to that of the whole Society. . . .
>
> An auxiliary desideratum for the melioration of the Republican form is such a process of elections as will most certainly extract from the mass of society the *purest and noblest characters* which it contains; such as will at once feel most strongly the *proper motives* to pursue the end of their appointment, and be most capable to devise the proper means of attaining it. (MP 9, 357, emphasis mine)

Despite the brief and decidedly pessimistic treatment afforded the subject of political leadership in "Vices," from these private notes there can be little doubt that Madison considered the selection of leaders who would act on the basis of the higher political motives (the public good, enlightened self-interest, reputation) an important objective to be addressed in designing republican constitutions. He did *not* take the conditions he observed in the state governments—officeholders motivated primarily by the narrower forms of ambition and interest—as given or as the necessary starting point for his reflections on how to design institutions for a more extensive federal republic.

In contrast to the more systematic treatment of political motives in "Vices," Madison does not provide a separate treatment of the motivations of political leaders in *The Federalist*. Motives of officeholders are addressed in the discussion of controlling factions in Number 10 and in other essays in which the different offices are taken up. However, the same theory of motives underlies Madison's arguments in defense of the Constitution. Motives attributed to officeholders include the higher motives of the public good, and a concern for reputation (character), as well as the lower motives of ambition, interest, and passion. Madison argues in Number 10, for example, that representatives selected under the forms of the Constitution will be more likely to be "proper guardians of the public weal" and to "discern the true interest of their country" and "least likely to sacrifice it to temporary or partial considerations" (MP 10, 268). Members of the Senate will be motivated, at least in part, by a sense of "national character" because their own individual reputations will be "incorporated with the reputation and prosperity of the community" (*Federalist* 63, MP 10, 544–45).

Recall that ambition was the one motive Madison had observed to be common among officeholders but not ordinary citizens. We can infer from the well known treatment of separation of powers in Number 51 ("Ambition must be made to counteract ambition. The interests of the man must be connected with the constitutional rights of the place") that he considered ambition a motive that would be common among the holders of most national offices (MP 10, 477). Both here and in Number 57, Madison makes the case that properly designed institutions can channel even the narrower form of ambition (the desire for power for its own sake) into advantageous behavior. An ambitious executive and ambitious legislators keep one another within the boundaries defined by the Constitution; "ambition itself" is one of the "cords" by which members of the House of Representatives who wish to retain power "will be bound to fidelity and sympathy with the great mass of the people" (*Federalist* 57, MP 10: 523). Personal interest and passion give rise to less beneficial behavior on the part of officeholders. Observing that interest corrupts judgment when judging one's own case, Madison asks his reader: "[W]hat are the different classes of legislators but advocates and parties to the causes which they determine?" (*Federalist* 10, MP 10, 266). Arguing for the need in every republican constitution for an institution such as the Senate, Madison observes that otherwise "national councils may be warped by some strong passion or momentary interest" (*Federalist* 63, MP 10, 544).

As with the earlier treatments of political motives, Madison's contributions to *The Federalist* recognize the existence and importance of the higher motivations among officeholders, but characterize the lower motives as more common and powerful. Thus, in the same number in which he argues that national representatives will be more likely to be motivated by the public good than those elected from smaller constituencies, Madison also concedes that "[e]nlightened statesmen will not always be at the helm" (*Federalist* 10, MP 10, 266). Likewise, in the discussion of how separation of powers is to be maintained in the proposed constitution, he endorses the "policy of supplying, by opposite and rival interests, the defect of better motives" (*Federalist* 51, MP 10, 477). However, these statements are certainly misunderstood if taken to mean that Madison's political science focuses single-mindedly on designing institutions to check or channel the lower political motivations of ambition for power or personal interest. As we shall see below, at least as much attention is devoted by Madison to the question of how to design institutions to increase the probability that leaders with better motives *would* be at the helm more often than had been the case under the republican governments Americans had experienced during the 1780s.

To summarize, three features of Madison's theory of political motives are most important for understanding his analysis of political leadership within republican constitutions. First, Madison considered the motives he observed in politics to be of two types: the better or higher, but weaker and less common motives (reason, enlightened self-interest, reputation), and the lower but stronger motives (ambition, personal or immediate interest, passion). A second important distinction for Madison is between the lower motives that have a rational or calculating element (ambition and interest), and motives based in passions, which are less common in politics but can produce irrational or self-destructive behavior, as well as behavior calculated to advance an ideology, religious orthodoxy, or favored leader.[16] Finally, Madison's view of popular majorities was that they could be based on broad, longer-term public interest, or "reason," as well as passion or narrower interests. Effective republican institutions would respond to the former but resist or control the latter.

The Ends of Government

Along with this theory of the hierarchy and varying influence of different political motives, a second fundamental element of Madison's political science was its focus on securing certain specific political objectives. Throughout his writings and speeches of the 1780s Madison makes clear that the purpose of his political investigations was to gain understanding of how to design institutions that could better secure the fundamental ends of republican government, which he termed private rights and the public good. As difficult as these ends may have been to realize in practice, each has a fairly precise and consistent meaning within Madison's political science.

In his notes on "Vices of the Political System of the United States," Madi-

son observes that one of the most "alarming" defects of the political system
under the Articles was the injustice of laws enacted by state governments.
This problem was more alarming than others, "because it brings more into
question the fundamental principle of republican government, that the majority who rule in such governments are the safest Guardians both of the
public Good and of private rights" (MP 9, 354). In *The Federalist* Number 10,
Madison states explicitly that the purpose of his political science is to secure
these ends—the public good and private rights—thereby vindicating the
fundamental principle of republican government:

> When a majority is included in a faction, the form of popular government . . . en-
> ables it to sacrifice to its ruling passion or interest, both the public good and the
> rights of other citizens. To secure the public good and private rights against the
> danger of such a faction, and at the same time to preserve the spirit and form of
> popular government, is then the great object to which our enquiries are directed.
> (MP 10, 267)

Madison uses this same formulation to characterize the ends of republican
government repeatedly in his earlier writings and throughout *The Federalist*.[17]

By "private rights," "the rights of other citizens," or sometimes simply
"justice," Madison refers to individual rights of property and conscience.
David Epstein has argued persuasively that Madison understood securing private rights to involve primarily *preventing* actions that involve violations of individual or private rights (see Epstein 1984, 100–101, 162–63). This logic is
visible, for example, in Madison's discussion of the benefits of large republics:
"Extend the sphere and you take in a greater variety of parties and interests;
you make it less probable that a majority of the whole will have a common
motive to invade the rights of other citizens" (*Federalist* 10, MP 10, 269).

By "the public good," Madison refers to the broad, collective, long-term
interests of society. Other formulations used to refer to this second basic end
of government in Madison's writings include "the general harmony," "the
permanent and aggregate interests of the community," "the great and aggregate interests," "the real welfare of the great body of the people," "an enlarged
and permanent interest," "the common good of the society," and "the general good." For Madison, as for his coauthors in *The Federalist*, the public
good primarily involves two broad objectives that benefit all members of society: safety or security, and economic prosperity.[18] In contrast to private
rights, which were protected primarily by preventing factional majorities or
government officeholders from taking certain actions, securing the public
good was understood by Madison more often to require positive action by
government. Note his comment in Number 45: "[T]he public good, the real
welfare of the great body of the people, is the supreme object to be pursued;

... no form of government whatever has any value than as it may be fitted for the attainment of this object" (MP 10, 429). As Epstein (1984, 163) argues: "[W]hile private rights must be respected by government, it is the public good which is to be 'pursued' by government."

Madison's political science took as its principal task the design of constitutional forms that could secure private rights and the public good more effectively than those that had been established during and immediately after the Revolution. Unlike his predecessors, who had displayed a "mistaken confidence" in "the justice, the good faith, the honor, the sound policy" of officeholders in republican governments, Madison brought to the task a more systematic—and realistic—understanding of the motives animating both political leaders and citizens (MP 9, 351). Applying his more scientific understanding of politics to the problem faced by Americans in 1787, Madison sought to design republican constitutional forms that could protect private rights from the effects of the lower political motives *and* select and develop leaders who would be motivated by the broader or higher motives to advance the public good.

Constitutional Forms and the Public Good

The conventional understanding of James Madison's political science among contemporary political scientists is that it focuses on the design of institutions that protect liberty by controlling and channeling self-interest. This understanding of Madison is not so much incorrect as it is incomplete. As we have seen, Madison's own observations of American politics and study of history led him to the conclusion that selfish motives—originating in the personal interest and ambition of officeholders and in the material interests and passions of ordinary citizens—are the most common and powerful forces that motivate political action. It should therefore come as no surprise that some of the main arguments Madison advanced about constitutional design do *not* depend on the higher, more public-regarding motives. However, Madison's science of institutional design does not stop with the problem of how to check power to prevent violations of private rights, but also addresses the problem of generating positive action to advance the public good. In this section I review briefly the best known Madisonian arguments about the importance of the narrower forms of self-interest in the design of republican constitutions, but then take up in greater detail Madison's less well known arguments about the ways institutions can be designed to increase the likelihood of selecting public-spirited officeholders, and encourage those officeholders to advance the public good while in office.[19]

In both "Vices of the Political System of the United States," and *The Federalist*, Madison cites the same two issues as the central problems of constitutional design for modern republics.

> The great desideratum in Government is such a modification of the Sovereignty as will render it sufficiently neutral between the different interests and factions, to controul one part of the Society from invading the rights of another, and at the same time sufficiently controuled itself, from setting up an interest adverse to that of the whole Society. (MP 9, 357)

> It is of great importance in a republic not only to guard the society against the oppression of its rulers, but to guard one part of the society against the injustice of the other part. (*Federalist* 51, MP 10, 478)

Because leaders "of factious tempers" as well as "enlightened statesmen" may win positions of power, the principal means of protecting one part of society (the minority) from the other part (a factional majority) is not public-spirited leadership but the creation of an extensive republic. "Extend the sphere and you take in a greater variety of parties and interests; you make it less probable that a majority of the whole will have a common motive to invade the rights of other citizens; or if such a motive exists, it will be more difficult for all who feel it to discover their own strength and to act in unison with each other" (*Federalist* 10, MP 10, 269). Note that the effect of the extended republic, according to Madison's argument, is primarily to *prevent* action, in this case the formation of national majorities motivated by interest or passion to pursue some objective adverse to private rights or the public good.[20]

Similarly, because ambition to exercise power will often be a motivation of officeholders, and citizens cannot always maintain control of them through elections, the abuse of power by rulers cannot be prevented by a reliance on better motives or respect for constitutional limits. Instead, to quote one of the best known passages in Madison's contributions to *The Federalist*:

> [T]he great security against a gradual concentration of the several powers in the same department consists in giving to those who administer each department the necessary constitutional means and personal motives to resist encroachments of the others. . . . Ambition must be made to counteract ambition. The interest of the man must be connected with the constitutional rights of the place. (*Federalist* 51, MP 10, 321–22)

This institutional arrangement is also oriented primarily toward the prevention of action—in this case encroachments of one branch on the powers of another, especially encroachments arising from the "enterprising ambition" of the legislative branch (*Federalist* 48, MP 10, 457).

As important as these arguments are to Madison's understanding of the proper design of republican constitutions, there is another series of institutional design arguments present in Madison's writings and speeches that does *not* rely on the lower or narrowly self-interested political motives, and focuses instead on securing positive action to advance the public good. In a passage that echoes the concluding section to "Vices of the Political System of the United States," Madison observes in *The Federalist* Number 57 (MP 10, 521): "The aim of every political constitution is, or ought to be, first to obtain for rulers men who possess the most wisdom to discern, and most virtue to pursue, the common good of the society; and in the next place, to take the most effectual precautions for keeping them virtuous whilst they continue to hold the public trust." This passage draws our attention to two additional problems addressed by Madison's political science: selecting properly motivated officeholders and configuring institutions in ways that evoke and reinforce the motivations that incline individuals to seek out and act on the public good.

Madison believed that the institutional arrangement most likely to lead to the selection of public-spirited officeholders was election from large electoral districts. His first statement of this view appears to have been in comments on Jefferson's draft of a new constitution for the state of Virginia in the mid-1780s (see Morgan 1974, 863). During the Federal Convention Madison opposed selection of either house of the national legislature by the legislatures of the states. Early in the debates (June 6, 1787) he argued that election "by the people immediately" was "a clear principle of free Govt. and that this mode under proper regulations had the additional advantage of securing *better* representatives" (Farrand 1966, 1, 134; emphasis mine).[21] Delegate Rufus King recorded in his notes that Madison had specified large districts as the "proper regulation" necessary to produce this effect: "Madison—The election may safely be made by the people if you enlarge the Sphere of Election—Experience proves it—if bad elections have taken place from the people, it will generally be found to have happened in small Distracts (ibid., 143–144).

In *The Federalist* Number 10, Madison offers a detailed explanation of how an extensive republic with larger districts would tend to produce better legislators, "proper guardians of the public weal." First, in a larger republic, there would be a larger pool of quality candidates that would create a "greater probability of a fit choice." Second, larger districts would make it more difficult for "unworthy characters to practice the vicious arts by which elections are too often carried." Elections would become "more likely to center on the men who possess the most attractive merit and the most dif-

fusive and established characters" (MP 10, 268). As Madison argued in a 1788
letter recommending very large (statewide) districts for the senate of Kentucky: "[In] free Governments, merit and notoriety of character are rarely
separated, and such a regulation would connect them more and more together" (MP 11, 286). Finally, small districts make legislators "unduly attached" to "local circumstances and lesser interests"(*Federalist* 10, MP 10,
268).

Madison elaborates on the benefits of larger electoral districts in the same
1788 letter recommending constitutional provisions for Kentucky:

> The appointment of Senators by [small] districts seems to be objectionable. A
> spirit of locality is inseparable from that mode. The evil is every where displayed
> in the County representations; the members of which are every where observed
> to lose sight of the aggregate interests of the Community, and even to sacrifice
> them to the interest or prejudices of their respective constituents. . . . The most ef-
> fectual remedy for local biass is to impress on the mind of the Senators an atten-
> tion to the interest of the whole Society, each citizen voting for every Senator.
> (MP 11, 286)

Thus Madison believed that "representatives chosen from large, heterogeneous districts are likely to be independent of any single interest" (Morgan
1974, 861). Or as James Q. Wilson (1990, 559) has characterized Madison's
expectation, rather than being strictly controlled by a homogeneous group
of voters, "each representative would now become the agent of many different and perhaps competing principals." In turn, it is the greater leeway representatives would enjoy, and the greater probability that voters would select
public-spirited legislators in large districts, that primarily explain the capacity of a properly designed "scheme of representation" to provide an important auxiliary check on factions: "to refine and enlarge the public views by
passing them through the medium of a chosen body of citizens, whose wisdom may best discern the true interest of their country . . . and will be least
likely to sacrifice it to temporary or partial considerations"(*Federalist* 10, MP
10, 268).

Regarding the constitutional forms Madison thought would help to keep
officeholders "virtuous" while in power and encourage positive action to advance the public good, it is important to note that not all of these institutional arrangements rely exclusively on the higher political motives. While
recognizing its limits, Madison believed that the motive of personal ambition
could be put to useful work in a properly designed constitution. As noted
above, Madison considered ambition useful as a motive that would cause the
legislature and the executive (especially the latter) to resist encroachments on
their respective constitutional powers. In the series of papers in *The Federal-*

ist on the House of Representatives, Madison also cites ambition as one of the motives that would help preserve the virtue and prevent the "degeneracy" of members of that body once elected to office. Citing ties that would develop to constituents from duty, gratitude, and pride, he acknowledges that all of these "would be found very insufficient without the restraint of frequent elections." To those concerned that members of the House would have insufficient "sympathy with the mass of the people," Madison observes that the House is

> so constituted as to support in the members an habitual recollection of their dependence on the people. Before the sentiments impressed on their minds by the mode of their elevation can be effaced by the exercise of power, they will be compelled to anticipate the moment when their power is to cease, when their exercise of it is to be reviewed, and when they must descend to the level from which they were raised; there forever to remain unless a faithful discharge of their trust shall have entitled their title to a renewal of it. (*Federalist* 57, MP 10, 352)

It also seems likely that one additional dimension to Madison's argument in support of larger electoral districts was that this change in electoral institutions would also have the beneficial effect of focusing the personal ambition of legislators on the representation of broader interests, even if legislators did not feel any real attachment to the public good. Succeeding politically in larger, more diverse electoral districts would require even those officeholders motivated strictly by officeholding ambition to develop skill at brokering and adjusting a wider range of interests. Those who did not develop these skills would also descend from power fairly quickly in a system with large electoral districts and frequent elections.[22]

However, in his analysis of the Senate, both in the Convention and in *The Federalist*, Madison develops a very different institutional logic. As Jack N. Rakove (1990, 51) has pointed out, Madison viewed the Senate as "the critical institution" in a republican constitution because of the dominant power he expected the legislative branch to wield and the volatility that could be present in the lower chamber. It is thus revealing that Madison's explanation of how the upper chamber should work relies much less on the motive of personal ambition or the negative incentive of possible electoral defeat, and more on the positive effects that could be expected from the higher political motives in a legislative body with fewer members who serve longer terms.

The smaller size of the Senate encourages its members to take positive actions to advance the public good for two reasons, each of which follows directly from Madison's understanding of individual motives. First, recall the general principle that the higher political motives that incline individuals to

advance the public good tend to be weakened or undermined when individuals act in large groups. Madison approached the design of legislative institutions with the same principle in mind. "In all very numerous assemblies,
of whatever characters composed, passion never fails to wrest the scepter
from reason. Had every Athenian been a Socrates, every Athenian assembly
would still have been a mob" (*Federalist* 55, MP 10, 505). Recognizing that
the House would have to be a fairly large body, Madison opposed proposals
in the Convention that would have increased the size of the Senate. As he argued on June 7: "The use of the Senate is to consist in its proceeding with
more coolness, with more system, & with more wisdom than the popular
branch. Enlarge their number and you communicate to them the vices
which they are meant to correct" (Farrand 1966, 1, 151). Being few in number, according to Madison's theory of personal motives, members of the Senate would be more likely to act on the basis of reason, rather than motives
arising from interest or passion.

In addition, Madison considered the members of a smaller, more permanent body to be especially inclined to advance the public good out of a concern for reputation, both their individual reputations and their country's reputation in the world—what Madison termed "a due sense of national
character." Recall that he had recorded in his private notes in advance of the
Convention that, the motive of reputation might be strong in particular individuals, "but is diminished in proportion to the number which is to share
in the praise or blame" (MP 9, 355). A smaller legislative body therefore
makes this motive much more likely to manifest itself in a legislator's behavior. In cases where "the national councils may be warped by some strong passion or momentary interest," Madison observes, "the presumed or known
opinion of the impartial world may be the best guide that can be followed"
(*Federalist* 63, MP 10, 382). However a sufficiently strong concern for the nation's reputation, Madison reasons,

> can never be sufficiently possessed by a numerous and changeable body. It can
> only be found in a number so small that a sensible degree of the praise and blame
> of public measures may be the portion of each individual; or in an assembly so
> durably invested with public trust that the pride and consequence of its members
> may be sensibly incorporated with the reputation and prosperity of the commu-
> nity. (*Federalist* 63, MP 10, 544–45)

Madison devoted less attention to the design of executive institutions,
conceding in a letter written just before the Convention that he had
"scarcely ventured as yet to form my own opinion either of the manner in
which it ought to be constituted or of the authority with which it ought to
be cloathed" (MP 9, 385; see also 370). However, as Alexander Hamilton ar-

gued in *The Federalist*, the logic of Madison's institutional solution of keeping the numbers of officeholders small and giving them longer terms as means of enhancing the importance of reputational motives applies even more powerfully to a unitary executive who can expect to serve an extended term in office.[23] Against those who had wanted to make the president ineligible for re-election, Hamilton argued in Number 72 that such a provision would weaken motivations to advance the public good as a means of leaving a personal mark on history:

> [E]ven the love of fame, the ruling passion of the noblest minds, which would prompt a man to plan and undertake extensive and arduous enterprises for the public benefit, requiring considerable time to mature and perfect them, if he could flatter himself with the prospect of being allowed to finish what he had begun, would, on the contrary, deter him from the undertaking, when he foresaw that he must quit the scene before he could accomplish the work, and must commit that, together with his own reputation, to the hands which might be unequal or unfriendly to the task. The most to be expected from the generality of men, in such a situation, is the negative merit of not doing harm, instead of the positive merit of doing good. (Rossiter 1961, 437)[24]

The letter advising on a constitution for Kentucky suggests that by 1788 Madison had come to hold a similar view of the executive office. He also counsels against making the governor ineligible for re-election: "By rendering a periodical change of men necessary, it discourages beneficial undertakings which require perseverance and system" (MP 11, 289).[25]

Finally, in Madison's treatment of the Senate we also see the importance he placed on this institution for helping to provide the capacity needed in a republican constitution to resist popular passions or majority factions until a more reasonable popular majority could emerge. "In order to judge the form to be given to this institution," Madison explained to the Convention on June 26,

> it will be proper to take a view of the ends to be served by it. These were first to protect the people agst. their rulers: secondly to protect the people agst. the transient impressions into which they themselves might be led. . . . [The reflection of the people] would naturally suggest that the Govt. be so constituted, as that one of its branches might have an oppy. of acquiring a competent knowledge of the public interests. Another reflection equally becoming a people on such an occasion, wd. be that they themselves, as well as a numerous body of Representatives, were liable to err also, from fickleness and passion. A necessary fence agst. this danger would be to select a portion of enlightened citizens, whose limited number, and firmness might seasonably interpose agst. impetuous counsels. (Farrand 1966, 1, 421–22; see also *Federalist* 63, MP 10, 546)

In Madison's political science, then, republican constitutional forms serve both to check the abuses of power that threaten private rights, and to increase the probability that officeholders will take positive actions to advance the public good. Institutions are designed to select officeholders who will be responsive to certain types of popular majorities or preferences (those based on reason or the public good) but resistant to others (those based on passion or partial or short-term interests). Institutional arrangements intended to check abuses of power can operate primarily on the basis of the lower or more selfish political motivations. While Madison believed that ambition could sometimes be channeled in ways beneficial to the public good, institutions designed to advance the public good rely primarily on the more public-spirited motivations of reasoned attachment to the broader public good and concern for one's own or the nation's reputation.

Madison and Contemporary Political Science

Leaving aside for a moment Madison's old-fashioned talk about passions and politicians motivated by the public good, his awareness of the power of self-interested motivations in politics and close attention to the interplay of self-interest and institutional incentives make him seem remarkably up to date. These same concerns provide the foundations for the rational choice theories that underlie the most influential work in contemporary political science. Citing the explanations provided by *The Federalist*, one leading proponent of the rational choice approach, Morris Fiorina, has noted that "the self interest assumptions that underlie . . . [his own work] are much the same assumptions that underlie the architecture of the American political system" (Fiorina 1989, 105). Thomas Schwartz has advanced a similar claim of direct intellectual lineage from Madison and his coauthors: "Evinced more than stated, the *Federalist* principles of political analysis are strikingly similar to those of the contemporary public choice school" (Schwartz 1989, 32). Taking Madison's analysis of political leadership and comparing it with work on political leadership by rational choice scholars confirms the existence of some striking similarities, but reveals some equally, if not more striking, contrasts.

One body of theory that has been widely applied in recent rational choice scholarship, especially work on political leadership, is the theory of agency or principal-agent theory.[26] As this theory is usually stated, a principal or group of principals select an agent and delegate authority to the agent to carry out some specialized task. Regarding the agent's motivations, "there is no guarantee that the agent, once hired, will in fact choose to pursue the principal's best interests or to do so efficiently. The agent has his own interests at heart, and is induced to pursue the principal's objectives only to the extent that the incentive structure . . . renders such behavior advantageous" (Moe 1984, 756). Agents often prove hard to control because their interests may diverge from those of the principals, and the principals often lack sufficient information to ensure that the agent is truly acting in their interest. When agents fail to act in accordance with the preferences of their principals, this behavior is known as "shirking." As the theory has been applied to leadership within democratic political institutions, leaders are viewed as agents of those who select them. "The reward structure of leadership ties ambition (to remain leader in the next period) to performance (in the current period)" (Shepsle and Bonchek, 1997, 382). This framework has been applied to a wide range of political institutions, and has been especially influential in recent scholarship on leadership in Congress (see Rohde 1991; Sinclair 1995; Cox and McCubbins 1993).

Parts of Madison's analysis of political leadership do bear an unmistakable resemblance to the logic of principal-agent theory. Madison believed that popular election (either direct or indirect) would provide a strong incentive for officeholders to remain attentive to the interests of citizens, but also recognized that ambitious officeholders would still attempt to expand and abuse their powers. As Madison states in *The Federalist* Number 51: "A dependence on the people is, no doubt the primary control on government; but experience has taught mankind the necessity of auxiliary precautions" (MP 10, 477). Regarding the importance of electoral incentives for controlling self-interested officeholders, note again Madison's treatment in *The Federalist* Number 57 of ambition as a "cord" that binds members of the House of Representatives "to fidelity and sympathy with the great mass of the people." Due to their short terms, members of the House would "be compelled to anticipate the moment when their power is to cease, when their exercise of it is to be reviewed, and when they must descend to the level from which they were raised; there forever to remain unless a faithful discharge of their trust shall have established their title to a renewal of it" (MP 10, 522–23). Still, Madison recognized that citizens still might encounter difficulties in controlling their elected agents, hence the concern with "auxiliary precautions," such as separation of powers in which elected agents are given incentives to check one another's attempts to violate their principals' interests.

While it is therefore clear that Madison understood the logic that underlies modern principal-agent theory, and applied that logic to the design of some important features of the Constitution, on closer inspection some important points of divergence between these approaches begin to appear. The first point of divergence involves how leaders' motivations are understood. Most applications of agency theory assume a single mode of rational, opportunistic behavior on the part of agents. As Fiorina and Shepsle have explained: "[It] is taken as a given that A [the agent] will behave opportunistically in her own interest, and the challenge to P [the principal] is to structure the situation so that, as though there were an invisible hand, she will nevertheless be guided to act in his interest as well" (Fiorina and Shepsle 1989, 20). Seeking the clear deductive predictions that can be gained by simple motivational assumptions, most applications of the theory to political officeholders assume that representatives or leaders are motivated primarily by personal officeholding ambition. As Barbara Sinclair (1995, 18) describes this assumption in the case of congressional leaders: "To the extent that leaders value their positions and want to retain them, they have an incentive to try to fulfill members' expectations." Cox and McCubbins's application of agency theory to congressional leadership likewise focuses strictly on the electoral motives of legislators and their "desire for internal advancement" (1993, 125–26). While these scholars acknowledge the existence of other goals or motivations, including a concern for good public policy, these broader motives play at most a peripheral role in their theoretical explanations of the politics of leadership. More generally, while it is often noted that rational choice theories need not posit narrowly self-regarding motives for political actors (only that behavior is rational and goal-oriented), in contemporary research in this vein it is fairly rare to find theoretical explanations that posit motives of leaders other than personal ambition or re-election.

Madison's theory of political motives resembles contemporary rational choice theory and principal-agent models of leadership in recognizing the power of narrowly self-regarding motives and the importance of institutional incentives. However as we have seen, Madison's political science also incorporates a theoretically important distinction between higher and lower motives in politics, with the higher being those that incline officeholders to advance the public good over short term or partial interests. In addition, Madison's understanding of political motivations incorporates passionate motives that produce behavior that may be self-destructive or vindictive rather than rationally calculated to achieve some political goal ("where no substantial occasion presents itself the most frivolous and fanciful distinctions have been sufficient to kindle their unfriendly passions and excite their most violent conflicts," *Federalist* 10, MP 10, 265). Although Madison recognized that the higher political motives are weaker and less common than the lower, his own experience in politics and his study of history had convinced him that public-spirited motives were important in explaining the political behavior of political leaders and could become *more so* if political science could be better employed in the design of constitutional forms. And in his attention to passion as a distinctive type of political motivation Madison also took theoretical notice of motives that are in some respects lower and more dangerous than self-interest and less predictable in terms of the political behavior they can produce.

A second point of divergence is related to the first, and involves how institutions should be designed to ensure that officeholders act to secure citizens' best interests. In principal-agent theories, a well-designed institution is one that ensures alignment between the principals' interests and the agent's. When the actions of the agent do not reflect the preferences of the principals the theory interprets this behavior as a problem—as shirking that occurs because of the opportunism of the agent. Madison was concerned about this type of agency problem, but was equally concerned about the possibility that the preferences of the principals would not always reflect *their own* best interests. In a well-designed constitution, Madison believed officeholders would distinguish passionate or factional popular majorities from reasonable ones and have some capacity to resist the former. James Q. Wilson has pointed out (as the Anti-Federalists had in Madison's day) that some of the institutional arrangements Madison endorsed most strongly actually "worsen the principal-agent problem from the point of view of the citizen" (1990, 559). For example, large electoral districts in effect create multiple principals by incorporating a broader range of interests and allowing the possibility for representatives to play groups of citizens off against one another, rather than being under the close control of a smaller, more homogeneous electorate. If short terms keep legislators in mind "of their dependence on the people," the longer terms Madison strongly favored for the Senate undoubtedly weakened that same "cord."

Here again we see the central importance of the higher, public-regarding political motives in Madison's political science. If Madison shared the understanding of motives that underlies most applications of principal-agent theory—that agents always act opportunistically when given the chance and well-designed institutions should induce agents always to be responsive to their principals' preferences—his support for intentionally creating "slack" in some of the linkages between citizens and officeholders would seem puzzling. However, as we have seen, Madison's understanding of political motivations is more subtle and complex than this. Madison's theory, while recognizing the power of narrower motivations, does *not* imply that insulation from citizens' preferences will always produce more opportunistic behavior by officeholders. Instead, Madison thought that these types of institutional arrangements created the possibility for officeholders to "refine and enlarge" public preferences. Hence Madison's view that, if properly designed to evoke the higher, public-regarding motives, an institution more insulated from popular control (i.e., the Senate) would actually have a *greater* capacity to secure the long-term public good.

While the resemblance between Madison's explanation of political leadership and contemporary principal-agent theories is striking in some respects, the differences between the two approaches are at least as important. Madison certainly understood the importance of narrowly self-interested motives in politics and how institutions and incentives could be designed to limit the harmful effects of those motivations, or in some cases even channel them toward beneficial political action. The most significant differences involve the wider range of motivations incorporated in Madison's theory, the hierarchy of motives that distinguishes higher from lower, and the importance placed on officeholders refining preferences and deliberating rather than simply reflecting or aggregating preferences.[27]

Conclusion

How we view Madison from the perspective of today's political science depends on the importance placed on the features of Madison's political science that lay outside his analysis of the interplay of the narrower forms of self-interest and institutional incentives. If the features of his political science that most resemble contemporary rational choice theory constitute its major contributions to the study of politics, the significant advances in that branch of political science since Madison's time suggest that Madison himself now holds a similar position in political science to the one he in 1792 accorded the "celebrated" Montesquieu:

> Montesquieu was in politics not a Newton or a Locke, who established immortal systems. . . . He lifted the veil from the venerable errors which enslaved opinion, and pointed the way to those luminous truths of which he had but a glimpse himself. (MP 14, 233)

Using Madison's own scale, I would argue that his achievements as a political scientist should be ranked much closer to those of a Newton or a Locke. Not because all of the elements of his political science have proven to be immortal or even correct in the short run, but for having shown how self-interest and public-spiritedness can exist side by side in the politics of modern constitutional republics, and how different constitutional forms can lead to greater or lesser attention to the public good on the part of both citizens and their political leaders. Taken seriously as political science, Madison's realism counsels us to remain attentive in our explanations not only to political leaders who are motivated primarily by the narrower forms of self-interest but also to those whose motives may include, or hold the potential for developing, a genuine concern for the public good. Madison the politician, and founder of the American republic, provides an important case in point.

Notes

The author gratefully acknowledges helpful comments on earlier versions of this chapter from the editor of this volume, Samuel Kernell, and from Robert Bartlett, James Ceaser, Charles O. Jones, Steven Kautz, Iain McLean, Daniel J. Palazzolo, David Robertson, and Rick Wilson.

1. "Of Parties in General," in Miller 1987, 54.

2. It probably goes without saying that few political scientists have been influenced by interpretations of Madison that place him within the civic humanist or classical republican traditions, in which civic virtue and a selfless attachment to the common good throughout society were viewed as necessary conditions for the success of republican polities.

3. See for example, Riker 1982, 9–11; Wilson 1990.

4. The only uses of the term "leader" in a positive light in Madison's contributions to *The Federalist* involve two references that look back to leaders of the Revolutionary period. See *The Federalist* Numbers 14 (MP 10, 288) and 49 (MP 10, 462); Engeman, Erler, and Hofeller 1988, 295. On the types of leadership Madison and his *Federalist* coauthors considered beneficial, see Ceaser 1979, 52–61.

5. Robert Dahl argued that Madison's writings cannot be read in the same way we read works by most other political theorists, because Madison "was up to his ears in politics, advising, persuading, softening the harsh word, playing down this difficulty and exaggerating that, engaging in debate, harsh controversy, polemics and sly maneuver" (Dahl 1956, 5). In a similar vein, Douglass Adair (1974b, 102) noted Madison's reticence to reveal his complete thoughts on some issues taken up in *The Federalist*: "There was a certain disadvantage in making derogatory remarks to a majority that must be persuaded to adopt your arguments."

6. An interesting exception to the ancient mode may have been the famed Spartan lawgiver Lycurgus, who, before establishing a new constitution for that city, undertook comparative research in Crete, Egypt, and Asia, "to examine the difference betwixt the manners and rules . . . just as physicians do by comparing healthy and diseased bodies." Lycurgus did not neglect to have his plan reviewed by the oracle of Apollo at Delphi, who is said to have accepted it without revision. Plutarch, "Life of Lycurgus," in Clough 1899, 87–91.

7. The literature on the influences of earlier political thought on Madison is extensive. For a recent overview, see Rosen 1999, 3–6. On the influence of

Hume, see, Adair 1974b; Pangle 1988, 68–72; Howe 1987; Epstein 1984, 13–14, 70–71, 90, 101; Zuckert 1992. On Locke, see Pangle 1988; Weaver, 1997. On liberal contract theory more generally, see Rosen 1999.

8. Madison wrote out these notes to organize his own thoughts and in preparation for drafting correspondence to George Washington, Thomas Jefferson, and Edmund Randolph on his plans for the Constitutional Convention (see Rakove 1990, 46–50).

9. Madison's theory of political motives strongly resembles Hume's earlier treatment of the same subject in his essays "Of Parties in General" and "Of the Parties of Great Britain." See Adair 1974b, 103–6; Miller 1987, 54–72.

10. See the parallel use of the term "character" to mean reputation in *The Federalist* (*Federalist* 10, MP 10, 268; *Federalist* 62, MP 10, 539; Federalist 63, MP 10, 544–45).

11. Compare with Hume's essay "On the Independency of Parliament" (Miller 1987, 42–46). See also Adair 1974b, 101–2.

12. Jefferson had previously written Madison (June 20, 1787) stating his opposition to the idea of a national veto over state laws: "Prima facie I do not like it. It fails in an essential character, that the hole & the patch should be commensurate. But this proposes to mend the hole by covering the whole garment" (MP 10, 64).

13. Madison did state in his discussion of political motives in his Constitutional Convention speech of June 6, 1787, that religion "*may* become a motive to persecution and oppression" (Farrand 1966, 1, 135, emphasis mine). See also Epstein 1984, 90.

14. On this point, see Howe 1987, 491–93.

15. Andrew Sabl, in his illuminating analysis of the politics and ethics of political leadership in democratic regimes, refers to this orientation among officeholders as "democratic constancy." On the views of Madison and others on the importance of this trait for democratic political leaders, see Sabl 2002, 45–49, 55–95.

16. On this distinction in the thought of Hume and other figures who may have influenced Madison's understanding of political motives, see Holmes 1990.

17. On the distinction between the public good and private rights in *The Federalist,* see Epstein 1984, 60–61, and the numerous passages cited at 207, n. 6.

18. Unfortunately Madison never provides a single explicit definition of this term in his writing. His use and that of his coauthors in *The Federalist* indicate that it refers primarily to matters of national security and economic prosperity (Epstein 1984, 163–64; Bessette 1994, 29–30). In addition, in "Vices," the subjects of national security and the state of commercial affairs provide the focus for Madison's analysis of the inability of the Confederation to secure the common interests of the states (MP 9, 348–51). For the view that Madison may have meant by the public good something broader and more akin to long-term public opinion, see Sabl 2002, 78–80.

19. In this section I follow fairly closely the interpretation of Madison's thought in David F. Epstein's *The Political Theory of the Federalist* (1984), especially his ch. 7.

20. As previously noted, Madison would have preferred also to have a national veto over state legislation as a further check on the violation of private rights within the states.

21. Gordon S. Wood (1969, 471–518) has argued that the Federalists, including Madison, were primarily concerned with restoring the influence of a social elite that had been losing influence in politics since the Revolution. This may have been true of others aligned with the Federalist cause, but it is a misreading of what Madison meant by "better" representatives. See, for example, Madison's objections in the Convention (July 26, 1787) to the proposal to make landed property a condition of officeholding: "It was politic as well as just that the interests & rights of every class should be duly represented & understood in the public Councils. It was a provision every where established that the Country should be divided into districts & representatives taken from each, in order that the Legislative Assembly might equally understand & sympathise, with the rights of the people in every part of the Community" (Farrand 1966, 2, 123–24).

22. I am indebted to Samuel Kernell for bringing this implication of Madison's argument to my attention.

23. On the parallel logic of Madison's analysis of the Senate and Hamilton's analysis of the presidency, see Sabl 2002, 72–83.

24. On the importance of the motive of historical reputation among Madison and his contemporaries, see Adair 1974a.

25. In this case Madison is considering not only how re-eligibility might evoke reputational motives, but ambition and interest as well. Ineligibility for re-election, he continues, "takes away one powerful motive to a faithful & useful administration, the desire of acquiring that title to a re-appointment. . . . Add to the whole, that by putting the Executive Magistrate in the situation of the tenant of an unrenewable lease, it would tempt him to neglect the constitutional rights of his department, and connive at usurpations by the Legislative department, with which he may connect his future ambition or interest" (MP 11, 289).

26. For overviews of the main features of principal-agent theory as it applies to leadership in political settings, see Fiorina and Shepsle 1989; Shepsle and Bonchek 1997, 380–404; and Kiewiet and McCubbins 1991, ch. 2.

27. Wilson (1990), Cain and Jones (1989), and Chappell and Keech (1989) have also noted similar discontinuities between Madison's thought and modern rational choice scholarship.

Chapter 5

"The True Principles of Republican Government": Reassessing James Madison's Political Science

SAMUEL KERNELL

Since Thomas Jefferson made *The Federalist* required reading for all University of Virginia students, professors have enlisted these essays to instruct each generation of undergraduates in the principles of American government. The two favorites in today's classroom are James Madison's *Federalist* Numbers 10 and 51. Each essay identifies an essential and distinguishing characteristic of the American political system. Number 10 offers an ingenious rationale for the nation's pluralist politics, while Number 51 dissects the formal constitutional system. The first grapples with the tyrannical impulses of society's factions and the second with self-interested politicians who might be tempted to usurp their authority. In both cases concentration is the threat for which Madison finds similar solutions in "divide and conquer," a principle he had once described as the "reprobated axiom of tyrants." In Number 10 his solution takes the form of an extended republic containing numerous, diverse factions whose representatives reconcile their competing interests in a well designed, deliberative national legislature. In Number 51 a republican equilibrium requires a strong form of separation of powers containing checks and balances. Given that factional competition and checks and balances are based on the same strategic idea and the fact that Number 51 closes with a recapitulation of the main points of Number 10, it is not hard to see that these twin principles should be regarded as establishing the theoretical foundation of the Constitution.

Harder to understand is how this "Madisonian model" went unrecognized for so long, from shortly after ratification until Charles A. Beard reintroduced it more than a century later in his classic *An Economic Interpretation of the Constitution of the United States* (1912). According to Beard, Madison and his nationalist allies fused these principles in a scheme to hamstring government action and prevent national majorities from raiding the purses of the propertied class. While Beard was not the first to level these charges, he appears to have been the first since the ratification campaign to fashion these two principles into a unified theoretical model.[1] Beard's class conspiracy long ago lost favor, but the Madisonian model and its conservative bias remain the conventional wisdom of modern scholarship on James Madison and the Constitution's founding.

Subsequent scholars, many of whom rank among the Who's Who of twentieth-century political science, have relied on Beard to berate the Madison model. "If the multiplicity of interests in a large republic makes tyrannical majorities impossible," complained E. E. Schattschneider (1942), "the principal theoretical prop of the separation of powers has been demolished." By the 1950s, even those students of American pluralism who might be expected to number among Madison's most faithful boosters had joined the ranks of critics. Citing the presumed duplication of these principles, Robert A. Dahl (1956) concluded that the Constitution goes "about as far as . . . possible [in frustrating majority control] while still remaining within the rubric of democracy." And a few years later James MacGregor Burns (1963) joined the chorus, again charging that Madison "thrust barricade after barricade against popular majorities."[2] Madison's critics have been matched by his admirers (Diamond 1959; Carey 1978; and many others) who have defended or sought to repair the model, typically by reinterpreting these *Federalist* essays in various ways. Both sides, however, accept Beard's insight that the Madisonian model represents its namesake's blueprint from which the Constitution was constructed.

In this essay I will leave it to others to appraise how well the Madisonian model describes essential features of the Constitution. Instead, we shall limit ourselves to the more problematic issue of how well it represents the theoretical views of its author. In short, I argue that the Madisonian model is a misnomer. It does not represent Madison's sincere theoretical views on the Constitution—at least before and during the Constitutional Convention, when they were consequential. Instead, the Madisonian model was formulated after the fact, specifically in *Federalist* Number 51 and its companion essays, in order to promote the Constitution's ratification. In parrying the nearly apocalyptic Anti-Federalist charges that the Constitution took a short path to tyranny, the nationalist campaign needed desperately to show that the new plan was constructed on sound republican principles and assuage the worries of fence-sitting delegates to the states' ratification conventions. The Madisonian model fulfilled that need.

I arrive at this conclusion after examination of several kinds of evidence—the internal validity of the central arguments of Numbers 10 and 51 and the consistency between them; similarities and differences between the Madisonian model and Madison's previous political science on constitutional reform, including arguments tendered at the Constitutional Convention; and the model's value as campaign rhetoric during the ratification debates. In the next section (I), I argue that the Madisonian model is fundamentally flawed. Beyond the familiar charges of duplication—which, after all, may amount to no more than "too much of a good thing"—the Madison model contains a serious contradiction between its core principles. One simply cannot design a constitution that optimizes the performance of both factional competition and checks and balances. While the former prescribes essentially a majoritarian solution to the potential dilemma of majority tyranny, separation of powers—as implemented with the Constitution's strong checks and balances described in Number 51—succeeds only to the extent it frustrates this same majority control. We begin in the next section by reviewing the arguments of Numbers 10 and 51, in which we draw out the contradictory implications.

This raises the question of how Madison could embrace a contradictory argument. The answer is simply that he did not. Although at various times Madison enlisted factional competition and checks and balances as alternative solutions to the majority tyranny problem, a review in Section II of Madison's relevant writings and activities fails to turn up an instance where he combined these principles prior to Number 51.

The joint appearance of factional competition and checks and balances in his *Federalist* essays might, as some have argued (Banning 1995), reflect the continuing development of Madison's theoretical views. Perhaps so, but there is little evidence from Madison's subsequent writings that he seriously revised his theoretical views on institutional design from those he took to the Convention (Riley 2001, 176–82). At least as strong an argument can be made that Number 51 springs from a strategic desire to dress up the Constitution in familiar principles in order to reassure delegates who were deliberating its fate at their states' ratification conventions. In section III I test this possibility by examining its value as campaign rhetoric. The Madisonian model presents a compelling case for ratification that is both different from the standard nationalist position and one Anti-Federalists probably found difficult to refute.

I conclude that Madison went to Philadelphia committed to replacing the Articles of Confederation with a constitutional system capable of positive action, both responsive to national majorities and protective of minorities in the states. He left Philadelphia with something quite different in hand. Despite privately expressing disappointment and lingering misgivings with the Constitution, he accepted it as superior to the Confederation and defended it vigorously in the ratification campaign. In doing so he combined the principles of factional competition and separation of powers into a rationale for legitimizing a Constitution born of politics and its contradictions.

I. The Disparate Logics of Number 10 and Number 51

The Federalist Numbers 10 and 51 are canon. And yet, I argue, they contradict each other. Nowhere is this more evident and destructive for the Madisonian model than in these essays' treatment of the House of Representatives. In Number 10, Publius unconditionally reposes government authority in a well designed legislature, which closely resembles the House of Representatives in all of its essential features—membership composition, size and extent of its constituencies. (Below we will trace an unambiguous lineage from the theoretical construct stated in Number 10 to the actual construction of the House of Representatives at the Philadelphia convention.) Yet writing Number 51 several months later, Publius singles out the House as posing the greatest potential threat to liberty and against which the Constitution must array the full force of checks and balances. To understand how these principles could generate such contradictory prescriptions, we need to understand their disparate logics.

I.A. NUMBER 10: INSTITUTIONALIZING FACTIONAL COMPETITION

Madison opens this famous essay by declaring that the chief virtue of a "well-constructed Union" lies in "its tendency to break and control the violence of faction." He defines faction as "a number of citizens, whether amounting to a majority or minority of the whole, who are united and actuated by some common impulse of passion or of interest, adverse to the rights of other citizens, or to the permanent and aggregate interests of the community." After exploring its properties, Madison concludes: "The inference to which we are brought is that the *causes* of faction cannot be removed, and that relief is only to be sought in the means of controlling its *effects.*" This lays the groundwork for a government founded on factional competition.

Madison then constructs a constitutional system from some simple, mostly unobjectionable assumptions about the effects of size and diversity. He begins by noting that the advantage of representative over direct democracy lies in conveniently incorporating a large number of citizens. Greater numbers mean greater variety of interests, or factions, that will participate in the nation's collective decisions. As factions compete they hold each other in check and enact only those policies that command broad support. It is a simple yet profound idea. In that an extended republic supplies the diversity of interests vital for keeping factional tyranny in check, this argument allowed Publius to counter the favorite Anti-Federalist shibboleth that only small republics could endure.

As for institutional design, Number 10 presents two mechanisms for containing and aggregating preferences of numerous, potentially "turbulent" factions. These are representation and a deliberative legislature. On the former, Madison introduces a theoretical novelty, "a scheme of representation" that "promises the cure for [faction] which we are seeking." Republican theorists had traditionally regarded representatives as serving essentially as agents of a particular interest. Members of Britain's House of Lords, Montesquieu explained, were selected in such a manner as to guarantee their undistracted representation of the aristocracy. When Alexander Hamilton and John Adams explored possible constitutional arrangements in America, they had held fast to this conventional republican principle in formulating an American variant of "mixed government" in which the lower house of the legislature would represent the poor; the upper, the rich; and at least for Hamilton, the disinterested executive, the public good. For Madison, however, multiple-cleavaged constituencies implied a more complex role for politicians. These actors, he sensed, would embody "a change in the principle of representation" (Hunt 1900, 338). Like present-day members of the House of Representatives, but unlike all models of representation that preceded this essay, Madison's politicians succeeded electorally by building consensus (i.e., coalitions) across factions by discovering common policies that served their constituencies' competing interests.[3]

On the legislative process, Madison again enlists pluralism to take the rough edges off factionalism. He is clearly sanguine about the moderating effects of this new scheme of representation but allows that even were representatives "of factious tempers, of local prejudices, or of sinister designs" elected, they would be constrained by their need to coalesce with differently minded representatives. The only additional ingredient required was a sufficient variety of interests so that none could dominate. This fortuitously came in precisely the form that responded to the Anti-Federalist fears of a large republic. "Extend the sphere," Publius reassures us, "and you take in a greater variety of parties and interests; you make it less probable that a majority of the whole will have a common motive to invade the rights of other citizens." All three of Number 10's key features—representation, a well-proportioned legislature, and an extended republic—follow logically from the presence of multiple factions whose divergent and conflicting interests must be represented and combined. Moreover, by identifying these institutional attributes as desirable, the argument served the ratification cause by highlighting prominent features of the House of Representatives as well as by rendering the Constitution suitable for a growing nation.

More problematic in Number 10 is its failure to deal with the states and with the other branches in the new governmental plan, both of which had appeared as prominent potential sources of tyranny in Convention debates. Number 10 has the ideal constitution generating factionally moderated national policy that, among other goals, would check tyrannical impulses arising in the more homogeneous states. Publius hints at this in noting an "advantage . . . in controlling the effects of faction . . . enjoyed by the Union over the States," but with federalism entrenched in the new Constitution and with Anti-Federalists projecting the specter of a distant, inadequately bridled national government, he necessarily soft-peddles the Constitution's supremacy clause and dares not mention that James Madison, a known booster of ratification, was still quietly promoting a national veto over state policy.

Certainly if factional competition *is* the solution, then it should be the criterion for judging the internal design and power relations among the other branches of government as well. Of course, the Constitution did not implement the logic of factional competition beyond the House of Representatives, which undoubtedly explains why Publius failed to continue his exercise beyond a well-proportioned, popularly elected legislature. After all, the presidency, the Supreme Court, and even the Senate fall far short of satisfying the design requirements identified in Number 10 for generating moderate policy.[4] This raises the question, how in the absence of factional competition do these other branches avoid capture by some faction or inappropriately configured coalition bent on pursuing immoderate policies? The answer, at least for the second part of the question, is offered in Number 51's checks and balances.

I.B. NUMBER 51: INSTITUTIONALIZING
SEPARATION OF POWERS

Where Number 10 makes a tightly reasoned, deductive argument, Number 51 approaches its task in a more empirical, discursive, and speculative fashion. Experience and widely accepted republican notions of good government are summoned to endorse the Constitution's provisions and to rule out governmental arrangements that do not survive in the final plan. Consequently, the constituent parts of Number 51's overall argument depend less

Rationale for Separation of Powers

From Number 47: "The accumulation of all powers, legislative, executive, and judiciary, in the same hands, whether of one, a few, or many, and whether hereditary, self-appointed, or elective, may justly be pronounced the very definition of tyranny."

Par. 1: With "exterior provisions found to be inadequate" in the earlier essays, the solution must lie in "contriving the interior structure of the government as that its several constituent parts may, by their mutual relations, be the means of keeping each other in their proper places."

Par. 2: "Each department should have a will of its own." Among other things, this requires that "members of each [branch] should have as little agency as possible with the appointment of the members of the others." Ideally, members of each branch would be elected directly by the "same fountain of authority, the people," but this may not be practical and would involve "additional expense." Especially for the judiciary whose members have special qualifications, elections would be awkward. Anyway, their "permanent tenure" would "soon destroy all sense of dependence" on popular authority.

Par. 3: Equally important, "members of each department should be as little dependent as possible on those of the others, for the emoluments annexed to their offices."

Par. 4a: But the best way to keep the branches separate "consists in giving to those who administer each department the necessary constitutional means and personal motives to resist encroachments." Then comes the most quotable of Madison's passages: "Ambition must be made to counteract ambition. The interest of the man must be connected with the constitutional rights of the place." Of course, were men angels, he reminds us, none of this would be necessary. "You must first enable the government to control the governed: and in the next place oblige it to control itself."

Transition 1: From Rationale to Specific Separation of Powers Provisions

Par. 4b, the last sentence: "A dependence on the people is, no doubt, the primary control on the government; but experience has taught mankind the necessity of auxiliary precautions."

The Constitution's Separation of Powers

Par. 5: Ideally, each branch would have the capacity to check the others.

Par. 6: But this is not possible. "In republican government, the legislative authority necessarily predominates." One solution is bicameralism, in which each chamber is independent by virtue of "different modes of election and different principles of action." An additional check on the legislature could be found in an absolute executive veto, but perhaps this would give too much to the executive. Instead, the same benefits might be obtained by arming the executive with a veto that can be backed up by the Senate, "a weaker branch of the stronger department." Clearly, the House of Representatives is the problem branch.

Par. 9: Madison finds a third check in federalism. "The different governments will control each other, at the same time that each will be controlled by itself."

Transition 2: Review of Factional Competition Thesis

Par. 10: It is of great importance in a republic not only to guard the society against the oppression of its rulers but also to guard one part of the society against the injustice of the other part.

Remainder of essay (about 45 percent of text): Madison recapitulates argument of Number 10.

TABLE 5.1. Synopsis of Number 51

on one another than did those in Number 10. Where all of Number 10 rests or falls on the integrity of factional competition, here particular claims or causal statements stand more on their own. To map Number 51's various arguments and their critical connecting statements, we will refer to the outline of this argument in Table 5.1.

This essay proceeds from a definition (stated in Number 47) that tyranny is tantamount to the "accumulation" of government power. Madison does not initially explain just why this should be so, but later in Number 51 he elliptically hints at two possible reasons. First, despite factional competition, aggrandizing majorities might occasionally materialize to endanger the civil rights of those factions in the minority (par. 6). Below we shall see that Madison hedges his bets on factional competition by stating probabilistically (the only instance where he ever does so) the efficacy of factional competition in preventing majority tyranny. Second, politicians pursue their self-interests (par. 2), just as do their constituents, and if left unchecked, they will exploit their authority to the detriment of the general welfare. So, "first government must control the populace and then control itself." In the language of modern principal-agency theory, the problem of tyranny from politicians represents a severe form of "agency loss." This is an apt expression capturing Madison's conception of citizens as principals who delegate authority to representatives who act as their agents.[5] We adopt it here to distinguish it from Number 10's majority tyranny.

For the most part, Publius concentrates on agency tyranny in fashioning checks and balances as a system of "auxiliary" controls. This prompted George W. Carey (1978, 156) to read Madison as saying: "At no point does separation of powers play a role in curbing majority factions." If this were so, and at the outset it certainly appears to be the direction the essay is heading, it might rebut any charges of contradiction between factional competition and separation of powers. Each would tackle a different kind of tyranny—majority and agency, respectively—and thereby complement each other. But Number 51 veers off this parallel path, and by the conclusion, there is little prospect of these principles avoiding a collision, much less complementing one another.

As early as paragraph 2, Publius acknowledges that in a democracy direct popular election is the preferred method for keeping politicians responsive to the citizenry. This passing homage to democratic creed immediately throws into question the need for separation of powers and, ultimately, wreaks havoc on the seemingly neat division of labor between Numbers 10 and 51. Why not minimize agency loss by simply electing everyone? Indeed, this was standard practice in the states at the time and, much to Tocqueville's bemusement (Jardin 1988), remained so decades later. Moreover, in his essay

"The Vices of the Political System of the United States," written shortly before the Constitutional Convention, Madison appeared to judge direct and
indirect elections as fully adequate to the task of checking agency tyranny.
After distinguishing these two forms of tyranny in much the same way as he
would in Number 51, Madison observes that though agency tyranny is a particular curse of monarchies, republics may not be immune from it either.[6] Yet
it is less likely to pose a serious threat to republics because "the melioration
of the Republican form is such a process of elections as will most certainly
extract from the mass of the Society the . . . noblest characters . . . [who] will
at once feel most strongly the proper motives to pursue the end of their appointment, and be most capable to devise the proper means of attaining it."
Elections are at the core of Madison's new scheme of representation developed in this pre-Philadelphia essay—just as they are in Number 10, but not
in Number 51—and are presented as adequate for solving the agency problem. Equally revealing, while setting up a tripartite division of government,
"Vices" ignores the opportunity that separation of powers presents for introducing checks and balances to address agency loss.

Writing Number 51 eight months later, Publius finds elections to be
problematic. The difficulty they present has more to do, I suspect, with political strategy than with any newly discovered theoretical concerns. Specifically, if elections sufficed to keep politicians in line, they would threaten to
terminate the argument before Publius can make his case for the Constitution's checks and balances. Clearly, if Number 51 were to promote ratification, Madison had to get past the electoral solution to the one actually provided in the Constitution. He tries to extricate himself from this bind with
what must be one of the most anemic (and charitably ignored) arguments
Madison ever authored. He discounts the utility of universal elections as
causing "some difficulties" and "additional expense" (par. 2).[7] If that were the
only problem, he might still have combined factional competition with
checks and balances. He illustrates these points, for example, with reference
to judges' job qualifications and life tenure. So, here, where the primary controls are awkward or would prove ineffective, is a logical place to apply the
"interior controls" of checks and balances. To check a band of life-tenured
judges who might pursue a repudiated political agenda (as some Federalist
partisans had briefly contemplated in the aftermath of their 1800 election
debacle) Madison could have found safeguards in Congress' explicit authority (Article III. Section 1) to reorganize the federal judiciary, withhold salary
raises, and mount impeachment proceedings. Similarly, the Constitution explicitly reserves for Congress the power of the purse and numerous other
mechanisms for tethering some future president who might covet a mon-

arch's robe.[8] Oddly, provisions such as these go unmentioned because this is not where Publius is headed.

He forges on, but a little later (in Transition 1) returns to elections as if to suggest a reconciliation. Again, Madison the democrat reminds us that elections must constitute the "primary" control mechanism in a republic, but here, unlike his "Vices" essay, checks and balances appear as a useful "auxiliary" safeguard (par. 4b).[9] Foregoing better targets, paragraphs 5 through 9 apply these "auxiliary" controls exclusively to the only branch of the new American government that will already be subject to direct elections, the House of Representatives. Publius endorses a presidential veto that can be sustained by a one-third minority of the Senate. Even this check, he cautions, might prove inadequate to rein in a House of Representatives inclined, by virtue of its singular popular mandate, to act "with an intrepid confidence in its own strength."

In sum, writing as Publius, Madison developed a rationale for a strong form of separation of powers best suited for checking the ambitions of unelected politicians in the executive and judiciary, but then, he turned it against the popularly elected House of Representatives. As a result Number 51 simply fails to follow through in the fashion needed to keep factional competition and checks and balances on the parallel and complementary tracks preventing the two kinds of tyranny to which republics are susceptible. In the end, separation of powers is brought to bear on the same institution that factional competition has already moderated. No wonder twentieth-century critics complain that the Madisonian model is overkill.

Ironically, in directing checks and balances against the House of Representatives, Number 51 highlights the inherently contradictory effects of these principles. Yet, in truth, even had this essay limited its application of checks and balances to unelected and indirectly elected agents, the president's veto and the coequal malapportioned and state-controlled Senate would still have restricted the capacity of the House of Representatives to legislate moderate policy. To see this we need to step outside the texts of Numbers 10 and 51 to consider the variety of ways in which a political system constructed on checks and balances could prevent gains from factional competition.

I.C. THE DAMAGE CHECKS AND BALANCES POSE FOR FACTIONAL COMPETITION

Where does the Constitution's separation of powers leave factional competition as *the* "republican solution?" It is unclear that factional competition will have more than an incidental, moderating influence on national policy. Given the vetoes held by the Senate and presidency, successful policy will have to pass through these institutions whose members are neither selected via the carefully configured representational scheme of Number 10 nor subject to the countervailing pressures from politicians representing other interests. Policies arising from the Senate and presidency can be expected to deviate frequently from the preferences of the median member of the House of Representatives, and where they do they will be less desirable. The likely results are gridlock and bad public policy.

One can easily read *The Federalist* as arguing that a little gridlock is a good thing. The damage checks and balances pose for collective action is irrelevant in assessing the Madisonian model, so the argument goes, because Numbers 10 and 51 posit a single public good—the prevention of majority tyranny. As long as checks and balances block immoderate House policies, they are performing their intended function. One might ask, however, why if the reformed government is configured to produce gridlock—confirming the suspicion of the Constitution's twentieth century critics—did Madison labor so ardently—first at Annapolis and then against initially indifferent responses to his proposed Philadelphia meeting—to reform a constitution that had already demonstrated its capacity for gridlock?

Clearly, fear of national-level tyranny did not bring Madison or any of the other delegates to Philadelphia. From across the political spectrum the delegates had come to realize the unacceptable costs of continuing to struggle with their collective concerns through the Articles of Confederation's weak national government. Although Madison's and his nationalist colleagues' commitment to install "energetic" national institutions has been exhaustively documented, it offers an admittedly unsatisfying rebuttal to the claim that beyond the prevention of tyranny, the Madisonian model was not designed to produce collective goods.[10]

These essays do, however, contain a rationale for positive government even within the narrow objective of preventing majority tyranny. From the vantage of the twenty-first century, one might assume that any limits on Washington's capacity to act serve to check potential tyranny. Yet, in 1787 whenever Madison and his nationalist colleagues expressed concern with majority tyranny, they were referring to majorities in the states. "It can be little doubted that if the state of Rhode Island was . . . left to itself," ponders Publius in Number 51, "the insecurity of rights under the popular form of government within such narrow limits would be displayed by such reiterated oppressions of factious majorities that some power altogether independent of the people would soon be called for by the voice of the very factions whose misrule had proved the necessity of it." This is what prompted Madison repeatedly to seek a national veto over the states at the Convention and later in the First Congress as a provision in his draft of the Bill of Rights. Gridlock threatens the capacity of the new government to shield the citizenry from tyranny arising in the states.

Even when gridlock does not occur, checks and balances might still subtly undermine moderate public policy. In addition to rendering factional competition irrelevant, the prospect of a checking action can be reasonably expected to intrude insidiously in the House's deliberations and shift policies from those moderated by factional competition. Before incurring the high transaction costs Madison laid out for them, House politicians will look down the decision tree to determine the prospects for each policy alternative in the Senate and presidency.[11] The president can threaten to veto legislation, and the Senate can pass alternative provisions strategically designed to strengthen its hand in conference negotiations. Where a legislative faction finds an ally in one of the other branches, it can inject this leverage in negotiations with the other factional representatives. The framers were fully aware of these strategic implications as evidenced in the remark of Madison ally James Wilson, that the veto "would seldom be used," but its "silent operation" would nonetheless be felt: "The Legislature would know such a power existed, and would refrain from such laws, as it would be sure to defeat" (Farrand 1966, 100).

In addition to corrupting the legislative process these "checking" institutions will discover at times that they can ignore the preferences of the House altogether and take independent action enlisting as necessary their agents in the bureaucracy and the judiciary. Opportunities for direct policy, authorized by the Constitution, include some of the major concerns that brought delegates to Philadelphia: trade treaties, westward expansion and security, and protection of American shipping on the high seas.

The issue is simple: only legislative supremacy of the kind contained in the Virginia Plan provides the republican solution to majority tyranny. One must give factional competition free rein over the political process rather than confining it to one of several independent branches. Either these checking institutions will themselves be subject to the same moderating forces, or the House of Representatives must have the capacity to trump opposition from these branches. The first is highly improbable given their intentionally dissimilar designs, and the Constitution disallows the second. How can one square this implicit requirement of legislative supremacy with Madison's long-standing reputation as "Mr. Separation of Powers?" There are several possibilities. Perhaps Madison failed to detect the contradictory implications of these principles. Or, perhaps, he was insincere in offering factional competition as a solution (Epstein 1993). Finally, our understanding of Madison's political science might be misinformed by an over-reliance on Number 51.

To search for the answer we turn to Madison's previous efforts at institutional reform. If the inconsistencies of the Madisonian model reappear in his earlier political science, they might confirm Dahl's assessment of Madison as a brilliant politician but a second-rate theorist. But if Madison's previous political science turns up free from the flaws revealed here, we would be on firmer ground in suspecting that under the guise of Publius, Madison promulgated these contradictory principles to promote ratification. There are four episodes that deserve close investigation: two occurring in the mid-1780s when Madison crossed swords with Virginia's political leader Patrick Henry over religious subsidies and revision of that state's constitution and two involving Madison's proposals for a new national constitution.

II. James Madison's Political Science Prior to Publius

Madison's officeholding career tracked the course of the nation's institutional development. Everywhere he served—the Continental Congress during the war, the Virginia legislature, and the Philadelphia Convention—reform loomed as an urgent yet thorny and seemingly intractable issue. Institutional design always attracted Madison's careful attention. Even as the youngest member of Congress during the Revolution, he gained colleagues' notice for his compelling arguments in behalf of a strengthened national government. These included proposals to give the government coercive authority to remedy states' chronic shirking of their contributions to the war effort and beefed up executive agencies to which Congress could delegate important administrative decisions (e.g., the number of uniforms to purchase), thus freeing its time for making war policy. Not until he was back in Virginia in the mid-1780s, however, did he find himself confronting systematic institutional reform.

II.A. VIRGINIA'S RELIGIOUS WARS: AN EDUCATION IN FACTIONAL COMPETITION

On his return to Virginia after the war Madison discovered Patrick Henry firmly in control of the state through his leadership in the Assembly and in turn through that chamber's domination of the other branches. The contrast with his recent experiences in the feeble national Congress was stark and instructive. And it helps explain the resolve with which Madison headed to Philadelphia in 1787 to strengthen national authority and set it up as a check on majority power in the states.

In the spring of 1784, Patrick Henry proposed a general tax on Virginians to support "teachers of the Christian religion." When a legislative majority appeared poised to pass this legislation, Madison rallied Methodist, Baptist, and Presbyterian leaders who had chaffed under years of Virginia's tax subsidy for the Episcopal Church and were understandably wary of any new proposals that would reintroduce state subsidies of religion (Ketcham 1990, 162–68). In the fall election they successfully challenged some of the bill's chief boosters and sent a message to other would-be supporters of the legislation. When the assembly returned to session the next spring, the leadership quietly dropped the measure.[12] Reporting candidly on the home front to Jefferson in Paris in August 1785, Madison (*The Papers of James Madison* [hereafter MP] 8, 345) noted, perhaps for the first time, the political benefits of factional competition: "The mutual hatred of these sects has been much inflamed. . . . I am far from being sorry for it, as a coalition between them could alone endanger our religious rights."

During the next several years leading up to the Convention, Madison frequently returned to this theme. According to his first biographer and next door neighbor, Madison often recited Voltaire: "If one religion only were allowed in England, the government would possibly be arbitrary; if there were but two, the people would cut each other's throats; but, as there are such a multitude, they all live happy and in peace" (Ketcham 1990, 166). Not until the spring of 1787, however, in his penetrating essay "Vices of the Political System of the United States," did Madison fully secularize this principle: "The Society becomes broken into a greater variety of interests, of pursuits, of passions, which check each other, whilst those who may feel a common sentiment have less opportunity of communication and concert." Establishing the desirability of a "greater variety of interests" allowed Madison to then conclude that an "extended" republic would limit the power of imprudent majorities.

James Madison was not the first to offer this rationale favoring large over small republics. Credit for that belongs to David Hume, who had made a similar argument nearly a half-century earlier. Until Douglass Adair (1974b) identified striking similarities between the language of several of Hume's essays and Number 10, however, few scholars fully appreciated Madison's debt to this Scottish philosopher. So similar are some passages of Number 10— particularly, those defining factions—with those in Hume's essays "Of Parties in General" and "Idea of a Perfect Commonwealth," one might be tempted to conclude that without Hume's coaching Madison might not have made the transition from sects to factions or recognized the advantages of a large republic.

Hume undoubtedly influenced Madison's thinking, probably beginning with his undergraduate course work at Princeton under Professor John Witherspoon, a student of the Scottish Enlightenment. Yet Hume did not lead Madison toward factional competition as offering the "republican solution" to the conundrum of majority tyranny. To appreciate the development of Madison's political science and its original contribution to republican theory, consider what Hume had to offer on the subject and where his thinking stopped. Declaring "democracies are turbulent," Hume proposed an elaborate (and to Madison nonsensical) constitutional order designed to isolate society's different interests from one another as much as possible. The representatives to the political institutions that ultimately controlled decisions would not meet, but would vote from their communities, as if in a referendum. For Hume the virtue of an extended republic lay exclusively in its expanse (Hume 1985, 528): "The parts are so distant and remote, that it is very difficult, either by intrigue, prejudice, or passion, to hurry them into any measures against the public interest." Only by disengaging politics could a peaceful republic, "steady and uniform without tumult and faction," be realized.[13]

In a little noted passage of "The Perfect Commonwealth," Hume caught a glimpse of the path Madison would take nearly a half-century later. "The chief support of the British government is," Hume admits, "the opposition of interests; but that, though in the main serviceable, breeds endless factions." His own scheme (ibid., 525), conversely, "does all the good without any of the harm." This passage offers a rare instance in which an earlier generation theorist, locked in a paradigm based on the cultivation of virtue rather than interest, discerns a critical, anomalous fact but does not know what to make of it. Whether standing on Hume's shoulders or not, Madison is the first to examine pluralism unflinchingly and to discover within it the "remedy for the diseases most incident to republican government." He traveled to the Convention armed with this insight and a plan for the new government derived from it. One need search no further than Number 51 to confirm the impact of Virginia's brief denominational battle on Madison's republican views: "In a free government the security for civil rights must be the same as that for religious rights. It consists in the one case in the multiplicity of interests, and in the other in the multiplicity of sects. The degree of security in both cases will depend on the number of interests and sects." Both, he adds, will consequently gain security to the "extent of the country and number of people comprehended under the same government."

II.B. REFORM OF VIRGINIA'S CONSTITUTION:
AN APPLICATION OF SEPARATION OF POWERS

With roots extending back to Aristotle's balanced polity and serving as a key design element for Montesquieu and other contemporary republican theorists, separation of powers enjoyed unimpeachable certitude among the delegates at Philadelphia. Everyone sought to associate his favorite constitutional reform with this design principle. Alexander Hamilton, one of the Convention's most ardent nationalists, casually summoned the language of separation of powers to argue in behalf of an active and authoritative presidency. With similar ease, George Mason and others, worried about a too powerful national government, favored separating authority into several independent and disconnected branches as a way of stifling all but the least controversial national policies. The only two constitutional features these and other plans had in common were bicameralism and the division of the government into legislative, executive, and judicial branches. The semantic slipperiness of separation of powers gave delegates, including Madison, the latitude to change their positions on specific institutional arrangements without having to recant their principles. It cannot be too surprising, then, to find references to separation of powers sprinkled liberally throughout Madison's speeches, letters, and scholarly writings.

The particular strain of separation of powers that interests us contains a strong form of checks and balances. Madison's only important sponsorship of such a system before late summer in Philadelphia came in 1784 in a failed effort to reform the Virginia constitution. His proposals bore a close resemblance to the Constitution as described in Number 51, both in their specific checks and balances provisions and in the arguments summoned in their behalf.[14] In a speech on the floor of the state legislature, Madison decided to "stir the matter" (Ketcham 1990, 159) by labelling the Assembly's "union of powers that is tyranny." Untouched by checks and balances, this chamber elected the governor, appointed the judges, and held exclusive power to initiate legislation. Madison's proposals in Virginia, which were elaborated on the next year in correspondence with a friend seeking advice on Kentucky's state constitution, gave each branch independent authority and separate recruitment of its officeholders. The Senate would have been placed on an equal footing with the Assembly and its members insulated from external pressures with six-year terms. As long as the governor was appointed by the legislature, Madison reasoned, it could offer no counterbalance to intemperate legislation. Therefore, the governor should be popularly elected and a Council of Revision that included the governor created to review and veto imprudent state laws. With judges' salaries closely supervised by the legislature, constitutional interpretation fell back onto the chamber enacting the laws. Madison sought to insulate judges with executive appointment, life terms, and "liberal" salaries. With Patrick Henry implacably opposed and publicly haranguing against these reforms, Madison got nowhere. Henry even persuaded the Assembly to bar their reconsideration during the remainder of the session. Thoroughly defeated, ally Thomas Jefferson proposed to Madison that their only recourse was to "devoutly pray for his [Henry's] death."[15]

Service in the wartime Congress and the Henry-dominated state assembly provided Madison with the kind of education to which Henry Adams always aspired and never got—insight as to what was required next. Soon Madison took on the formidable task of revising the nation's constitution. With an assist from Daniel Shays, Madison found his opportunity in May, 1787.

At the Constitutional Convention, Madison can be read as having promoted two distinct constitutional plans neither of which corresponds to the Madisonian model. From the opening day until July 14, he ardently pursued the Virginia Plan. This constitutional blueprint closely follows the logic of factional competition with only modest employment of checks and balances. After its defeat with the adoption of the Grand Compromise, Madison abruptly switched principles. With a Senate controlled by the states, he began to search for ways to salvage independent national authority and fence in the Senate's jurisdiction; he found it in checks and balances. At the same time factional competition became irrelevant and disappeared from Madison's discourse for the remainder of the summer.

II.C. THE VIRGINIA PLAN

In the spring of 1787, after months of scholarly research and with the Convention drawing near, Madison approached fellow Virginia delegates on the need to prepare a substitute plan of government that would be capable of "positive" action. Madison's correspondence sketches out a popularly elected legislature whose members would be apportioned across the states by population. This legislature would possess unequivocal authority to veto state laws to prevent them from "oppressing the minority within themselves by paper money and other unrighteous measures which favor the interests of the majority."[16] This passage and others like it show Madison arriving at Philadelphia, preoccupied with immoderate factional majorities in the states. In none of this preparatory correspondence does he address agency tyranny, the problem that subsequently motivates much of his discussion in Number 51. Madison arranged for the Virginia delegation to assemble in Philadelphia a few days early to draft a reform proposal and probably to plot strategy. The product of their collaboration (Matthews 1995) soon came to be known as the Virginia Plan.[17]

In this plan Madison envisioned a government organized around an elective, bicameral National Legislature with representation to both chambers based on population. Members of the second chamber—soon to be referred to as the Senate—would be elected by those in the first from nominations provided by the state legislatures. Each chamber could originate laws "to legislate in all cases to which the separate states are incompetent." This included the authority "to negative [veto] all laws passed by the several States, contravening in the opinion of the National Legislature the articles of the Union; and to call forth the force of the Union" against any state failing to perform its constitutional duties.

Nowhere is the National Legislature's supremacy more apparent than in the organization of the other branches diagrammed in Figure 5.1. The National Legislature would elect the National Executive for a fixed term and without eligibility for re-election. This officer (or officers) would exercise general authority to administer national laws. Similarly, the National Legislature would create a national judiciary and elect its members, who would then serve for a term of good behavior. Together, the executive and a "convenient number of judges" would constitute a Council of Revision with the sole task of vetoing imprudent legislation.[18] If legislative selection of the executive and judiciary did not ensure the Council's sympathetic oversight, the National Legislature's ultimate authority was secure in a provision for a veto override.[19]

Remarkably, the vast literature on Madison's contribution to the Constitution's development fails to credit the Virginia Plan with faithfully and ox tensively implementing the principle of factional competition. Perhaps the five-month interval between presentation of the plan and Number 10 obscures their association. Yet at the Convention, Madison offered early, partially developed versions of Number 10's argument in defense of the Virginia Plan. In one of his most important and, for us, theoretically revealing speeches, Madison employed factional competition to counter claims by Delaware's John Dickinson and others that tyranny could be avoided only through strict separation of powers with "the legislative, executive and judiciary departments . . . as independent as possible." Madison beat back strict separation of powers and defended legislative supremacy with factional competition.[20] During floor debates on June 4, Madison unveiled the argument that would become Number 10. William Pierce from South Carolina discerned in it "a very able and ingenious" outline of "the whole scheme of government" (Rakove 1996, 61). During the next four days, Madison repeated the argument no less than four times, and fellow nationalists picked it up in their speeches. At one point, after listening to the familiar recitation of the small state arguments, James Wilson (ibid., 67) reminded everyone: "No answer has been given to the observations of [Madison] on the subject."

A. Organization of National Government

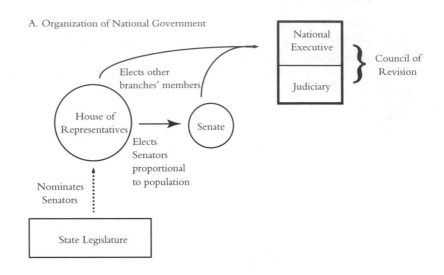

B. A Bill Becomes a Law

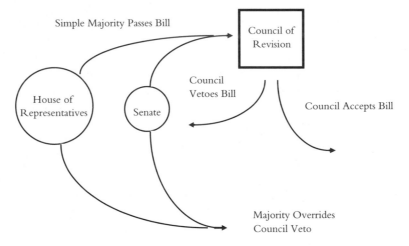

FIG. 5.1. The Virginia Plan

Madison, no less than anyone else, also wanted to associate his proposals with separation of powers, but during these early deliberations, he employed it mostly to describe the division of labor that would strengthen the capacity of the new national government. Reminding his colleagues of the wartime Congress's dismal performance in administering the government with legislative committees, Madison commended separation of power as fostering government efficiency.

There are elements of checks and balances in the Virginia Plan. These remained implicit in the general outline in "Vices," but Madison drew them out more explicitly during the Convention's deliberations. In that these mild checks were tendered in response to other delegates' insistence for creating truly "separate" branches, one might be tempted to dismiss them as rhetorical embroidery offered to allay some small state delegates' misgivings. Yet, the weak form of checks and balances Madison offers at the Convention is wholly consistent with the Virginia Plan's legislative supremacy. The two constitutional features that Madison emphasized as checks are the Council of Revision with its weak veto and the Senate with nearly coequal legislative authority. On June 4 (Farrand 1966, 1, 608) he defended a veto lodged in the Council of Revision: "A negative in the Executive is not only necessary for its own safety, but for the safety of a minority in danger of oppression from an unjust and interested majority." As to the Senate, its "use . . . is to consist in its proceeding with more coolness, with more system, & with more wisdom, than the popular branch." Clearly, in Madison's view the checking benefits from the Senate derived not from representing different interests, since these men would in fact be elected by the "popular branch." Rather it came by representing the same interests in a different deliberative setting. "Enlarge their number," added Madison in the next sentence, "you communicate to them the vices which they are meant to correct."[21] The upper chamber's "coolness" and "system" buys time and opportunity for reconsideration.[22] This is not the robust bicameralism proposed for Virginia with its separate recruitment of independent officers. Indeed, the Virginia Plan remarkably resembles the Virginia constitution Madison had sought to reform several years earlier.[23]

Note that Madison recommends neither the Council of Revision nor the Senate as trimming potential agency loss. In fact, during this phase of Convention deliberations the only time Madison acknowledges this as a potential problem comes in response to a proposed amendment to the Virginia Plan that would allow a majority of the states to instigate removal of the president. In that small states would enjoy an equal vote with more populous states, it would "enable a minority of the people to prevent the removal of an officer who had rendered himself justly criminal in the eyes of the majority" (ibid., 1, 86). It appears majority control is as essential for properly monitoring agents as it is for ameliorating factional differences.

With the demise of the Virginia Plan, Madison's interest in separation of powers turns from efficiency and a system of modest checks to a radically different form of checks and balances. He had worked against a hemmed in Congress when the Virginia Plan was under consideration, but now needing a means to quarantine the state-infested Senate he switched to a dispersion of governmental authority—stronger on some checking provisions, in fact, than those contained in the final Constitution.

II.D. AFTER THE GRAND COMPROMISE

After losing the legislature and the national veto over the states in the Grand Compromise, Madison sought unfettered national authority in a more independent executive and judiciary.[24] To achieve this Madison continued to invoke separation of powers during the second half of the Convention and apparently succeeded in that no one in the sometimes heated exchanges accused him of changing his mind.[25] From Madison's numerous statements, proposals, and votes during this period one can fashion a second plan—a plan that does not so much add up to a formal system of government as a collection of provisions that consistently worked to shift authority away from the poorly designed Congress. Most directly, he endorsed the proposed enumeration of powers for Congress, an idea he had resisted during consideration of his Virginia Plan. When the states' rights delegates advocated state election of the president, Madison countered with direct national election. The result was yet another compromise, the Electoral College. Similarly, some states' rights supporters wanted the president to serve at the pleasure of Congress. Madison had equivocated on this matter earlier, but now he insisted that separation of powers required a fixed term without term limits. Others wanted administrative and judicial officials appointed by Congress, but Madison, sounding increasingly like Hamilton, countered that the appointment power struck to the core of executive responsibility. By late July this recent proponent of legislative supremacy was fashioning an independent, assertive president. Noting the tendency of a "legislature to absorb all power in its vortex," Madison (ibid., 2, 586–87) defended a veto with a three-fourths override provision as necessary "to check legislative injustice and encroachments."

When it came to the judiciary, neither side appears to have decided which arrangement best served its interest. Early on, the nationalists won adoption of a judicially enforceable supremacy clause—consolation, they were reminded, for losing the national veto over state laws. Subsequently, Madison and his allies faced down a half-hearted attempt to leave constitutional interpretation and enforcement of federal laws to the separate state judiciaries. During the late days of the Convention, as the Virginia Plan and its theoretical rationale of pluralism faded from view, Madison used these numerous, small victories to fend off additional state incursions and to stamp onto the Constitution his nationalist preferences, at least as best one could with the negative instruments of checks and balances.

II.E. RECONCILING MADISON'S FOUR
REFORM PROPOSALS

This chronology of Madison's reform politics from 1784 through 1787 includes every instance in which he enlisted either factional competition or separation of powers doctrine before sitting down to write Numbers 10 and 51. Clearly, by the fall of 1787 the arguments in these essays had been applied to reform both state and national governments. For the most part, the concepts, phrasing, and logic were well established by the time Madison wrote these *Federalist* essays. This helps to account for the alacrity with which he was able to churn out cogent arguments in the heat of the campaign. Yet there are some important differences, especially with respect to Number 51, that caution us from assuming that their arguments were the sincere extensions of ideas well tested elsewhere.

On two of the four occasions reviewed above, Madison appears to have employed one or the other principle opportunistically. In staving off re-establishment of religion we found him hurriedly assembling fundamentalist preachers to lobby members of the assembly and where necessary replace them in the next election. Similarly, in July after recovering from a disappointing setback at the Convention, Madison grasped for alternative institutional mechanisms to achieve his goals of blocking state dominance via the Senate. On the other two occasions, however, where Madison had the luxury of initiating constitutional revision, he was able to prepare and argue for more comprehensive and theoretically grounded reforms. In Virginia it took the classic form of Montesquieu's checks and balances directed against the popularly elected assembly, as it would again with Number 51. At the Convention, factional competition provided the blueprint.

Summarizing the analysis, Figure 5.2 shows that unifying Madison's political science was not so much a preference for particular constitutional architecture as it was the goal of frustrating majority tyranny in the states, and collaterally, of strengthening national authority. One way or another, Madison consistently pursued the rearrangement of federal-state power. From the sheer volume of endorsements in his speeches and writings, as well as from private correspondence, one may reasonably conclude that Madison did sincerely favor factional competition where the requisite pluralism was present. He did, after all, rely on it almost exclusively in the Virginia Plan. But clearly, where conditions were unsuitable—as in the states—or prior decisions precluded this avenue—as with the post–Great Compromise deliberations— Madison was fully prepared to fashion interior controls to advance his goal.

The only lapse in pushing institutional reform in the direction of promoting national over state power occurs in Number 51, when Publius enlists

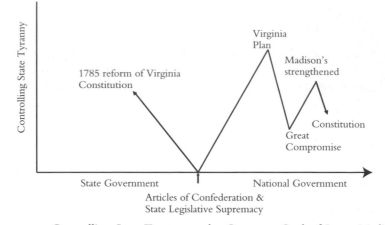

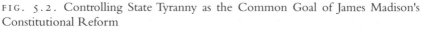

FIG. 5.2. Controlling State Tyranny as the Common Goal of James Madison's Constitutional Reform

both factional competition and separation of powers for the purpose of restraining national majorities and their politicians from intruding on the rights of the states and the citizenry. Of course, even this deviation can be reconciled *strategically*, in that it promoted ratification of the Constitution, which Madison acknowledged privately offered a heavier counterweight to imprudent state policies than currently provided by the Articles of Confederation.

Classifying Number 51 as highly sophisticated campaign rhetoric introduces its own difficulties. Why should Publius have believed that he could win popular support by having nonelective offices block the authority of a popularly elected House of Representatives? With Anti-Federalists charging that the new government would quickly transmogrify into a distant, unresponsive Leviathan, this kind of appeal would appear especially problematic. Before judging Number 51's core argument to be strategic, we must ascertain that it did, indeed, offer the target audience a compelling rationale for ratifying the Constitution.

III. Federalist Number 51 as Campaign Rhetoric

Right up to the time he began writing his *Federalist* essays, Madison privately expressed reservations about the Constitution and could bring himself to muster only tepid support for the overall plan. In his letter (MP 10, 163–64) to Jefferson on September 6, 1787, in which he explains the Convention's work during the summer, Madison devoted more space to excusing the Constitution's deficiencies than to celebrating its strengths. The new national government will "neither effectually answer its national object nor prevent the local mischiefs which everywhere excite disgusts against the state governments."[26] This and other private statements reveal Madison working for ratification mostly from an aversion to the Articles of Confederation. They certainly give a hollow ring to Publius's boosterism.

From his private views and public activities before and during the Convention one can reasonably surmise that Madison's *sincere* public endorsement of the Constitution would have gone something like this: "The nation is presented with a choice between two imperfect governmental systems. Unquestionably, the Constitution *is* superior to the Articles of Confederation and therefore, deserves ratification. Its advantages include a popularly elected and fairly apportioned House of Representatives, federal taxation authority, and provisions for amendment that will allow it to be strengthened as the need arises." This halfhearted endorsement would have befitted Madison's modest won-lost record at the Convention, but it would not, of course, have served the ratification cause.[27] All this adds up to an image of Madison wanting Publius to succeed, but not having much to offer in the way of compelling, sincere arguments.

Normally, politicians' issue stances are anchored in the vicinity of core constituency commitments and by the threatened loss of credibility were they to drift too far from their established positions. But the guise of Publius relaxed these constraints and freed Madison to tailor his message closely to the preferences of his audience. Thomas Jefferson (*The Papers of Thomas Jefferson* [hereafter JP] 11, 353) thought he had detected such strategic writing in Madison's *Federalist* essays and averred to his friend: "In some parts it is discoverable that the author means only to say what may be best said in defense of opinions in which he did not concur." If so, the contradiction that arises in Number 10 and Number 51 might reflect Madison's need to modify his sincere views with campaign rhetoric to appeal to fence-sitting voters and delegates.

The absence of public opinion data for this eighteenth-century, national election severely handicaps our ability to assess the relative merits of campaign arguments. The situation is not hopeless, however. If one assumes that each side's campaign strategists knowledgeably adapted their issue stances to the median voter or delegate, we can by tracking the course of campaign rhetoric discover which issue stances received the greatest play and required a response from the other side.[28] By examining the shifting positions and issues over the seven-month campaign we can evaluate the merits of Number 10 and Number 51 as campaign statements.

The data for this exercise comes from William H. Riker (1991, 1996), who systematically compiled and analyzed all of the pro and con arguments that appeared in the nation's newspapers during the ratification campaign.[29] The antiratification side conducted essentially a negative, single-issue campaign. More than 90 percent of their published arguments raised the specter of tyranny.[30] Clearly, the untested Constitution gave the Anti-Federalists superior material for imagining hypothetical dangers, and wherever they searched among the Constitution's provisions, they uncovered a potential source of tyranny.[31] Ultimately, the Federalist had to answer these charges. "Just as the plaintiff-like position of the Anti-Federalists forced them to be negative," observed Riker (1996, 244), "so the defendant-like position of the Federalists forced them to be positive in the sense that they had to refute the Anti-Federalists' criticisms." The Constitution's provision for a standing army supplied early fodder for Anti-Federalist attack. They dropped it after the nationalists successfully answered that with America flanked by three foreign powers, this feature of the Constitution remedied one of the glaring vulnerabilities of the defenseless confederation. A little later the antiratification forces discovered that the missing Bill of Rights exposed a major chink in the nationalists' armor. After initial insistence that "paper guarantees" were neither effective nor necessary in a limited government, Madison and his allies recognized that these responses were not working and agreed to introduce appropriate constitutional amendments as soon as the new government was under way.

A careful examination of the charges and countercharges flying back and forth when Numbers 10 and 51 were written shows both essays directly responding to a variant of the tyranny currently being advanced by the Constitution's opponents.[32] On October 17, 1787, Brutus (probably Robert Yates, who served as one of New York's delegates to the Constitutional Convention) published an article in a New York paper charging "a free republic cannot succeed over a country of such immense extent, containing such a number of inhabitants, and these encreasing in such rapid progression." Hamilton quickly countered (Ball 1988, 162) with *Federalist* Number 9, arguing that Montesquieu's prescriptions, on which Brutus relied, were based on societies with aristocracies that had to be accommodated. Shortly thereafter, Madison issued Number 10. Fortunately for Madison, Brutus's essay limited its attack to the "extended republic" variant of tyranny and did not venture into the structure of new national government for which factional competition could offer no justification. Brutus's narrow argument allowed Madison to truncate his factional competition discussion precisely at the point where this principle's institutional prescriptions diverge from the Constitution's provisions.

Later in the fall, the Anti-Federalist campaign began hammering the new government as providing insufficient checks and balances against national tyranny. The arguments took a variety of forms, from name-calling to informed theoretical exposition. One widely reprinted Anti-Federalist article, "Dissent of Pennsylvania Minority," stated a familiar mainstay of the opposition to which the ratification forces clearly needed to respond.

> The constitution presents . . . undue mixture of the powers of government: the same body possessing legislative, executive, and judicial powers. The senate is a constituent branch of the legislature, it has judicial power in judging on impeachment, and in this case unites in some measure the character of judge and party, as all the principal officers are appointed by the president-general, with the concurrence of the senate and therefore they derive their offices in part from the senate. . . . Such various, extensive, and important powers combined in one body of men, are inconsistent with all freedom; the celebrated Montesquieu tells us, that "when the legislative and executive powers are united in the same person, or in the same body of magistrates, there can be no liberty." . . . The president general is dangerously connected with the senate; his coincidence with the views of the ruling junta in that body, is made essential to his weight and importance in the government, which will destroy all independence and purity in the executive department. (*Debate* 1993, 1, 546)

Of the various charges in "Dissent," possibly the most damaging is the image of a "junta" forming between the president and the Senate. Riker (1996) logged more Anti-Federalist references to a presidency that might evolve into an elective monarchy than any other dire scenario. As with the extended republic variant on the tyranny argument, one can imagine a couple of rebuttals available to proratification strategists. They could, as did Hamilton in Number 9, deny the premise from which tyranny could be deduced. In the following passage, fellow nationalist Americanus (John Stevens, Jr.) adopts this approach and ices it with a vivid ad hominem.

> Montesquieu's *Spirit of the Laws* is certainly a work of great merit. . . . On an attentive perusal, however, of this celebrated performance, it will manifestly appear, that the main object of the author, and what he seems ever to have most at heart, was to mollify the rigors of Monarchy, and render this species of Government in some degree compatible with Liberty. . . . But tho' his work has been of infinite service to his country, yet the principles he has endeavored to establish will by no means stand the test of the rigid rules of philosophic precision. . . . It ever has been the fate of *system mongers* to mistake the productions of their own imaginations, for those of nature herself. (*Debate* 1993, 1, 487–93, emphasis added)

Madison could have sincerely signed his name to this argument, including the slap at Montesquieu.[33] Instead Publius takes a more ambitious, if circuitous, approach by reconciling Montesquieu and separation of powers doctrine with the Constitution. The volume and variety of pro-ratification campaign arguments suggest that this issue had to be neutralized, but could it be by simply denying its validity for the American case?[34]

Consider, in comparison, the gambit Number 51 offers. After elevating Montesquieu as "the oracle who is always consulted," Publius stipulates that tyranny is indeed a serious threat for which a well configured separation of powers is the preferred solution. No problem so far, since he has matched Anti-Federalist arguments almost word for word. Only late into the argument does Publius depart from the path taken by the Constitution's opponents. Sizing up the distribution of authority across the branches differently, he reassures readers that they need not worry about a coalition forming between the president and a Senate junta. These politicians, if they are lucky, might manage to stave off an overreaching House of Representatives prone to act with "intrepid confidence." If they are not so lucky, the Constitution might need to be amended to bring interbranch relations into balance. But certainly, one need not worry that the executive and judiciary possess the kind of authority that would allow them to usurp a democratic government.

This is a terrific campaign argument. First, Publius shifts the debate to safer ground for engaging his adversaries. He takes exception to Anti-Federalist conjecture over the operation of a hypothetical government rather than by arguing against the universally accepted separation-of-powers principle and needlessly picking a fight with the illustrious Montesquieu. Second, Publius adroitly configures his argument to avoid a variety of possible Anti-Federalist rebuttals. He might, alternatively, have invoked the judicial branch in its acknowledged role—with or without judicial review—as referee over jurisdictional disputes, but he would have opened the door to a favorite Anti-Federalist retort that Publius was prepared to entrust the fate of the Republic on unelected justices. Or he could have discounted the danger by stressing the asymmetric character of the veto. But instead, he minimizes the president-Senate threat by introducing the possibility that all of its authority might be insufficient to withstand an overreaching House of Representatives. He knows full well, as Riker's analysis verifies, that the Anti-Federalists will not attack the House of Representatives, the one popular branch.

Whatever difficulties Number 51 presents Madison's political science, its strategic value cannot be doubted. Clearly, the generality of separation of powers doctrine opened the way for this tactic, but its success depended on a sophisticated understanding of subtle, institutional design arguments, a talent for which Madison was peerless. He, more than anyone else, could figure out a way to abduct Montesquieu and steal the separation-of-powers issue from the opposition.[35]

To test Madison's (and to a lesser extent Hamilton's) specialized role in the ratification campaign, I counted all references to Montesquieu and separation of powers published in an exhaustive five-volume compilation (Kaminski and Saladino 1988) of extant newspaper and pamphlet arguments for and against ratification. The results show that Publius summoned Montesquieu twice as frequently as did the other proratification writers, although only half as often as did the Anti-Federalists. With respect to separation of powers, however, Publius eclipsed everyone—three times as frequently as the other Federalists and nearly twice as frequently as the Anti-Federalists. Moreover, unlike the other proratification references including Hamilton's *Federalist* essays, Madison's Publius consistently invokes these sources favorably. There was a constitution to be won, and Number 51 appears to have been masterfully contrived to respond to critics.

IV. Conclusion: Madison, a Nationalist and Pluralist

Several weeks after the close of the Constitutional Convention in September 1787, James Madison (MP 10, 163–65) wrote a long letter to Jefferson in Paris reporting the results of the recently concluded Constitutional Convention. After singling out various provisions of the new Constitution for praise and criticism, Madison noted that on balance private rights would be more secure "under the Guardianship of the General Government than under the State Governments." Madison then posed to his friend a riddle: why should this be so, assuming both levels are "founded on the republican principle which refers the ultimate decision to the will of the majority, and are distinguished . . . by extent . . . than by any material difference in their structure?" Solving this puzzle, Madison averred, would "unfold the true principles of Republican Government." Indeed it does. Without explicitly solving the puzzle, Madison proceeded to lay out the rationale for factional competition. The puzzle fully encapsulates the goal orientation of Madison's political science. The stated goal of republican government is to protect private rights while empowering majority rule. Moreover, the "principles" for achieving this goal are found less in the "interior" design of institutions (as in Number 51) than in the quality of pluralism. Where this condition is satisfied, the task of institutional design is to harness this pluralism with factional competition.

This is a riddle composed by a nationalist and pluralist. The former label is a familiar one for Madison. His nationalist credentials were well established among his contemporaries. Calling Madison a pluralist is more controversial. It squarely disputes familiar critiques of Madison and the Constitution that began most prominently with Beard and continued with Dahl (1956), both of whom judged Madison as embracing "the goal of avoiding majority control." He "goes about as far as possible," Dahl added, without having to drop the republican label, but in reality he belongs "in the camp of the great antidemocratic theorists." Both critiques rely chiefly on Number 51.

Madison's pluralism does not make him a majoritarian democrat in the modern sense of the phrase. He accepted unfettered representative democracy only in circumstances that imposed serious collective action problems for the formation of governing majorities. These conditions could be satisfied in an extended republic in which governmental institutions gave full expression to the nation's pluralism. When these conditions were met, the design requirements of America's national government could be simple: representation that reflected the preferences of the population and a fairly apportioned, well designed national legislature. This Madison implemented, not in the Constitution, but in the Virginia Plan. In the confined territory and comparatively homogeneous population of Virginia and the other states, the transaction costs to majority formation were naturally lower and so, Montesquieu's mechanical controls had to be superimposed onto politics.

Where does this leave the Madisonian model, the presumed theory behind the Constitution? First, associating it with Madison is a misnomer, since Madison does not offer it until late in the ratification campaign in Number 51, and then only behind the cloak of Publius. It might not represent Madison's political science, but the model does describe the Constitution. Number 51's combination of factional competition and checks and balances should be recognized as Madison's brilliant effort to justify theoretically a Constitution born of politics and facing an uncertain future. The Madisonian model (or perhaps more felicitously, the "Publius model") rationalizes a plan created from numerous logrolls and compromises that reconciled competing interests. So understood, the presence of contradictory elements poses no problem. After all, the contradiction between factional competition and checks and balances describes well the ever-present tension between America's transient, rarely dominant majorities and the irrepressible claims of entrenched, particularistic interests. To conclude, Numbers 10 and 51 carry a division of labor quite different from that with which we opened the discussion. Number 10 states James Madison's prescriptions for republican government, when the necessary conditions are present, while Number 51 explains the Constitution.

Notes

1. Beard reintroduced readers to the long neglected Number 10, "the most philosophical examination of the foundations of political science"; then, several pages later he grafted it onto the already famous checks and balances provisions of Number 51. Beard characterized Number 51's argument as "fundamental theory . . . the basis of the original American conception of the balance of powers."

2. Dahl also questioned the quality of Madison's theorizing. The concept of tyranny in Number 10 proved to be so differently defined from Number 51, he could not interchange them and have the rest of the argument make sense. He concluded, "as political science rather than as ideology the Madisonian system is clearly inadequate" (31).

3. Perhaps these actors are not the fully realized, modern-day professionals— Madison, after all, throws out the prospect that the process will favor the recruitment of virtuous officeholders—but their success would hinge in part on their success as brokers. For a comparison of Madison's with other contemporary views on representation see Pitkin (1967). Morgan (1974) finds in this new class of self-interested political entrepreneurs the need for checks and balances, but I dispute here that Madison shared Morgan's inference.

4. Constitutional law professor Richard A. Epstein (1993) suggests that this missing discussion reveals that Madison did not take factional competition seriously. After all, if he had found this argument convincing, why would the Constitution's chief architect have lavished attention throughout the *Federalist* on the composition and authority of the executive and judicial branches, on bicameralism and on federalism? He concludes that Madison offered it as a "bit of legerdemain" inspired to promote ratification.

5. One familiar passage of Number 10 illustrates Madison's agency perspective. In distinguishing democracy from republic Madison notes "the delegation of the government, in the latter, to a small number of citizens elected by the rest." Wood (1969, 543–53) cites numerous instances of the widespread use of agency theory at the Philadelphia convention and in the ratification debates. In the Virginia ratification convention, John Marshall maintained that since the citizenry could not "exercise the powers of the government personally," they "must trust to agents."

6. "The great desideratum in Government is such a modification of the Sovereignty as will render it sufficiently neutral between the different interests and factions, to controul one part of the Society from invading the rights of another, and at the same time sufficiently controuled itself, from setting up an interest adverse to that of the whole Society."

7. Although he explains why this might be justified for the judiciary, Madison is silent on the matter of the presidency. Number 51 even offers a curious endorsement of direct elections: "Perhaps such a plan of constructing the several departments would be less difficult in practice than it may in contemplation appear."

8. And Publius could have described the protective wall the Constitution constructs around this vital chamber by making its members ineligible for the

kinds of corrupting executive appointments and other emoluments that the Framers universally viewed as suborning the British House of Commons.

9. Carey reads this passage differently (Carey 1978, 160): "Clearly the phrase 'auxiliary' precautions refers to additional obstacles to governmental abuses [that is, agency loss] and not to majority tyranny."

10. Biographer Ralph Ketcham (1990, 301) emphasizes Madison's positive view of government power: "In seeking separation of powers, Madison meant not only to prevent simple tyranny but to tap more fully the latent increment to power for constructive action afforded by the republican principle. In this insight Madison transcended the traditional dogma . . . that freedom meant *release* from the authority of government. Under a government of consent, properly constructed to prevent domination by faction, freedom could mean the *use* of power in the public interest." See also Diamond (1959).

11. As Riker (1992) noted, the aggregation of constituencies in the Senate should not lead to different median preferences across the two institutions. Rather it is their differences in mode of election and distribution of seats without regard to population that should generate differences between the House and Senate.

12. Sensing his sudden advantage in the backlash, Madison dusted off Jefferson's stalled "Bill for Establishing Religious Freedom" and won its speedy enactment. Three years later at the Virginia ratification convention, Madison (Miller 1992) reminded delegates of this recent controversy while defending the absence of a bill of rights from the Constitution. Declarations are merely "parchment barriers." "The utmost freedom of religion" rests with the "multiplicity of sects ... which is the best and only security for religious liberty in any society."

13. Adair p. 148. David Epstein (1984, p.102) also stresses the fundamental dissimilarities of Madison and Hume. To achieve such a solution, Hume constructs a dubious, three-tiered system of government. The nation is divided into 100 equally populous counties whose citizens elect 100 county representatives (for 10,000 in all), who in turn elect eleven county magistrates and one senator. Only the 100 senators ever convene as a deliberative body, and any policy they adopt must be ratified by a majority of the county magistrates or representatives meeting in their separate locales. Ultimate authority would reside with officeholders who never meet.

14. The most direct evidence of Madison's reliance on the same separation of powers doctrine as stated in Number 51 is a topical outline he proposed for a speech in the House of Delegates in June 1784. It consists of two lists of phrases and sentence fragments—e.g. "Judiciary dependent for am. of salary"—almost all of which covers some aspect of the division of power among the several branches of the state government. Hunt 1900, II: 54–55.

15. Undaunted, Madison came back the next session and led the legislature to modernize the state's legal code—117 statues in all. Reflecting on this one legislator wrote another, "Can you imagine it possible that Madison can shine with more than the usual splendor in this Assembly? . . . He has astonished Man-

kind and has by means perfectly constitutional become almost a Dictator . . . . His influence alone has . . . carried half . . . the revised code." (Ketcham 1990, 161).

16. Madison listed other advantages of the "negative" over state policies: resolve state boundaries; "guard the national rights and interests against invasion"; and restrain the states from "molesting each other." (*Papers*, March 19, 1787, 9: 318–19). In his subsequent letter to Randolph, Madison suggests that the veto be lodged with the upper chamber (the Senate) because its membership would be more divorced from politics. (*Papers*, April 8,1787, 9:369). Hobson (1979) persuasively places this frequently neglected federal veto at the center of Madison's republican theory.

17. Historians agree (Miller 1992; Ketcham 1990) that it represents Madison's ideas for the new Constitution.

18. Madison's paternal preference for the Virginia plan is revealed in the extent to which he resisted proposed changes. Early on, he opposed the convention's decision to substitute a presidential veto for the Council of Revision. He subsequently sought to reinstate it. See Farrand (1937, 1:236 and 2: 74, 298).

19. Unlike Madison's endorsement of a three-fourths supermajority override rule later in the summe, after the Great Compromise, the Virginia Plan did not broach a supermajority requirement.

20. Moreover, he used this tactic on other occasions, but once the Great Compromise was narrowly adopted, he dropped the argument until Number 10. In his record of the day's events, William Pierce of Georgia described it as "a very able and ingenious speech." (Farrand 1937: 1, p.110). On June 26 Madison returned to this argument in defending a population basis for representation in the Senate. Jillson and Eubanks (1984) examine the theoretical novelty of Madison's ideas.

21. In the same speech, Madison emphasizes that the Senate's value as a check on the lower house lies in institutional design and not the recruitment of philosopher kings: "When the weight of a set of men depends merely on their personal characters: the greater the number the greater the weight. When it depends on the degree of political authority lodged in them the smaller the number the greater the weight. These considerations might perhaps be combined in the intended Senate; but the latter was the material one" (June 7, Farrand, 152).

22. This conclusion is little different from that reached by William H. Riker (1992) who similarly assumes that the median voter preference in the two chambers is the same.

23. On this issue, and perhaps only this issue, I disagree with Rakove (1996), who finds in these remarks Madison's abiding suspicion of the popular branches at any level of government.

24. The loss of the national veto came in two stages. Over Madison's objection, the Convention limited it to instances when national and state authority intersected. Then the *coup de grace* came when any mention of this essential feature was left out of the Grand Compromise.

25. His success continues today as scholars locate Madison's *Federalist* arguments in his Convention speeches but fail to recognize that he was enlisting the same language to promote much different conceptions of the Constitution. Carey (1978), for example, enlists passages of Madison's June Convention speeches in behalf of the Virginia Plan to validate for Madison's support in Number 51 for provisions of the Constitution that are inimical to the Virginia Plan.

26. It would probably soon require fixing, he added. In fashioning a rationale for the actual Constitution—whether designed to be persuasive or not—many of Madison's sincere views on republican governance were simply irrelevant. In *Federalist* Number 37, he speculates, "the convention must have been compelled to sacrifice theoretical propriety to the force of extraneous considerations."

27. Lance Banning (1995), one of the few scholars to confront the striking inconsistencies between Madison's earlier writings and his *Federalist* essays, asserts that this is precisely what happened. "Madison's opinions changed *as he was working on the series*," Banning (1995, 400) concludes, "a possibility that ought to seem entirely likely to anyone who has completed a major piece of writing." The main evidence Banning offers for this claim is that Madison never subsequently retracted or contradicted positions taken in these essays. The absence of evidence, however, does not offer a very compelling case for anything other than a null hypothesis. Moreover, this explanation does not resolve the contradictions that appear within Madison's *Federalist* essays.

28. This assumption does not strictly require their perceptions to be accurate in order for them to generate strategic appeals, but at the same time, we presume that ratification strategies actively enlisted less precise technology to arrive at approximately accurate measurements of their campaigns' success.

29. Riker's analysis covered some 617 entries ranging from "minor squibs" to *The Federalist*. These he decomposed into 3268 segments which he then weighted according to the frequency with which they were reprinted across the states.

30. Riker's (1996) classification found 49% of Anti-Federalists' appeals concerned tyranny:

General threat stated	14%
With respect to civil liberties	14%
With respect to governmental structure	14%
With respect to national authority	7%
Total	*49%*

31. In a frequently cited essay, Cecilia Kenyon (1955) judged Anti-Federalists to be "men of little faith." If one considers the decision facing the nation, a negative campaign has a lot of strategic merit. Why make promises, on which Anti-Federalists might disagree, when a negative campaign succeeds in keeping one's adversaries on the defensive? This, and not the absence of core beliefs about the character of government, might explain the distinct differences that emerged across the two sides' campaigns. Perhaps the best known Federalist effort at scare

tactics is John Jay's *Federalist* Number 2 in which he predicted the nation would splinter into regional, competing confederacies if the national government were not strengthened.

32. New York's support was critical and yet most of the delegates elected in the fall had publicly stated varying degrees of displeasure with the Constitution. When the Anti-Federalist governor, George Clinton, delayed consideration in the hope that Virginia and other states would vote down ratification, making it easier to do so, the state became one of the most hotly contested battlegrounds of ratification. Campaign editorials, essays and letters flowed daily through New York City's five newspapers—three of which were declared supporters of ratification, one opposing and one neutral. In addition to reprinting articles published outside the state, the New York campaign spawned substantial local campaign writing enterprises that included some of the most persuasive and theoretically ambitious essays from both sides of the issue. See Eubanks (1989).

33. In the February 18, 1792, issue of the *National Gazette*, Madison was more reserved: "Montesquieu was in politics not a Newton or a Locke, who established immortal systems, the one in matter, the other in mind. He was in his particular science what Bacon was in universal science: He lifted the veil from the venerable errors which enslaved opinion, and pointed the way to those luminous truths of which he had but a glimpse himself." See MP 14: 233–34.

34. Evidence of this issue's durability can be found in amendments to their ratification resolutions adopted by the last four states to ratify the Constitution reminding everyone that "the legislative, executive and judicial powers of Government should be separate and distinct" (Carey 1978, 152–53).

35. This is not all the nationalists stole. They had beaten the more deserving opposition to the Federalist label, occasioning Patrick Henry's complaint that the nationalists would be better named the "Rats," presumably because they favored ratification.

Chapter 6

Madisonian Separation of Powers

JOHN FEREJOHN

Madison's ideas about separation of powers and checks and balances are often located in a collection of specific texts, written during the period of the Founding. And, of course, he did have particular ideas about how the powers of the new national government ought to be allocated. But it is a mistake to take these ideas as his last word on the subject. In this essay I shall argue that what we might call Madisonian separation of powers ought not to be understood as a fixed set of institutions or rules for allocating authority among the departments of the new government. Rather, it is best seen as an attempt to set in place a set of normative and institutional processes that would permit rearranging departmental powers in light of experience. His initial ideas—those found in his *Federalist* essays for example—are best seen as provisional or experimental attempts to establish a new republican government, based on the best knowledge available at the time. As experience with these new institutions grew, he expected that adjustments would need to be made, but such adjustments would need to be consistent with the underlying principle of the Constitution: popular sovereignty.

Madison's experimental attitude toward constitutional government is well reflected at the very beginning of *Federalist* 51, where he confronts the issue of how to maintain a system of separated powers. There, Publius asks: "To what expedient then shall we finally resort for maintaining in practice the necessary partition of power, as laid down in the constitution?" (Rakove 1999, 294). He recognized in that number that his argument in *Federalist* 10 had not yet convinced New Yorkers, or at least not a sufficient number of them, that it was safe to trust a new and powerful national government. It was necessary to try something more: to arrange the "interior structure of the government" as a means of keeping its departments in their "proper places" (*Federalist* Number 51, quoted in ibid., 294). And while he recommended the proposed Constitution as having accomplished this task tolerably well, Madison recognized that the new institution represented a pragmatic effort to control constitutional dangers as well as these could be foreseen.

Thirty years later, he was still struggling with the same question, and still with the same attitude. When, for example, John Adams wrote to him in 1817 about Condorcet's endorsement of a centralized republic, he replied that

> the great question to be decided in the Unites States . . . is whether "checks and balances sufficient for the purposes of order justice and the general good," might be created by dividing and distributing power among "different bodies, differently constituted, but all deriving their existence from the elective principle and all bound by a responsible tenure of their trusts." On the national level . . . the American experiment was favored by "the extent of our Country," which above all "prevents the contagion of evil passions." (quoted in McCoy 1989, 64–65)

Even then, Madison was only moderately sanguine about the fate of the republican experiments in the states, some of which had even tried something resembling a principle of legislative supremacy. But, he was reassured that, as of 1817, most of the states had overthrown these innovations in favor of "assimilating their constitutions to the examples of the other states, which had placed the powers of Government in different depositories, as a means of controlling the impulse and sympathy of the passions" (cf. ibid., 64). So, he saw reasons for optimism even as the particular ways that checking institutions were implemented varied from state to state.

The justification for the Constitution's elaborate system of checks and balances is to maintain a proper separation of governmental powers. So, it is somewhat surprising that Madison did not say very much about how separate governmental powers could or should be. Following Locke and Montesquieu he favored the idea that legislative, executive, and judicial functions ought not to be mingled too much and that it would be improper, for example, if the legislature were to attempt to adjudicate disputes (that would be to exercise the whole power of another branch). But, he pointed out in *Federalist* 47, strict separation was neither desirable nor possible. The British government—which was thought by Montesquieu and others to be particularly favorable to political liberty—did not effect anything resembling a complete separation. The Crown not only exercised legislative functions but, in addition, its ministers were dependent on Parliament for funds and authority. And of course, though the judges were appointed by the Crown, from the beginning of the eighteenth century they could be impeached in parliament for bad behavior. Moreover, in *Federalist* 48, he demonstrated that none of the new American state constitutions had secured either complete separation or the full independence of the branches of government. In each of these governments, there was a mixture of powers in which the executive, for example, not only exercised some fraction of legislative powers but was also dependent on the legislature and the judiciary to fulfill his constitutional functions. So blending governmental powers had ample precedent in those regimes that were most favorable to promoting liberty. In this light it is not surprising that he defended the proposed Constitution as achieving the most appropriate degree of intermixing of governmental powers.

Indeed, to many political scientists, Madison's reputation as a constitutional designer rests most heavily on his writings on checks and balances and specifically on *Federalist* 51. In that number, we find his defense of the system of checks and balances embodied in the proposed Constitution. There he lays out his principles of institutional design: the justification of government itself is human imperfection (if men were angels there would be no need for it). He emphasizes the importance of exploiting these imperfections in service of constructing and sustaining good government: using ambition against ambition in order to restrain the encroachments by the various departments of governments. In that essay he also expresses his conviction that in a republic, it is the legislative power that is the most dangerous to control (even if the most essential). So, in *Federalist* 51, he emphasizes the need for dividing that power both internally, and between Congress and the other branches. There too he worried that even these checking measures might not be adequate to protect the other branches from what he thought would be the inevitable encroachments of the legislature.

The structure of the Constitution reflects these assumptions. The relatively greater length and detail of Article I compared with Articles II and III is only the most superficial manifestation of these concerns. Article I, first of all, identifies the powers of the federal government with those of the legislature, and it places numerous restrictions on this power. Some of these restrictions—those found in the enumeration of powers in Section 8, for example—Madison was later to call "parchment barriers," while others were more structural, such as the division of legislative powers between the House and Senate and the provision for a limited presidential veto. In comparison, Articles II and III are both shorter, and the qualifications they impose on executive and judicial powers are less precise. Given Madison's assumptions, and those of the other Framers, this imprecision with respect to the executive and the judiciary is understandable. These were simply less powerful and less dangerous departments, and it was not nearly as important to limit their authority as it was to control what the legislature could do.

In any case, events were soon to demonstrate how inaccurate these assumptions were. The first decade of the new republic saw two developments that had not been fully anticipated: first, the nation was embroiled in a series of annoying and dangerous foreign entanglements that had several times brought it to the point of war. The centrality of foreign and military issues had the effect of making the president and his ministers far more powerful than anyone perhaps expected (save Alexander Hamilton). Second, the new executive branch agencies, especially the Treasury Department, turned out to be much more effective and active than the Constitution-makers had thought possible. These two developments had the effect of enlarging the executive power and of increasing the executive's power to initiate as well as veto legislation—something that had not been contemplated in Philadelphia.

Madison himself opposed these developments on both partisan/ideological and constitutional grounds. It is not always possible to separate these motivations. He was quickly forced to recognize that the Constitution was defective and incomplete in important ways. While the Constitution did establish a functioning national government, the limits on its powers were imprecise and soon subject to interpretive disputation. And though the Framers had been careful to limit the dangerous authority of the legislative, they had been much less careful in spelling out which powers were to be included in the executive authority, nor did they worry overmuch about how much legislative authority the president or his ministers might exercise. As a result, Madison rapidly found himself embroiled in a series of conflicts with executive officials as to the proper limits of both governmental powers in general and presidential powers in particular. And at this point, the Constitution was already in place, and so he was forced to adopt new strategies to deal with these circumstances.

The first strategy he tried was to appeal to what I shall call "constitutional morality"—to attempt to develop interpretive principles to guide the "construction" of the Constitution. The principles he sought sometimes involved appeals to the "intentions" of the Founders, to the notion of strict construction, to the concept of popular sovereignty, and sometimes simply to ordinary logic or common sense. But over the course of the 1790s, each of these casuistical attempts failed to check the ambitions of executive officials or their congressional friends, largely because they were overwhelmed by the stronger attractions of party. At that point, Madison began turning to the states—especially his own state of Virginia—and asked that they play an active role in regulating the constitutional order. This appeal was very much in the spirit of *Federalist* 51, in that it attempted to use ambition against ambition. But it failed too, not only because the states lacked the (constitutional) capacity to act as Madison wanted,[1] but also because partisan passions undermined any will the states might have had to play this role. As a result, therefore, Madison and his followers were forced to move "out of doors" and give meaning to the idea that the people could play a pivotal role in resolving deep constitutional disputes. This role was not regulated by any fixed or underlying substantive idea—of truth or justice—but was grounded on the simple notion that, ultimately, in a republican government, only the people can regulate the balance of institutional powers.

The way this regulation was to be done was not through invoking constitutional mechanisms or processes but through appeals to the people in regular elections. Appeals to the people to rectify constitutional crisis were extraordinary and required an unusual kind of campaign and electoral mobilization. Somehow the people needed to be made aware of the seriousness of the constitutional violation and of the futility of seeking other remedies. But at least the institutional prerequisites for such campaigns were in place both formally, in the constitutional provisions for electing federal officials, and informally, in the new institution of political parties capable of articulating thematic and national campaigns and connecting them to popular sovereignty.

That, at any rate, is the thesis of this essay, and to examine it I shall look at the experience of the new national government in its first decade. The 1790s, the period of this study, is short, too short to prove a case, but it provides plenty of evidence, I think, of the empirical and pragmatic Madison as he attempted to assimilate new and unexpected information about how and how well the new government worked and where it was in further need of repair and redesign. In particular, this history provides an opportunity to see how Madison responded to the alarming development of the powers of the executive in these early years, powers that had been only vaguely envisioned in the design of the Constitution. It is in this area, as much as any other, that Madison began to develop constitutional interpretations that look, to many, strikingly different from ideas he had espoused only a few years earlier. I argue that the best explanation for these shifts is not any change in his fundamental political beliefs, but is instead to be found in his enduring commitment to erect and maintain a stable system of separation of powers in rapidly changing political and institutional circumstances.[2]

Republican Starting Points

Madison came to the issue of separation of powers from a fairly orthodox eighteenth-century Whiggish viewpoint that had been well articulated by Montesquieu,[3] in Book XI of the *Spirit of the Laws.*[4] Like Montesquieu, he thought that the separation of legislative, executive, and judicial powers was vital to the protection of liberty. Montesquieu believed that in a republican government, the legislature was most dangerous to liberty.[5] Partly this is because legislation—authoritative rule-making—is in its nature flexible and open-ended and hard to confine. In part, too, the danger arose from the close connection of the legislature to the people, and from the resulting susceptibility to popular passions. And part of the danger was due to the fact that the authority of a republican legislature is drawn wholly from the people, and is unmixed with any aristocratic or monarchic sources.

Examples of popular or legislative interference with other governmental powers were widely known to eighteenth-century readers, especially from ancient Athens but also from the diverse republics in Renaissance Italy. Republics and democracies were thought to be especially susceptible to populist passions, stirred up by effective orators, taking over the lawmaking powers. And the particular danger in a republic is that popular passions will overwhelm the administration of justice. For Montesquieu, in fact, tyranny was virtually defined as the circumstance in which legislative and judicial functions are commingled, where the power to make law is confounded with its application to particular cases, so that people will be unable to know in advance when they are acting within the law or to foresee with any accuracy when they may be punished. In such a system everyone is vulnerable to arbitrary or whimsical rule. Montesquieu's famous examples of tyrannies illustrate many of the ways in which liberties are insecure when the legislative and judicial powers are combined.

Montesquieu thought that the British constitution, which he took to be essentially republican, though masked under a veneer of mixed government, maintained an adequate separation of powers in various ways. He emphasized the role of juries in separating the exercise of judicial power from the legislative. Indeed, his description of judicial power in Book XI, where he says that the judicial power is a *pouvoir nulle,* seemed to confuse juries, which are made up of lay people who come together to decide a particular dispute and then disperse, with judges, who are continuing officials of government.[6] In any case, English judges had been made substantially independent of Parliament by the time of his sojourn in that country, so he was justified in seeing the judicial process generally, as well as its separate components, as having a good deal of independence from parliamentary or Crown influence.

Montesquieu himself never really explained how it was that the English managed to maintain their system of separated powers. The protections for judges (continuing service on good behavior, rather than at the pleasure of the Crown) and, indeed, the use of juries, were secured by statute and could be amended by Parliament, as could any other aspect of legal procedure. Besides, such judicial independence as there was had been recently invented when Montesquieu wrote and had been vigorously contested by the Crown for a century prior to its establishment. Somehow, though, during the same period, the English managed to develop and successfully defend a robust conception of political liberty, well before republican elements—such as a freely elected Parliament sharing in legislative powers and independent judges—crept into her "constitution."

Perhaps, then, Montesquieu was wrong to think that the protection of English liberties was due to its (virtual) republican elements; perhaps, as Tocqueville was to suggest about nineteenth-century America, those liberties were protected despite the popular elements of the English constitution and not because of them.[7] In fact, the monarchy and the House of Lords represented distinctly nonrepublican sources of authority that might well have mitigated popular impulses dangerous to liberty, within the balanced model of the Crown in Parliament. If that is so, then whether the protections of liberty achieved by the British under their mixed constitution could be maintained in a pure republic—in which all authority is traceable to the people, one way or another—remained an urgent and open question.

Madison shared many of these ideas. He regarded the legislative power as difficult or impossible to place under external limitations. So he saw an urgent need to devise means to ensure that the legislature would not encroach on the other powers. Like Montesquieu, he also entertained a distinctive theory of institutional power in a republican government that we might call a "popular proximity" theory: the idea that the most powerful republican institutions are those closest to the people. We can see an explicit instance of this theory in his writings on federalism (in *Federalist* 45–46), where he argued that the states and localities, because they are close to the people, will understand and sympathize with their problems and respond effectively to them.[8] For this reason, these governments will tend to be trusted and to enjoy popular affections, and therefore tend to retain power and vigor. The people will look first to these nearby and friendly governments as they confront problems requiring public coordination and assistance.

Madison is best understood as entertaining this theory with respect to institutions more generally. The legislature—especially its popular chamber—

being closest to the people, will be highest in their affection and therefore the most vigorous and most dangerous to other institutions "[in] a representative republic . . . where the legislative power is exercised by an assembly, which is inspired by its supposed influence over the people with an intrepid confidence in its own strength; which is sufficiently numerous to feel all the passions which activate a multitude; but not so numerous as to be incapable of pursuing the objects of its passions. . . . [It] is against this department that the people ought to indulge all their jealousy and exhaust all their precautions" *Federalist* 48 (Rakove 1999, 283). This closeness to the people may be maintained by frequent elections, relatively small electoral districts, and by electing this body on a wide suffrage. The Senate, then the president, and finally the courts would then, lacking as frequent and intense contact with the people, enjoy successively less popular affection and trust and could be less active and dangerous to liberty. The power of institutions in a republic is tied, in this way, to closeness to the people. In this sense, the people themselves remain the chief source both of authority and of instability in republican government and therefore the chief threat to liberty. Ironically, because the people are sovereign in republican government as well, they are also the ultimate source of a solution to this threat.[9]

These were Madison's starting points. He understood that the American republics could rely on nothing but popular sovereignty—institutionalized in various ways—and the processes and mechanisms built from it, to guarantee liberties. There were no other recognizable bases of authority than the people and therefore no other principle of choosing a government but election. Because of this monolithic source of legitimation, the legislature, and especially its popular branch, remained the principal source of difficulty to be tamed and controlled in a successful republican government. The question is whether and how this might be done.

Checking Powers: Madison's Constitutional Moment

Madison recognized, certainly by the mid-1780s, that liberties were not well protected in the American states.[10] State laws were dangerously unstable and lacking in wisdom, especially in their assaults on rights of property and on religious liberties. The state governments, on his view, were failing in this respect: as he was to argue in *Federalist* 10, the states were too small and homogeneous, and therefore their legislatures were very susceptible to majoritarian capture. A larger national government would not be so easily taken over by the majoritarian spirit and would be much less likely to yield to tyrannical impulses. The state constitutions were defective in failing ade-

quately to separate governmental powers and functions in various ways. Not
all the states had bicameral legislatures, and the legislatures were too often
unchecked in exercising their legislative powers; also they infringed too easily on the executive and judiciary. Specifically, the judiciaries in the states
were inadequately insulated from political forces, lacking both tenure guarantees and salary protections. Partly because of his lack of faith in vulnerable
state judges, he urged in the Philadelphia Convention that the national legislature be given an absolute veto over state legislation. And, when that proposal failed, he supported the development of federal judicial power that
could regulate defective state legislation. Indeed, as with other elements of
the Constitution, the judicial power emerged from Philadelphia as a product
of piecemeal political compromise rather than design.

Not surprisingly, the structure of the proposed Constitution reflected
many basic republican ideas, as can be seen in the detail and structure of the
first three Articles.[11] The legislative powers were carefully enumerated and
divided between two chambers elected on different principles, between
Congress and the president and, more controversially, partially allocated to
courts in their interpretive and reviewing capacities. This was to be expected:"In republican government, the legislative authority necessarily predominates. The remedy for this is to divide the legislature into different
branches; and to render them by different modes of election and different
principles of action, as little connected with other, as the nature of their common functions, and their common dependence on society, will admit" (Federalist 51; Rakove 1999, 295).

But the powers of the judiciary and, especially, of the executive were
much less clearly set out and regulated. While the "executive power" was
vested in the president, the extent of that power—what it includes and excludes—is not very clearly defined.[12] This imprecision would soon invite
some interpreters to look to the prerogative powers of the British Crown as
being implicitly given under this phrase. Similarly, the president's obligation
to "take care" that the laws be executed is imprecise and open to conflicting
constructions. The judicial power was similarly undefined. We now think
that its exercise is carefully confined to cases and controversies, but it was
(and is) unclear what it takes to make a justifiable case or a controversy that
courts could legitimately decide. Courts themselves rapidly began narrow-
ing these meanings (as, by refusing to give advisory opinions), but the original grant of authority was opaque and incompletely defined. Some thinkers
even thought that federal courts had inherited from Britain the power to apply and make common law.

The relative vagueness of executive and judicial authority is explicable if
the drafters and ratifiers shared what I have called the republican view of the

threats to liberty. If the legislature is seen as the most powerful and danger-ous branch, it is especially important to carefully limit its powers, and to put in place regulatory mechanisms that can keep it within bounds. But limiting the range of executive or judicial powers was both unnecessary and possibly counterproductive. Madison and the other Framers had little interest in weakening these new departments—especially in view of the necessity that they be made vigorous enough to stand up to the popular branch. "As the weight of the executive authority requires that it should be thus divided, the weakness of the executive may require that it should be fortified" (*Federalist* 51; Rakove 1999, 295). "The executive power being restrained within a nar-rower compass, and being more simple in its nature; and the judiciary being described by land marks, still less uncertain, projects of usurpation by either of these departments would immediately betray and defeat themselves" (Rakove 1999, 282).

By the time that the *Federalist* was written, Madison had adopted a dis-tinctive principle of constitutional control: we might call it the principle of institutional self-interest.[13] By dividing up the legislative power and giving some share of it to the other branches, the Constitution provides these branches with the means to protect themselves against congressional en-croachments. He did not doubt that occupants of these offices would have the will to use these devices to protect the authority of their own depart-ments, blocking bills, giving them narrow interpretations, or even striking them down altogether as inconsistent with the Constitution. In this respect, then, the distribution of powers given in the Constitution appeared to be self-enforcing, almost mechanical, and there would be no need to rely either on the self-restraint of officials, or on an external enforcement mechanism (such as appeals to the states or to the people).[14] This, at any rate, is widely taken to be the genius of the Madisonian constitution, at least as understood by contemporary political scientists and economists.

It seems clear in retrospect that the analysis of the various powers pre-sented in *Federalist* 51 was at least ambiguous, if not fatally flawed. The text of the Constitution itself distinguishes pretty clearly between the govern-mental departments and powers. It speaks, for example, of vesting the exec-utive power in the president and of placing the judicial power in "one su-preme court, and in such inferior courts as Congress may . . . ordain and establish." This distinction between powers and institutions lies at the heart of Madison's theory of checks and balances. The notion of dividing the leg-islative power among the departments plainly rests on this idea. Madison could still think, in 1788, as Montesquieu did forty years earlier, that, as the executive power is inherently simple and self-limiting, there is little danger in placing all or most of it in a single pair of hands. Indeed, Madison's worry was that holding the executive power by itself would not be enough to enable the president to maintain his constitutional position, and for that reason his powers needed to be beefed up by adding to them some legislative authority.

Viewed in this light, it may appear surprising that Madison recommended some sharing out of executive authority, such as requiring the president to obtain the consent of the Senate in making treaties and high-level appointments. But there seem to be better explanations of this than any desire to weaken the new president. Relying on the records of the Philadelphia Convention, Jack Rakove has demonstrated that many of the Framers were actually more concerned to limit the powers of the more aristocratic (and potentially conspiratorial) Senate by limiting its capacity to make the president its dependent. From this perspective, it seems as likely that giving the president a role in treaty making was an attempt to limit the capacity of the Senate to conspire in the conduct of foreign affairs and was, in this sense, parallel to giving the president a limited veto over ordinary legislation. Moreover, the creation of a separate treaty power would place additional limits on the influence of the House of Representatives over foreign policy. In these respects, the design of the treaty power can be seen more as another effort at fragmenting legislative powers than an effort to tether the president. In effect, the Constitution creates two separate legislative processes and gives the president an ex post veto over one, and an ex ante proposal power over the other. And, while Rakove does not explore this idea, it also seems possible that connecting the president and the Senate in ministerial appointments was yet another way of driving a wedge between the Senate and the popular chamber and of encouraging it to ally itself with the executive. From this perspective, then, perhaps the least likely point of the allocation of the appointment and treaty powers to the Senate and president acting jointly, was to further weaken an already weak executive.

In any event, it is clear that Madison did not think or wish that the executive would merely exercise executive power. He would exercise legislative powers as well and in this respect would become a part of the legislature. And if the president was to exercise some fraction of legislative powers, one might think that these powers might make his office dangerous, on Madison's own terms. Why wouldn't the president have an institutional incentive to ally with some fraction of Congress, or perhaps of the Senate, to aggrandize powers to the executive? What institutional impediments would forestall such an alliance? The text of *Federalist* 51 is, in retrospect, baffling in its failure to treat the presidency as an institution with a heterogeneous mixture of powers, rather than merely the holder of the executive power.

Controlling Presidential Power

Madison and others soon discovered that the elegant structure of checks and balances put in place in the first three articles of the Constitution and defended in Madison's *Federalist* was no barrier to the expansion of presidential authority. Almost as soon as the Constitution went into operation, Madison was forced to recognize the very incomplete manner in which the executive powers had been defined. We may trace this recognition through several distinct events centering on the extent of the executive power that was to be vested, with some qualifications, in the president. In each case, Madison's response was to try to define and invoke a kind of "constitutional morality" according to which actors would restrain themselves to correct constitutional interpretations.

We begin with the first dispute over the powers of the executive to remove high officials that arose in 1789, while Congress was in the process of enacting statutes to establish executive branch departments. Did the power to appoint ministers with the advice and consent of the Senate imply that the president must also seek senatorial consent before such officials can be fired? In this case, Madison rejected that fairly natural implication on both practical and theoretical grounds. Practically, needing Senate consent for removal would require that the Senate be in session continuously (more or less), something that seemed unwieldy and politically impossible. Theoretically he argued that a wide reading of the grant of executive power to the president was appropriate to the conduct of a vigorous national government. Madison regarded the president as the most responsible officer in government—"[He] is impeachable for any crime or misdemeanor, before the senate, at all times . . . and he is impeachable before the community at large every four years." (ibid., 454). If the president could be stuck with ministers with whom he could not work, he could hardly be held responsible to see that the laws are carried out—which is the reason for having a separate executive. Giving this wide reading to the executive powers of the president is consistent with Madison's previous views in favor of buttressing the weak president. In a letter explaining the advantages of his favored position, he reminded his reader that, in any case, the legislature retains other ways to influence the conduct of the administration (it can appoint ministers for fixed terms, set their salaries, control appropriations). Moreover, he wrote, "if the Federal Government should lose its proper equilibrium within itself, I am persuaded that the effect will proceed from the Encroachments of the Legislative department. If the possibility of encroachments on the part of the Ex. or the Senate were to be compared, I should pronounce the danger to lie rather in the latter than the former" (letter to Edward Pendleton, June 17, 1789, in ibid., 467). This is vintage Madison, of course, but of an early vintage.

Importantly, on this occasion, Madison articulated a new fundamental interpretive principle: that *limitations* on departmental powers should be narrowly construed. The Constitution vested the executive power in the president, subject to particular qualifications: specifically, it required that the Senate shall have a role in appointments of high ministers and in treaty making. As nothing was said about removals, Congress has no authority to add additional qualifications to those enumerated in the document. This principle is actually in some tension with the doctrine of strict construction that Madison and his Republican colleagues were to develop and defend over the next decade. In the case of the removal power, there was a choice of whether to construe either the executive power or its limitation broadly or narrowly. Evidently, in this instance, Madison chose to give an expansive reading to executive power, and construe limitations on that power strictly. Nothing in the idea of strict construction mandates that this particular choice be made.

One can imagine two justifications for this new interpretive principle: Madison argued in this case, as he had in *Federalist* 51, in favor of investing the various powers (legislative, executive, and judicial) substantially in their respectively named branches, subject to particular and specific exceptions and qualifications. Therefore, interpretive precedence should be given to this primary assignment as a way of preserving as much separation of powers as the Constitution could support. Each branch is presumed to be competent to exercise its proper power, subject to checks that keep it from encroaching on the others. An alternative theory would separate out the weaker branches for special treatment. As we have seen, up until 1789, Madison assumed that it was the president and not Congress that needed institutional buttressing, and so he might have preferred to limit this new interpretive principle to the executive branch (and possibly to the judiciary had the issue arisen). It is hard to say which account is to be preferred, and in any case events soon moved beyond this dispute.

Those events were largely driven by the fact that the United States was surrounded by arrogant and often hostile European powers. Revolutionary happenings in France had set in motion a global confrontation, at once material and ideological, between that country and the European monarchies, and that led to the outbreak of a general war in 1792. For the United States, this confrontation mostly involved Britain, France, and, to a lesser extent, Spain, and the American interests that were most threatened concerned commercial shipping to Europe and the Caribbean.[15] War in Europe was a favorable and tempting circumstance for American farmers and traders, and there was much eagerness to supply American products to belligerents on all sides. But, as can be imagined, neither the British nor the French looked with favor on U.S. shipping to their enemy, and there was, as a result, much interference with American commercial intercourse. At the same time, revolutionary events in France had excited the enthusiasm of many Americans who saw the emerging French republic as a natural ally and the vanguard of a general republican transformation in Europe. Moreover, the United States had a long-standing trade treaty with France, dating to 1778, that assured her of most-favored nation treatment and incorporated other commercial understandings as well. Madison and Jefferson were particularly sympathetic to this pro-French policy and hoped that the United States would continue to follow it. And they expected that President Washington shared their sentiments on these matters.

It came therefore as a surprise to Madison when the president issued a proclamation of strict neutrality that seemed favorable to British control of Atlantic trade and implicitly to undercut prior agreements with France. Madison had learned from Jefferson of the tense cabinet deliberations on the subject. Hamilton had argued in cabinet that the treaty with France had been made with a monarchical government and had become, with the revolutionary transformation of that nation, a dead letter. Moreover, he thought that American commercial interests were so closely aligned with the British that it was pointless to risk them by taking the hopeless course of opposing British navigation policy by insisting on moribund treaty obligations. Jefferson responded, again in cabinet, that there were no grounds in international law for Hamilton's claim that a change in government voided a treaty and that, in any case, he thought the president could not constitutionally declare neutrality without involving the Senate. Insofar as a neutrality declaration voided a treaty, it involved the exercise of treaty power that was to be governed by Article II procedures.

Writing under the pseudonym Pacificus, Hamilton answered with an argument superficially reminiscent of Madison's view of the removal powers: "[As] the participation of the Senate in the making of treaties and the power of the legislature to declare war, are exceptions out of the general executive power, vested in the President, they are to be construed strictly" (quoted in Madison's *Helvidius* No. 1, in ibid., 538) In effect, Hamilton claimed the whole territory of foreign affairs—what Locke had called the federative power—for the president, subject only to narrow exceptions.[16] It was left to Madison to argue against this last point in his Helvidius essays.

The issue was simple. The Constitution conferred the power to declare

war on the Congress, and it placed the treaty power in the hands, jointly, of
the president and two thirds of the Senate. The power to make war is essentially legislative: The power to declare a war "is one of the most deliberative
acts that can be performed; and, when performed has the effect of repealing
all the laws operating in a state of peace, so far as they are inconsistent with
a state of war. . . . In a like manner a conclusion of peace annuls all the laws
peculiar to a state of war" (Rakove 1999, 541) Put this way, it is clear why
Madison and Jefferson believed that the president had overstepped his constitutional authority in issuing the Neutrality Proclamation. The declaration
of neutrality had, in effect, put American ships under new (legislative) regulations—subjecting captains and crews to new legal obligations—without
any congressional participation at all.

As he had in the case of the removal power, Madison used this occasion
to develop and extend principles of constitutional interpretation. As the
President's prerogatives in the realm of foreign affairs have an essential legislative component, the presumption must be in favor of requiring congressional participation—either of two-thirds of the Senate, or of the whole
Congress: "[T]he powers of making war and treaty being substantially of a
legislative, not an executive nature, the rule of interpreting exceptions
strictly, must narrow instead of enlarging executive pretensions on these subjects" (ibid., 542). While Hamilton had claimed the terrain of foreign policy
as nearly exclusively presidential, Madison claimed the same ground mostly
for Congress, at least as regards making rather than executing policy. The executive was to be concerned solely with executing laws and treaties, and perhaps with proposing and negotiating them, but to have no independent authority beyond that.

Madison's revised interpretive principle may be stated as follows in two
parts: the "vesting" clauses—the clauses that establish the "core" powers of
the three branches—of the three articles should be given wide interpretation, and so the president is to have wide latitude in exercising properly executive powers. But if a department has a constitutionally prescribed part in
exercising a power that is not substantially vested in it, that part must be interpreted narrowly and not extended to areas not specifically conferred on
that department. Thus, the president's legislative role, given in Article I, section 7, ought to be a narrowly construed exception to Congress's legislative
power. I think enough has been said to notice how far this principle takes us
from the notions that Madison advanced in the *Federalist* or even in the 1789
debates on the removal power. On this doctrine, the president's role in treaty
making ought to be subordinated, interpretively, to that of the Senate—a
view that he implicitly opposed in 1789. By 1793, then, Madison had been

forced by events to recognize the enormous authority that the president could assume, especially in times of war or near war.

Then there was the question of the breadth of the treaty power itself. The continuation of the European war had led to great hardships for American merchants. And, despite the provisions of the 1783 Paris Treaty, the British retained several forts on American territories, from which they could maintain contacts and alliances with various Indian tribes. The particular circumstance was produced by an escalation of the British policy of preventing trade with the French in the second half of 1793. American vessels were routinely searched and impounded, and its sailors were impressed into service in the Royal Navy. The result was general popular reaction against the British and increased talk of war. Hamilton and his congressional allies were concerned to head off these developments. They recognized that American neutrality policy ran against the British effort to prevent supplies reaching France, as American merchants were busily engaged in that trade. Such trade hardly seemed neutral to the British. Hamilton's party also recognized the futility of war or even hostile relations with Britain. Our trade took place mostly with the British and, in any case, our military was too weak to even consider force as an option.[17] The Federalists therefore favored a negotiated agreement instead. And, despite opposition from the Republicans, President Washington finally decided to send John Jay to London to try to negotiate a treaty settling these and other matters.

No doubt the British recognized the weakness of the American bargaining position, and Jay ended up agreeing to a treaty that did little to resolve the issues important to most Americans. It did nothing to settle the impressment issue; it granted Britain favorable trading status and effectively implicated the American government in British navigation policy; and it gained as concessions mainly things that Britain had already agreed to in prior treaties. At most Jay had found language to get the British to withdraw from forts on American territory (something they had agreed to do in 1783), to set up commissions to resolve continuing war-related claims, and that promised to keep the United States from getting into a war with Great Britain, by restricting the freedom of American merchants to trade with France. And, though the treaty had been agreed to in November 1794, its terms were kept secret until after the Senate ratified and the president signed it. Indeed, Madison did not learn of the details until the following summer, and he was dismayed on learning of the terms, especially the procedures that had been followed. To the Republicans, the treaty, when it was made public, was a disaster: not only did it permit the British to continue interfering with American shipping but it also granted numerous concessions that the French were sure to take as a departure from neutrality. It risked a break with France, the nation that Madison and others thought our natural republican ally, in favor of a humiliation by the overbearing British.

In any case the deed was done. Obviously the Federalists had control of the Senate, and there seemed, on the face of things, little that the House could do. The treaty required, however, the creation of several commissions that would investigate and resolve disputes among British and American citizens, and that required money. The Constitution, it will be recalled, entitles the House to originate money bills, and so the House might claim to exercise authority over the fulfillment of treaty obligations. The House requested President Washington to turn over the papers relating to the negotiations so that it might decide what course to take. The president refused, saying that he could see no constitutional purpose behind such a request. So, here was the conundrum: the Constitution vests the treaty-making power in the president and the Senate. But what if a treaty requires appropriations? Does the fact that the House has a constitutional role in appropriations give it a role in treaty making, at least with respect to treaties that require money?[18]

Madison recognized that there is no clear line that can be drawn between treaties and statutes: things that can be accomplished by statutes may be done by treaty instead. Speaking to the House on the Jay Treaty, Madison pointed out that the "President and Senate by means of a Treaty of alliance with a nation at war, might make the United States parties in the war: they might stipulate subsidies, and even borrow money to pay them: they might furnish Troops, to be carried to Europe, Asia or Africa: they might even undertake to keep up a standing army in time of peace" (ibid., 562). Treaties are, indeed, a species of statute—they simply have different procedural requirements. Consider for example a treaty for mutual defense that obligates the United States to go to war if its treaty partner is attacked. The Constitution gives to Congress (including the House) the authority to declare a state of war but no influence over a treaty bringing a state of war into existence. Madison worried that the House would have an obligation both to declare the war that had come into existence and, as the originator of revenue bills, appropriate the funds for it. To behave otherwise would, he worried, be deemed treasonable. Congress would be, in this instance, "mere heralds proclaiming [war]" (ibid., 563) But an obligation of the nation to go to war is only a special instance of what might be undertaken by treaty. The executive and Senate might commit us to regulate rivers, commerce, or populations or, with a little imagination, almost anything else.

Both treaties and statutes are law, and under the Constitution, each is the supreme law of the land. True, getting two-thirds of the Senate to vote for the same proposition can be tricky, but whether to prefer one or another course of action is a contingent matter for political judgment. As a matter of constitutional practice, treaties are negotiated (drafted) by the executive, subject to two-thirds senatorial approval, and there is no role for the House of Representatives at all. Moreover the president and his ministers play the leading role in negotiating treaties with foreign powers, and such negotiated agreements cannot easily be amended. So, in treaty making, the president has assumed a power to propose legislation, and essentially the power to propose, under what we would now call a "closed rule." In these respects then, not only do we have two separate legislative processes, but the procedures by which the two processes are to work are remarkably disparate. This fact makes it likely that treaty and ordinary legislation will overlap and conflict. That was the political basis for the Constitutional question that Madison posed on this occasion.

On Madison's account of the treaty power, the Jay Treaty was constitutionally defective. Its enactment had the effect of imposing (legislative) regulations on American merchants. These regulations were put in place secretly and without any participation or legislative process involving the House of Representatives and had, indeed, been carried out and executed in secret. The secrecy by which the treaty was ratified had the effect of excluding the House of Representatives from playing its proper constitutional role in making appropriations. Moreover, the president, by refusing to forward papers that the House thought it needed to do its job, had arrogated to himself the right to decide what were the constitutional responsibilities of another department of government.

Madison's proposed solution was this: where treaty legislation overlaps with congressional authority—when for example it requires expenditures or regulates foreign commerce—Congress retains its authority to legislate to accomplish these things. In particular the House has the constitutional duty to deliberate and legislate where treaties require action that is within congressional powers. In other words, where a treaty power overlaps congressional authority, congressional action is still required to bring the treaty into effect. Unless such legislation is agreed to, the treaty would remain a dead letter, even though it was validly ratified. Madison dismissed the notion that this view would emasculate the nation's capacity to enter into treaties with others. Characteristically, he argued: "The several powers vested in the several Departments form but one Government; and the will of the nation may be expressed thro' one Government, operating under certain checks" (ibid., 566). The fact that both legislative processes are expressions of a popular sovereign would supply sufficient unity.

In effect, Madison argued that the House of Representatives had a kind of limited veto over some of the treaties that might be agreed to by the president and the Senate. It was limited in the sense that only those treaties that encroached on governmental powers given to Congress would be subjected to "veto." If a treaty could accomplish its objections without doing this, it would not be subject to any action from the House. Of course, there remained the question of who was to decide. Madison clearly worried that each department retain the authority to determine for itself what its obligations were under the Constitution. So, whether a treaty did or did not require congressional rather than merely senatorial action, must remain an issue for the House as well as the Senate to decide.

Obviously, the events surrounding the Jay Treaty had pushed Madison a long way from his initial views of presidential power. The president had authorized his ministers to enter into partisan negotiations with Britain, had claimed the right to keep those negotiations secret, had sealed off the ratification process in the Senate from popular deliberation, and had usurped congressional powers in the process. Needless to say, Washington's presidency did not seem the weak and fragile institution that Madison had envisioned up until 1789. And, far from needing more protection, means had to be found to prevent the presidential office from taking over rightfully congressional powers.

Controlling the President's Legislative Powers

The fact that the Constitution did not adequately define and, perhaps, limit presidential powers might not seem very surprising to modern Americans. To the Framers, the executive power consisted mostly in what was needed to carry out congressional commands. While they foresaw that when Congress was out of session, the executive might have to take actions in unanticipated circumstances, and that he might have information not easily shared with Congress as a whole, the essence of the power was executory. Most important, the constitutional Framers really had very little experience with issues of foreign policy in which the executive's informational advantages over the legislature are chronic. Europeans, having been much earlier forced to recognize notions of "reason of state," could have told Americans of the necessity of rapid and flexible responses in foreign affairs, of the need for secrecy and flexibility, and of the necessity of someone taking responsibility for the fate of the nation in extreme conditions. Washington, and later John Adams, were perhaps doing no more than was necessary in insisting on the capacity of the president to formulate and execute an effective foreign policy. Indeed, as Americans have come to recognize (again) since September 11, foreign policy cannot always be tidily cabined within the restrictive forms of the rule of law that might be insisted upon in the case of domestic legislation. When the Republicans took power after 1801, Jefferson and Madison were soon to learn of these necessities themselves.

The president's role in negotiating treaties has already been discussed, but as commander-in-chief of the military forces, the president is inevitably put in the position of recommending changes in military policy and readiness (witness the repeated and disturbing discussions of a standing army). And, of course, the authority of the executive in foreign and military affairs raises the question of the intersection of foreign and domestic policy. What happens when the president, or his copartisans, decide that foreign policy requires the restriction of domestic liberties? The president or his agents may urge internal legislation, such as the Alien and Sedition Acts, which are supposed to be necessary to the conduct of foreign policy. "[An] ... actual war is not the only state which may supply the means of usurpation. The real or pretended apprehensions of it, are, sometimes of equal avail to the projects of ambition" (ibid., 605). This gives the executive a powerful and unanticipated role in domestic legislation. Madison had understood the president as merely the enforcer of laws enacted by the legislature, but when foreign issues dominate the agenda, the president is often required to be the initiator. This presidential advantage is not, however, a constitutional one but arises from circumstances of danger or "necessity" and from the willingness of the public or of congressmen to follow his lead. This presidential advantage is, as Madison came to realize, a profound threat to the constitutional structure. As he wrote in the *Aurora Advertiser* in 1799: "A ... war is among the most dangerous of all enemies to liberty; and that the executive is the most favored by it, of all the branches" (ibid.).

Moreover, the advantages of the executive are by no means confined to issues of foreign affairs. The point of establishing executive branch agencies is to permit the effective use of information in a timely fashion, and such information can be as valuable to Congress as it is to the president. It is perhaps ironic that, in the legislation establishing the Treasury Department, Congress had insisted that the secretary had special duties to report to Congress directly and was not merely responsible to the president. Indeed, so convinced were House leaders that the first secretary, Alexander Hamilton, would provide them with adequate information to carry out their constitutional responsibilities in enacting taxing and spending legislation, that they abolished the first Ways and Means Committee as unnecessary for the exercise of the powers of the purse.

In modern terms, Congress's insistence that Treasury owed it direct responsibilities accomplished two things: Congress created itself as a principal, separate from the president, to which Treasury was to be directly responsible. While this may have increased congressional leverage over the agency, it also gave Secretary Hamilton a degree of independence from both Congress and the president. Secondly, by giving Treasury the duty to report to Congress, the secretary was given the opportunity and the incentive to develop detailed legislative proposals to which Congress was obliged to pay attention. In effect, the Treasury secretary was to have the power to propose domestic legislation; a power that was, in effect, already enjoyed by executive branch officials in foreign and military policy.

We can see now that there was an inadequacy in Madison's political science, or at least the version he offered in the *Federalist*. The constitutional plan was for the president to share in the exercise of legislative power only passively, through the use of the veto. But legislation, especially important legislation, requires information, analysis, and coordination of a kind that a heterogeneous and understaffed Congress can rarely manage. The early fights over Hamilton's proposals for a national bank and for funding the debt revealed that executive branch officials had enormous advantages over the legislature in formulating and coordinating plans for action, even in the domestic sphere. This meant, of course, that the president and the executive branch inevitably had a vastly larger share in legislation than either the Framers or ratifiers had anticipated.

Moreover, Madison's republican theory of institutional power rapidly proved inadequate too. While the president is remote from the people in some sense, he can serve a role of symbolizing, articulating, and focusing popular expectations about government in a way that a heterogeneous legislature cannot. The enormously respected and popular George Washington gave early evidence of the president's capacity to symbolize and articulate national plans and programs, and to permit the emergent executive branch to develop and promote elaborate legislative programs. Even John Adams, hardly a populist lightning rod, could keep public attention focused on the continuous and dangerous possibility of war with either Britain or France, and arouse anxiety of insidious plots and infiltration by foreign agents. So, in some respects, the president has a kind of closeness to the people that permits him to attain the public ear, to focus public attention, and to interpret remote concerns in ways that Congress cannot.

As Madison came to recognize that both the executive powers and the president himself posed serious constitutional threats, he tended to respond by appealing to constitutional morality. Thus, his response to Hamilton's bank was to argue that the Constitution did not give Congress the power to establish a bank. His response to Washington's Neutrality Proclamation was to deny that the president had the constitutional authority to declare peace any more than war. And his response to the Jay Treaty was to claim that the president and Senate had encroached on the constitutional role of the House of Representatives. None of these appeals worked, of course, and Madison was later driven to seek other remedies. His quest is best illustrated by tracing his response to the Alien and Sedition Acts.

Those acts were passed in 1798 to restrain the activities of pro-French activists as American policy tilted increasingly in favor of the British. Their targets were, principally, republican newspaper editors who were publishing attacks on the Adams administration and its policies. Each was constitutionally defective in various ways. One Alien Act, for example, gave the president unreviewable judicial powers to decide whether a foreigner posed a threat warranting deportation. Madison wrote in his Virginia Report of 1800: "[It] is the president whose will is to designate the offensive conduct; it is his will that is to ascertain the individual on whom it is charged; and it is his will, that is to cause the sentence to be executed. It is rightly affirmed therefore that the act unites legislative, and judicial powers to those of the executive" (ibid., 631). Allocating such powers to the president is inconsistent with Madison's principle of separation of powers according to which a whole or complete power appropriate to one branch ought not be bestowed on another. Madison would probably have had less grounds for objection to the act had the president's power been subject to judicial review.

The Sedition Act seemed, in the first place, a plain violation of the First Amendment by imposing direct congressional restrictions on the press. Second, Madison claimed that whatever authority Congress has to prevent insurrections cannot extend so broadly as to prohibit libels that might have a mere tendency to lead to such disturbances. Defenders of the act responded that it did no more than to modify the prior common law of sedition. But Madison denied that there was any such thing as federal common law; if there was such law the whole doctrine of enumerated powers would have been meaningless. Congress would, under common law, be permitted to legislate over the whole domain within which common law applied, and would not be confined to its enumerated objects. And finally, and perhaps most important, the Sedition Act, which is aimed at preventing political dissent, is supposed to be in effect during congressional elections. That would prevent those elections from fulfilling their function, "intended by the Constitution to preserve the purity, or to purge the faults of the administration" (ibid., 652–53).

Despite these objections, neither Congress nor the judiciary raised any real impediments to the Alien and Sedition Acts and, indeed, were enthusiastic in their enactment and enforcement. That, as Madison argued in the Virginia Resolution, these acts plainly violated both structural and rights-protecting aspects of the Constitution was no hindrance at all. Plainly, the protections and checks built into the constitutional scheme had failed to prevent tyrannical and unjust governmental action. And the efforts of Madison and others to develop a constitutional morality did not work either.

There are various and well known reasons for these failures. The most important was probably the deep and growing ideological divisions among the leading Framers of the Constitution as to what kind of nation the United States should become. The period from the formation of the First Bank of the United States to the enactment of the Alien and Sedition Acts is a record of how political parties—even the relatively weak and ad hoc formations of the 1790s—can override both the insightful political sociology of *Federalist* 10 and the delicate political science of *Federalist* 45–51. In light of this history, it would be easy to dismiss Madison's views, either as expressed in the design of the Constitution or as expressed in his texts in the *Federalist*, as a failed and anachronistic vision that had become outdated almost before they were written. While there is no doubt that political parties were the most significant unforeseen and unappreciated elements in the new constitutional order, Madison's deeper failure was theoretical. He and the other Founders had acted on a very incomplete and partial understanding of how the new government would actually work, one that placed far too much emphasis on controlling the legislature and paid too little attention to other potential sources of usurpation. As events unfolded in the first decade of the new republic, the president and his ministers turned out to be a much more potent source of power, and therefore, of constitutional danger, than the Framers had anticipated.

New Strategies for Separating Powers

Madison began to recognize after 1789 that the system of checks and balances articulated in *Federalist* 51 was not working in the mechanical or automatic way that he had envisioned. True, political officials were ambitious and generally wanted to protect the powers of their offices and institutions, but the constitutional framework had not taken account of developments that began to appear from the first Congress. As I have already argued, the insistent crises of foreign and military conflicts placed far more weight on the executive than had been foreseen and opened up new political opportunities for the executive branch. Perhaps even more important in the long run, the congressional creation of executive agencies rapidly shifted legislative advantages in the direction of the president and his henchmen. In view of these transformations a response was called for, and it is possible to see it taking place at three levels.

One answer to these new developments could be found in principles or norms of constitutional interpretation, or what I have called a constitutional morality. Madison and others, as they learned of new dangers to the constitutional order, repeatedly urged on political officials particular interpretations of congressional powers. In a way, the reliance on interpretation reminds us of Madison's derisive characterization of "parchment barriers"; both relied on the occupants of political office to be restrained in the interpretation and exercise of their powers. Second, there was a constitutional response: a call for amending the Constitution in view of developments (the passage of the Eleventh Amendment is an example, as is that of the Twelfth), or a resort to less well defined constitutional possibilities that were invoked in the Virginia and Kentucky Resolutions. Or, finally, we can imagine a reconceptualizing or retheorizing of the constitutional order, but within the frame of the Constitution itself.

Madison's most significant constitutional innovation in the 1790s was found in his (and Jefferson's) responses to the Alien and Sedition Acts. The failure of the constitutional order to forestall tyrannical legislation led Madison to rethink the role of the states, and then of the people, in a well functioning federal republic. In the Virginia Resolution he resorted to first principles of political contract and argued that the states, as parties to the constitutional compact, "have the right, and are in duty bound, to interpose . . . for maintaining within their respective limits, the authorities, rights and limits appertaining to them" (quoted in Rakove 1999, 589). Precisely what interposition meant was not obvious, but it was clear that the states had some rights and duties that arose from their being the contracting parties (acting in convention as direct agents of the people rather than through their ordinary institutions) that formed the federal government. Thus, however it was to be understood, interposition was plainly intended as an indirect appeal to the people, assembled in the states, to help police a breakdown in the constitutional machinery.

To be sure, this argument was not created out of whole cloth. In arguing for the stability of federal arrangements in *Federalist* 45 and 46, Madison had already envisioned a role for the people in the event of usurpation by either states or the national government. So, one could say that Madison was simply invoking a mechanism that was always contemplated in the constitutional scheme. This seems pretty unconvincing, however. The role of the people in those early essays as well as in the Virginia Resolution does not seem to be exercised within the constitutional framework at all but is antecedent or foundational to that framework. The authority of the people is pre- or meta-constitutional. They, acting through the states, are the original compacting parties and, as such, do not surrender or alienate their rights to interpret the compact but only delegate powers to their created institutions for as long as the compact is in force.

This does not imply that the state governments or legislatures should be seen as having delegated powers to the national government. Such institutions have at most an interpretive role to play, perhaps by sounding the "clarion" call that Madison anticipated in *Federalist* 45–46. That is the role that the Virginia and Kentucky legislatures asked their sister legislatures to play. The final determination is to be made by the people, acting in their sovereign capacity. Should the national institutions attempt to exercise powers not granted under the Constitution, the people retain the right to "interpose, for arresting the progress of the evil" or finally dissolve the compact (quotation from 1800 Report on the Alien and Sedition Acts, in ibid., 609).

In any case, these desperate attempts failed. The other state governments were mostly in Federalist hands, and they dismissed Virginia's and Kentucky's pleas. It was left to Madison and Jefferson to craft a role for the people more plainly and regularly situated within the Constitution. This they accomplished by running an electoral campaign aimed at asserting, through ordinary electoral processes, the fact that the people did not accept the conduct of the national government. This the people did by removing the Federalists from executive and legislative power and leaving them in control only of the judiciary.[19] This assertion of a popular role was never really articulated in the high constitutional discourse of the Virginia Resolution or indeed of the interpretation of venerable clauses of the Constitution. Rather it was accomplished on the ground, through an electoral appeal. The most ordinary kind of electoral politics was summoned and proved sufficient to reconfigure the constitutional balance. In the event, the appeals to a republican morality of self-restraint, or to preconstitutional principles, were unavailing. The people themselves played the needed role.

Ironically, the resulting configuration of republican control of the elected branches and Federalist control of the judiciary was to lead to the eventual development of a judicial role in the enforcement of separation of powers. Madison as a political actor had a lot of problems with the early stages of these developments. But Madison as a political scientist ought to have been able to appreciate how it was driven by the empirical experiences of the new republic.

Conclusions

It is important to separate Madison's contributions to government from his contributions to political science and political theory. To political science Madison contributed a vision of institutional design that was based on a realistic, if pessimistic, view of human nature—one that regarded a competent and well structured government as a means to pursue genuinely common interests. From this viewpoint, it is a virtue of a set of institutions that they are stable or self-enforcing, and, given his view of human nature, it seemed natural to seek to obtain this stability by enlisting man's lower capacities—ambition and self-dealing—to accomplish these necessary tasks. Institutions, so designed, seem well suited to work among individuals who must be taken largely as they are found. This vision of institutional design—the Madisonian vision—still inspires us even if, as I have argued, it distorts Madison's own views in various ways.

Madison gave to government a clear normative conception of the importance of securing liberty within a framework of popular rule or sovereignty. He also contributed a willingness to study and learn from a wide range of governmental experiences both near and distant in time, and a practical willingness to build on new experiences in finding how to combine liberty and popular rule. It would be to dishonor these contributions to associate with his thought a fixed set of ideas about separation of powers or federalism. It is true that he believed that separation of powers is essential to the maintenance of liberty. But how to maintain and enforce that separation depended on where the threats to it arose. The story in this paper is that the president and the executive branch turned out to be much more potent threats to the separation of powers than Madison had foreseen. Partly this was due to the urgency of foreign affairs and the danger and cost of wars. Partly it was due to the unanticipated advantages of the president within the legislative process. Obviously, in the last century this last advantage has ramified many times over.

Madison tried two strategies to deal with this specter. First, he embarked on a course of urging institutional self-restraint. He argued, against Hamilton, that the Constitution did not authorize the creation of a bank, and so Congress ought not to legislate one into existence. He urged the president and Senate to stay within a narrow construction of the treaty powers. These can be seen as appeals to political or institutional morality and not to the kind of institutional self-interest that we see in *Federalist* 51. To respond to such appeals, men had better be at least somewhat angelic and government had better be more than an expression of man's fallen condition. But perhaps it is too great a strain on human nature to expect men to respond morally to every new circumstance. Perhaps, therefore, we should understand the message of *Federalist* 51, in retrospect, as an attempt to put into place self-enforcing restraints so that we don't need to rely solely on political morality.

In any case, both the mechanical and moral appeals failed, and Madison was forced to look for an external enforcement device. The judiciary—solidly and enthusiastically in Federalist hands—was unavailable (should he have wanted to appeal to it; a doubtful proposition, I think), and so the only possibility was to be found in the very conception of popular sovereignty itself. Sometimes, if all else fails, the people—We the People—have to play an essential role in restoring an appropriate balance of governmental powers. But, as the events of 1798–1800 were to illustrate, it was unclear how the popular role could be played or if it could be played at all. With Jefferson, Madison tried to invoke the preconstitutional processes he described in *Federalist* 45–46, and call to the people through the states (acting in their sovereign capacity) to restore the balance by interposition. The failure of that appeal led to a more direct, and regular, appeal to election as a device by which the people might express their disapproval of poor government. In hindsight, the availability of this appeal seems more attractive and perhaps less desperate than it must have seemed to Madison.

Notes

I wish to thank Larry Kramer, Pasquale Pasquino, and Sam Kernell for comments on earlier drafts of this paper, and Jack Rakove for pushing my thinking about Madison in ways too numerous to recount. None of them are responsible for the views expressed here; each can speak for himself.

1. There was, of course, a real problem with finding authority for the states within the Constitution. This problem is manifested in the controversies over the notions of "interposition" found in the Virginia Resolution, or "nullification" that was proposed for the Kentucky Resolution. These ideas were both undefined within the Constitution and, as later events were to show, dangerous. At best they can be seen as extra-Constitutional ideas that are based in the notion that the people's consent to any government is not inalienable. This is treacherous stuff.

2. As is well known, Madison's ideas changed substantially during the 1790s. As generations of historians have noted, he went from being a vigorous and clear-sighted nationalist profoundly critical of the state governments, generous in his recommendations for expanded and open-ended federal powers, to a defender of states rights committed to a strict construction of federal authority. All this happened quickly, embarrassingly quickly. By the second term of the first Congress he declined to support Hamilton's scheme to assume state war debts (appearing to reverse his earlier position on that issue). He went on to oppose

plans for the creation of a national bank, and to ally with Thomas Jefferson in creating an opposition to administration policies. Historians are divided in the interpretation of these events, and some claim that Madison never really changed his basic political positions or ideas. According to Lance Banning, for example, Madison never was the thoroughgoing nationalist that Hamilton was, and his alliance with Hamilton was contextual: a response to the specific and critical problems of the new nation in 1787 and 1788. After that, the problems changed, Madison's role changed, and his political recommendations changed as well. After 1789, there was a new national government with imperfectly defined powers, and Hamilton, who really was a committed nationalist, was in position to exercise profound influence over how those powers would be interpreted and exercised.

3. I am not claiming that Montesquieu could be ideologically identified as a republican but that he offered a "positive theory" of republican government that was largely accepted by Madison, among others. This theory stressed the importance of maintaining a separation of legislative and executive from judicial powers, if republican liberties are to be preserved. He also anticipated later writers in defending something like checks and balances in order to preserve adequate separation of powers. See Vile 1967, 83–106.

4. "When legislative power is united with executive power in a single person or in a single body of the magistracy, there is no liberty, because one can fear that the same monarch or senate that makes tyrannical laws will execute them tyrannically.

"Nor is there liberty if the power of judging is not separate from legislative and from executive power. If it were joined to legislative power the power over the life and liberty of the citizens would be arbitrary, for the judge would be the legislator. If it were joined to the executive power, the judge could have the force of an oppressor" (Montesquieu 1989, 157).

5. Montesquieu makes this point rather obliquely, in saying: "If the executive does not have the right to check the enterprises of the legislative body, the latter will be despotic." But "the legislative power must not have the reciprocal faculty of checking the executive . . . As execution has limits of its own nature, it is useless to restrict it" (Book XI of the *Spirit of the Laws*, 162). Elsewhere, of course, he points out that the judicial power is "null."

6. I doubt that Montesquieu was confused in this way. I believe it is better to read his text as referring to judicial power and not to judges as institutional officials. Such a reading is consistent with Roman institutional practices with which he was very familiar. In Roman law, there was a separation of the institution of the praetor, who prepares a legal question out of the actual dispute, and the *iudex*, who decides the dispute. The praetor was a high-ranking elected official who held office for a term of years, whereas the iudex was appointed only for a single trial. The power of the iudex was, in Roman law, the judicial power, and corresponded closely to the power of the jury in an English trial. A similar distinction is made between prosecuting magistrates and those sitting as decid-

ing judges within the judiciaries of civil law systems, though both magistrates are state officials in this case. See esp. ch. 18 of Book 11, in which Montesquieu describes the exercise of the judicial power in Rome and notes that the English practice is "quite similar."

7. Tocqueville emphasized the importance of an American "Aristocracy" of lawyers, and especially judges, in creating and protecting a system of rights within a system that was otherwise open to egalitarian sentiment and majoritarian government.

8. "The first and most natural attachment of the people will be to the governments of their respective states. . . . With the affairs of these, then people will be more familiarly and minutely conversant. . . . [On] the side of these, therefore, the popular bias may well be expected most strongly to incline" (*Federalist* 46; Rakove 1999, 266–67). And, in the same number, Madison argues that their popularity gives the states overwhelming advantages in resisting federal encroachments.

9. A reviewer of this paper was puzzled about Madison's role in pushing the Virginia Plan with its rather expansive allocation of powers to the new Congress. Why, if Madison thought that Congress would be the most dangerous branch of the national government, would he place so much unchecked power at its disposal? There are two responses. First, the Virginia Plan was the first move in a complicated process of negotiation and probably ought not to be taken as Madison's fixed and final views on this subject. He was, after all, an experienced legislator by this period, and he could not have expected the Convention to adopt his own recommendations without amendment. More important, the popular proximity theory would see the state legislatures as far more dangerous to liberty than the new Congress (with its larger districts, and more able and virtuous members), and the expansive congressional powers of the Virginia Plan were mostly intended to check the state legislatures. Madison's tenacious insistence throughout the Convention on a congressional negative on all state legislation (not merely state laws trespassing on federal jurisdiction) is the clearest evidence of this. Moreover, he did not think that the state constitutions had been very effective in limiting the powers of the state legislatures. As a member of the federal convention, therefore, he was forced to rely on the tools at his disposal to correct this systemic deficiency. This concern may well have moved him to allocate more power to Congress than he might have wished, had the states adequately cabined the power of their own legislatures.

10. Obviously this statement is overbroad. There was variation among the states in this respect, as Madison recognized. Indeed, such variability was a reason that Madison was to draw on the experiences of the state constitutions to develop his ideas for the federal instrument.

11. Of course, insofar as Madison's ideas were common at the Convention, it would be wrong to attribute the structure of the Constitution to a single man.

12. It was left to Hamilton to provide the Federalist explanation of executive powers, and, while he generally stayed within Madison's theoretical framework,

Rakove points out several junctures where his exposition of those powers probably departed somewhat from Madison's more classical (Montesquieuian) understanding. "From his later conduct it is possible to discover in The Federalist those conceptions of the executive which seem most avowedly Hamiltonian" (Rakove 1996, 283).

13. Modern readers sometimes ascribe to Madison the idea that human beings are inherently venal and self-seeking in a materialist sense. His assertion that men are not angels can certainly support such an interpretation. I think a more "cognitive" reading is better, however: the weakness of human beings lies not in their venality but in their limited imaginative and empathic capacities. So, when people assume a governmental office, they tend to assume its perspectives and interests as their own. A later political observer of bureaucratic politics coined the expression "where you stand depends on where you sit." Indeed, much of the dispute between Madison and Hamilton in the early 1790s can be explained by the fact that one was a member of the House and the other a minister in government.

14. Madison did envision the possibility of extra-Constitutional appeals to the states or to the people organized in the states. In *Federalist* 45–46, he tried to reassure skeptical New Yorkers that the states had the strength to successfully oppose usurpations of power by the national government. The usual means for such opposition would be the organized state governments, but ultimately, appeal could be made to the people, organized in the state militias.

15. Westerners were affected as well, because the European powers each had allies among the Indian tribes.

16. We may lay part of the confusion on this point to Montesquieu. Although he started his famous ch. 6 of Book 11 with an allusion to Locke's federative power, the topic disappeared immediately behind the now familiar conception of separation of powers into the legislative, the executive, and the judicial. Conduct with foreign powers fits poorly in this classification, as it contains uneliminable elements of both legislative and executory powers. Nowadays, of course, we are less scrupulous in attributing legislative authority to the executive, so this eighteenth-century debate has a rather abstract feel to it. I owe this point to Pasquale Pasquino in private conversation.

17. Ironically, Madison and other republicans had successfully opposed the creation of a credible naval force. Such a force, if it were able to protect American ships, might well have given Jay a stronger hand to play in London.

18. A dispute of this kind had arisen earlier in treaty negotiations with the Barbary powers. Those treaties were agreements to pay ransom for American hostages or to purchase free passage for American ships. As such, these treaties were concerned with money and nothing else. The Americans had, at that point, no way of actually threatening to retaliate against the Barbary states.

19. Even this concession was insecure. Congress repealed the 1801 Judiciary Act and fired the sixteen federal judges who had been appointed by its authority.

Chapter 7

Madison's Dilemma: Revisiting the Relationship between the Senate and the "Great Compromise" at the Constitutional Convention

DANIEL WIRLS

James Madison's relationship to the Senate, the institution he called "the great anchor of the government," was replete with irony.[1] Madison believed that a Senate was the crucial institutional innovation needed to prevent the disease endemic to state legislatures, and he worked diligently at the Constitutional Convention to create one according to his vision. Although the Convention's work on the Senate greatly disappointed Madison, he defended it most vigorously in the *Federalist* during ratification. Madison was denied admission to the Senate, though he served in the House and as secretary of state and president; and by the time of his death the Senate was the institutional embodiment of his warning at the Convention that the true division in the country was between North and South, free and slave.

This paper uses the records of the Constitutional Convention to re-examine the relationship between the construction of the Senate and the resolution of the representational question—proportional representation in the House and equal representation in the Senate—commonly referred to as the Great Compromise. James Madison is the central figure in this interpretation. A properly constructed Senate and proportional representation were the keystones of Madison's institutional architecture for a national republic. The deliberations of the Constitutional Convention quickly showed, however, that these two keystones could not fit in the same edifice. Madison and some of his fellow delegates were vexed by the dilemma he helped create, a dilemma that ultimately aided the decision in favor of equal representation for the Senate. While it would be stretching the truth to argue that the representational compromise came into existence because of the Senate, or more precisely, because of the near consensus on the need for an upper house, I demonstrate the significant ways in which the widespread agreement on the need for a republican Senate in a stronger national system helped to shape and produce the compromise, rather than the other way around. A Senate was crucial to the new system, regardless of any struggles for political power. The Convention made sure that there would be a Senate, even if it was not exactly the Senate Madison had sought.

Understanding the Senate at the Constitutional Convention

The structure of legislative representation was the most vexing issue of the Constitutional Convention. The Convention came close to collapsing against this obstruction; once it was overcome, though other difficulties remained, the Convention appeared certain to produce a final document. As James Madison lamented during the debates: "The great difficulty lies in the affair of Representation; and if this could be adjusted, all others would be surmountable" (Farrand 1966, 1, 321). At the center of this struggle was the composition of what would be called the Senate. That the U.S. Senate, the world's "greatest deliberative body," was created by one of the world's greatest deliberative assemblies, is no accident. A properly constructed Senate was intended by Madison and others at the Convention to be foremost among the institutional innovations they produced. Although these facts are common knowledge, the richness and complexity of how the Senate affected, and was affected by, the struggle over representation are lost or obscured in many accounts of the process. In most accounts the goal is to describe or explain the politics of the Convention more generally, not of the Senate in particular, and even in the few accounts that emphasize the Senate, the complete picture often escapes a focus on either the large state–small state struggle or the alleged class interests of the Framers.[2]

Views of the Senate's creation tend to fall into the familiar schools of thought about the Constitutional Convention as a whole, and it is unnecessary to offer a standard review of the literature on the Convention and the arguments in behalf of the relative influence of ideology and interests (Jillson 1988, 1–17; Hutson 1987). Suffice it to say that in recent years, scholarship has centered around more subtle, if not more correct, arguments about the interplay of interest and ideology. If there is a consensus in the more recent literature, it is on the notion that principle and interest mixed freely at the Convention and that the distinction is, often, a difficult if not false one

(Wolfe 1977; Nelson 1987; Jillson 1988; Onuf 1989). Or as Jack Rakove notes:"It is not difficult to see that both [ideas and interests] affected the deliberations at Philadelphia in 1787. What is elusive is the interplay between them" (1996, 15). The interesting thing, then, is to show how the two mixed.

If the Convention was not simply a meeting of great and disinterested minds, it certainly was not a predetermined clash of interests in which ideas were tossed about as thinly disguised rationalizations. We tend to acknowledge that Madison, however mindful of or biased by being a Virginian, was not simply advancing principles in service of his state or regional interests. I think, albeit to a lesser extent than with some, the same can be said of most of the other delegates. Moreover, the delegates, including Madison, learned as the weeks and months progressed. That is, the analytic difficulties associated with attempts to understand the Convention's decisions are multiplied insofar as both the principles and interests at stake were being defined as the Convention proceeded. Neither was brought to bear on the deliberations as exclusively exogenous factors; instead, both interests and principles were being defined in the process and were to that extent endogenous. In particular, as far as principles were concerned, the debate about republicanism on a continental scale was wholly novel, and even Madison seemed to be adapting to new formulations (Banning 1987, 1995). Likewise, though many of the interests at stake were familiar to the delegates coming into the Convention, there were several categories of interests from which to choose, and the Convention did much to shape and reshape delegates' perceptions of which interests might matter the most. The problems of social choice presented by the Convention were formidable indeed, and nothing shows that better than the debates and decisions about the composition of the Senate.

Madison's Republican Dilemma

The extent and superiority of Madison's preparation for the "business of May next" has long been recognized and often noted.[3] Madison engaged in a concentrated effort to educate himself and come up with a sensible plan for national reform. His preparation was both strategic and dynamic: he knew he wanted a stronger national government and felt obliged to offer an agenda, but his studies and writings reflect an evolution in his thoughts about the form that should take. His efforts produced the set of resolutions offered at the beginning of the Constitutional Convention by the Virginia delegation, often referred to as the Virginia Plan. In contrast to the final product of the Convention, the Virginia Plan can seem more like a skeleton than a blueprint of a constitution. It was relatively short and not very specific about many of the powers or institutional structures of the new government. Madison, however, knew that the few fundamentals in the Virginia Plan were the "ground-work" for the creation of a truly national system.

It is beyond the purpose of this essay to provide a detailed sketch of the evolution of Madison's thoughts that became the Virginia Plan (Banning 1995; Rakove 1996). Three dimensions of change dominated his correspondence on reform as the Convention approached. Like many reformers he sought additional power for the national government, including exclusive power over trade. Unlike many, Madison believed it necessary to invest the national government with a "negative in all cases whatsoever on the Legislative Acts of the States" (*The Papers of James Madison* [hereafter MP] 9, 370). As the Convention drew near, the negative on state laws and the question of powers, which had loomed large in his thinking, took a back seat to what he referred to as the "first step to be taken" and the "ground-work": "a change in the principle of representation" (ibid., 369, 383). This was in Madison's mind the one overarching transformation: the nationalization of the government by changing the principle of representation from representing states as states to representing national citizens as individuals, with national laws, in turn, acting unmediated upon individual citizens. This principle was directly embodied in the lower chamber of the legislature, with election "by the people." Direct election by the people presupposed the application of proportional representation among the states.

The enhancement of national power and the revolution in the constituent basis of the national government entailed the third major reform: a functional separation of powers and checks against legislative excess and abuse of power. As Madison explained it to Washington: "A Government composed of such extensive powers should be well organized and balanced." First on his list was the division of the legislature into two branches, with a more popular branch to be balanced by the other, which was "to consist of fewer members, to hold their place for a longer term, and to go out in such a rotation as to always leave in office a large majority of old members." In short, a Senate. A Senate was as close as Madison came to locating a solution to one of his central concerns: "The great desideratum which has not yet been found for Republican Government, seems to be some disinterested and dispassionate umpire in disputes between different passions and interests in the State" (ibid., 383–84). Madison's chief criticisms of the state legislatures were the volume, poor quality, and mutability or instability of the legislation they produced (ibid., 353–54). Democracy, in the form of these supposedly tumultuous state legislatures, had to be balanced to produce republican government. This combination of popular will and sovereignty balanced by distance, disinterest, and dispassion is the core of republican dualism.

The Virginia Resolutions directly embodied this dualism. Immediately after the one-sentence introduction resolving that the "Articles of Confederation ought to be so corrected and enlarged" as to accomplish their stated objectives, the second article stated "that the right of Suffrage in the National Legislature ought to be proportioned to the Quotas of contribution, or to the number of free inhabitants, as the one or the other may seem best in different cases" (Farrand 1966, 1, 20). Here was the change in the principle of representation upon which Madison staked the rest of his project of reform. The institutional expression of the dualism came in the next three resolutions, which called for a divided national legislature and defined the composition of the first and second branches of that legislature. Although some details were left unspecified, the contrast between the two branches of the legislature was stark. If one keeps in mind that the Virginia Plan was designed for an unprecedentedly large republic, the provisions for direct election, recall, and mandatory rotation, envisioned a *radically* democratic lower house. And while some of these stipulations might not have been to Madison's liking (and indeed the Convention narrowed the differences considerably), during the Convention he defended the democratic nature of the first chamber, and even moved to double the number of representatives![4] In sharp contrast, the upper house was to be selected by the lower out of nominations made by state legislatures and to consist of a smaller number of members with a long tenure and staggered terms to "ensure their independency."

Proportional representation based on direct elections and a smaller, insulated Senate were Madison's two fundamental features of institutional reform in the new government. They were in tension automatically by the dictates of republican theory. But there was a practical tension as well. Could Madison get both institutions as he envisaged them, or did the characteristics of the two chambers in their ideal forms make them, in practice, mutually unattainable? Jack Rakove puts the problem this way: "[T]he Senate's representative character was incidental to its substantive functions and deliberative qualities" (1996, 78). In other words, proportional representation was not essential to the republican purpose of the Senate, which was its independence and detached judgment. While proportional representation was explicitly tied to what would become the House of Representatives, the representative basis of the Senate was rather different and did not require proportionality among the states. The fifth resolution stated that "the members of the second branch of the National Legislature ought to be elected by those of the first, out of a proper number of persons nominated by the individual Legislatures" (Farrand 1966, 1, 20). Proportionality was not required in outcomes, but only in the influence on the selection process through the election by the lower house. And even this effect was tempered by the states' role in nominations. In fact, the nomination by the state legislatures, though intended by Madison to be part of the process of elevation, independence, and detachment, immediately introduced, instead, the idea that the Senate was tied, more than the House, to the states, as states (though in theory the House could pick whomever it wanted to out of the nominations). In this way, two of Madison's primary republican objectives—direct representation of national citizens and a refined selection process for the Senate (which were to provide tension and balance in the actual workings of government)—immediately came into conflict in the attempt to design the government. Madison, as he would discover, was in danger very early in the Convention of being hoisted by his own republican petard.

More than any other delegate, Madison had, so to speak, "gamed" the Convention beforehand by anticipating the divisions based on state size and counting the probable votes accordingly. Madison could do this because, unlike the other delegates, Madison had a plan by which to judge potential reactions. Madison's strategic calculations centered on the change in the basis of representation with proportional representation at its core. Anticipating an equal vote by each state at the Convention, Madison predicted a victory for the new principle of representation based on a coalition between the currently large states and the prospectively large states.[5] States would be for or against this new principle, not so much on the basis of abstract principles, but because of rather straightforward calculations of political advantage and disadvantage. Power and principle mixed freely in Madison's view of the crux of the matter. But it is worth bearing in mind that proportional representation was a logical corollary to the representation of national citizens as individuals; it was not simply or even primarily a power grab by the large states.

Not everything in the Virginia Plan had to be accepted simultaneously, but Madison seemed to think that once the grand (and most controversial) principle of the new basis of representation was accepted, the Senate would follow as a derivative of that acceptance (with bicameralism taken for granted). What Madison did not foresee, at least publicly, was how delicate the relationship was between his two key goals (the basis of representation and a select, insulated Senate). Madison apparently did not anticipate that the change in the principle of representation would not find its serious opposition in general principle or even in its application to the lower chamber, but in the specific application to the other chamber of the legislature. In particular, he did not anticipate how an alteration in the basis of the selection of the Senate could upset everything else in the bargain.

In no other institution did power and principle come together in such a direct way. The institution that enjoyed a near consensus on its desirability on pure republican grounds (so much so that Madison perhaps did not think as carefully about its constitution as he should have), nevertheless became the principal point of contention during that summer. Thus did the power struggle that he anticipated, and the institution he took for granted, collide. Once it became clear, early in the Convention's proceedings, that most of the delegates were amenable to a centralizing alternative to the Articles of Confederation, the real difficulty became the place of states as corporate entities in a more national system, and the key to the resolution of that problem was in the structure of the legislature. The devil was in the details when the agreement in principle on bicameralism and a strong and independent Senate confronted the political realities of constitution-making.

Consensus

Although they confronted a daunting task, the delegates who convened in Philadelphia were not without some advantages. The formidable talents of many of the participants notwithstanding, it just so happened that the formidable talents who were opposed to the project of fortifying the national government decided to boycott the meeting partly in the expectation that it would collapse under its own weight. The Convention was, as a result, populated by many of the most nationally minded among the political elite. This not only greatly enhanced the prospects for something more than a mere reformation of the Articles of Confederation, it broadened the level of agreement on several features of a good government. The delegates shared similar conclusions based on their republican beliefs and experiences in their state governments. One such conclusion was a widely shared belief in the desirability of a two-chamber legislature, with an upper house to check the more popular lower house.

At several points during the debates, the delegates expressed confidence about the self-evident appeal of bicameralism. As Virginia's George Mason argued, "Much has been said of the unsettled state of the mind of the people. He believed that the mind of the people of America, as elsewhere, was unsettled as to some points; but settled as to others. In two points he was sure it was well settled. 1. in an attachment to republican government. 2. in an attachment to more than one branch in the Legislature" (ibid., 1, 339). Even the democratic soul of the Convention from unicameral Pennsylvania, James

Wilson, vigorously defended the need for a two-chamber legislature: "Is there no danger of a Legislative despotism? Theory and practice both proclaim it. If the Legislative authority be not restrained, there can be neither liberty nor stability; and it can only be restrained by dividing it within itself, into distinct and independent branches. In a single house there is no check, but the inadequate one, of the virtue and good sense of those who compose it" (ibid., 1, 254).

The extent of this accord on bicameralism is evident from the opening actions of the Convention. A two-house legislature based on proportional representation was the fundamental innovation of the Randolph or Virginia Resolutions, which became, without debate, the agenda for the Convention. The plan's proposal for a two-house legislature was the opening item on May 31, and it engendered no debate or opposition. As Madison recorded in his notes: "The Third (3d) Resolution 'that the national Legislature ought to consist of two branches' was agreed to without debate or dissent, except that of Pennsylvania, given probably from complaisance to Doc. Franklin who was understood to be partial to a single House of legislation" (ibid., 1, 48). But Pennsylvania's dissent on this issue disappeared thereafter. This effectively unanimous vote on bicameralism took place even after it was clear that the Virginia Plan intended proportional representation for both houses, something to which at least Delaware, the smallest of the small, took exception only the day before. Yet Delaware, with its explicit instructions to protect state equality, did not object on this first vote on bicameralism. Small states, it would seem, at first saw the need for bicameralism, not the threat to state representation. It would take more debate before the intractable relationship between these two facets of the Convention's work—the number of legislative chambers and the ratio of representation—became apparent to the delegates and the crux of the proceedings. After the connection is made and the battle joined between the so-called large and small states, bicameralism faced its only threat in the form of the New Jersey Plan and its adherence to a unicameral legislature based on state equality. The turn against bicameralism came when the small state coalition realized that it could hope to preserve state equality only in a one-chamber legislature similar to that of the Confederation. There was no chance of agreement to equal representation in both chambers. And, as we shall see, the delegates rejected the largely tactical unicameral threat rather easily.

The accord on bicameralism was based in no small part on the delegates' also widely shared assumptions about the distinct and special purposes of the upper house. While the lower house was to be simplicity itself in its democratic form and purpose, a carefully constructed Senate was essential to bal-

ancing and enhancing the legislative process. To demonstrate the nature of
the consensus on the general design and functions of a republican Senate, I
found and categorized every remark or speech that made reference to a desired or ideal trait or purpose of a properly designed Senate.[6] From the beginning of the proceedings to July 16 and the vote on the Great Compromise, nineteen delegates, most of the active participants during the period,
offered at least some opinion about what they felt were the important characteristics of a Senate. Some only hinted at their preferences; others expounded repeatedly and at some length. The total number of remarks or
speeches on the subject is forty, citing sixty-five preferred traits or purposes
of a Senate (Table 7.1).[7] The table displays the list of speakers in chronolog-
ical order and the classification of their comments (page numbers refer to
Farrand 1966, vol. 1).

Although the delegates cite a number of desired characteristics, the list is
a harmoniously interrelated one, and the level of agreement is evident. The
trio of ideal traits—small size, select appointment, and independence—account for nearly half the references to an ideal upper house and elicited no
dissent beyond Dickinson's claim that small size was not important (see below). At fourteen references, small size is the most frequently invoked trait.
The remarks about size manifest concern for producing the quality of debate in which—the delegates believed—only a small group can engage. This
appears to have been so self-evident to most delegates that no one felt compelled to expound at any length on the logic of small size and its relationship
to deliberation. Most of the delegates would have agreed with Publius's later
and trenchant summary of the logic of numbers: "In all very numerous assemblies, of whatever characters composed, passion never fails to wrest the
scepter from reason. Had every Athenian citizen been a Socrates, every Athenian assembly would still have been a mob."[8] It is worth noting that the
modern functionalist literature on bicameralism does not address the effect
of chamber size on deliberation, which was so important to the Convention
delegates.[9]

A relatively small number of senators was, from the republican perspective, essential. Nevertheless, it helped, of course, to have as many Socrates-like
statesmen as possible in this small assembly. The process of selection and the
longer term for senators would also mitigate the passions and precipitation
to which more numerous assemblies were alleged to be prone. A small number of senators, who would be, by and large, better men because they had
achieved their positions through some refining mode of selection, and who
were elected for relatively long terms, could best achieve the purposes or

TABLE 7.1. Comments on the Ideal Traits and Purposes of a Senate, May 29–July 16

Speaker	Records page	small size	select appointment	independent	quality of deliberation	wisdom	stability	check on democracy	bicameral check	represent property
Randolph	51	1			1			1		
Butler	51	1								
King	51	1								
Wilson	52	1		1						
Madison	52		1							
Dickinson	86								1	
Madison	120	1		1			1			
Dickinson	136		1	1						
Pinckney	150	1								
Dickinson	150		1							
Williamson	150–51	1							1	
Read	151		1							
Madison	151	1			1	1				
Gerry	152			1				1		
Wilson	154		1			1				
Madison	154		1							
Pinckney	155	1		1			1			
Randolph	218			1				1		
Madison	218–19						1			
Madison	233	1	1							
Butler	233		1							
Madison	233						1			
Sherman	234								1	
Wilson	254								1	
Hamilton	288–9						1	1	1	
Ellsworth	406					1				
Williamson	407	1								
Randolph	408					1	1			
Madison	421–2	1				1		1	1	
Sherman	423					1	1			
Hamilton	424					1	1			
Wilson	426						1			
Madison	426–27			1						
Gen Pinckney	426									1
Dayton	428			1						
Mason	428									1
Baldwin	469–70									1
Davie	487	1								
Wilson	488	1								
Morris	512							1	1	1
		14	8	8	2	8	8	6	7	4

goals of a Senate. All three traits promoted superior deliberation, characterized by wisdom and a value for stability. This stability and wisdom would be
primarily a check on the democratic excesses of the lower chamber (the
comments on stability often implied a check on democracy). A properly
constructed Senate would provide some institutional memory, a knowledge
of and experience with various proposals and policies, and, as a result, reduce
the likelihood of constantly fluctuating laws and policies.

The tabulation also clarifies what most of the delegates did *not* believe was
the essence of the Senate. First, the Senate was not just a second chamber intended to provide a merely mechanical check on the legislative process.
While several delegates linked the Senate to a general or bicameral check, a
few of the comments I have so categorized are somewhat ambiguous. The
vast majority of comments explicitly or implicitly designate a properly designed Senate the sine qua non of a republican legislature, not simply a necessary check. In most of these comments, the lower house is taken for
granted as the essential democratic component, but never accorded any real
respect, except through fear of its power. A small and independent Senate is
required to balance and refine the legislative process. Second, the nature of
the balance represented by the Senate was not intended to be merely the
counterweight of property against the masses. Although four delegates linked
the Senate to representation and protection of property, their views constitute a small minority, even amid the secret deliberations. And some were not
so obvious in their preferences. For example, by the end of Morris's speech
on this topic, he has implied that the rich should have their own chamber so
that others can watch and check them (Farrand 1966, 1, 512). No doubt, men
of property are implicit in the refined selection, but not primarily to represent the interests of property; instead their possession of property imbues
them with the wisdom and independence to form an effective Senate. Property, independence, education, and breadth of experience, in the beliefs of
most of the delegates, came together as a package in society.

Because the Senate was the linchpin of the compromise that resolved the
problem of state representation in the new government, and thereby saved
the Convention, there is a mistaken tendency to conflate the origins of the
Senate with the Great Compromise. As we have seen, the vast majority of
delegates agreed on the need for a two-chamber legislature before state representation in the legislature became the pivotal issue that summer. They
likewise shared similar views about the structure and purposes of an upper
house. But the idea of an upper house designed to carry through the principles of republican government, as we shall see, gets muddied by the issue of
representation. Despite the general agreement in favor of a bicameral legis-

lature and a strong and independent upper house, legislative design was the central issue from the start, because the basic nature of the republic would be embodied in the form and structure of legislative representation.

Conflict

Movement toward what would become the Great Compromise, and the role of the Senate in solving the Convention's central dilemma, began to develop fairly quickly, but indirectly at first. The delegates initially resorted to the tactic (perhaps a necessary one) of delaying the issue of proportionality or equality of representation in favor of resolving as many of the other issues of legislative structure and powers as possible before having to confront in any final fashion the crucial issue. This strategy was only partially successful insofar as the representation issue refused to disappear—it was important to, or implicit in, the other issues of legislative design. But this bit of indirection may have helped the compromise develop and impress itself on the delegates in a manner that tempered opposition, as will be shown. This long gestation of the compromise also forced the delegates to reveal their sentiments about the form and functions of a Senate. In short, the debate shows how the Great Compromise was not only a settlement between state or regional interests but also a compromise of many delegates' vision of a properly constructed upper house.

The conflict and the indirect approach to compromising over representation arose almost immediately. On May 30, the first day of substantive deliberation, the proposal to end equal state representation, in the national legislature as a whole, sparked the initial controversy. After circling around direct language about proportional representation, the delegates closed in on language that called for an end to the "equality of suffrage established by the articles of Confederation . . . and that an equitable ratio of representation ought to be substituted" (ibid., 36). This was, perhaps surprisingly, generally agreeable, but George Read of Delaware objected and reminded the delegates of Delaware's explicit instructions to adhere to equal representation—in general—or abandon the proceedings. Although Madison responded with the first speech on why equal representation was no longer necessary or justifiable, the delegates decided to postpone the resolution because of Delaware's resistance (ibid., 36–38).

This quick evasion did not get the delegates very far. The next day, the issue quickly resurfaced in the discussion of how the two legislative chambers would be selected, a discussion that *preceded* any explicit discussion of equal representation in any part of the legislature. The Virginia Plan called for the people of the states to elect the first branch and for the first branch to select the membership of the second from nominations submitted by the state legislatures. After some debate about the merits of direct public participation and democracy, the delegates agreed to popular election of the first branch (ibid., 50–51). But according to the notes of Georgia's William Pierce, before they had even voted on this, an objection was raised by delegates who thought the two chambers so interrelated that they could not vote on the mode of selection of the first without knowing the mode of selection of the second. Pierce records that Richard Spaight of North Carolina interrupted the discussion of the first branch to argue that the mode of selection of the upper house was linked to any decision on the lower house, and he proposed that the second branch be selected by the states, no doubt to ensure that at least one branch would be tied to the states as corporate entities. South Carolina's Pierce Butler seconded the proposal and insisted that he could not decide on the mode of selection without knowing more about the "number of Men necessary for the Senate" (ibid., 58). Whether this debate actually preceded the vote on House selection or came after (according to Madison's notes) is not crucial; either way it shows that delegates began to protect the place of states within the system prior to an explicit discussion of equal representation (both Spaight and Butler *opposed* state equality). Both Madison's and Pierce's notes agree that Butler's objection took the delegates off in a somewhat different direction. In his demurral, Butler asked Randolph to explain his resolution and, in particular, "the number of members he meant to assign to this second branch" (ibid., 51, 58). Why Butler felt the number of senators was crucial to determining the mode of appointment is unclear, but it allowed Randolph to provide the first endorsement of a Senate whose membership

> ought to be much smaller than that of the first [branch]; so small as to be exempt from the passionate proceedings to which numerous assemblies are liable. He observed that the general object was to provide a cure for the evils under which the U.S. laboured; that in tracing these evils to their origin every man had found it in the turbulence and follies of democracy: that some check therefore was to be sought for against this tendency of our Governments: and that a good Senate seemed most likely to answer the purpose. (Ibid., 51)

Massachusetts delegate Rufus King drew the logical conclusion: if Spaight's proposal to have the state legislatures select the second branch were to be adopted, the Senate would be, from the outset, too numerous, unless "*the idea of proportion* among the States was to be disregarded" (ibid.). The concern that the Senate would get too big apparently caused Spaight to withdraw forthwith his proposal for state selection. James Wilson then offered a radical alternative. To Wilson both state nominations and selection by the first house were objectionable: the second branch "ought to be independent of both." Wilson, the Convention's most ardent democrat, favored election of both by the people, but with the smaller and more select upper house created by combining states into larger districts, analogous to the combination of counties used to select New York's upper house. Madison immediately objected on behalf of the small states that would be ignored when combined with larger states. But the point about independence was made: selection by the House would compromise the Senate's independence. The debate concluded with a 3–7 vote rejecting the Virginia Plan resolution to have the first branch select the second from state nominations (ibid., 52).

Two problems have thus far emerged to undermine Madison's principle of proportional representation for the new government, at least as far as the Senate is concerned. The first is the impact on the size of the Senate. This will surface several times during the debate, showing the strong sentiment for a small Senate, significantly smaller than strict proportional representation would produce. The second problem is the independence of the second branch. Selection by the first branch would create too close a connection and undermine the bicameral check. It was rejected partly on that basis, and of course partly on the basis of delegates from large and small states alike wanting to give states direct representation. Having eliminated selection by the lower house, the delegates are pushed toward states as the obvious solution. Any scheme such as Wilson's district system, however abstractly sensible, was unworkable and probably unacceptable to the country. Moreover, the Virginia Resolutions had already proposed that state legislatures nominate the candidates for the upper house. Thrown back to the states for the primary role in selection and constricted by the nearly universal desire for a small Senate, the delegates were on the road toward the Great Compromise whether most knew it or not at the time. As support for proportional representation in the Senate was eroded by the problem of size and the role of state selection, equal representation emerged as the only viable alternative. And as it did so, the nature of the nascent Senate began to change as the ideals of independence, elite membership, and the checking function, merged with the direct representation of states. To Madison and his allies this potential perversion of the Senate was anathema. But to the nascent coalition of those interested in protecting states and especially small states, state selection became a wedge for redefining and expanding the purpose of the Senate to accommodate state influence.

The idea of combining state selection with state equality in the Senate evolved rapidly. As early as May 31, Connecticut's Roger Sherman made the initial, brief, and unpursued suggestion that each state legislature select one senator.[10] This was followed on June 2 by John Dickinson's foresight that, "[as] to the point of representation in the national Legislature as it might affect States of different sizes, he said it must probably end in mutual concession. He hoped that each State would retain an equal voice at least in one branch of the National Legislature" (ibid., 87). Neither of these suggestions was considered because the primary issue was still the mode of selection, not the ratios of representation. And, in fact, Dickinson, Sherman, and other advocates of state equality made their case for state selection primarily in terms that did not demand or even evoke equality. The first goal was to secure direct state selection as one way of ensuring state influence, even if some delegates, including Sherman and Dickinson, were merely laying the groundwork for making Senate equality an inflexible demand.[11] As the two features—state selection and equality—merged, the small state advocates developed a new logic for the Senate, one that attempted to combine what Madison and others saw as oil and water: state control of the Senate and the Senate's role as an independent upper house.

Dickinson began the amalgamation by uniting state selection with a core principle of Senate design, the elevation or refinement of membership selection:

> Mr. Dickinson considered it as essential that one branch of the Legislature should be drawn immediately from the people; and as expedient that the other should be chosen by the Legislatures of the States. This combination of the State Governments with the national Government was as politic as it was unavoidable. In the formation of the Senate we ought to carry it through such a refining process as will assimilate it as near as may be to the House of Lords in England. (Ibid., 136)

Dickinson saw selection by state legislatures as fully compatible with the principle of an elite and independent Senate. In fact, in the same speech he acceded to concerns about possible Senate dependence on the states by suggesting a long and "irrevocable" term of three, five, or seven years. He was supported both by Sherman, and more important, by Massachusetts's Elbridge Gerry, who likewise argued:

> It was necessary on the one hand that the people should appoint one branch of the Government in order to inspire them with the necessary confidence. But he wished the election on the other to be so modified as to secure more effectually a just preference of merit. His idea was that the people should nominate certain persons in certain districts, out of whom the State Legislatures should make the appointment. (Ibid., 132)

Pierce then summarized the emerging principle by advocating "an election by the people as to the first branch and by the States as to the second branch; by which means the Citizens of the States would be represented both individually and collectively." Roger Sherman and South Carolina's Pinckney followed Pierce by raising one more point in support of state selection. They asserted that state selection also would have the effect of quelling state fears of the new government and creating loyalty to the new government (ibid., 78, 82). In this way a small number of delegates attempted to merge the ideal with the necessary and pragmatic, much to the chagrin of Madison and his allies.

On the decisive day for Senate selection, June 7, Dickinson proposed selection by state legislatures, with Sherman seconding the motion. Neither of these small state stalwarts suggested anything about the ratio of representation, but Charles Pinckney immediately noted that proportionality would produce too large a Senate, even if the smallest state got only one senator. Dickinson responded with another attempt to blend state representation with a powerful and elite upper house:

> Mr. Dickenson had two reasons for his motion. 1. because the sense of the States would be better collected through their Governments; than immediately from the people at large; 2. because he wished the Senate to consist of the most distinguished characters, distinguished for their rank in life and their weight of property, and bearing as strong a likeness to the British House of Lords as possible; and he thought such characters more likely to be selected by the State Legislatures, than in any other mode. The greatness of the number was no objection with him. He hoped there would be 80 and twice 80 of them. If their number should be small, the popular branch could not be balanced by them. The legislature of a numerous people ought to be a numerous body. (Ibid., 150)

Dickinson, the only delegate to express a lack of concern for the size of the Senate, again posited a unity of purpose between state selection and his ideal Senate, obviously without equal representation foremost in mind (his cavalier comments about 80 and twice 80 left plenty of room for proportional representation). Hugh Williamson of North Carolina replied by endorsing a small Senate, of twenty-five, with each state getting at least one. Madison expanded on Williamson's idea in a blunt attack on Dickinson's logic:

> If the motion (of Mr. Dickinson) should be agreed to, we must either depart from the doctrine of proportional representation or admit into the Senate a very large number of members. The first is inadmissible, being evidently unjust. The second is inexpedient. The use of the Senate is to consist in its proceeding with more coolness, with more system, and with more wisdom, than the popular branch. Enlarge their number and you communicate to them the vices which they are meant

to correct. He differed from Mr. Dickinson, who thought that the additional number would give additional weight to the body. (Ibid., 151)

Although he would resist equal representation to the end, Madison was painting himself and his allies into a corner. Equal representation was inadmissible and a large Senate was inexpedient, but others had pointed out forcefully that proportional representation and a small Senate were mutually exclusive. The Senate would simply become too large under any form of proportional representation. A large Senate violated the first principles of republican legislative theory, which insisted that the second chamber be more deliberative, and to most delegates this required that it be smaller. This dilemma worked in favor of the Great Compromise. It made exact proportional representation all but unacceptable, even to a few of the staunchest large state delegates, though some like Madison would hold fast on the issue. The contradiction between size and proportional representation may have been influential, if not decisive, in pushing some other delegates toward compromise, as we shall see. Again, however, the discussion had strayed from the issue on the floor, which was the mode of selection. So the relationship between size and proportionality was pushed aside to make the final decision on selection. As a last alternative, Wilson offered his proposal for direct election of the Senate by the people combined into large districts (to keep the Senate small). This was defeated 10 to 1. Not only were new districts thought by some to be politically unacceptable and impracticable, the proposal was inextricably linked to popular election, which clearly a majority of the delegates were against when it came to the Senate. This remaining option eliminated, the delegates voted 11–0 in favor of state selection (ibid., 149, 155–56).

And once decided, state selection was here to stay, despite its increasingly obvious relationship to equal representation. The delegates would later, amid the rancor and peril of the representation debate, reaffirm their support for state selection of the Senate by a 9–2 vote, with only Pennsylvania and Virginia in opposition. This shows that many large state delegates believed that state selection was the best way to pick the Senate and that state representation (the emerging principle of federalism) was vital, despite the obvious opening this gave to equal representation. Commitment to state selection was, for many of these delegates (Gerry and Pinckney among them) out of conviction rather than political expediency. For Gerry, this conviction would help push him to compromise; for others like Pinckney, the belief in state selection did not require compromise. Pinckney, as we shall see, tried until the last moment to salvage proportional representation for a state-selected Senate.

Crisis and Compromise

With the issue of who would select Senators settled, the ratio of representation loomed even larger, and could not be long postponed, though the delegates attempted to settle other matters. As each day passed, however, the delegates had less success trying to do other business. The issue of representation intruded with increasing persistence until it threatened to break up the Convention. The debates and decisions during this period show, first, how the consensus on bicameralism was tested but survived with broad support; and, second, how shared principles of the ideal Senate continued to move the delegates toward compromise.

Following the decision to have state legislatures elect the Senate membership, the delegates could not manage even two days of business without returning to the issue of representation. June 9 began with the issue of the selection of the executive, but ended with William Patterson of New Jersey calling for a return to the issue of suffrage in the legislature. During his long speech that day, Patterson most vehemently opposed a system he believed would be dominated by the large states (Virginia, Massachusetts, and Pennsylvania, in his view) and declared that New Jersey "will never confederate on the plan before the Committee. . . . He had rather submit to a monarch, to a despot, than to such a fate." "If N.J. will not part with her Sovereignty," retorted Wilson, "it is vain to talk of Govt." (ibid., 179–80). The next day of business—Monday, June 11—foreshadowed the next five weeks. King and South Carolina's John Rutledge opened the day with a motion to affirm the Virginia Resolutions' call to scrap equal representation established by the Articles of Confederation and substitute for the first branch "some equitable ratio" of suffrage. This passed 7–3–1.[12] The quick and decisive victory of proportional representation in the first branch was immediately followed by Sherman and Oliver Ellsworth's motion that in the second branch of the national legislature each state have one vote. This lost 5–6, despite Sherman's warning that "[e]very thing . . . depended on this. The smaller States would never agree to the plan on any other principle than an equality of suffrage in this branch" (ibid., 201). Wilson and Hamilton immediately proposed that the second branch have the same rule of representation as the first branch. This passed 6–5, in a mirror image of the previous vote, thus establishing the close division between the large (Massachusetts, Pennsylvania, Virginia, North Carolina, South Carolina, and Georgia) and small state coalitions (Connecticut, New York, New Jersey, Delaware, and Maryland). "Large" and "small" are, of course, overly simplistic terms: "[T]he average population of the large states, exclusive of heavily populated Virginia, was 307,000; of the small states, excluding tiny Delaware, it was 278,000, a relatively small difference."[13] An important part of the large-small dimension of conflict was not current population but prospective population based on current physical size. The geographically large states, especially ones with western lands, were assumed to be, sooner or later, the most populous. A direct reference to this assumption was made by Delaware's Bedford, who in commenting on Georgia's alliance with the large states noted: "Though a small State at present, she is actuated by the prospect of soon being a great one" (ibid., 491).[14]

Despite the initial victory of proportional representation, Madison's nationalist Senate had been significantly distorted by the victory of state selection, the first step in what would become a process of combining and confusing the structure and purposes of the upper house. Moreover, the temporary vote in favor of proportional representation in the Senate was based more on principle than practicality: the advocates of proportional representation had not solved the problem of size.

Only after the 6–5 vote in favor of proportional representation in the Senate did the small states rally and offer an alternative to the Virginia Resolutions, when William Patterson presented the New Jersey Plan on June 15. Up to this point, the opposition had no clear alternative. In part this was because there was broad agreement on the overall thrust of the Virginia Plan—the only significant dispute had been over the issue of equal representation of states. The need for a more effective response on this principal point of contention necessitated a more complete alternative. The New Jersey Plan, which called for a moderately strengthened Congress of the Confederation, retained the unicameral, equal representation legislature of the Articles. This aspect of the design did not imply a philosophical preference for a single house legislature. Patterson and his small state supporters advanced unicameralism less on principle than as a means to the end of equal representation. They all voted, it should be remembered, for bicameralism at the beginning.[15]

Despite these arguments, this protest against proportional representation was rejected fairly easily on June 19 (ibid., 322). The tactical opposition to bicameralism ended on June 21, with the consideration of the revised Virginia Plan and the final vote on the bicameralism resolution (with dispute over the ratio of representation still to be resolved). This final endorsement of bicameralism reproduced the 7–3–1 division that had rejected the New Jersey Plan two days earlier (ibid., 358).

With unicameralism eliminated, the remaining battleground was the Senate. And Sherman once again reminded the delegates: "If the difficulty of representation can not be otherwise got over, he would agree to have two

branches, and a proportional representation in one of them, provided each
State had an equal voice in the other" (ibid., 343). While some delegates
would keep the door to compromise open, others threatened to slam it shut
and gave intransigent voice to their willingness to end the proceedings on
this issue. During this period Madison made two longer speeches in an increasingly desperate attempt to persuade his colleagues that equal representation in the Senate was neither "just, nor necessary for the safety of the small
States agst. The large States" (ibid., 446). In the first, Madison tried to show
that small states and large states did not form distinct and natural coalitions
on the material issues that would be before the government. It followed that
equality was an unnecessary precaution, in addition to being manifestly unjust (ibid., 446–49, 455–56). Two days later, the day before the Convention
would deadlock on the representation issue, Madison unleashed a new argument. The true division of interests in the country, he said, did not lie between small and large states but between free and slave, North and South,
"and if any defensive power were necessary, it ought to be mutually given to
these two interests" (ibid., 486).[16] This "important truth" had compelled him
to search for "some expedient that would answer the purpose," and he suggested, but did not propose, a modified version of proportional representation with one branch apportioned counting free inhabitants and slaves (according to the three-fifths ratio) and the other free inhabitants only.
Madison's reluctant invocation of the slave issue evinced his anxiety. The tactic did not seem to help; in fact, it might have bolstered the equal representation coalition (Rakove 1996, 75).

    This contentious phase ended on July 2 with another vote on the issue of
equal representation in the Senate. This time, however, the states deadlocked
in a 5–5–1 vote, in which Georgia cast the crucial indecisive vote, the only
change from the 6–5 victory for proportionality on June 11.[17] The gravity of
the situation expressed itself vividly in the immediate and almost desperate
decision of the delegates to appoint a committee of one member from each
state to produce a compromise proposal. The committee, composed of mod-
erates from the large states and some staunch advocates of small state interests, was stacked in favor of equal representation in the Senate.

    The committee produced, in Gerry's words, the "ground of accommoda-
tion" that paired state equality in the Senate with vesting the House with the
exclusive power over the origination and amendment of money bills (leaving the Senate with the equivalent of a veto power) (Farrand 1966, 1, 527).
This compromise is generally seen as having little effect on the eventual
agreement to Senate equality, and not without good reason. To begin with,
the delegates had, three weeks earlier, by a 3–8 vote, rejected a proposal to

"restrain the Senatorial branch from originating money bills" on its own merits (ibid., 233–34). So it is somewhat odd that this should have resurfaced as the basis of compromise, the concession by small states, the quid pro quo to save the Convention, and not surprising that it was greeted with scorn by several delegates, including Madison, Butler, Morris, Williamson, Wilson, and Pinckney. Even Gerry, presenter of the compromise committee's work, noted that "he had very material objections to it." Wilson and North Carolina's Williamson (who ultimately became a key vote for the compromise) remarked that if one house should have exclusive rights of origination, it should be the more deliberative Senate. Pinckney reminded the delegates that "the restriction as to money bills had been rejected on the merits singly considered by eight States against three; and that the very States which now called it a concession were then against it as nugatory or improper in itself." But the delegates quickly voted—albeit by one of the most divided votes of the Convention—to keep the money bills provision as part of the package, by 5–3–3, with Massachusetts dividing and North Carolina voting in favor (ibid., 527–32, 543–47).[18]

Having accepted the committee's package deal, the delegates confronted the decision on equal representation. On July 14, after heated debate and uncompromising words from both sides, Charles Pinckney offered the final motion to salvage proportional representation for the Senate with his modified plan to give the states one to five senators each, which Madison supported as a reasonable compromise (Farrand 1966, 2, 5). This was defeated by the slim margin of 4–6. Maryland, now joined by Daniel Carroll, voted for this compromise, while North Carolina and Massachusetts voted against it. This was the last action of the Convention prior to the Great Compromise on Monday the 16th, when by a 5–4–1 vote the Convention accepted equal representation in the upper chamber of the legislature.

The motivations behind the key vote changes that produced the Great Compromise vote remain somewhat of a mystery. Decades of scholarship have produced a list of usual suspects but no smoking guns. Certainly the most persuasive is what can be called the coercion theory. The small state coalition's insistence on equal representation in the Senate, to the point of putting the whole Convention at risk, compelled some large state delegates to agree to a compromise to salvage the project. This is sometimes portrayed as nearly a game of chicken, with the reluctant and last-minute votes of a few delegates producing the compromise and saving the day. Other alleged interest- or faction-based causes include North vs. South (eased by the three-fifths compromise on slavery and representation in the House), conflict over the disposition of western lands (eased by Congress's timely agreement on the North West Ordinance), other wheeling and dealings among some delegates outside the Convention hall, and the particular situation of North Carolina. The substantiation for each of these interest-based arguments is slim and often based on assumptions or deductions about their effects rather than direct evidence (Hutson 1987). The record of the Convention offers little support for them, especially when it comes to the crucial changes in voting. In fact, even coercion theory has some trouble explaining why only certain votes in the Massachusetts and North Carolina delegations change, or why Georgia changes back to opposing a compromise.

I do not seek to construct a new explanation for the compromise vote. Instead, I have shown the ways in which widely shared principles about bicameralism and a Senate helped to shape the compromise instead of the Senate's simply being shaped by the compromise. Concerns about Senate selection and size pushed the delegates toward the compromise, and the agreement on bicameralism withstood the counterattack by the small state coalition. This put the delegates at the brink of the compromise but did not compel them to agree to it. In addition, these same shared principles may have influenced some of the key vote switching that produced the compromise vote.

After New York's departure (a solid vote for equal representation), the crucial changes were the division of the Massachusetts vote and the switch by North Carolina to favor equal representation. The North Carolina vote made up for the loss of New York, and the Massachusetts division prevented another tie vote. There is significant evidence that key members of both the North Carolina and Massachusetts delegations were increasingly inclined toward compromise, with equal representation as the only viable alternative. Part of the evidence comes in the expressions of concern, voiced as the dilemma became apparent, by the four crucial delegates whose votes produced the compromise: Elbridge Gerry and Caleb Strong of Massachusetts, and William Davie and Hugh Williamson of North Carolina.

The division of the Massachusetts vote on the Great Compromise vote is not that surprising, given the record of the delegation on earlier votes and the remarks of delegates like Gerry. Massachusetts had divided on thirteen votes prior to the Great Compromise, and "whenever the individual votes were recorded Gorham and King stood against Gerry and Strong" (Jillson and Anderson, 1978, 544). Gerry, in particular, was one of the early supporters of state selection on the dual merits of preserving independence from the other chamber and preserving a strong role for the states. State selection of the Senate was also a way of elevating senatorial selection and producing a more fit body of men.[19] Although the Massachusetts delegation stayed with the large state coalition through the July 2 deadlock vote of 5–5–1, it is clear that Gerry and Strong decided as a result and thereafter that equality was all but inevitable and probably necessary to save the Convention.[20] So firm was their conviction that they, Gerry and Strong, voted against Pinckney's eleventh-hour modified proportional scheme. Massachusetts was (with King voting yes and Gorham absent) the crucial vote against it.

The behavior of the North Carolina delegation is more mysterious and subject to more elaborate explanations based on more complicated motivations. North Carolina was the only Southern state to shift ground completely on the crucial question. With William Blount absent, and Spaight voting against the compromise, North Carolina's decision was determined by Williamson, William Davie, and Alexander Martin. While Martin said nothing of his motivations either during or after the Convention, his colleagues Williamson and Davie evinced strong concern for the problem that plagued proportional representation from the start—that it would produce too large a Senate. Although troubled by the same dilemma, some delegates such as Pinckney, King, and Madison did not change their votes. For Williamson and Davie, who did vote for the compromise, these concerns might have been more influential.

Hugh Williamson, a defender of proportional representation, "preferred a small number of Senators, but wished that each State should have at least one. He suggested 25 as a convenient number. The different modes of representation in the different branches, will serve as a mutual check" (Farrand 1966, 1, 151–52).[21] Later, as the pressure built, Williamson professed that he wanted to preserve state governments but "was at a loss to give his vote as to the Senate until he knew the number of its members. In order to ascertain this, he moved to insert these words after '2d branch of the Natl Legislature'—'who shall bear such proportion to the no. of the 1st branch as 1 to '" (ibid., 407). Although he was not seconded in this motion, it shows the extent of his concern for a small Senate. Moreover, Williamson expressed some conflicting sentiments with regard to both the need to compromise and the actual quid pro quo produced by the committee. Williamson spoke in favor of forming the compromise committee and called for concessions on both sides, or "our business must soon be at an end" (ibid., 515). However, after the committee produced the trade, Williamson said: "He was ready to hear the Report discussed; but thought the propositions contained in it, the most objectionable of any he had yet heard" (ibid., 532). The proposition he specifically criticized was not equal representation, but the money bill monopoly. As was noted earlier, Williamson argued that such an exclusive power was better vested in the more deliberative Senate rather than the popular house. This would seem to contradict his later remark (on August 9, as the money bill provision got significantly weakened), which is sometimes taken as an explanation for North Carolina's vote: "The State of N.C. had agreed to an equality in the Senate, merely in consideration that money bills should be confined to the other House" (Farrand 1966, 2, 233).

Likewise William Davie gave passionate voice to his concern for a small Senate. Indeed when faced on June 30 with the choice between equality and proportionality in the Senate he seemed nearly vexed:

> Mr. Davy was much embarrassed and wished for explanations. The Report of the Committee allowing the Legislatures to choose the Senate, and establishing a proportional representation in it, seemed to be impracticable. There will according to this rule be ninety members in the outset. . . . It was impossible that so numerous a body could possess the activity and other qualities required in it. Were he to vote on the comparative merits of the report as it stood [with proportional representation], and the amendment [Ellsworth's equal representation motion], he should be constrained to prefer the latter. (Ibid., 487)

Later in the same speech, Davie changed his perspective:

> On the other hand, if a proportional representation was attended with insuperable difficulties, the making the Senate the Representative of the States looked like bringing us back to Congs. again and shutting out all the advantages expected from it. Under this view of the subject he could not vote for any plan for the Senate yet proposed. He thought that in general there were extremes on both sides. We were partly federal, partly national in our Union. And he did not see why the Govt. might (not) in some respects operate on the States, in others on the people. (Ibid., 488, 498)

Although ultimately indecisive in his remarks, Davie clearly considered the size of the Senate to be a central concern, one that outweighed proportional representation almost to the extent of agreeing to equal representation. Davie was also North Carolina's representative on the compromise committee, and this may have reinforced his role as a compromiser in bringing North Carolina around.[22] Size does not provide the smoking gun in North Carolina's case. But Williamson and Davie were clearly influenced by the size dilemma as well as the need to compromise, and were not obviously swayed by the money bills concession.

While perhaps not decisive, the widely shared sentiments of an ideal Senate—independent to be an effective check, small to promote deliberation, and selected (rather than elected) to enhance both deliberation and the check—pushed the Convention toward the compromise, in the ways I have described. Efforts to elaborate purely interest-based explanations mistakenly overlook this evidence from the record. I cannot, given the limited evidence, conclude that ideals or principles of good government were decisive, but among the factors that shaped the compromise and swayed the votes of a few individual delegates, these shared principles manifested their importance throughout the deliberations, even at the brink of compromise.

Whatever the exact motivations that produced the compromise, the Senate was, as a result, a compromised institution, intended to embody two potentially incompatible purposes, and no one felt this more keenly than Madison. Rufus King reminded the delegates of this dilemma on the last day of debate before the compromise vote: "According to the idea of securing the State Govts. There ought to be three distinct legislative branches. The 2d. was admitted to be necessary, and was actually meant to check the 1st. branch, to give more wisdom, system, & stability to the Govt. and ought clearly as it was to operate on the people to be proportioned to them. For the third purpose of securing the States, there ought then to be a 3d. branch, representing the States as such and guarding by equal votes their rights and dignities" (Farrand 1966, 2, 6–7).

Conclusion

Madison's dilemma—the incompatibility between a small Senate and a proportionally representative Senate—helped to bring about one of Madison's principal disappointments in the Convention's work.[23] Equality in the Senate had ironically combined the characteristic Madison wished most of all to eradicate from the new government, the representation of states, with the institution he believed was essential to produce a truly national government. Did the compromised Senate represent the states, or was it still the national institution and steward of governmental policy? Could the two functions be combined? Confusion and disagreement about both questions were evident for the rest of that summer's deliberations as the delegates tried to complete other aspects of the Senate's design and to decide what powers to give it. Madison's own ambivalence about the Senate, as structured by the representational compromise, was expressed by his actions during the remainder of the Convention and during ratification. After the compromise vote, Madison led the counterattack against granting the Senate exclusive powers (for example in treaties and appointments) because it now seemed to represent states as states. Madison and his allies came to look more favorably upon the executive as a counterweight to state influence, and they argued and voted to shift powers in the president's direction. Yet, when he sat down that fall to argue the case for the proposed Constitution, Madison forthrightly defended the Senate's republican purpose. "The equality of representation in the Senate," wrote Madison, "is another point which, being evidently the result of compromise between the opposite pretensions of the large and the small States, does not call for much discussion." And despite his misgivings, "the advice of prudence must be to embrace the lesser evil; and instead of indulging a fruitless anticipation of the possible mischiefs which may ensue, to contemplate rather the advantageous consequences which may qualify the sacrifice" (Hamilton, Madison, Jay 1961, 377). Madison devotes a mere 12 percent of his words in *Federalist* Numbers 62 and 63 to either equal representation or state selection.[24] The rest are dedicated to an honest and direct defense of the republican role of a Senate. Madison, it would seem, was holding out hope that the Senate of state equality could still be the "great anchor of the government."

Notes

1. Madison referred to the Senate in this manner in a letter to Jefferson dated October 24, 1787 (see appendix).

2. Specific treatments of the Senate's creation can be divided between generally brief, almost pro forma reviews (Kerr 1895; Rogers 1926; Haynes 1938; Swanstrom 1985) and a few recent and more analytic accounts (Eidelberg 1968; Swift 1996; Lee and Oppenheimer 1999).

3. As the editors of Madison's papers put it: "The period between the spring of 1786 and the spring of 1787 was perhaps the most creative and productive year of JM's career as a political thinker" (MP 9, 346).

4. Farrand 1966, 1, 568–69. Madison's motion lost on a vote of 9–2 in probably the only vote in which Virginia and Delaware together formed the minority (1, 570).

5. He does so three times, in letters to Thomas Jefferson (March 19, 1787), Edmund Randolph (April 8, 1787), and George Washington (April 16, 1787). See MP 9, 318–19, 371, 383.

6. The search for comments was done in three ways: 1) a direct reading of Madison's notes (Farrand 1966); 2) a cross-check with Benton's (1986) topical collation of Madison's notes; and 3) an electronic CD-ROM search of Madison's notes in *American Reference Library*, which contains the searchable text of *Journal of the Federal Convention*, E. H. Scott, ed. (Chicago: Albert, Scott & Co., 1893).

7. Comments ranged from brief allusions to one characteristic or goal, to lengthy commentaries that referred to three or four. Most of the comments are clear and direct in reference. Others, of course, are open to interpretation. The main categories that potentially overlapped were "check on democracy" and "stability." Speakers sometimes were specifically referring to stability as a virtue in policy-making; others seemed to be referring to stability as a check on de-

mocracy's tendency to rapid change or as part of the general bicameral check (for example, Dickinson: Farrand 1966, 1, 86). I tried to judge on the basis of the full commentary and context. Also, I classified stability as a purpose or end, rather than a characteristic because that is the way most of the speakers used the term— stability as an end in itself. The following were excluded from the tally for being too vague or indirect to classify, or for being too directly related to state repre- sentation: Madison: 1, 50; Madison: 1, 490; Ellsworth: 1, 484; Pinckney: 1, 429; Davie: 1, 542. Butler's somewhat indirect reference to size (1, 51) was included because of the context provided by Pierce's notes (1, 57–59), which clarify But- ler's concern about the size of the Senate. Dickinson's comments that a large Senate was fine (1, 150, 153) were not included, in part because he was the only delegate to express that opinion but, more important, because he did not seem to be expressing his ideal as much as commenting that size was not so impor- tant.

8. Hamilton, Madison, and Jay 1961, 342; see also Eidelberg's excellent dis- cussion of how size influences personal conduct and deliberation (1968, 85–86).

9. For example, see the rational choice literature: Tsebelis and Money 1997; Miller, Hammond, and Kile 1996; Levmore 1992; Riker 1992; Hammond and Miller 1987; Gross 1982. Baker (1995) offers one of the few exceptions in the empirical literature. Others examine the effect of chamber size indirectly through the effects of equal representation (Lee and Oppenheimer 1999; Baker and Dinkin 1997).

10. For Sherman this was no spur-of-the-moment idea. He had suggested essentially the same bicameral arrangement during the 1776 deliberations of the Second Continental Congress on the Articles of Confederation, advocating the need for concurrent majorities of both citizens as individuals and states as units (Collier 1971, 262).

11. Given the eventual crisis over this issue, many scholars assume that the small state delegates knew what they were aiming for from the beginning. How- ever probable, it is still an assumption, and one that can lead to errors. For ex- ample, in his account Irving Brant (1950, 46) claims that Dickinson's comment on June 7 about the need for a Lord-like upper house was him "jockeying for state equality." Why then would Dickinson, during the same debate, dismiss con- cerns about the size of the Senate? "The greatness of number was no objection with him. He hoped there would be 80 and twice 80 of them" (Farrand 1966, 1, 150).

12. This general resolution was immediately specified by Wilson and Pinck- ney's motion to base the ratio on the number of free citizens "and three fifths of all other persons" (the same as the ultimately unsuccessful 1783 rule of revenue contributions proposed by Congress under the Articles of Confederation), which was agreed to 9–2.

13. Kelly, Harbison, and Belz 1983, 97.

14. See also Luther Martin's post-Convention assessment of the same issue

(Farrand 1966, 3, 187). On the general question of state size and politics during the Founding, see Zagarri 1987.

15. Lansing, Patterson, Martin, and Sherman are the only delegates during the Convention to speak in favor of a single-chamber legislature (Farrand 1966, 1, 249–52, 340–43).

16. Yates's notes record that Madison invokes the North-South division on June 29, not June 30 (Farrand 1966, 1, 476).

17. Georgia, with only Houston (no) and Baldwin (yes) present, divided. The other Georgians, Pierce and Few, had left for Congress in New York. On Baldwin's vote, see Luther Martin's assessment (Farrand 1966, 3, 188). Scholars have debated the significance of this. Some credit Baldwin with saving the Convention. One problem is that Georgia switches back to opposing the compromise on the July 14 final vote on the representation question.

18. CT, NJ, MD, DE, NC (5)–PA, VA, SC (3)–MA, NY, GA (3). This in some ways presages the compromise vote, with North Carolina the lone large state voting yes and Massachusetts divided on the issue. See Farrand 1966, 1, 547. This vote could also imply that the money bills compromise was not meaningless, at least to North Carolina, or that North Carolina had, by this time, been persuaded of the inevitability of the compromise. But as we shall see it is the votes of the key delegates that matter, and here the evidence is somewhat mixed.

19. See Gerry's remarks on June 6, as well as June 7, during which he rejected selection by the first branch as destructive of senatorial independence; whereas selection by state legislatures would produce a refinement of selection in favor of commercial interests (Farrand 1966, 1, 132, 152).

20. On July 2, in calling for a compromise committee, Gerry makes some of the most impassioned remarks about the need to compromise or risk "war and confusion" (Farrand 1966, 1, 519). See the remarks by Gerry on July 6 (1, 545) and Gerry and Strong during the July 14 debate, the day before the Great Compromise vote (2, 5–7), which also show that to the end Gerry preferred proportional representation in the Senate, but felt even a modified version (Pinckney's scheme) would not be acceptable to the small states. Likewise, Strong tells the Massachusetts Convention that "the Convention would have broke up" if it had not agreed to Senate equality (3, 261–62).

21. Williamson later defends proportional representation by analogy to states and counties within states (Farrand 1966, 1, 180).

22. Without substantiation, William Peters (1987, 127) asserts that North Carolina was "swayed by William R. Davie ... who had served on the compromise committee."

23. The other candidate is the lack of a national power to veto state laws (see appendix, "James Madison to Thomas Jefferson"). The veto, however, never enjoyed anything close to majority support.

24. Using a standard word count, the texts of Federalist 62 and 63 yielded 5,415 words, of which 638 were devoted to state selection and state equality.

Chapter 8

Constituting a National Interest:
Madison against the States' Autonomy

DAVID BRIAN ROBERTSON

An Economic Policy Perspective on the Founding

America's leading politicians came to Philadelphia in 1787 chiefly to correct the path of American economic policy. Independence, war, and depression had compelled state officials quickly to develop the capacity to tax, to borrow and print money, to regulate credit and commerce, and to charter corporations. These thirteen new states were endowed with widely varied economic assets. Naturally, the states were pursuing different economic policies, often at the expense of other states and the Continental Congress. Increasing economic rivalry, national government ineffectiveness, and economic and military insecurity had multiplied the number of state officials, nationalist patriots, landed elites, merchants, creditors, and manufacturers who were receptive to strengthening national economic policy tools.

James Madison seized on this political opportunity and developed a strategic agenda for the Constitutional Convention: he proposed a reconstituted national government capable of exercising extensive authority over the nation's economy, independent of the states. He criticized current decentralized economic policy as opportunistic, parochial, chaotic, fluid, uncertain, and menacing for prosperity and republicanism. Madison outlined a plan for a national government designed to motivate and empower national policymakers to pursue national economic goals. He wanted national policy-makers' ambitions to counteract state policy-makers' ambitions, so that policy-makers would have the means and the motive to pursue the economic interests of the nation as a whole, independent of the expressed interests of individual states or coalitions of states. Madison's plan would reconstitute the national government to make it the presumptive economic authority in the United States, to establish national policy-making processes that would motivate national policy-makers to pursue national economic interests rather than state interests, and to authorize the national government to veto state policies at will. The Virginia Plan embodied Madison's core ideas.

New Jersey, Connecticut, and Delaware—commercially vulnerable states in the middle of the Confederation—countered the Virginia Plan. Their agenda nationalized control over a strictly limited set of public goods, while it protected many of the economic prerogatives of the states and established a stronger national government whose economic policies would depend on the concurrence of the states. The final Constitution resembled this agenda more closely than Madison's. The Constitution expanded national authority by ensuring a financial base and providing for national coinage, trade, and related powers to protect interstate commerce, and it authorized state officials to maintain their control over decisions about their economic endowments, including policy choices about slavery, the regulation of domestic markets, resource use, economic development, and the encouragement of enterprise.

This argument differs from recent scholarship on the Founding by combining an older historical literature on the material origins of the Constitution (Beard 1913) with more recent insights from political science on agenda setting, representation, collective action problems, and American political development. In recent decades, historians have written many outstanding works on the Founding focused on intellectual histories of Founding-era ideas, particularly about republicanism and liberty (Bailyn 1967; Wood 1969; McCoy 1989; Matthews 1995; Rakove 1996). These studies, while inspiring as intellectual history, emphasize the breadth and flow of ideas in the Founding period, rather than the immediate policy crisis, interests, and compromises that occupy any policy-making process such as the Constitutional Convention (suggestive works in this vein, however, include McDonald 1958, 1985; Onuf 1983; and Banning 1995).[1] In political science, the rational choice (Mueller 1997), public policy (Sabatier 1999), and neoinstitutional scholarship (Dodd and Jillson 1994) that has contributed so much to understanding more recent periods of American political development has had limited impact on the analysis of the Founding itself. Scholars in the fields of public policy and American political development frequently refer to the Constitution's impact, but have not brought the field's perspective to bear on a systematic analysis of the political design of the Constitution. By focusing on the political entrepreneurship of James Madison, and his definition of the problems the Confederation faced, one can better understand what the Framers were reacting against, and how they attempted to change politics fundamentally while protecting material interests they viewed as critically important.

State Autonomy and Rivalry

When the states declared their independence of Great Britain, they also orphaned themselves from British policy supervision, including its benefits. Before the Revolution, the British had borne the costs of making and enforcing public policy for their empire. The British regime provided public goods for the Colonies, such as an army and navy, the Bank of England, advantageous trade rules within the British empire, basic commercial and property law, and some uniform administration. Some of this British policy infrastructure, such as common law, endured. But much of importance for the collective interest of the Colonies did not survive. Independence meant the loss of specie, British administrative expenditures in the Colonies, legal status within the trade of the British empire, and various British statutes. The states assumed control of economic policy within their borders.

Each colony reinvented itself as an independent, self-governing republic.[2] Each asserted sovereignty over the fundamental policy choices about war and peace, commerce and taxation that king and Parliament had made for them. Each state set up a public policy process suited to a self-proclaimed independent republic, and each established its own tariff, currency, land, and debt policy. "American public policy" almost entirely became the aggregate of these state policies.

Swept into power by revolutionary republicanism, the new state governments ensured that the mass of male white voters would exercise immediate influence on public policy. Popularly elected legislators made public policy largely unimpeded by upper legislative chambers, executives, or courts. These legislators had served single-year terms at the pleasure of electorates that by 1790 included 60 to 70 percent of adult white males (Nevins 1924, 139, 152–64; Main 1973, 192–208; Wilentz 1992, 35; Wood 1969, 166–67; Keyssar 2000, 24).

American state legislators, therefore, bore responsibility for virtually all American economic policy in the 1780s. These legislators governed trade, currency, credit, and public finance with little regard for citizens in other states or the national interest. Their control over economic policy tools enabled them to externalize policy costs to other states (for example, by taxing imports at a lower rate than neighboring states). State policy-makers sometimes took advantage of the cooperative self-sacrifices of neighboring states;

when New Hampshire, Massachusetts, and Rhode Island prohibited British vessels from unloading in their ports in 1785, Connecticut used the opportunity to welcome British ships (Nevins 1924, 564; Jensen 1950, 339; Davis 1977, 73–75, 100–101). The American states, in short, confronted a "prisoner's dilemma" (Hardin 1982; Axelrod 1984, 3–24; Lichbach 1996), much like nation-states in the contemporary international political economy (Yarborough and Yarborough 1991, 159, 164). No U.S. state was so economically and militarily dominant that it could unilaterally bring leadership and order to the 1787 American economy.

Substantial differences in the states' material interests severely exacerbated this inherent rivalry. The most important differences lay in agriculture, from which more than nine of ten Americans derived their income. Differences in agriculture created fundamental differences in the policy interests of three distinct regions—the South, the Middle States, and New England. Leaders in the South, dependent on exports and free trade, and the North, eager for merchant monopolies and tariff protections, already recognized that their regions were on a collision course.

Land-rich and endowed with a long growing season, the economies of Maryland, Virginia, the Carolinas, and Georgia were driven by cash export crops such as tobacco, rice, and indigo. In the 1770s, these Southern economies had remained the most colonial, in that they exported these few products to Great Britain in bulk and used the profits to import finished goods from Britain. The large size of many farms and the length of the growing season made slaves a profitable investment in the region. Slaves made it possible to expand the scale of export farms, facilitating the growth of large plantations more efficient in producing specialized export crops. Prices of these crops fluctuated substantially, and these price fluctuations favored the evolution of large plantations (with ten or more slaves) because larger units could more readily produce surplus crops to weather economic downturns (Walton and Shepard 1979; Walton and Rockoff 1998, 94–97). Slaves constituted about one-third of all of the private physical wealth in the South, compared with less than 5 percent in the Middle States and virtually none in New England (Jones 1980, 31). Southern states, then, had a stake in policies that protected slavery and minimized the costs of direct trade with Europe. These states had little interest in assisting the economic diversification that was occurring in states to their north. These states also favored free and competitive trade in general, and access to the Mississippi River as a trade route critical for the westward expansion of the Southern economy. Southern economic interests particularly were at cross-purposes with Northern merchants, who sought to protect American carriers and limit competition with them.

The Middle States of Pennsylvania, Delaware, New Jersey, and New York also had fertile land but provided a less hospitable climate for agriculture. In contrast to the South, the climate in these states was too cold to produce food during several months of the year. Instead of the year-round, large-scale cultivation of a few cash crops to the South, farms in this Middle region grew a more diverse array of crops, primarily wheat, but also corn, rye, oats, barley, some fruits, and vegetables (such as potatoes). These farms also raised livestock. In these areas, the typical farm was smaller than the Southern plantation. Slaves, then, were less cost-effective in these states because the scale was smaller and slaves could not contribute to production in the winter. Instead, the Middle State farmers tended to operate family farms, depending on a few indentured servants or itinerant workers for additional help. These farms produced some surplus for export, particularly bread and flour, but were not as dependent on European demand as the farms to the south (Walton and Shepard 1979, 81; Walton and Rockoff 1998, 97–99). New York and Philadelphia had become important ports, and nascent industries such as iron manufacture were growing. Middle states had a smaller stake in slavery and the protection of exports than the South, and had more stake in the development of internal markets, manufacturing, and trade.

New England had gone farthest to break with its colonial role and to develop a diversified market economy. New England's soil, terrain, and climate were much less hospitable for agriculture than were those of the other regions. In Connecticut, Rhode Island, Massachusetts, and New Hampshire, farming tended to be concentrated in small, subsistence farms that produced corn, wheat, and other hardy foodstuffs for household consumption. New England could not produce enough food for its own needs, and it had to import food. Its citizens, then, became accustomed to combining farming with other enterprises. New Englanders on the seacoast took advantage of the rich opportunities for whaling and fishing, particularly for cod. The existence of these fisheries, in combination with very high quality timber, prompted the development of a sizable shipbuilding industry in the Northern and Middle colonies. Domestic New England markets became more geographically extensive, and production more integrated, than those in other regions. New England merchants (protected by British mercantile laws) became heavily involved in the carrying trades, shipping goods among the Colonies and between the Colonies and their export partners (Main 1973, 76; Davis 1977, 16–19; Walton and Rockoff 1998, 94–113, 147–50). Plantation colonies shipped commodities that needed minimal processing, while New England produced and shipped products that "stimulated the growth of a wide range of related enterprises and financial services: the processing and milling of grain, timber, and turpentine; the building of special casks for provisions; the construction and capitalization of ships and equipment for the fisheries; and finally, the storage, financing, and transportation facilities needed to gather cargoes and ship them abroad" (Newell 2000, 46). The region had less interest in slavery than other regions (British carriers brought most of the slaves to the United States). It had a much greater interest than the South in a diversified, independent economy. It was developing an interest in the control of trade to benefit its own commercial and embryonic manufacturing interests.

New England also had become very accustomed to active government promotion of the economy, in contrast to the Southern states. From the 1630s, New England governments emulated the British government itself, encouraging market integration and economic diversification by building roads and bridges, providing subsidies, chartering corporations (including, in Massachusetts, a state bank), and in other ways actively supporting home industries (Handlin and Handlin 1969; Newell 2000).

Different economic endowments in each state created cross-cutting conflicts among states within each region. The economic influence of the states with large populations weighed heavily on neighboring states with fewer citizens. The 1790 census would show that 18 percent of the U.S. population lived in Virginia, and that half the population lived in four states (Virginia, Pennsylvania, North Carolina, and Massachusetts), which were scattered across the economic regions (U.S. Census Bureau 1975, 24–37). Most states were "small" from the perspective of Virginians like Washington and Madison, or the Pennsylvanian James Wilson.[3] Disparities in access to land also created political rivalries. Massachusetts, Pennsylvania, and the four Southern states enjoyed land in abundance, while Connecticut, New Jersey, Delaware, and Maryland lacked extensive lands (Nevins 1924, 598; Nettels 1962, 138; McDonald 1985, 218–19). At the beginning of the 1780s, Maryland refused to ratify the Articles of Confederation without concessions from Virginia on that state's western land claims; the Southern states sought a political alliance with New York on the issue of western claims to help to isolate the state from a closer political alliance with other Northern states (Nevins 1924, 578–83, 595).

Access to a supply of slaves split the Southern states, and access to ports split the North. Virginia and North Carolina had slaves in abundance and tended to favor a ban on the importation of slaves; such a ban would effectively limit the future supply of slaves and raise their value. South Carolina and Georgia depended on the slave trade and received three-quarters of the slaves imported into the South in the late Colonial period (Walton and Shepard 1979, 102). These Deep South states opposed a ban on the slave trade (McDonald 1985, 217–18). In the North, thriving port cities particularly advantaged two Middle states—Pennsylvania and New York—at the expense of their regional neighbors. Maryland, New Jersey, and Connecticut were highly dependent on the ports of New York and Philadelphia. New York's 1785 tariff law imposed duties on British goods brought in from neighboring states identical to those for goods brought in from England; port fees and tonnage duties were increased for vessels from Connecticut and New Jersey, increasing the effective price of produce from those two states in New York, to the advantage of New York producers. Some of the states imposed tonnage duties on any ship owned outside the state, including ships from other states (Giesecke 1970, 139). This state commercial authority grew more politically attractive to the port states, and more threatening to those that depended on outside ports. In the years 1784–87, New York was deriving more than half its revenue from its imposts (Cochran 1932, 167; Jensen 1950, 338; Robertson and Walton 1977, 69–70, 75, 87).

The economic and political vulnerabilities of smaller states in the geographical center of the Confederation—Rhode Island, Connecticut, New Jersey, Delaware, and Maryland—gave them a special stake in selective improvements in national policy capacity, even while it made them anxious to ensure their remaining policy autonomy. New Jersey, for example, had no public lands to sell to produce public revenues, and no ports large enough to produce substantial tariff revenues. Most of its farmers shipped through out-of-state ports, and thus were very exposed to rent seeking by Philadelphia and New York. New Jersey state leaders resented New York for paying its obligations to the national government with imposts on goods entering the port of New York and then passed along to New Jersey. While New York was rejecting a Confederation impost amendment as an intrusion on its impost revenues, New Jersey's legislature in 1786 passed a resolution to withhold its required contribution to the Confederation treasury (or requisition payment) until all the states had ratified the amendment. In effect, New Jersey by this action formally seceded from the congressional requisition system and defied the Articles of Confederation. New Jersey citizens held a larger than average share of the Continental debt, and the state announced that it was assuming direct control of payment of the debt within its borders (Ferguson 1961, 231; Dougherty 2001, 72–73). As the legislature made clear to Congress in 1778, New Jersey sought the nationalization of resources, notably national revenues, western lands, and tariffs, so that it could benefit financially from import duties currently extracted by Pennsylvania and New York (McCormick 1964; Murrin 1987, 4–5). New Jersey gave its delegates to the Annapolis Convention in 1786 the broadest mandate to overhaul the national policy-making system: "to report such an Act on the subject, as when ratified by them 'would enable the United States in Congress assembled, effectually to provide for the exigencies of the Union'" (Kurland and Lerner, 1987, 1: 186). However, its support for increased national power was contingent on retaining as much control as possible over its assets while guaranteeing that larger states would not institutionalize their existing commercial and financial advantage over New Jersey into permanent policy dominance.

The evaporation of unifying revolutionary ardor intensified these interstate conflicts. Economic depression in the 1780s (a downturn comparable to the Depression of the 1930s) increased pressures on state legislators to use state powers to relieve constituents (Nettels 1962, 93; McCusker and Menard 1985, 366–67, 375–76; Morris 1987, 134–37). Georgia, South Carolina, North Carolina, New Jersey, New York, Rhode Island, and Pennsylvania issued paper currency to help raise prices and aid the debt-ridden farmers, and paper money proponents were narrowly beaten back in four other states. When the currency depreciated rapidly, some states passed laws that required creditors to accept the paper bills as equivalent to gold and silver. Other states enacted "stay" laws that suspended debt payments for a period of time. The Pennsylvania legislature revoked the charter of the Bank of North America, affecting credit nationwide (Nettels 1962, 75–81, 138–46; Polishook 1969; McDonald 1985: 156). Some of these actions adversely affected creditors in others states, who could do little or nothing to defend their interests against state economic policy.

Commercial rivalries were becoming particularly ominous. New York, Massachusetts, Pennsylvania, Rhode Island, and New Hampshire erected tariffs in the 1780s that protected local industries against foreign competition. New York in 1787 put special duties on foreign goods imported by American vessels from Connecticut and New Jersey (Nevins 1924, 558–64; Nettels 1962, 69, 72–73; Jensen 1950, 339; Davis 1977, 73–75, 100–101). To strike back at New York's earlier trade restrictions and attract merchants from other states, New Jersey in 1784 had designated Perth Amboy and Burlington as free ports for twenty-five years (Delaware also created free ports two years later). When New Jersey complained to the Continental Congress about New York's escalation, Congress could do no more than instruct the state to retaliate (Nevins 1924, 558–561; Nettels 1962, 69, 72–73; Giesecke 1970, 126; Murrin 1987, 38; Dougherty 2001, 72–73).

The national government structurally lacked the means to motivate and effect a remedy for these problems. The Articles of Confederation protected state sovereignty, and established a national government that states could easily incapacitate (Jensen 1959, 131, 174–75; Wood 1969, 358; Jillson and Wilson 1994, 134–63). By the middle 1780s, interstate policy antagonism made it impossible for Congress to govern (*The Papers of James Madison* [hereafter MP] 9, 275; Wood 1969, 359; Morris 1987, 92–94, 99–101). The Confederation government could not enforce the collection of requisitions from the states, and could not make a credible commitment to back its currency debt (Calomiris 1988; Dougherty 2001) and other obligations. Coalitions shifted from issue to issue as states aligned and realigned kaleidoscopically. No stable coalition emerged in the national legislature, and in 1786, long-festering regional frustrations "broke the back of the Congress" (Jillson and Wilson 1994, 169, 267) as it tried to generate revenue for the national government and deal with the regionally divisive issue of trade on the Mississippi River. When Congress called on the states to amend the Articles to enable it to collect an impost, several states ratified only on the condition that all the other states do the same. Twice, a single state blocked a change in the Articles that would have permitted the Confederation government to have a more reliable and independent source of revenue than state contributions. New York's governor refused to call a special legislative session to permit the national government to assume responsibility for collecting a proposed national impost (Cochran 1932, 172–76; Nettels 1962, 95; De Pauw 1966, 34–43; Davis 1977, 37–39, 57; Riesman 1987, 143; Dougherty 2001, 70–72).

To many American leaders, the future looked worse. In June 1786 the Continental Board of Treasury reported that "nothing but an immediate and general Adoption of the Measures recommended by the Resolves of Congress of the 18th. April, 1783, can rescue us from Bankruptcy, or preserve the Union of the several States from Dissolution" (United States, *Journals of the Continental Congress* [hereafter JCC] 30, 359–66). Madison believed that the possibility of consensus would further erode as new states entered the union bringing "sentiment[s] and interests les[s] congenial with those of the Atlantic states than those of the latter are one with another" (Madison to Jefferson, March 18, 1786, in MP 8, 503).

These compounding policy problems were creating a loose, diverse, nationwide, and growing group of American leaders who shared support for some enhancement of national power. Conservatives and nationalists expressed growing opposition to parochial policy in the 1780s (Matson 1996, 382–83). Leaders in each section recognized that more uniform and effective national policy administration would improve the economic and political situation in each state, though disagreements about the nature of that policy created implicit disagreements among the leaders within and between the states. Merchants in Boston, New York, and Philadelphia demanded additional power for Congress to deal authoritatively with British trade restrictions (Madison to Jefferson, August 20, 1785, MP 8, 344; McDonald 1985, 217). New Jersey and Connecticut farmers wanted a national power to prevent New York from discriminating against their products. Western settlers wanted a national government with the power to open the Mississippi. Slave owners wanted national rules committed to helping them recover escaped slaves (Nettels 1962, 93). Many (though not all) merchants, manufacturers, and creditors shared an interest in enhancing specific national economic powers—establishing a large free trade area, creating a single national currency, protecting commercial credit, and providing sound public securities—and restricting state economic powers. Urban commercial interests sought uniform currency laws, tender laws, and transport and quality regulations to overcome the discriminatory, self-protective legislation of the states that were meant to impede commerce and protect home industries (Matson 1996, 384). Holders of national and state government debts were especially vocal supporters of establishing sound currency policies on a national basis, as well as a predictable revenue base for funding the Confederation government (Ferguson 1961, 242–43; Jensen 1965, 344–45; Brown 1993, 171ff).

Proponents of stronger government were united by diverse material interests, not by a theoretical commitment to an abstract, unqualified strengthening of government. As long as the details were sketchy, a stronger national government could serve as a fuzzy common goal to unite political actors whose interests differed and often conflicted; after the Convention, even the opponents of the Constitution generally conceded that the Confederation government was ineffective and that the nation needed an effective national government (Storing 1981, 28). Rarely was there support for an undefined and undifferentiated strengthening of national power divorced from impact. Nationalists advocated the enhancement of specific national powers for specific national ends, and nationalist rhetoric could be used strategically to paper over these differences and keep the coalition united. To the extent that it became apparent that a stronger government could be as useful for harming their interests as for advancing them, consensus crumbled, as it did at the Constitutional Convention. Madison himself helped to articulate these differences when he gambled that a plan for nationalized economic authority would compel these interests to coalesce. Instead, Madison's agenda crystallized the fears and fault lines of state leaders inclined to greater national economic power.

Madison's Strategy: Engineering an Independent National Policy Interest

James Madison was positioned superbly to tailor a strategic reform agenda to this confluence of economic and political problems.[4] One of the nation's most experienced politicians, Madison also was the most knowledgeable and respected American policy authority (Farrand 1966, 3, 94–95). He had helped draft Virginia's Constitution of 1776, served in the state's House of Delegates, and represented Virginia in Congress (Ketcham 1990; Wood 1987; Banning 1995; Matthews 1995, 1–3). He had emerged as a leader in the Continental Congress in the early 1780s, served on many key committees, worked behind the scenes to broker national policy coalitions,[5] and played a major role in initiating the Annapolis Convention of 1786 (MP 9, 115–19; Banning 1995, 422 n 47). His writings and speeches provide ample evidence that he was a shrewd, experienced observer of fellow politicians, an astute theoretician who confidently drew on his experience to generalize about political behavior. He was skilled in the legislative arts, including manipulating agendas, locating points of policy compromise, and building coalitions. Madison articulated his Constitutional strategy in private letters to Jefferson, Randolph, and Washington (MP 9, 317–22, 368–71, 382–87), in "Notes on Ancient and Modern Confederacies" (hereafter, "Notes"), written in 1786, and in "Vices of the Political System of the United States" (hereafter, "Vices"), written in the months immediately prior to the Convention (MP 9, 3–24, 345–58; Rakove 1996, 46–56). The Virginia Plan, which set the initial agenda of the Convention, embodied nearly all of Madison's ideas and aimed to implement his vision of appropriate policy-making reform.[6]

As a principled republican, an economic liberal,[7] a political pragmatist, and an advocate for Virginia, Madison had invested considerable effort to improving economic policy by making incremental changes within the framework of the Articles of Confederation. The Articles underwrote republicanism in America, and Madison expressed unyielding dedication to republican values in private letters and speeches to Convention delegates (MP 9, 286; Farrand 1966, 1, 135; Banning 1995, 77–107). Madison used Confederation policy-making rules skillfully and vigorously to protect Virginia's economic interests in political disputes over western lands, war debts, the admission of Vermont, and commerce (MP 3, 307–8; 4, 38–39; Banning 1995, 17–19, 50–51, 178–81).[8] By 1786, however, incremental adjustments had failed to pull national economic policy out of the downward spiral that threatened Virginia, the nation, and the republican experiment itself.

Madison's frustrating personal efforts to reform specific Confederation economic policies most profoundly shaped his strategy for national government reform. Barely a month after taking his seat at the Confederation Congress in March 1780, the "confused and critical state" of national finance shocked the twenty-nine-year-old legislator, who wrote: "Our great danger at present arises from the dilatory proceedings of the States and the real difficulty of drawing forth those resources from which the new System is to operate upon" (MP 2, 21–22). Madison served on three-member congressional committees that aimed to obtain the states' requisitions and to establish a national impost (JCC, Nov. 8, 1780, 28, 1033–1035; Feb. 3, 1781, 29, 112–13), on committees to discourage Pennsylvania and New Jersey from assuming the payment of federal obligations (MP 5, 363), and on a committee that insisted on using "the force of the United States" against states that shirked their obligations (JCC, May 2, 1781, 20, 469–71). Madison often supported Superintendent of Finance Robert Morris in his efforts to ensure the government's solvency in the early 1780s, and was associated with Morris, Hamilton, and other nationalists seeking to strengthen the political position of the Confederation government (Morris 1973, 1, 20–21; Ferguson 1961, 1969; Banning 1995, 13–42). Initially more reluctant to interfere with the states' commercial powers than their finances, Madison was driven by interstate commercial rivalries and the Mississippi controversy to make effective national commercial power a top reform priority by the mid-1780s (MP 8, 333–36; Banning 1995, 54–55, 72). As late as August 1786, Madison had become deeply skeptical about both the Annapolis Convention (limited officially to commercial reform) and an openly discussed, wider-ranging "Plenipotentiary Convention for amending the Confederation" (MP 9, 96).

After repeated efforts to correct national economic problems with incremental adjustments to the Articles, Madison in 1787 reversed course, determined to address all the faults of the Confederation systematically. Madison's political instincts suggested to him that the national political crisis and the repeated failures of patchwork solutions created a unique window of opportunity in which a sweeping proposal for enhanced national policy authority could forge a decisive coalition from the growing but amorphous political discontent with the Confederation. Incremental reform proposals failed because they were partial; the forthcoming Convention "will only be useful in proportion to its superiority to partial views and interests" (MP 9, 307). Madison had experience in strategically expanding agendas. In the Confederation Congress just three months before the Convention, he had used national security to justify Confederation aid to Massachusetts for suppressing Shays' rebellion. Although "there might be no particular evidence in this case of such a meditated interference, yet there was sufficient ground for a general suspicion of readiness in [Great Britain] to take advantage of events in this Country, to warrant precautions agst. her" (MP 9, 277–78).

To support a comprehensive agenda for reconstituting the national government, Madison had to convince himself that the plan could succeed and remain consistent with economic liberalism and the protection of Virginia's economic interests.[9] For Madison on the eve of the Convention, economic liberalism dovetailed perfectly with Virginia's comparative advantage, which he seemed to equate with that of the entire nation: "The general policy of America is at present pointed at the encouragement of Agriculture, and the importation of the objects of consumption. The wid[er] therefore our ports be opened and the more extensive the privileges of all competitors in our Commerce, the more likely we shall be to buy at cheap & sell at profitable rat[es]" (MP 7, 58–64). If representation in the national legislature were based on population, Virginia, the largest state and a Southern state, could bring order to national policy-making as the broker of a coalition between the growing South (Georgia and the Carolinas) and the most populous states (Pennsylvania and Massachusetts). Before the Convention, Madison insisted to fellow Virginians Washington, Jefferson, and Randolph that the representation question had to be the first issue resolved at the Philadelphia Convention, for just such strategic purposes. Eastern states would support the proposal for proportional representation because of their current population advantage, and Southern states could support it because their populations were expected to overtake those of the Eastern states in the foreseeable future. "And if a majority of the larger States concur, the fewer and smaller States must finally bend to them. This point being gained, many of the objections now urged in the leading States agst. renunciations of power will vanish" (MP 9, 318–19, 369–70, 383).

Building on the foundation of proportional representation, Madison's plan for constitutional revision followed from three premises, expressed in private writings and advanced in Convention debates. First, state policy autonomy was undermining the American political economy because state legislators' policy authority gave them the means and the motive (or the "ambition") to pursue economic policies that undermined the national interest. Second, the diagnosis implied the cure: it was necessary to redesign national government so that national policy-makers effectively would pursue purely *national* economic interests completely independent of the states. Third, to establish this independent national interest, the national government would have to exercise sovereign authority over national economic development and wield a veto over state laws.

According to Madison, selfish parochialism was the fundamental flaw in

American economic policy in the 1780s, autonomous state legislation the instrument, and collective economic bad the result. "[M]ost of our political
evils," he wrote to Jefferson, "may be traced up to our commercial ones, as
most of our moral may to our political" (MP 8, 502). The historical record
of confederacies, Madison believed, proved that the lack of a central trade
policy was an endemic and fatal problem for them (MP 9, 11, 17; Farrand
1966, 1, 317). "The practice of many States in restricting the commercial intercourse with other States, and putting their productions and manufactures
on the same footing with those of foreign nations, though not contrary to
the federal articles, is certainly adverse to the spirit of the Union, and tends
to beget retaliating regulations, not less expensive & vexatious in themselves,
than they are destructive of the general harmony" ("Vices," MP 9, 350).

Madison's "Vices of the Political System of the United States" heavily emphasized the economic problems that state policy autonomy created for the
national economic interest. Madison ranked the failure of the Confederation
requisition system as the first of these "Vices," and blamed it on "the number and independent authority of the States."[10] Madison ranked "Encroachments by the States on federal authority" as the second "Vice," and at the
Convention he elaborated, listing unauthorized state treaties with Indians,
interstate compacts, and Massachusetts's raising of troops (Farrand 1966, 1,
316–17). "Vices" does not allude to the state assumption of federal debts as a
state encroachment on the Confederation government, but an earlier congressional committee headed by Madison had noted that, to the extent that
states assume the union's debts, "the federal constitution must be so far infringed" (JCC, Oct. 1, 1782, XXIII, 630), and the problem had worsened
considerably in the ensuing years. The third "Vice" involved state violations
of treaties with foreign nations, and at the Convention Madison elaborated
that "[t]he files of Congs. contain complaints already, from almost every nation with which treaties have been formed" (Farrand 1966, 1, 316). The
fourth "Vice," "Trespasses of the States on the rights of each other," distinguishes a national market for credit and commodities, and describes state
laws that interfere with those markets as "destructive of the general harmony." The fifth "Vice" addressed the "lack of concert" in economic policy;
the sixth the inability of the states to engage the national government in protecting themselves against such economically driven violence as Shay's rebellion; the seventh the inability to implement rules such as national requisitions (MP 9, 348–50).

These economically self-defeating policies followed from the short-term,
parochial incentives that motivated the state legislators who bore responsibility for most American economic policy. The policy-makers used state au-

thority to provide expedient "base and selfish measures" for constituents, even at the expense of other Americans. "Is it to be imagined that an ordinary citizen or even an assembly-man of R. Island in estimating the policy of paper money, ever considered or cared in what light the measure would be viewed in France or Holland; or even in Massts or Connect.? It was a sufficient temptation to both that it was for their interest: it was a Sufficient sanction to the latter that it was popular in the State; to the former that it was so in the neighbourhood" (MP 9, 354–56). State legislators' short-term, narrow perspective even threatened the Revolution's republican victory. Excessive and volatile lawmaking sometimes threatened basic rights, such as freedom of religion, and made republican policy-making appear ineffective (MP 9, 348–50, 353–54). The multiplicity, mutability, injustice, and impotence of state laws constitute "a dreadful class of evils" that "indirectly affect the whole" nation (Farrand 1966, 1, 318–19). Madison captured the spirit of the "prisoner's dilemma" when he generalized about the counterproductive effects of nearly unlimited interstate rivalry.

Madison emphasized that these economic policies followed logically from the structure of state legislators' incentives. He held it as fundamental that politicians pursue the interests that their public offices empower them to pursue. This premise is most clearly articulated with respect to the separation of powers in *Federalist* 51, in which Madison states that protection against the concentration of political power must depend on giving policy-makers "the necessary Constitutional means, and personal motives," to resist encroachments. "Ambition must be made to counteract ambition. The interest of the man must be connected to the Constitutional rights of the place" (*Federalist* 51, in Hamilton, Madison, and Jay 1961b, 349). Madison premised his diagnosis and cure on this assumption. State policy-makers primarily were motivated by their self-interested use of parochial powers, in his view. Rhode Island legislators printed paper money because they had the power to benefit themselves politically, and they used it, regardless of the negative externalities for their neighbors. This problem was endemic and evident in every state. Rhode Island merely exemplified the economic perversity of unconstrained policy decentralization. State legislators everywhere were combining trade restrictions, emissions of paper currency, or debtor relief laws to further their ambitions and help their constituents, because they had the means and motive to do so.

National policy-makers, in contrast, lacked the will or ability to make authoritative decisions for the nation's interest, independent of the interest of their states. They lacked the motive and means—they lacked the ambition—to act in behalf of the collective good of the nation. Thus no policy-makers

had the capacity to defend effectively the fundamental values of republicanism, individual liberties, or commercial liberalism. On the eve of the Convention, in identical language in letters to the nationalist Washington and his
state's governor, Edmund Randolph, Madison summarized his position: the
"fundamental point" was that the "individual independence of the States"
was "utterly irreconcilable" with "the idea of aggregate sovereignty" (MP 9,
369, 383).[11]

It followed that, if vesting power in state policy-makers invites the pursuit
of state economic interests, then vesting power in the national policy-makers should invite the pursuit of a national economic interest. If a policy-
maker can pursue narrow interests but cannot pursue broad national interests, he will harness his ambitions to the pursuit of narrow interests. Although
Madison did not make the premise explicit, the logical implication is that it
is necessary to give national policy-makers broad and independent powers to
motivate policy-makers and give them the means to pursue the national interest (assuming, of course, that all these powers would be limited and exercised according to republican principles).[12] This assumption makes the significance of expanded national powers, including a veto over state law, readily
apparent.

Confederation policy-makers lacked the economic authority that would
instill in them the means and motive to pursue the interests of the national
political economy. The Confederation was merely a "treaty of amity of
commerce and of alliance, between so many independent and Sovereign
States." The architects of the Confederation originally had "a mistaken confidence that the justice, the good faith, the honor, the sound policy" of the
state legislatures would make it unnecessary to protect the national interest.
But in practice, state legislators could not escape their parochial shackles.

> It is no longer doubted that a unanimous and punctual obedience of 13 inde-
> pendent bodies, to the acts of the federal Government, ought not be calculated
> on. . . . How indeed could it be otherwise? In the first place, Every general act
> must necessarily bear unequally hard on some particular member or members of
> it. Secondly the partiality of the members to their own interests and rights, a par-
> tiality which will be fostered by the Courtiers of popularity, will naturally exag-
> gerate the inequality where it exists, and even suspect it where it has no existence.
> Thirdly a distrust of the voluntary compliance of each other may prevent the
> compliance of any, although it should be the latent disposition of all. . . . If the laws
> of the States, were merely recommendatory to their citizens, or if they were to be
> rejudged by County authorities, what security, what probability would exist, that
> they would be carried into execution? Is the security or probability greater in fa-
> vor of the acts of Congs. which depending for their execution on the will of the

state legislatures, wch. are tho' nominally authoritative, in fact recommendatory
only. ("Vices," MP 9, 351–52)

One could anticipate state encroachment on the small remaining sphere
of national power "in almost every case where any favorite object of a State
shall present a temptation." Note that states are encroaching on policy authority, not physical territory. The erosion of national power foreshadowed
the union's division into smaller, politically rivalrous regional confederacies
(MP 9, 295, 299; Farrand 1966, 1, 320–21).

Madison in effect proposed to reconstitute the national government so
that national policy-makers' ambitions would be driven by a material concern for *national* advantage. When Madison traced the roots of unjust state
policies mainly to the material interests of citizens in "Vices,"[13] he argued
that the nationalization of policy authority can protect republican policy-
making from being hijacked by selfishness. In words similar to those he used
in *Federalist* 10 in late November 1787 (in Hamilton, Madison, and Jay 1961b,
60–61), Madison noted in "Vices" that sovereign power must attend to the
"public good and private rights" of the *entire* society (that is, the nation as a
whole): "The great desideratum in Government is such a modification of *the
Sovereignty* as will render it sufficiently neutral between the different interests
and factions, to controul one part of the Society from invading the rights of
another, and at the same time sufficiently controuled itself, from setting up
an interest adverse to that of *the whole Society*" ("Vices," MP 9, 357; emphasis added).[14]

Immediately following this sentence in "Vices," however, Madison
claimed that national government redesign must animate the motive to
achieve a *national* interest to "temper" the natural "evils" arising from the
parochial rivalry of confederated small republics. He did not state this view
explicitly, but given his belief that there is an interest of the whole society
and that government can pursue it,[15] this interpretation is a most reasonable
way to understand why constitutional means and motives are so important
to him. This interpretation also explains why he contrasted the design of incentives in a monarchy to those in a republic, in a passage in "Vices" that
never appears in the *Federalist*:

> In absolute Monarchies, the prince is sufficiently neutral towards his subjects, but
> frequently sacrifices their happiness to his ambition or his avarice. In small Re-
> publics, the sovereign will is sufficiently controuled from such a Sacrifice of the
> entire Society, but is not sufficiently neutral towards the parts composing it. As a
> limited Monarchy tempers the evils of an absolute one; so an extensive Republic
> meliorates the administration of a small Republic. (MP 9, 355–57; compare *Fed-
> eralist* 51 in Hamilton, Madison, and Jay 1961b, 347–53)

Madison drew the analogy that, as a king's authority must be limited to achieve the public good, a republic's authority must be expanded to achieve the public good. In a monarchy, constitutional limits on a king's policy authority keep the national government attentive to the national interest (particularly the national economic interest); if it is not restricted, unlimited economic authority will tempt the king to use this power to enrich, immortalize, or otherwise benefit himself. Conversely (and rather glibly), Madison drew the conclusion that republics require precisely the *opposite* remedy: they need *expanded* national authority. A republic requires expanded national authority—not merely expanded geographical scope—to motivate and empower national policy-makers to pursue the national interest in the face of the powerful centrifugal force of parochial interest. He put it in a slightly different way to Washington: "The great desideratum which has not yet been found for Republican Governments, seems to be some disinterested & dispassionate umpire in disputes between different passions & interests in the State" (MP 9, 383–84).[16]

This logic led Madison to propose a national policy process that would instill an ambition to pursue the national interest and the power to turn that ambition into authoritative national policy. If state policy authority resulted in the incentive to pursue parochial interests, then national authority could create the incentive to pursue purely national interests. Madison could have said that national ambition counteracts parochial ambition—an argument understandably absent in his later public letters advocating ratification to un decided New Yorkers. Even during the Convention, Madison may have retreated from the implications of this logic. Yet the logic informs the *Federalist Papers*. In light of his private analysis of the economic problems of the United States prior to the Convention, it is striking that Madison as Publius is so insistent about the need for national policy-makers to counteract each other, but is deafeningly silent about the obvious problem of national policy-makers' power to counteract their state counterparts.

Three fundamental reforms in national government could effectuate the motive to pursue the national interest: extending national policy jurisdiction, establishing a national veto over state policy, and creating governing institutions divorced from state interests. First, the national government should be the presumptive national economic policy authority, not the residual policy authority as at present.[17] In the polemical *Federalist* 10, written for an audience dubious about national power, Madison wrote of "extending the sphere" of government and defended "an extensive Republic"; in the essay, "extensive" clearly refers to a relatively large population and territory.[18] Prior to and during the Convention, however, Madison's meaning of "sphere" conflates two concepts: authority and geography. He sought to give the national government a relatively large area of policy jurisdiction and authority, not merely a large territory and population. He wanted to extend the sphere of government substantially in the sense of extending national power, not merely physical reach. The Confederation already had created a geographic entity "as cohesive and strong as any similar sort of republican confederation in history" (Wood 1969, 359), and had a national legislative body in which state representatives could make some national policy decisions. The problem was that the scope of these decisions was not sufficiently broad for the pursuit of an independent national interest. In his first major speech at the Convention, on June 6, Madison criticized the narrowness of Roger Sherman's proposal for authorizing a select few enumerated powers for the national government. Madison argued that enlarged national power would instill the will to pursue the national interest. A government with a very broad and open jurisdiction would provide "more effectually for the security of private rights, and the steady dispensation of Justice . . . evils which had more perhaps than any thing else, produced this Convention" (Farrand 1966, June 6, 1, 134–36).

> The only practical way to protect the interest of the nation against the oppressive policies supported by mere majorities is to enlarge the sphere, & thereby divide the community into so great a number of interests & parties, that in the 1st. place a majority will not be likely at the same moment to have a common interest *separate from that of the whole or of the minority*; and in the 2d. place, that in case they shd. Have such an interest, they may not be apt to unite in the pursuit of it. (Farrand 1966, June 6, 1, 136; emphasis added)

In these secret deliberations, Madison argued that "enlarging the sphere" of power and territory not only prevents majority oppression but also permits the otherwise fragile national interest (the "common interest . . . of the whole") to root itself in the premises of policy choice.

It followed that the reconstituted national government should "be armed with a positive & compleat authority in all cases where uniform measures are necessary" (MP 9, 317–22, 368–71, 382–87), and that the burden of proof for exercising any economic policy prerogative should fall on the states. Given his diagnosis, uniform measures were most urgent in finance and commerce. The ambitions of those who occupied national policy-making offices would be driven by a material concern for national economic advantage. It was their national position and the national policy power they wielded, not merely their selection, that made national policy-makers the obvious repository of economic policy. If, as he had written, "Every general act must necessarily bear unequally hard on some particular member or members of it," then it was imperative to have a national policy-making process that could make redistributive decisions in behalf of the national interest. The key to Madison was not merely to negate interests but to reduce the impact of local interests in guiding national policy, so that fewer obstacles impeded the pursuit of purer, national goals.[19]

What kinds of powers did Madison have in mind? Compared with his moderate positions on national authority before 1787, Madison had vastly expanded his vision of appropriate national economic policy beyond national finance and national commercial regulation. The economic problems of confederacies extended to "the want of uniformity in the laws concerning naturalization & literary property; of provision for national seminaries, for grants of incorporation for national purposes, for canals and other works of general utility, wch. may at present be defeated by the perverseness of particular States whose concurrence is necessary" (MP 9, 350). Madison believed that the national government should wield basic tools of national economic development: commercial law, corporate law, infrastructure development, and some role in higher education.

Madison tried to convince fellow delegates of these premises to the very end of the Convention, but to little avail in the face of fierce protectiveness of state economic prerogatives. On September 15, Madison expressed the view that "[he] was more & more convinced that the regulation of Commerce was in its nature indivisible and ought to be wholly under one authority" (Farrand 1966, 2, 624–25); it is almost impossible to imagine the development of the American political economy without recurring conflict over the boundaries of national and state commercial power. The previous day, Madison had attempted to include specific national powers to establish a national university and "grant charters of incorporation where the interest of the U.S. might require & the legislative provisions of individual States may be incompetent."[20] Both proposals were rejected. The proposal to nationalize corporate law would have profoundly altered the path of American political development. This provision could have made it much more difficult to defeat the creation of a national bank. It could have made the development of the national infrastructure in the nineteenth century—canals, roads, and railroads—a much more nationalized process, and completely nationalized the politics of infrastructure development. Most important, a national corporation law could have prevented the corporate charter-mongering that encouraged the growth of large corporations beginning in the late nineteenth century; these corporations became the distinguishing feature of the American political economy (Chandler 1977, 1990) and profoundly affected the formation of labor interests and party competition in the twentieth century (Robertson 2000).

Madison insisted that national policy-makers also have the power to veto state laws. In his letter to Washington, he drew the conclusion that a national veto power was a necessary condition for establishing a material stake in the national interest.

> [A] negative *in all cases whatsoever* on the legislative acts of the States, as heretofore exercised by the Kingly prerogative, appears to me to be absolutely necessary, and to be the least possible encroachment on the State jurisdictions. Without this defensive power, every positive power that can be given on paper will be evaded & defeated. The States will continue to invade the national jurisdiction, to violate treaties and the law of nations & to harass each other with rival and spiteful measures dictated by mistaken views of interest. Another happy effect of this prerogative would be its controul on the internal vicisitudes of State policy; and the aggressions of interested majorities on the rights of minorities and individuals. (MP 9, 383–84; italics in original)

He then repeated the analogy between the respective needs of monarchies and republics in "Vices," and he specified that the analogy led logically to the need for a national veto in republics: "Might not the national prerogative here suggested be found sufficiently disinterested for the decision of local questions of policy, whilst it would itself be sufficiently restrained from the pursuit of interests adverse to those of the whole Society?" (ibid., 384). The national veto required the constant monitoring of state policy, and that monitoring itself would build in the nation's policy-makers the sense of national purpose. The veto would make national policy-makers alert to predatory state economic policies. To Jefferson, Madison wrote: "The effects of this provision would be not only to guard the national rights and interests against invasion, but also to restrain the States from thwarting and molesting each other, and even from oppressing the minority within themselves by paper money and other unrighteous measures which favor the interests of the majority" (ibid., 318).

In the context of Madison's diagnosis and cure, the national veto played a central role in forming the national interest. The power to veto state laws would force national policy-makers to develop and use an independent notion of national interest. This belief explains why Madison had to fight so fiercely for the national veto, and why he identified the absence of that veto as the central flaw of the Constitution in a letter to Jefferson after the Convention. In that letter he again alluded to the royal veto: "If the supremacy of the British Parliament is not necessary . . . for the harmony of that Empire; it is evident I think that without the royal negative or some equivalent con-

troul, the unity of the system would be destroyed" (ibid. 10, 209–14; see also
Hobson 1979). Independence had made the American states policy orphans;
now they needed a surrogate, visible hand of national government to ensure
that the states would pursue fundamental national interests and rights. The
imperative need for a national veto was indispensable given Madison's assumptions, and was not merely driven by his alarm over state actions
(Rakove 1990, 52).[21]

The exercise of such extensive national powers required republican policy-making institutions controlled by voters, not the states. The presumption
of national policy authority could only be valid if republican policy-makers,
rather than a king, would exercise them. The legislature should be internally
divided, with one house chosen by popular elections. Separate, effective executive and judicial branches would also "extend national supremacy." The
experience of the state governments suggested that these separate institutions
could help energize an interest in national liberal policy outcomes (MP 9,
384–85, 370). In the Virginia Plan, though not in Madison's writings, voters
would elect the House of Representatives, and the House would elect the
Senate; both would elect the executive and the judiciary. The states had no
agency in the national government (though they produced the slate from
which the Senate was chosen). Madison intended that representatives in both
houses of the national legislature be apportioned on the basis of population.
Population-based representation would further nationalize policy by reducing the influence of states as units of representation, and substantially increase
the influence of Madison's Virginia in the national policy process.

The Virginia Plan and the Constitution

The Virginia Plan initiated substantive discussion at the Convention on May
29. Over the next two weeks, as the Convention discussed elements of the
plan, the broad agenda crystallized the opposition. The delegates, who were
obliged to advocate their states' interests (McDonald 1985, 186, 224; see also
Slonim 2000), now confronted the prospect of a government in which the
states they represented had little or no agency. Madison's central concern, the
states' agency in the new policy system, became the focal point of the Virginia Plan's opponents.

Within two days, Richard Dobbs Spaight, speaker of the North Carolina
General Assembly, moved that the Senate should be chosen by the state legislatures (Farrand 1966, 1, 51), and Delaware's John Dickinson took the opportunity to argue against "abolishing the State Governments" and for state
agency in national institutions and procedures (June 2, I, 85–87; June 7, I,

150–53). Roger Sherman seized the agenda decisively on Monday morning, June 11, with a motion that the lower house of Congress be apportioned by population, but that the states have an equal vote in the upper house. In a pair of key 6–5 votes on that day it became evident that Connecticut, New York, New Jersey, Delaware, and Maryland were coalescing into a block in opposition to Madison's projected coalition (ibid., 196–202). Four days later, the New Jersey Plan broke the Virginia Plan's monopoly on the Convention agenda. The New Jersey plan evolved from the block of states opposed to Madison, and resulted from the collaboration of delegates from New York and the commercially vulnerable Middle States of Connecticut, New Jersey, Delaware, and probably Maryland. The plan protected state agency in national policy-making by maintaining the existing Confederation Congress, provided for a Confederation revenue base, and established congressional power to govern interstate and foreign commerce. In effect, the New Jersey Plan dealt only with the minimal list of collective action problems that virtually all participants recognized as in need of reform and that particularly interested the vulnerable Middle States. Although the Convention rejected the New Jersey Plan on a vote of 7–3 (New York, New Jersey, and Delaware in the minority) on June 19, the Paterson proposal made two of Madison's top priorities—proportional representation and the expanded sphere of national authority—the central stumbling blocks of the Convention (ibid., 321) and brought it to an impasse.

Madison tried but failed to break the constitutional impasse by using the states' economic diversity to make his case. The delegates were not persuaded by arguments that different factor endowments would prevent the three largest states of Massachusetts, Pennsylvania, and Virginia from coalescing to the economic disadvantage of the smaller states (ibid., 447–48, 463; Rakove 1996, 78). When Madison implied protection for slavery, arguing that "if any defensive power were necessary, it ought to be mutually given" to the interests of the North and South (Farrand 1966, 1, 486), his Northern support began to drift away (Jillson 1988, 98–99). In the end, the Convention rejected the elements of reconstitution that Madison believed indispensable for creating an independent national interest: population-based apportionment of representatives in both houses of the legislature, the national veto, and expansive national authority. Connecticut, Maryland, New Jersey, and Delaware voted together on the Connecticut Compromise on July 16 and on rejecting the national veto on June 8 and July 17 (Farrand 1966, 1, 163; 2, 15, 21–24).

In making specific decisions about the scope of national policy authority, Convention delegations weighed costs and benefits for their constituents. In the words of one Constitutional scholar, it is "impossible to read the debates without realizing how much the mutual jealousies of the States contributed to render them jealous of a powerful central authority" (Nevins 1924, 625; for an empirical analysis, see McGuire and Ohsfeldt 1986). National authority on slavery and trade, two of the most fundamental issues separating the interests of the states, was decided through a supermajority logrolling agreement. The commercial states sought advantage through national authority to restrict trade, while Southern states wanted free trade and the southernmost states sought to protect the importation of slaves. By late August, a special committee had crafted a mutually advantageous agreement. For the Southern states, Congress would not be able to restrict the importation of slaves until 1800 (splitting the difference in the interests of the upper and lower South). For the Northern states, a simple majority, rather than the two-thirds majority many Southerners preferred, would be sufficient to enact "navigation" acts. Charles Cotsworth Pinckney of South Carolina attempted to break this deal by proposing that *all* commercial regulation require a two-thirds vote for approval. "States pursue their interests with less scruple than individuals," Pinckney argued. "The power of regulating commerce was a pure concession on the part of the S. States. They did not need the protection of the N. States at present." Pinckney's motion lost on a 4–7 vote, with his own South Carolina delegation joining New England and the Middle States in opposition (Farrand 1966, 2, 449–53; Rakove 1996, 86–89).

During the Convention, Connecticut's Oliver Ellsworth clearly and coldly articulated the position that the national interest required that states continue to govern their own economic assets: "[L]et every State import what it pleases. The morality or wisdom of slavery are considerations belonging to the States themselves—What enriches a part enriches the whole, and the States are the best judges of their particular interest" (Farrand 1966, 2, 364). After the Convention, Ellsworth told his constituents: "[No] state would have a right to complain about a navigation act which should leave the carrying business equally open to them all. Those who preferred cultivating their lands would do so; those who chose to navigate and become carriers would do that" (ibid. 3, 164–65). Upon this principle, the delegates forged a plan of government that reconciled economic liberalism with substantial state freedom to exploit their economic advantages. Madison could not persuade the delegates to authorize the national government to exercise powers he believed essential, such as national corporate charters and a national university, and the final document limited national authority to interstate and foreign commerce (ibid. 2, 615–16).[22]

In the end, the Constitution was neither a conscious plan nor a patternless accumulation of ad hoc compromises. The Constitution was a settlement on national economic policy authority, a treaty reflecting contingent compromises on a new national policy-making process, authorized to collect revenue and provide an imprecisely determined but limited set of public goods. The Constitution ensured the states would retain substantial control over existing policy prerogatives and remaining comparative advantages, and guaranteed state agency in the national policy process. In hindsight, this consensus position is understandable. Beyond reconstituting the national policy process, a majority of state delegates could agree only that they wanted to preserve their states' existing comparative advantages with minimal sacrifice of state autonomy. The delegates were disposed to resist an effective national power to pursue a national interest independent of the material interests of their states, and the Virginia Plan had made that possibility clear to them. Thus, the opposition to Madison's ideas unfolded in the defense of individual states on individual issues, in ensuring that the process would not obliterate their policy autonomy, and in engineering a series of mutually contingent compromises on authority and procedure that maintained a balance of economic power.[23]

The Constitution and American Political Development

Madison's proposals undoubtedly would have created a national government more capable of arriving at majoritarian resolutions of interregional economic disputes in the United States, and with much more national control over economic policy outcomes. It is difficult to judge whether such a Constitutional change in 1788 would have been salutary even if it were feasible politically.[24] It is not difficult to explain the failure of Madison's agenda. Madison failed because state officials already had the institutional will and the ability to prevent the surrender of their policy prerogatives and to ensure that national policy outcomes would depend heavily on the future protection of those prerogatives. State delegates to the Convention protected state policy authority in areas where national control could do their interests more harm than good. The final Constitution merely limited the sphere within which state officials could control their revenues, powers, and relative economic advantages, and empowered the states to impede the authoritative resolution of interregional conflicts. Within the sphere of power established by the Constitution, the states enjoyed substantial power to govern market relationships, economic development, resource use, business, and labor.

This view of the Constitution as a compromise on economic policy prerogatives helps explain the origins and institutional incentives that resulted in several unique aspects of American politics. Some of these unique aspects include the mixed record of the states as laboratories for mitigating the "creative destruction" of capitalist economic development; the rise of the business corporation as a distinct feature of turn-of-the-twentieth-century American capitalism, despite early working-class enfranchisement and antitrust laws; the absence of a programmatic labor party; and the fragmentation of American public policy.

This understanding of the Constitution suggests that, compared with those of national officials, state officials' policy choices are more heavily influenced by the immediate, short-term comparative advantages of their jurisdiction. States compete within a constitutionally established free trade zone in which capital and labor are mobile, states are prohibited from imposing substantial restrictions on commerce, but states retain substantial discretion over revenues, regulations, and other policy tools that can be used for the state's economic advantage (Weingast 1995). State policy-makers can induce investments, but they cannot use tariff and trade restrictions to protect domestic industries. National policy-makers enjoy a substantial arsenal of protectionist tools to use to extract rents to pay for distributive benefits. The Constitution, in short, imprisoned state policy-makers in a system of competitive federalism (Robertson 2000, 17–20). The difference between the priority given to comparative advantage by state and national policy-makers is not absolute; countervailing constituency pressures (the Greenback, Populist, Townsend, and environmental movements) regularly have caused state legislators to make laws that limit the consequences of capitalist growth. The difference is one of degree. Offsetting constituency pressures are uneven in the states. Indeed, the responsiveness of some states to popular measures itself creates new comparative advantages for other states. Interstate competition makes state policy-makers in progressive states immediately aware of the economic consequences of limits on policy affecting private investment.[25]

Given that so much of domestic policy, including economic development policy, was exercised autonomously by states for most of American history and all of American industrialization, the difference in state and national attention to short-term comparative advantage has had cumulative and far-reaching effects over time (on path dependence, see Pierson 2000). State policy-makers had less freedom than national policy-makers to treat workers, including female and child workers, as something other than factor endowments (and if constituents in Massachusetts and New York give lawmakers in those states some freedom temporarily, lawmakers in other states could advertise their comparative advantage). The record of states as policy laboratories is extensive. States have used their discretion to build canals, highways, universities, and prisons; to restrict business collusion and to entice business to incorporate and invest within their boundaries; to resist the entry of potential welfare recipients and hazardous waste; and to serve as policy laboratories, for both civil rights and Jim Crow laws, for old age, mothers' pension programs, unemployment and work injury insurance, and punitive workfare programs; for pioneering air quality standards and for the Sagebrush rebellion against federal environmental standards. Given the importance of economic competitiveness for the states, however, it should come as no surprise that innovations that remained in state hands have tended to accommodate states' short-term economic advantages.

Instead of the decisive, independent national policy-making that Madison envisioned, the Constitution made it likely that national policy decisions would reflect inventive, post hoc logrolling compromises among a supermajority of diverse regional interests. Tariffs, river and harbor improvements, antipoverty programs, economic development initiatives, defense contracts, and academic research spending all illustrate this tendency. The U.S. government was designed to impede the authoritative redistribution of national resources, and for better or worse, that design still shapes the development of American public policy. The Constitutional revolution of the New Deal was very real. It enabled the national government to assume control of many state redistributive and regulatory policy innovations that threatened the comparative advantages of states: social insurance, civil rights, and environmental laws provide three major examples. From the beginning, states' rights became a national political battlefield because it served as a proxy for so many fundamental policy conflicts in American history (see, for example, McDonald 2000).

The Constitution skewed politics by shaping the way business and labor advanced their interests as the republic industrialized. Beyond tariffs, states were the most important battlegrounds for economic development policy. America's antitrust laws of the late nineteenth century prevented American businesses from colluding in the way foreign governments allowed home businesses to collude. Business leaders, however, discovered that public officials in a few states (New Jersey and later Delaware) would permit businesses to consolidate with relatively little interference in return for taxes and fees (modest costs for a large corporation, but substantial revenue producers for small states). This interstate corporate charter-mongering permitted firms to merge into politically and economically formidable unitary organizations. Arguably, the dominance of corporations was the most significant distinguishing feature of the twentieth-century American political economy. The rise of the corporation led in turn to exceptional forms of business and labor political mobilization in the United States, and it contributed to exceptional domestic policy outcomes (Robertson 2000, 100–106).

Finally, the Constitution has profoundly shaped political party strategies for controlling policy-making processes and outcomes. While the Constitution created conditions that allowed American businesses to merge when they could not collude, it allowed American politicians to collude but not to merge into programmatic political parties. The protection of state comparative advantages focused party competition at the state level. In national government, politicians could gain by colluding with politicians from other states without subordinating themselves to a disciplined party organization. The fragmentation of policy authority rewarded elected officials for creating long-term alliances of office-holding (American political parties) and using short-term, opportunistic coalitions to advance specific policy outcomes. This persistence of sectional rivalry in American political development is not a completely unanticipated consequence of Constitutional design. The separation of public offices, constituencies, and interests severely limited the disciplined cross-state party control of candidates, money, or philosophy that were prerequisites of programmatic parties in wealthy democracies comparable to the United States.

Madison, too, became the willing prisoner of the Constitution that fell short of his hopes. His *Federalist* letters had to defend it in its entirety, despite private reservations he was expressing to Jefferson. He had to help engineer the first important logrolling agreement in American policy history, permitting the national assumption of debt in return for terms favorable to Virginia and the location of the national capital on the Potomac (see Kiewiet, this volume). He had to help create political parties, using states' rights to oppose an independent national antisedition law. And as president he had to defend a national interest in the military and a national bank. Madison's public career after 1787 is rich with strategic adjustments to the Constitution, adjustments that provide a revealing portrait of the opportunities and constraints the Constitution has imposed on the development of American politics.

Notes

The author much appreciates helpful comments, conversations, and insights from Sam Kernell, Dan Wirls, Emery Lee, Dennis Judd, Rogan Kersh, Lyman Sargent, Linda Kowalcky, and three anonymous reviewers.

1. Historian Donald J. Pisani (1987) recently observed: "Surprisingly, given the strenuous debate over Charles A. Beard's economic interpretation of the Constitution, little has been written about the direct relationship between the Constitution and American political development."

2. Bringing order to the territory controlled by a state sometimes required considerable effort. It was not simple for Massachusetts, for example, to establish state government authority within its jurisdiction; see Handlin and Handlin 1969.

3. Some of the Framers themselves discounted the small versus large state distinction as misleading. Both may be understood as strategic efforts to redefine interstate conflicts on more favorable terms. Madison noted that it was "[p]retty well understood that the real difference of interests lay, not between the large & small but between N. & Southn. States. The institution of slavery & its consequences formed the line of demarcation" (Farrand 1966, 2, 10); this comment may have been tactical (see below). Hamilton on June 29 observed: "The only considerable distinction of interests, lay between the carrying and non-carrying States, which divide instead of uniting the largest States" (ibid. 1, 466). The small versus large state distinction was politically useful to states other than Virginia, Pennsylvania, and Massachusetts—especially the commercially vulnerable Middle States (see below)—that sought a coalition of shared interests threatened by population-based representation plans (Paterson in ibid., 178). The shifting voting alignments of the Convention belie the claim that either the ten small states or the three large states shared a common purpose across issues.

4. In terms of a policy-making process, 1787 provided a "policy window" (Kingdon 1995) in which economic and political problems, solutions, and political incentives provided an opportunity for a policy entrepreneur such as Madison to couple problems, solutions, and interests. Mouw and MacKuen (1992, 102 n 1) use the term "strategic agenda" to refer to the ways that legislators frame policy choices, observing that "skillful politicians alter the attractiveness of any proposal by modifying its mixture of policy considerations."

5. For example, at the Annapolis Convention, Madison approached Abraham Clark, then a leading figure in the New Jersey state legislature, to persuade the state to instruct its congressional delegates to return to Virginia's coalition opposing Jay's proposed revision of the treaty with Spain (Murrin 1987, 59).

6. The private correspondence and secret Convention deliberations reveal more about Madison's ideas about the Constitution than his letters in *The Federalist*, because his arguments in these letters defended a plan he privately thought to be flawed and reflect a degree of post hoc rationalization (see below; also see Hobson 1979, 217; Matthews 1995, 15). When this paper refers to Madison's ideas, it refers to ideas that he expressed through September 1787; his political ideas evolved substantially as his political experience and the nation's evolved further. It may be fruitful to try to assemble a coherent political philosophy from "countless and unsystematic" writings (ibid., xvii), but that is not the point here. Here the goal is to reconstruct the basic elements of Madison's policy strategy for altering the American policy-making process and outcomes at the moment he exercised influence on the design of the Constitution. In that sense, it is a task of limited scope, though one that requires an equally systematic approach. The

effort is more akin to a systematic analysis of other American policy strategists such as John R. Commons, Florence Kelley, Hyman Rickover, and J. Edgar Hoover (on policy strategy, see Robertson 1988, and 2000, 13–16).

7. "[P]erfect freedom [of trade] is the System which would be my choice," he wrote to Monroe (MP 8, 334; McCoy 1980b, 121; Matthews 1995; Rakove 1996, 314).

8. The priority that Madison gave to Virginia's interests is indicated by his shifting position on the important issue of federal assumption of state debts. His support for the national assumption of state debts was firm in the 1780s, when that position worked to Virginia's advantage (but his position changed by 1790, when Virginia would no longer enjoy relative benefit from that action; Ferguson 1961, 210–11).

9. At no other point in his career would Madison's political economy be as close to that of Alexander Hamilton as in May 1787. He had traveled a marked intellectual distance away from his more limited nationalism of his early 1780s career in Congress. Circumstances had made Madison disposed to a stronger national hand in the economy. Madison could support national powers of incorporation and internal improvement in theory by imagining the way these could work for Virginia, and could not yet imagine the way Hamilton would propose to use national economic power as secretary of the Treasury. The notion that economic sovereignty was anything but indivisible, or could be split between the national government and the states, must have seemed theoretically impossible to Madison before the Convention, even though Convention debate and compromise soon turned dual sovereignty into a political necessity.

10. Keith Dougherty (2001) valuably uses the concepts of public goods and joint products to specify the collective action problem of the Confederation requisition system. Dougherty characterizes state interests as private goods, but from the states' point of view, their public initiatives also were public goods. It is as reasonable to characterize the conflict over requisitions payments as a struggle between levels of government for the control of public goods.

11. James Wilson and George Washington also would identify state officials' autonomy as a fundamental problem of American governance during the Constitutional Convention (Wilson in Farrand 1966, 1, 133–34; 3, 51).

12. In his "Notes on Debates" in Congress for January 28, 1783, Madison alludes to Alexander Hamilton's application of this logic to the appointment of revenue collectors: "As an additional reason for the latter to be collected by officers under the appointment of Congress, he [Hamilton] signified that as the energy of the federal Govt. was evidently short of the degree necessary for pervading & uniting the States it was expedient to introduce the influence of officers deriving their emoluments from & consequently interested in supporting the power of, Congress." In a footnote, Madison criticizes Hamilton's statement, not out of disagreement with it, but because it backfired politically at the time (MP 6, 142–43).

13. "All civilized societies are divided into different interests and factions, as they happen to be creditors or debtors—Rich or poor—husbandmen, merchants or manufacturers—members of different religious sects—followers of different political leaders—inhabitants of different districts—owners of different kinds of property &c. &c." (MP 9, 355).

14. In the preceding sentences, Madison states: "If an enlargement of the sphere is found to lessen the insecurity of private rights, it is not because the impulse of a common interest or passion is less predominant in this case with the majority, because a common interest or passion is less apt to be felt and the requisite combinations less easy to be formed by a great than a small number. The Society becomes broken into a greater variety of interests, of pursuits, of passions, which check each other, whilst those who may feel a common sentiment have less opportunity of communication and concert" (MP 9, 354–55). I am interpreting Madison here to use the terms "common interest," "sentiment," and "passion" as common to a majority, but not the entire polity.

15. The idea of a "true" polity-wide interest resurfaces in Federalist 51, where the possibility exists for the national interest to influence policy unimpeded by parochial concerns: "In the extended republic of the United States, and among the great variety of interests, parties, and sects which it embraces, a coalition of a majority of the whole society could seldom take place on any other principles than those of justice and the general good; whilst there being thus less danger to a minor from the will of a major party, there must be less pretext, also, to provide for the security of the former, by introducing into the government a will not dependent on the latter, or, in other words, a will independent of the society itself" (Hamilton, Madison, and Jay 1961b, 352–53).

16. What did Madison mean by a "disinterested & dispassionate umpire"? One view is that Madison, an eighteenth-century patrician, hoped that diverse interests would neutralize each other in a new national government "and thereby allow liberally educated, rational men . . . to promote the public good in a disinterested manner" (Wood 1987, 83–84, 92; see Matthews 1995, 85). It is not likely that a politician as thoughtful and experienced as Madison could find this simple answer satisfactory, however. He had more than enough firsthand evidence that "[e]nlightened statesmen will not always be at the helm" (Federalist 10, in Hamilton, Madison, and Jay 1961b, 60). His belief that angels would not govern men came from experience, not theology.

17. Lance Banning (1995, 209) directly challenges the notion that Madison ever "wanted and expected an increasing concentration of decision-making at the federal level." But Banning can only speculate about Madison's national emphasis before and during the Convention, and especially about the reasons that Madison supported a national veto of state laws. He holds that Madison's strong support for a large republic in Federalist 10 had few limits *when he was concentrating only on the need for new securities for 'justice'*"; Banning argues that this implicit limitation on Madison's nationalism "helps account for his determined

struggle for a federal negative on local laws." In Banning's view, the claim that Madison sought unlimited national power is necessarily linked to the view that national legislators would be inherently wiser than state legislators. The argument here is that Madison assumed that national legislators would have the same character flaws as state counterparts, but would be led by the structure of incentives, including a national veto, to promote the national interest. Madison's view of national powers, at least in the economy, was more likely limited by his view that free markets promoted the national interest, an assumption he shared with most other delegates. For example, when George Mason advocated national power to impose sumptuary laws, Elbridge Gerry responded that "the law of necessity is the best sumptuary law"; Madison's Virginia delegation voted with seven other states to defeat the proposal of their fellow delegate (Farrand 1966, 2, 344).

18. In a sense, *Federalist* 9 and 10 may be read as elaborate rhetorical exercises in begging the question. In these numbers, Hamilton and Madison respectively argue for the value of a confederation of small republics, in effect suggesting that their opponents occupied an extreme position of disputing the need for any kind of national policy-making. On the tendency of Federalists to argue publicly that the states would continue to dominate under the new Constitution, see Riker 1996, 41.

19. It would have been impolitic to extend the argument to the states in *Federalist* 51, since the function of these letters was to allay New Yorkers' fears that the Constitution would inhibit their state policy-makers' pursuit of economic advantages that were in their interest. After the Convention, and in public argument, he had to state the same point in a way that would persuade the New York constituency of the implausibility of the fear that national policy would threaten them. For New York readers, Madison necessarily emphasized the geographical dimension of the concept (*Federalist* 51, in Hamilton, Madison, and Jay 1961b, 351).

20. On August 18, Madison and Pickney each had proposed to add the power "To grant charters of incorporation" to the enumerated powers of Congress (Farrand 1966, 2, 325). When Franklin proposed to give Congress the specific power to cut "canals where deemed necessary" on September 14, Madison moved to enlarge the motion into a power to grant charters of incorporation. Randolph seconded the motion; Wilson defended it. Sherman opposed the canal motion, arguing that the costs would be nationalized, but the benefits would be local. King opposed the broader national power to incorporate, cautioning that it would cause political rifts in the states, raise the contentious issue of a public bank, and threaten ratification by associating the Constitution with mercantile monopolies. The question on the national authority to provide for canals was defeated, with only Pennsylvania, Virginia, and Georgia voting in favor. The broader motion to authorize national corporations then "fell of course" (ibid., 615–16).

21. The Virginia Plan permitted the new legislature to "legislate in all cases

to which the separate States are incompetent, or in which the harmony of the United States may be interrupted by" individual state enactments, and it proposed that the national legislature possess the right "to negative all laws passed by the several Sates, contravening in the opinion of the National Legislature the articles of the Union." Slonim (2000) sees a distinction between the national veto described in Madison's correspondence and the national veto in the Virginia Plan, but whether the distinction made a substantive difference for Madison is doubtful. Under either formulation, Madison's national policy-makers would be motivated to measure state policy by the standard of national policy interests.

22. The Constitution evidently gave the commercially vulnerable Middle States the settlement they desired. Delaware and New Jersey, the first and third states to ratify, approved the Constitution unanimously and expeditiously. Maryland and Connecticut were among the next four states to ratify, and they did so by margins of 76 percent and 85 percent, respectively. Other than Georgia, which ratified unanimously, none of the other states ratified by such high percentages.

23. A different but compatible view of the Convention might be that it crafted institutions that established ex ante incentive structures for long-term cooperative behavior among independent and opportunistic organizations (see Williamson 1983).

24. There is no reason to think that Madison's design would prove as stable and enduring as the Constitution, for example. Madison's national government might have found state secession a far greater threat in 1798 or 1832.

25. A Massachusetts manufacturer who was critical of his state's Progressive-era social policies acidly observed that "[f]or the last generation, Massachusetts has allowed itself to become the social laboratory in which all kinds of freak legislation has been tried out for the benefit of the rest of the country" (McSweeney 1917).

Chapter 9

The Madisonian Scheme to Control the National Government

JENNA BEDNAR

Madison's Testament on the Vices of the United States and Advice for Its Salvation

The title of this essay might be surprising. Certainly, Madison set out to control the state governments by *expanding* the powers of the national government. But no theory of federalism is complete without a provision to draw and maintain the boundaries on all governments, including the national government. Most likely, the proposed government would have failed ratification had the Constitution's opponents continued to believe that the state governments would be diminished to administrative subunits, as the political Madison well understood. Therefore, he devoted much thought to controlling the national government, and the resulting theory, especially the separation of powers component, has been his greatest contribution to the study of political institutions. This essay will examine the efficacy of Madison's plan.

Madison's scheme for controlling the national government is inseparable from his understanding of what was wrong with the state governments. After an extensive study of classical confederacies (*The Papers of James Madison* [hereafter MP] 9, 3–24), Madison observed that in all unions where the states retained their sovereignty, the union eventually collapsed from interstate rivalry. He then recorded his thoughts on the problems with the American government under the Articles of Confederation. Famously labeling the problems "vices," his notes are a laundry list of the intransigence of the state governments, in their trespasses on one another, in their wildly divergent laws, and in their encroachments on the national government (see appendix). It was imperative that any new government reduce the ability of the states to harm the union.

Madison's concerns extended beyond making federalism work: he was worried that state governmental opportunism would forever tarnish republican democracy.[1] Several state legislatures had shown tendencies to ignore the rights of their citizens and otherwise lean toward tyrannical behavior unbridled by their constitution or bills of rights to such an extent that some called for an end to the experiment with republican governance. While for Hamilton (and others) the solution was to establish a monarchical system similar to Britain's, Madison was reluctant to give up hope for representative democracy. If the institutions of aggregation could be perfected, he reasoned, then republican government would succeed.

To Madison, the solution to both problems, federal and democratic, was clear: a strengthened national government would overcome the vices of the present system, thereby serving as double-cure, both by stabilizing the union and relegitimizing republican government. A strong national government, with direct powers over the people, would be necessary to patrol conflict between the states. It would also field better politicians and reduce the problems of faction. Republics can be too small, Madison reasoned in *Federalist* 10 and 51.[2] The larger union would have two advantages: it could draw its candidates from a larger pool, increasing the chance of getting an excellent public servant, and the larger union would dilute the potency of factions.

Madison's primary point seems vindicated: the subordination of state governments to a strong national government does appear to reduce interstate conflict. And the experiment in republican government has long proven successful. But the two prongs of Madison's solution—a decentralized, layered system with a strong center—each create problems of their own. At the same time that it created a new interest—the national government—for the citizens to control, Madison's federal solution erected obstacles for effective republican government. Institutional mechanisms stitched onto electoral control as "auxiliary precautions" (*Federalist* 51) do not make a seamless federal fabric; flaws remain that can doom the union. At its conclusion, this essay will suggest how judicial review is consistent with Madison's objectives and can repair some of these weaknesses of interbranch conflict and electoral control.

Section 2 examines Madison's political science to control the national government, beginning with his arguments that the national government would not need to be controlled. Sections 3 and 4 follow by addressing the weaknesses of institutional mechanisms and electoral control, respectively. Section 5 concludes by advocating the usefulness of judicial review to perfect federalism's operation.

The Control Mechanisms

Despite his focus on the states' propensity for shirking on their obligations to the federal union and burden-shifting on one another, Madison had to answer to critics of the Constitution who were worried about the strength of the new national government. As a political pragmatist, his first responses were strategic: he tried to calm fears about the center's power with assurances that the national government would have little motivation to encroach upon the states or upon citizen rights. But as political theorist, he carefully constructed an institutional framework to guarantee through structure that the federal government would not behave opportunistically. His institutional mechanism combined institutional checks and balances at the federal level and—less important—incorporation of states into the decision-making process. Finally, and most fundamentally, through the institutional mechanisms the electorate could be the ultimate watchdogs of federalism.

SELF-REGULATING FEDERALISM

In most of his rhetoric, Madison forcefully rejected the possibility that the national government would encroach on the state governments by constructing a theory of self-regulating federalism. Madison and his colleagues often tried to deflect concerns that the national government would trespass on the rights of states and citizens by suggesting that the national government would have little opportunity or motivation to do so. Writing long before the welfare state was imagined, Madison and Hamilton both argued that the national government was needed primarily to promote the defense of the union,[3] while normal police powers and day-to-day government functions would be performed by the states. Madison wrote in *Federalist* 45: "The operations of the federal government will be most extensive and important in times of war and danger; those of the State governments, in times of peace and security. As the former periods will probably bear a small proportion to the latter, the State governments will here enjoy [an] advantage over the federal government." To this defense he appends an equilibrium-based argument nudging citizens to arm the federal government as completely as possible: "The more adequate, indeed, the federal powers may be rendered to the national defense, the less frequent will be those scenes of danger which might favor their ascendancy over the governments of the particular States." He cleverly inverts fears of the national government's power into a call for supporting it all the more: the stronger the national government's defense capacity, the less need we have for defense; therefore, the less need we will have for the federal government generally, and the less it will come to dominate the state governments.

In the blustery beginning of *Federalist* 45, Madison argues that in light of the bloodshed of the Revolution, it is "preposterous" to think that the federal government would derogate state powers, so dearly bought. He diverts attention from the concern at hand—central government encroachment— by saying that the states are much more likely to threaten the center than the center do harm to the states. This was not a sentiment he reserved for the newspapers. In debate, too, he argued that the national government would have little incentive to overwhelm the states. While allowing that the central government would have augmented powers, he introduced and rejected the hypothetical that "indefinite power" be vested in the national government, and the states reduced to "corporations dependent on the Genl. Legislature":

> Why should it follow that the Genl. Govt. wd. take from the States any branch of their power as far as its operation was beneficial, and its continuance desireable to the people? In some of the States, particularly Connecticut, all the Townships are incorporated, and have a certain limited jurisdiction. Have the Representatives of the Townships in the Legislature of the State ever endeavored to despoil the Townships of any part of their local authority? . . . The relation of a Genl. Govt. to the States is parallel. (MP 10, 67–68)

The states had little to fear from the federal government: no precedent exists for a higher level of government usurping power from a lower. The federal government would have no motivation to encroach.

While the remainder of this section will detail Madison's scheme for controlling the center, it is helpful to keep in mind Madison's denial of a federal encroachment problem. While Madison, as a nationalist, was not opposed to a greater centralization of the government, he consistently expressed confidence that a combination of interinstitutional oversight, state government involvement, and electoral control were sufficient devices to check whatever stray motivations for usurpation might possess the federal government.

INTERINSTITUTIONAL OVERSIGHT

In Madison's scheme of harnessing conflict to invoke obedience, separation of powers is without question the crown jewel—Madison's most enduring contribution to the theory of political institutions. Breaking with the parliamentary model, Madison advocated the fragmentation of executive, legislative, and judicial power at the national level. In so doing, Madison implicitly acknowledged that federalism, in its rawest form as decentralized government, is not self-regulating but needs institutional support.

Institutions create incentive environments; rules and organizational structures affect individual behavior by changing the means to achieve desired ends. One theory of human motivation posits that we are all essentially selfish. We would be unlikely to deny ourselves opportunities and therefore are incapable of self-restraint, but our jealousy prompts us to monitor one another's actions closely. Madison applies this theory of human nature to government; governments are groups of selfish men and therefore also likely to act selfishly. Brilliantly, he transforms vice into virtue by manipulating the institutions of government to mimic the forces of selfishness in society: "[A]mbition must be able to counteract ambition." Madison's theoretical trick is to fragment government, while leaving the components partially dependent on one another through checks and balances. The antagonism within governmental parts induces a self-regulating whole.

To Madison, separation of powers was necessary for "preservation of liberty" and the prevention of tyrannical laws.[4] Madison fused protection of the people with maintenance of federalism, and separation of powers could help achieve both ends, by providing a "double security" (*Federalist* 51): "[So] it is to be hoped . . . the two governments possess each the means of preventing or correcting unconstitutional encroachments of the other" (MP 14, 218). While separation of powers might contribute to governmental efficiency because of task specialization, it seems far more likely to stall government action as the distinct interests bargain. For this reason, stagnation is evidence that separation of powers is working according to theory, because gridlock means that no one interest is able to overwhelm another. By frustrating attempts to dominate, separation of powers preserves federalism and protects people from tyranny.

In Madison's theory, separation of powers has two necessary ingredients: distinct but partially overlapping power, and independence. Overlapping power allows one branch to oversee the actions of another. In a 1785 reply to questions asked by his friend Caleb Wallace, in the course of agreeing with Wallace that amendment was necessary, he slipped in a comment about the importance of having some remedy available to one branch that believes another has superseded its powers (MP 8, 355): interbranch conflict was on his mind, and rather than promote a unified government, he sought an institutional outlet for internal disagreement. The cousin to separate powers, bicameralism, further unravels the monolith of parliamentary government by fragmenting power within the legislature. In the same letter to Wallace, Madison denigrated the design of the existing Senate, but "bad as it is, it is often a usefull bitt in the mouth of the house of Delegates" (MP 8, 351). In the Constitutional Convention, speaking on the proposed Senate, Madison argued: "[A]ll business liable to abuses is made to pass thro' separate hands, the one being a check on the other" (ibid. 10, 76).

Separation of powers can work only if the institutions have a motivation to cry foul. Task specialization is not enough to break the team mentality of the government. Their objectives and incentives must be independent as well. "Each department should have a will of its own," writes Madison in *Federalist* 51. His appreciation for the difficulties in achieving independence grew. The Virginia Plan called for the lower legislative house to appoint an upper, and the two chambers together would appoint the other branches. Staggered terms would "ensure" independence. Following the Convention, he was much more supportive of fragmenting the elections and the constituencies of the separate branches and the two legislative houses. Electoral separation prevents the coagulation of interests, thereby exploiting institutional self-interest by inducing the branches to be watchful of one another's actions. In a unified government, whistle-blowers lose their jobs when their party is punished at the polls. With separation of powers, constituents are not restricted to such a blunt instrument; they may retain their district's representative while rejecting their president.

Even when the prudence of independence and overlapping powers is seen, it is still difficult to work out in practice a combination of institutions that can carry it off. Certainly Madison's vision of the government evolved with experience: he seems to have grown more convinced of the necessity to disentangle the branches and put them on much more equal footing. If the mechanisms to provide independence are functioning correctly, a consequence is conflicting interests that need to be aired and reconciled. One feature that the remainder of this section will highlight is different mechanisms proposed to mediate intergovernmental disputes.

While separation of powers promotes contest and compromise, if it is at all imbalanced, it alone does not provide a means to halt interbranch encroachment, nor does it guarantee the Constitution. A complete institutional recipe must include some method of binding government action through constitutional review. Instinctively, the judiciary seems a likely candidate, but Madison and his colleagues were wary of vesting so much power in an unelected body,[5] and Madison doubted that the judiciary alone would be strong enough to counter the other two branches (Rakove 2002). Instead, Madison was intrigued by an institution in the 1777 constitution of New York, a Council of Revision (MP 8, 351). The Council of Revision joined the judiciary to the executive in a body that would have power to veto national legislation, as well as reject the legislature's vetoes of state legislation.

The Council of Revision has its roots in the British model. New York altered the British institution in two ways, and Madison seems to have supported both revisions. First, under the British model, the executive had the exclusive power to veto legislation. Madison favored including the judiciary, where the benefit of its "wisdom and weight" would be "incontestable" (MP 10, 36). At the same time, he did not propose transferring the whole power to the judiciary. Even apart from Madison's doubts about the judiciary's capacity, including the executive was critical to the political success of the proposal. Some Convention delegates opposed the measure, believing that to give the judiciary review powers was to give it the power to legislate.

A second change that New York made to the British model was in the potential to override the veto. The British model had an absolute veto: the New York legislature could override the veto if two-thirds of its members repassed the legislation.[6] While the Council of Revision failed to get enough support in the Convention, it demonstrates further Madison's dual scheme of interinstitutional checks and electoral control: the mechanism is purely institutional, but is careful to include the popularly controlled executive, rather than the judiciary alone.

With the demise of the Council of Revision, attention returned to the judiciary for legislative review. Madison never was a strong proponent of judicial review. He fails to mention it in the Virginia Plan.[7] When he did write about it, he was wary of granting power to a branch so removed from the people, but at the same time, worried that it was too weak to intermediate government disputes. Later in life, he also expressed frustration that the court tended to develop broad constitutional theories from specific cases.

Madison and his contemporaries viewed the court as the natural arbiter in interstate disputes and also thought the court could monitor state transgressions on federal jurisdictions, although in this latter capacity Madison was dubious about the judiciary's ability to enforce its rulings, without force to back up its words. If Madison had had his way, of course, the national legislature would have had the bite of the negative on state legislation, so judiciary weakness wouldn't matter.[8] Despite his expression of confidence in *Federalist* 39,[9] Madison worried that the judiciary still would not have enough influence to control the state governments.[10]

Madison's concerns about the judiciary were more complex: he also worried that it might have too *much* power relative to the other branches. He attributes to it a last-mover advantage: "[As] the Courts are generally the last in making their decision, it results to them, by refusing or not refusing to execute a law, to stamp it with its final character. This makes the Judiciary Dept paramount in fact to the Legislature, which was never intended, and can never be proper" (ibid. 11, 293).

Statutory interpretation extends to the judiciary legislative power reserved for the popularly controlled legislative branch, a threat that touched a particularly sore nerve with Madison, who wanted to ensure that republican democracy would work, by making the people's voice as effective as possible. Were the judiciary to grow too accustomed to intervening in intragovernmental disputes, it "might subvert forever, and beyond the possible reach of any rightful remedy, the very constitution, which all were instituted to preserve" (ibid. 17, 312).

Madison's confidence in the judiciary did seem to grow over time, as did his sense of the urgency of having effective checks on the legislature. The Alien and Sedition Acts of the Adams administration taught him that other structural safeguards could not be relied upon. In an 1830 letter to Edward Everett he cites the turnover in the next election as vindication that political safeguards work anyway, through the electoral process. At the same time, he allows more room for the judiciary to review the constitutionality of federal legislative and executive action, although he cannot help but in the same breath write that "the power has not always been rightly exercised" (Hunt 9, 393). Of this, he was perhaps referring to the Court's decision in *McCullough v. Maryland*, which he criticized in a series of letters to Spencer Roane in 1821 (ibid. 9, 55–63, 65–68). While Madison did not fashion himself to be an expert on the intricacies of law, he believed that constitutional interpretation ought to arise from a series of decisions, rather than the court expounding its own theory, abstractly, in the midst of reconciling a specific dispute. The court is particularly at fault when it embellishes its own power in this manner. The means to alter the power structure is available in the Constitution, and Madison believed that the court should not circumvent the established procedure of amendment.

In sum, interinstitutional oversight works through a combination of independence and dependence. Institutions should have distinct wills but need one another to act. When this balance is achieved, the federal government is less likely to behave opportunistically, whether by encroaching on the state governments or by tyrannizing its citizens.

STATE SUPERVISION

Madison's skepticism of the abilities of state governments is well known, and so we must unravel his theory here with care. Without a doubt, much of his writing is rhetoric to gain support for the Constitution. However, the theory is consistent with interinstitutional oversight because it works through a combination of independence and dependence, and while it is the least elaborated component of Madison's system of constraints on the federal government, it is one of the most cited today.

Although we remember *Federalist* 51 as a defense of separation of powers, in it Madison describes a parallel system for maintaining the power balance between state and federal governments: "the different governments will control each other, at the same time that each will be controlled by itself" (*Federalist* 51). States supervise federal action both from within and without the federal apparatus because the Constitution has made the national government dependent upon them to act. In correspondence with Thomas Jefferson, Madison wrote: "This dependence of the General, on the local authorities, seems effectually to guard the latter against any dangerous encroachments of the former" (MP 10, 211). The entanglement of state and federal interests in the national legislature makes it unlikely that a federal interest will evolve. Reminiscent of his earlier assurances that the national government will have no desire to encroach on the states, he submitted in later correspondence that: "encroachments of [state sovereignty] are more to be apprehended from impulses given to it by a majority of the States seduced by expected advantages, than from the love of Power in the Body itself, controuled as it *now* is by its responsibility to the Constituent Body" (Hunt 9, 58). Federal encroachment, if it occurs, is likely to be from state capture of the federal government. The federal government itself has no desire to increase its power.

Within the government, states have many avenues to express their interests. In *Federalist* 39, Madison describes how the Constitution is both federal and national: by federal he means that the states are involved in the central level decision-making, and he cites the Senate, the electoral college, and state ratification of the Constitution, as well as the "natural attachment" (*Federalist* 46) that citizens have to their own state, as evidence. The American formulation of bicameralism protected state interests in two ways: it provided for equal representation of the states, and until the 17th Amendment, state legislatures appointed the senators.

Madison blamed the state legislatures for the anemic performance of the union under the Articles; if he had had his druthers, the last thing he would have advocated was perpetuating their power in the new federal union.[11] Yet we remember him (disguised as Publius) as one of equal representation's more eloquent advocates, and state representation in the federal decision-making structure is considered by many to be an integral part of the Madisonian vision for governmental reform.

The resolution of this inconsistency is to be found in Madison's practicality and political skills: he believed that the institutional structure would minimize the danger posed by state intervention in the federal government, and he knew that equal representation was very popular and would increase the Constitution's chance for ratification. So we find him writing persuasive passages in the *Federalist* in support of the institutionalization of state input in the federal government. In *Federalist* 62 he alludes to the compromise that brought about equal representation and praises it for maintaining state autonomy, and especially that it is a useful mechanism for incorporating state input in national decision-making: "In this spirit it may be remarked, that the equal vote allowed to each state, is at once a constitutional recognition of the portion of sovereignty remaining in the individual states, and an instrument for preserving that residuary sovereignty."

Ever the statesman, he continues the thought by criticizing the position he had held prior to the vote on July 16: "So far the equality ought to be no less acceptable to the large than to the small states; since they are not less solicitous to guard by every possible expedient against an improper consolidation of the states into one simple republic. . . . No law or resolution can now be passed without the concurrence . . . of a majority of the states" (*Federalist* 62). Equal representation in the Senate will help to stabilize the union by ensuring the balance of power between state and federal governments.

Several other institutions incorporate state input in federal decision-making, as Madison delineates in *Federalist* 45. Not only will states be represented in the Senate, but the president cannot be elected without the states, and the House members, although directly elected by the people, will likely have state legislative experience.[12]

Structural political safeguards were just the first stage in the system of state protection as envisaged by the Founders. The states could also work outside of the formal structure by protesting when the federal government overstepped its bounds. James Wilson, delegate of Pennsylvania, describes the following chain reaction:

> The States having in general a similar interest, in case of any proposition in the National Legislature to encroach on the State Legislatures, he conceived a general alarm wd. take place in the National Legislature itself, that it would communicate itself to the State Legislatures, and wd. finally spread among the people at large. The Genl. Govt. will be as ready to preserve the rights of the States as the latter are to preserve the rights of individuals; all the members of the former, having a common interest, as representatives of all the people of the latter, to leave the State Govts. in possession of what the people wish them to retain. (Farrand 1966, 1, 356)

Wilson refers to the state legislatures responding to the cry of alarm from the U.S. senators. Madison echoes this argument in *Federalist* 45: "But ambitious encroachments of the federal government, on the authority of the State governments, would not excite the opposition of the single State, or of a few States only. They would be signals of general alarm. Every government would espouse the common cause." Ignoring any collective action prob-lem,[13] much less the possibility that the federal government's encroachment may be welcomed by some of the states, Madison argued that the states would watch federal action closely and jointly protest any violation.

When the Adams administration's passage of the Alien and Sedition Acts infuriated Madison for its encroachments on civil liberties, he federalized a political issue by enlisting the Virginia assembly (along with his colleague Thomas Jefferson, in Kentucky) to challenge the administration's moves (MP 17, 189–90, 303–351). States not only had the right to protest unconstitutional federal activity; it was their duty as an obedient member of the union to protect the union and maintain the constitutional covenant with the people.

Later in life he continued to support his position and the decision to write the Virginia Resolutions, although he regretted South Carolina's reference to the Resolutions while it attempted to nullify congressional legislation (Hunt 9, 383–403). While it seems that Madison believed in the protective force of political safeguards, particularly state involvement, on balance it is a poorly worked out component of his theory. Its greatest impact was no doubt as the rhetoric expressed to win over the states' rights constituency.

ELECTORAL CONTROL

If in his writing Madison had mentioned popular sovereignty only occa-sionally, or only in the propagandist *Federalist*, we might surmise that he praised the Constitution's protection of the electorate for strategic reasons, to quell the fears of dissenters distrustful of the power of the new national government. Instead, he was concerned about the future of republican gov-ernment. He planned to rescue popular sovereignty by perfecting the means by which people control their government. Inarguably, his was a federalism pulled by a joint team of national and state governments, but the people held the whip and reins. "The federal and State governments are in fact but dif-ferent agents and trustees of the people, constituted with different powers, and designed for different purposes" (*Federalist* 46). Even interinstitutional competition had its limits: in his proposed Council of Revision, if the pop-ularly controlled legislature could muster a supermajority, then it could over-rule the executive and judiciary and proceed with its proposed legislation.

The people were not to blame for the poor performance of the union un-der the Articles of Confederation. He was confident that if the people had the right instruments for governance—those that captured their reason while controlling their passion—then no government could better guaran-tee individual rights than a representative democracy (MP 14, 426–27). His faith in the people extended beyond appropriate use of the tools available to an ability to correct outcomes in the infrequent moments when the institutions fail. He relished the electorate's rejection of the Adams administration after its transgressions (Hunt 9, 392).

Madison favored elections by ballot (to preserve the election's integrity) with suffrage granted to as many citizens as practicable, although he was concerned that the poorer citizens might be tempted to sell their votes (MP 8, 353). While Madison stopped short of advocating that public officials be beholden to the instructions of their constituents (MP 12, 340–41), the design of the federal institutions and his rhetoric in support of it reflect his commitment to popular sovereignty. Indeed, as stated above, Madison's federal project was motivated by the desire to preserve electoral control.

Directly or indirectly, the people controlled all national institutions. Congress's bicameral structure tempered the House's passionate impulse with the Senate's longer view, and the executive might recruit seasoned leadership, but all were subject to electoral review (the Senate and president indirectly). And rather than construct a Bickelian criticism of the undemocratic judiciary, he optimistically pointed out that the people had indirect control over appointments, and underscored (twice repeating it in *Federalist* 39) that the judges would retain office only in cases of good behavior. The Constitution itself could be amended by the people, although only indirectly (through Article V). He did not support direct popular constitutional amendment. In *Federalist* 49 he criticized Jefferson's proposal for frequent or periodic review of the Constitution by the people, as it implied some flaw in the government and reduced the legitimacy of the Constitution. Here, his fear is not so much with the people's involvement, but the method of their involvement. He feared that passion had the potential to produce imperfect results that the people might later regret. Fully consistent with the rest of his proposals, a rejection of popular amendment is a means of perfecting republican democracy.

With so much control over the various engines of government, the people could become the ultimate protectors of the Constitution and of their own rights. If they did not approve of the activity of one of their governors, they had the power to remove him. State sovereignty was guaranteed through the watchful eyes of the general population, who would not tolerate federal encroachment unless they decided that it was in their own interest.

In sum, this brief review of Madison's proposals reveals a two-pronged system to control the national government, through interinstitutional competition (including state oversight) and electoral control. The next two sections consider the weaknesses in these approaches.

Credit Assignment and Federal Encroachment:
The Weakness of Interinstitutional Competition

Interinstitutional competition works through Madison's thesis of intertwining independence and dependence. Antagonism, spurred by independence, is necessary for the government to be self-regulating. But the branches of government might not always have an incentive to arrest one another's efforts to encroach; they are not automatic adversaries.

Consider the following argument about why states would serve as watchdogs. Madison records the following speech from James Wilson, delegate from Pennsylvania (and generally a supporter of Madison's plans): "He insisted that a jealousy would exist between the State Legislatures & the General Legislature. A private Citizen of a State is indifferent whether power be exercised by the Genl. or State Legislatures, provided it be exercised most for his happiness. His representative has an interest in its being exercised by the body to which he belongs. He will therefore view the National Legisl: with the eye of a jealous rival" (Farrand 1966, 1, 343–44).

Because the states are jealous of the attention that the federal government might receive from additional power, the states rebuke any federal attempt to encroach. Wilson, echoing Madison's sentiments, argues that the state legislators have incentives to be the providers of policy pleasing to its constituents, suggesting motivations for state encroachment.[14] The same drive for constituency service exists at the national level, and so Wilson's argument can be reversed, applied to the federal government to identify a motivation to encroach.

Political and institutional safeguards can depress or eliminate this motivation. These safeguards work in two ways: 1. by state interest penetration in the Senate and 2. by ambition counteracting ambition—that is, the branches checking one another's activity, presumably prepared to denounce one another. When these two conditions hold, states participate in the formation of federal interests or at the least can redraw any plan contrary to state interests. If state penetration fails to affect all of the federal branches, interbranch conflict will stifle any federal encroachment. This section will show how the federal structure and electoral connection work against these two conditions.

Political safeguards depend upon the infiltration of state interests in federal decision-making. Senators must remain true not just to their own state but also to *all* states, preserving state power against a greedy central government. Equal representation in the Senate was pitched (and still is) as a vertical federalism issue, as a way to maintain the balance of power between federal and state governments, an interpretation promulgated by some legal theorists and even the Supreme Court. In truth, equal representation in the Senate was always a small state–large state concern: the small states wanted protection from the large. While this is a federalism issue, it is a horizontal one about interstate rivalry, connected to the central government only through fears that the large states would, by their weight, capture the national government and discriminate against small state interests. It may be the case—perhaps, even, it often is—that one collection of states is able to capture just one branch of government at a time, thereby creating heterogeneous interests at the federal level, but this diversity is not automatic.

Madison's solution of state protest, exercised against the Alien and Sedition Acts, is an ineffective control on the center. It ignores the collective action problem inherent in expecting all states to band together in a costly exercise; it ignores that some federal encroachment may be welcomed by some states. It introduces the danger of misapplication (as with the Virginia and Kentucky resolutions), and worst, it has no teeth. Even when it works (and we must bear in mind that the most famous example, the protest against the Alien and Sedition Acts, was really about party politics and not about federalism), it does so only by enlisting some other institution for support, primarily by alerting the voters to the federal government's intransigence. It is symbolic, unsustainable, and therefore an ineffective deterrent.

The demands political safeguards place upon the electoral system contradict the system's design. Electoral competition causes each politician to act as Wilson suggested he would: to do what he can to please his own constituents. Each representative wants to be the one to provide demanded services. Naturally, when services are demanded in jurisdictions his level of government holds no responsibility over, he will do what he can to get his government involved. At times his objective will cause him to envy the successes of his compatriots in other levels of government; wherever possible, he will try to claim credit for those accomplishments. At some point, it is likely that the politician will be tempted to encroach upon the jurisdiction of another level of government, despite rules to the contrary.

Madison might counter that the second component of interinstitutional competition, separation of powers, would ensure that the House or executive would block Senate moves to encroach. But counteracting ambitions work only if interests are disparate, and these elected representatives have the identical urge to provide policy pleasing to their voters. Absent any ideological divisions over centralization, the branches of government are perfect partners to encroach upon state jurisdictions, and separation of powers (ironically) helps smooth any potential turf rivalries that might block (or highlight) the encroachment. At times, therefore, it is appropriate to treat the branches as agents differently abled but identically motivated. Federalism creates an *alignment* of interests in the electorally responsible federal branches; House, Senate, and president are motivated to work as a team to please their constituents, and sometimes they will be collectively motivated to pursue policy that encroaches on state jurisdiction.

Using decision-theoretic analysis,[15] we can define conditions favorable for encroachment.[16] Most intuitively, we think that a struggling central government would encroach upon a dimension where the states have been successful, to claim credit. Logically, the argument works as follows: assume retrospective voting and an optimal distribution of powers where the central government is more efficient at policy in its own jurisdiction than it is when it encroaches on state jurisdictions.[17] Voters have some threshold that defines their expectation for government performance; if performance falls below that threshold, they fail to re-elect. We might be tempted to think that any government whose expected evaluation lies below that re-election threshold would be a candidate for credit-claiming encroachment, but we can pursue a slightly more sophisticated analysis, in which we consider not just the expected value—the mean—but also the variance associated with the government's current policy. Because policies are plans adopted in a noisy—uncertain—environment, policies have distributions over the likelihood that they are successful. A tried-and-true policy might have a tight band of potential outcomes, where little can disrupt the outcome, while a new policy in an emerging problem area may have a broad range of possible effects, some feasible outcomes being beneficial, but others dismal failures.

When we consider both mean and variance, we see two conditions that make encroachment attractive to the central government. First, if its mean is already below the voter's re-election threshold, and its variance is low, then even random good shocks are unlikely to lift its performance to a level required for re-election. If the state is successful, or pursuing a high-variance policy that makes it more likely that it will please the voters, the central government might encroach to introduce some policy in a higher variance jurisdiction that allows it to share credit should the state succeed.

Even when the federal government's expected evaluation is above the threshold it may have an incentive to encroach. If it is pursuing a policy that has high mean, but also high variance, it may decide to encroach on state activity with a lower mean (but still above the threshold) and lower variance, as an insurance policy. The potential win-big payoff is lower, but it might reduce the probability of failure dramatically.

Notice that in this analysis the central government behaved as a single unit. All elected divisions of the government have the same set of interests:

please the voters. If the central government has a chance to give money for extra police on the streets and thereby have a chance to claim credit for reducing crime, president, Senate, and House will all support the program. Madison's scheme of interinstitutional competition works only if interbranch interests are diverse; here, as is often the case with federalism issues, they are identical.

In short, federalism is different from other concerns, especially from protection of individual liberty. The institutional structure designed to protect liberty cannot be relied upon to protect federalism, as the electoral mechanisms create a competition of sorts between the state and federal governments with the potential to destroy interinstitutional competition by aligning federal interests.

The Federal Paradox: The Weakness of Electoral Control

The structural weakness of the institutional safeguards, as laid out in Section 3, is minimized in Madison's theory because the institutions are backed up by the people. In *Federalist 46*, he writes:

> The adversaries of the Constitution seem to have lost sight of the people altogether in their reasonings on this subject; and to have viewed these different establishments not only as mutual rivals and enemies, but as uncontrolled by any common superior in their efforts to usurp the authorities of each other.... [T]he ultimate authority, ... resides in the people alone, and that it will not depend merely on the comparative ambition or address of the different governments whether either, or which of them, will be able to enlarge its sphere of jurisdiction at the expense of the other.... [T]he event in every case should ... depend on the sentiments and sanction of their common constituents. (*Federalist 46*)

In Madison's federalism, the people are sovereign. The secret to the efficacy of the political safeguards is that they express the people's will; the safeguards are backed by a public watchful that the union operates according to plan. Federalism creates a dual expression of their will: the people's needs are broken into tasks allocated to state and federal levels of government, and their will is determined through electoral mechanisms and administered through political institutions at both levels. If the federal government initiates legislation or executive action that violates the federal bargain, disrupting the balance of power between state and federal governments, the people will punish the federal government. Only if the people believe that the federal government would be better able to handle the jurisdiction than the states will the people fail to punish. Otherwise, as he writes in *Federalist 45–46* (and see Kramer 2001: 42), their "natural attachment" to the states causes them to prefer state empowerment and be suspicious of federal encroachment.

Madison's defense of the Constitution depicts the people holding the reins on their team, knowing the joint product they expect from their federal and state governments. They can balance each government's talents and ambitions to produce the best joint effort for union good; the allocation of powers between state and federal governments is efficient, or at least meets with public approval. Any federal encroachment is disarmed by an electorate loyal to the states. There are two problems with this argument: the impermanence of allegiance to the states, and the difficulty of managing a federation.

Madison argued that the citizens are most naturally attached to their states, considering themselves to be citizens of Virginia or New York first, and of the United States second. As the importance of the union grew, identities shifted; now, indisputably, we are Americans first: state identification, for some, is reduced to "currently, resident of Michigan." Riker fingered the upward shifting loyalties of citizens as the glue that binds a federal union together and makes centralization inevitable (1964, 108–16). At any rate, citizen attachment to the state is transient and cannot be relied upon to maintain the balance between federal and state powers. It is perhaps best understood as a product of the distribution of powers. It is not a reliable barrier to federal encroachment.

A second problem for the electorate is the complexity of managing a federation. While no one would argue that the federal system is straightforward and uncomplicated, many, including Madison, praise it for the increased opportunity for democratic control. By delineating jurisdictional responsibilities, the system takes advantage of specialization; requisites for national office are different than for state because the jobs are very different, and the people can elect those most suited for the specific job at hand. When coupled with staggered elections at one or both levels, as in the United States, it offers a compromise between consistency and reform. The frequency of elections and the number of offices on each ballot increase the importance of parties, and some have argued that parties contribute to stability in a federal system (Kramer 2000; Ordeshook and Shvetsova 1995; Ordeshook 1996). Parties that are most likely to prevent federal encroachment are integrated party systems, with a commonality of interests between organizational levels created by upward mobility and mutual dependence. When parties are decentralized, as in Canada, or weak, they are less successful at sustaining federalism.

Layering the political system introduces a problem for republican government underexamined to date: voters have no direct means to control the overall performance of their union. Instead, federalism's two-level republican system forces voters into a piecemeal articulation of the public interest. The central government cannot be relied upon to promote the most effective or efficient union. Central government representatives are rewarded when they provide policy pleasing to the voters; at times they will be motivated by electoral gain to encroach upon state powers in order to create ambiguity over policy responsibility, even in cases when such encroachment harms the overall efficiency of the union. While this is a moral hazard problem, it is one not handled by separation of powers, which depends upon "opposite and rival" interests: elected representatives in the central government have a common interest to claim responsibility for outcomes pleasing to the voters. This federal paradox diminishes the potential for electoral control.

Unfortunately, the Madisonian model of electoral control exceeds the capacity of boundedly rational voters; the federal system is complex, with a prism of responsibilities doled out between federal and state government, some shared, some separate. The allocation in some dimensions may be justified by a principle—for example, provision of public goods at the level required to absorb all externalities; but more often the assignment is somewhat haphazard, based upon historical precedent or, frankly, political convenience. Without defending optimality of the allocation of powers between state and federal governments, or even wanting to pretend that any frozen allocation can be considered perfect, there is much to be said for consistency and stability in the allocations in maintaining federal stability. But voters are not up to the task.[18] While they do seem able to spot major transgressions and respond, most federal opportunism pushes the boundaries of fuzzy parameters, often justifiable in the short-run (matching the voter's vision) or simply invisible until too late.

Even in the moments when the voters have a clear notion of what they want from the union, translating those orders into a division of tasks allotted to each level of government is more difficult than simple task specialization might indicate, as the governments are designed to compete with one another ever so subtly but quite importantly, as argued in section 3. Voters simply have no means of derailing the intergovernmental competition detrimental to the union, as this competition was designed into the system.

Federalism offers the appearance of republican government—it provides the instruments of democratic representation and popular sovereignty—but has it satisfied our requirements for a successful republic? Ought it not also be necessary that the government provide the ability for the people to form a general intention and articulate it to their government? Federalism poorly satisfies these two conditions, and therefore poses a serious challenge to republicanism. As a control mechanism on federal encroachment, elections are not efficient, and definitely not reliable.

Consequence: The Neglected Potential of Judicial Review

We know of the weaknesses of Madison's theory of factions: Madison himself supplied evidence of it, in pointing out to his Convention colleagues that the North–South division would be perpetuated by equal representation in the Senate (Rakove 1996, 68–69, 74–75). The last two sections probed this weakness more deeply, concluding that Madison's institutional and electoral theory of federal stability incompletely transforms self-interest into public good. Either mechanism works well under some conditions, perhaps even the majority of the time. But the coverage is incomplete, the constraint on the federal government is imperfect, and so the possibility of encroachment persists. Federalism's division of powers creates a national governmental interest distinct from the state government interests. It also erases any potential for the people to formulate, let alone express in a coherent fashion, their notion of the public interest. These two problems are closely related: at the same time that federalism establishes a new government in need of control, it makes it impossible for the people to say for themselves what they expect from the union. Federalism is a special topic; it is different from protection of individual rights, and the solutions that work for the latter we cannot assume will work for the former.

The gap in the protection of federalism might not be sufficient to endanger the polity's stability. Often the electorate and other political safeguards catch deviations that slip through cracks in the institutional structure. And often the institutional structure helps guide the electorate into formulating a vision for their federation. The overlap in failures may be rare, but a complete theory of federal stability needs insurance for infrequent threats as well as the mundane.

In *Federalist* 49, Madison describes a characteristic he would like to see in any body that would regulate intergovernmental dispute: "[It] is the reason, alone, of the public that ought to control and regulate the government. The passions ought to be controlled and regulated by the government."[19] The judiciary alone stands removed from public passion. Madison says so himself not two paragraphs earlier: "[T]he [judiciary], by the mode of their appointment, as well as by the nature and permanency of it, are too far removed from the people to share much in their prepossessions."

The judiciary is a viable solution for both of the problems created by Madison's federalism. It is not subject to electoral approval, so is freed from the motivation shared by the legislature and executive to encroach. While it cannot—and should not—decide the people's will for them, it is the guardian of the Constitution, which is the only expression we have of what we as a people want our federalism to look like. It can recover the second form of failure by promising a coherent practice of federalism according to our Constitution, offering the possibility that time and perspective might do what an instant's decision cannot: we can tinker (but not frivolously!) with our Constitution as we gain experience with its effects. Therefore, the judiciary has much to offer to federal stability.

But Madison's way of viewing federalism, as a self-enforcing system constrained by competition and electoral control, meant that the judiciary was neglected as an important stabilizing force. The U.S. Supreme Court is now reining in the federal government, with mixed reviews from legal and lay observers alike. Apart from the criticism of the doctrine the Supreme Court is developing, criticisms of its involvement at all ring loudly and point most often to Madison, championing his institutional and political safeguards.

Political safeguards are most explicitly laid out in *The Federalist*, especially Numbers 45, 46, 51, and 62, and modern analysts strengthen the theory. Neatly turning the tables, Wechsler (1954) argues that Congress does not threaten state power but instead helps to protect it. In his theory, not only is the Senate a forum for states to express and protect their interests, but the House, through state control of elections, also can be twisted to represent state interests. Choper (1977, 1980) urges us to consider the court's finite institutional capital: as a nonelected body, the court has limited leverage; it is best to reserve what power it has, and not test its legitimacy, by allowing it to focus on the protection of individual rights. In agreement with Wechsler, he argues that the court need not concern itself with federalism disputes because the states are protected through political institutions; he adds to Wechsler's list lobbying organizations such as the National Governors' Association. Kramer's (2000) political safeguards argument is not so much an addition to Wechsler as a transformation of it. In his argument it is the informal political institutions, particularly the political parties, that ensure state institutional input in the national decision-making process.[20] These Madisonian arguments have been used extensively to criticize judicial interference with federalism disputes, especially in curtailing federal encroachment; they have even been employed by Supreme Court justices to support their decision not to intervene.

Political safeguards is the meat of the dissent in *National League of Cities* [1976] (426 U.S. 833), which cites Madison in *Federalist* 45 and 46 and Wechsler. It also becomes the basis of the majority decision in *Garcia*, where, citing as evidence *Federalist* 45, 46, and 62, it is argued that: "the Framers chose to rely on a federal system in which special restraints on federal power over the States inhered principally in the workings of the National Government itself, rather than in discrete limitations on the objects of federal authority. State sovereign interests, then, are more properly protected by procedural safeguards inherent in the structure of the federal system than by judicially created limitations on federal power."[21]

The same reasoning continues to be employed in recent arguments, mostly in dissent, in *Seminole Tribe*,[22] in *Kimel*,[23] and in *Morrison*,[24] to protest judicial intervention when the justices believed that political institutions were designed expressly to incorporate state interests and form an adequate protection against national encroachment. The heart of the political safeguards argument can be summed up in Madison's words in *Federalist* 62: "No law or resolution can now be passed without the concurrence, first, of a majority of the people, and then, of a majority of the states." The political safeguards thesis believes that the electorate and the state governments, on independent patrols, stop federal encroachment. It ignores altogether the federal problem of credit assignment, it ignores the paradox of republican government in a federation, and above all it uses Madison's words out of context and written before the benefit of experience.

Are these Supreme Court references to the *Federalist* a near-criminal misreading of Madison, an over-reliance on his propagandist writings? No, not really. He did not think much of judicial review and he did believe that the states were effectively protected, although perhaps not for the reasons we think he did today. But by failing to understand the weakness of Madison's argument, the Court long accepted the role of executive handmaiden that Riker (1964) assigned it. Instead, the Court could bolster political safeguards, not replace them, by filling in where they have the potential to fail.

Madison knew that the federal government would have an incentive to embellish its power, but at the time of Founding he believed that the destructive motivation was sufficiently constrained by institutional design. He quickly learned otherwise, and when his backup plan of state protest backfired with the nullification crisis, he began to have more faith in judicial review. But it remained underappreciated by him and definitely by Madisonian scholars.

What he left unprotected was the Constitution, ultimately. The Constitution established the rules of play, established the incentive scheme that set in motion the web of competition and check that would create a self-enforcing federation. But federalism is not self-enforcing; it is because of electoral and interinstitutional competition that the governments will try to tweak the rules to their own advantage. The Constitution needs an advocate who is independent from the electorate. The judiciary is prone to errors, like all other institutions, but its errors are not correlated with counterfederalist motives. John Marshall did not meddle with the institutional balance and federalism; instead, he might have saved it. As the Court works out a federalism doctrine, rather than be impatient with its mistakes and criticize it for its countermajoritarian tendencies, we should remember Madison in his later wisdom, and accept that it might be useful to put our federation back on track (or keep it from derailing). The judiciary's infrequent, important interventions are what make the rest of Madison's theory work.

Madison was a nationalist and a populist, albeit perhaps not according to today's standards. He wanted a stronger national government and qualified democratic control significantly, but all with the aim of making republican democracy work. He pragmatically accepted the faults of men and designed a government to transform those flaws into virtues. When transformation was impossible, his mechanisms suppressed them. Madison believed that a vigorous federalism was necessary for a healthy democracy.

Notes

For thoughtful comments I am indebted to Andreas Kalyvas, Sam Kernell, and two anonymous referees.

1. Hobson (1979) describes this crisis as more important to Madison than the problems of controlling the state legislatures. He writes: "Madison regarded the crisis of the Confederation in the 1780s as foremost a crisis of republican government. The question at stake for him was whether a government that derived its authority from the people and was administered by persons who were directly or indirectly appointed by the people would prove to be more than a vain hope or merely theoretical ideal" (pp. 218–19). This essay agrees with Hobson that Madison most wanted to create a government of manageable popular sovereignty.

2. Madison first developed the size of states argument in his notes on the "Vices." Note 11 blames the poor quality of the laws on two factors: the representatives and the people themselves. Politicians seek office for three motives, Madison reasoned: ambition, personal interest, and public good, and he feared that the first two reasons outweigh the third, often causing the "honest but unenlightened representative [to] be the dupe of a favorite leader, veiling his selfish views under the professions of public good." *Federalist* 10 famously elaborates his position on faction, but Note 11 contains his early thoughts: the wider the sphere, the more difficult it is for factions to influence outcomes.

3. By no means did the Founders think that defense was a minor function. Riker (1964, 20–21) neatly summarizes the urgency of stabilizing the union: external threats from Great Britain and Spain meant that the American hold on the continent was tenuous. If the union could not be strengthened, its internal divisions would ease foreign encroachment. Citing the first papers of the *Federalist*

(written by John Jay, the diplomat), Washington's preoccupation with war pre-
paredness in letters, and Madison's own notes on the "Vices," where five of the
eleven deal with military weakness, Riker argues that the primary motivation for
reconstruing the union was external military threat.

4. See, for example, "Remarks in the Federal Convention on Electing the
Executive," July 17, 1787 (MP 10, 103), and *Federalist* 51. Note, however, the contributions of Kernell and McLean in this volume, arguing that Madison was
much less committed to separation of powers than we assume today.

5. For the modern edition of this concern, see Ely 1980 and Friedman 1993.

6. Madison reports that the British model was an absolute veto (MP 10, 36),
potentially a severe check on the legislature's authority. Madison was clearly intrigued by the New York revision of the British model, but the extent of Madison's commitment to harness the legislature is ambiguous.

In the Virginia Plan, widely attributed to Madison, the size of the majority
needed to override the veto is unspecified. The clause reads: "and that the dissent
of the said Council shall amount to a rejection, unless the Act of the National
Legislature be again passed, or that of a particular Legislature be again negatived
by [blank] of the members of each branch" (MP 10, 16). It is reasonable to assume that the condition "by [blank] of the members" indicated some supermajority, the exact proportion to be determined later. If not, the statement "again
passed" would suffice. The controversy is over the application of the condition
"by [blank] of the members." If it is intended to qualify overrides on the nega-
tives on state legislation alone, then the supermajority limits the use of the negative, but does not affect regular legislative action, which would then seem to require mere majority repassage. Circumstantial evidence indicates that Madison
supported a supermajority override requirement on national legislation.

In the Aug. 23, 1785, letter to Caleb Wallace, he praises the New York version
of the council in the midst of discussing the importance of legislative review to
protect against "fluctuating & indegested laws" (MP 8, 351). In his Oct. 24, 1787,
letter to Thomas Jefferson, he recounts the debate about the revisionary power.
The debate seemed to have been between the absolute veto and a supermajority requirement: simple majority repassage is not mentioned, and in fact he immediately supported a supermajority requirement when it was proposed in the
Convention (ibid. 10, 209). Finally, in his notes on "Draught of a Constitution
for Virginia," ca. Oct. 15, 1788, Madison offers two specific supermajority figures
for the Council of Revision: two-thirds and three-fourths (depending on if either or both of the executive and judiciary vetoed). As compelling as the specific
figures I find his reasons, both here: "a revisionary power is meant as a check to
precipitate, to unjust, and to unconstitutional laws" (MP 11, 293); and in 1785: it
is a "valuable safeguard" (MP 8, 351). It is not meant to be pro forma, or merely
a cry of alarm to the public.

Nevertheless, I must emphasize that this evidence is circumstantial. Certainly,
Madison's Virginia Plan did not advocate as strict a separation of powers as the

New York model: the New York executive, for example, was directly elected, while the Virginia Plan specified that the executive be chosen by the legislature. For an alternative interpretation that the Virginia Plan proposes a more unfettered national legislature, see the Kernell contribution in this volume. The Avalon Project at the Yale Law School has made the New York Constitution of 1777, as well as many other important Founding documents, available to anyone with access to the web at: *http://www.yale.edu/lawweb/avalon/avalon.htm*.

7. In its point 9 he details his conception of the judiciary's role, which includes no powers of review, unless you creatively interpret "questions which may involve the national peace and harmony" (MP 10, 17).

8. The supremacy clause was added to the Constitution as a weak compromise once the negative was lost.

9. Here I refer especially to the third-to-last paragraph of *Federalist* 39, regarding the necessity of a federal-level tribunal to resolve disputes between the levels of government. Although much later, in an 1830 letter to Edward Everett, Madison refers to this essay as early support for judicial intervention (discussed below), I think that when writing *Federalist* 39 he had in mind only state encroachment on federal power, and not the inverse; I do not consider it to be a recommendation of judicial involvement in federal encroachment claims.

10. See the discussion in Rakove 1996, 171–77; and Rakove 2002.

11. As a large state delegate, and moreover because of his suspicions of the state governments, Madison fought against equal representation in the Senate. He searched in vain for some principle other than state representation to guide Senate membership once his Virginia Plan proposal, in which the second chamber would be elected by members of the first chamber (who were themselves directly elected by the people), was rejected by the Convention. In the weeks preceding the "Great Compromise" (the July 16 vote for equal representation in the Senate), Madison's arguments against equal representation accelerate in bitterness and desperation. On June 7, Madison complained in debates that rather than serve as a useful check on inexpedient governmental practices in the national legislature, state appointment of senators might *promote* it, as the states had proven themselves to be prone to incompetent government (MP 10, 40); on June 21, he wrote that state governments are maintained, not to serve as checks on the national government, but instead because they are needed to attend to all the minutiae of local government that they can do more efficiently than a purely national one (ibid. 10, 68). His desperation showed on June 30, when in an attempt to frighten his compatriots into agreement, he spoke the unspeakable (and implicitly burst a hole in his theory of faction). He said that while equal representation might do no harm, it wouldn't help either, as "the Majority of the States might still injure the majority of the people" (ibid. 10, 90), and he introduced the possibility of sectional conflict, as a more important cleavage than the large state–small state division. As late as July 5, he was still protesting the proposed compromise, calling it "unjust" and saying further that he did not think it necessary to achieve ratification:

Harmony in the Convention was no doubt much to be desired. Satisfaction to all the States, in the first instance still more so. But if the principal States comprehending a majority of the people of the U.S. should concur in a just & judicious Plan, he had the firmest hopes, that all the other States would by degrees accede to it. (Ibid., 120–21)

On July 14 he made his final attempt to persuade his colleagues. He hotly delineated the fault with equal representation. With remarkable prescience, his closing argument reiterated his June 30 concern regarding the North–South division over slavery: "[T]he perpetuity it would give to the preponderance of the Northn. agst. the Southn. Scale was a serious consideration" (ibid. 10, 102).

12. Whether or not we should take seriously Madison's proclamation that because of the institutional incorporation of state interests the federal government would be politically dependent upon the state governments is unclear. We know how opposed he was to equal representation in the Senate and how disdainful he was of the competence of state representation. The connection between the Electoral College and state interests is weak, and his argument about the House contradicts his theory of enlarged republics.

13. Madison's logical slip here is worth noting because he well understood the collective action problem in state financing of war debt. We must assume that he believed protest was costless—that it was in each individual state's interest to protest—thereby skirting the collective action problem, or that he still did not believe that the federal government would encroach, so given the irrelevance of counterstrategies, he did not devote much thought to the protest mechanism.

14. He also reminds us of the limits of the public's scrutiny, which I take up in the next section.

15. Decision theory reduces the number of strategic agents to one: here, only the federal government's behavior is analyzed. Therefore, we exclude from consideration retaliatory encroachment by the states, strategic underperformance to reduce the attractiveness of encroachment and credit claiming, and advertisement of the center's encroachment activity. The first two state behaviors are far-fetched anyway: it is inappropriate to try to link decisions to encroach in a tit-for-tat sort of way, as encroachment is generally independent from dimension to dimension, and the second, intentional underperformance, is electoral suicide. The last behavior, public protest of federal encroachment, is the most likely reaction. Its efficacy depends on the electoral response, which I consider (and reject) in Section 4.

16. I make this argument formally in a manuscript titled "The Credit Assignment Problem," which first appeared as a chapter of my dissertation: *The Federal Problem: The Political Economy of Federal Stability* (Stanford University, 1998).

17. This second assumption rigs the problem against finding any encroachment and also allows us to think about federal behavior absent any specific assumptions about state competence or behavior.

18. Parties certainly provide helpful heuristics, so to the extent that they are free from interlevel competition, they may help voters to secure the federal balance.

19. Madison supplies a curious bit of food for thought regarding the legitimacy of unanimous decisions: he implies that they are an indication that the decision was governed by passion, not reason. "When men exercise their reason
coolly and freely on a variety of distinct questions, they inevitably fall into different opinions on some of them. When they are governed by a common passion, their opinions, if they are so to be called, will be the same" (*Federalist* 50).

20. Kramer transforms the political safeguards arguments of Wechsler and
Choper by arguing that the real source of political control is in the political parties, which of course constitute an informal organization of electoral control. In
so doing, he is much truer to Madison than most modern Madisonians. See also
Ordeshook's contributions.

21. 469 U.S. 528 at 43, 44 [1985].

22. 517 U.S. 44 at 183 [1996].

23. 528 U.S. 62 at 93 [2000].

24. 529 U.S. 598 at 639, 648 and 650 [2000].

Chapter 10

Madison at the First Congress: Institutional Design and Lessons from the Continental Congress, 1780-1783

RICK K. WILSON

Introduction

Madison took his seat as a delegate to the Continental Congress on March 20, 1780.[1] At the time Madison was an unknown politician, regarded by many as simply another of the young planters sent by Virginia to bear the burden of representing state interests. Very quickly, Madison proved his worth as a legislator. Within a year of being seated he was building legislative coalitions that would change the financing of the bankrupt government and add to its capacity to protect its fragile life.

Madison's concerns were similar to those that have been the focus of contemporary political science. Madison was enormously frustrated by the collective action problem inherent in the system of financing the war effort and paying down debts. The system allowed Congress to set requisitions for the various states. Each state, then, could choose to voluntarily pay that assessment. No contemporary political scientist would be surprised by the ineffectiveness of this voluntary contribution mechanism, and neither was Madison.[2]

Madison was also concerned with the collective choice problems inherent in Congress. There Madison found a system sometimes dominated by an open agenda, sometimes relying on simple majority rule and sometimes using a supermajority rule. Under an open agenda with simple majority rule, anything could happen and often did. Many of the same issues were revisited and often changed. Under supermajority rule, stalemate was the usual state of affairs. Again, neither of these things would surprise a contemporary political scientist, and Madison understood the institutional sources of such problems.

Finally, Madison entered an institution that was poorly designed to handle an increasing workload or otherwise process the demands on a fledgling national government. Balancing concerns for efficiency, expertise, and representativeness is always difficult. Madison found an institution that rarely met any of these goals in its day-to-day operations.

Few realized the role Madison would play in the Congress, and no one, including Madison, could realize the effect of the Congress on the ways in which Madison came to think of institutional design. This paper briefly discusses the organization of the Continental Congress, as Madison found it when he presented his credentials in 1780. Madison's role in the Congress is briefly sketched and data is brought to bear concerning his experiences in the Congress. Finally, his unpublished notes from 1786 and 1787, which reflected on the proper design of a new institution, are related to his experiences in the Congress. Although Madison returned to the Continental Congress in its dying years, that period is not touched on. Throughout, the claim is that Madison implicitly understood much of what is contemporaneously known as the "new institutionalism." While Madison never offered a theorem equivalent to one produced by Richard McKelvey, nonetheless his experiences in the Continental Congress led him to appreciate the central problems of social choice.

The Continental Congress

Within a week of taking his seat, Madison provided a candid assessment of what was wrong with Congress. In a letter to Jefferson he outlined a set of problems that were rooted in the design of the Continental Congress. While he claimed he could not determine which problem was the most critical, in retrospect two stand out. The first had to do with insufficient checks on the actions of less than noble statesmen.

> Congress from a defect of adequate statesmen [is] more likely to fall into wrong measures and of less weight to enforce right ones, recommending plans to the several states for execution, and the states separately rejudging the expediency of such plans, whereby the same distrust of concurrent exertions that has damped the ardor of patriotic individuals must produce the same effect among the states themselves. (Letter to Jefferson, March 27, 1780, quoted in Burnett 1921–36, V, 97)

Madison was concerned not only with the fact that members seemed to be squabbling over matters that were less than important, but worse, the inability of the delegates to articulate a plan that would carry forward to the states. As a loose confederation, it was a simple matter for the individual states to pick apart any major piece of legislation—especially weakly written legislation coming out of the Continental Congress. This was highlighted by a second concern that pertained to a system of financing the war effort (and covering old debts). Here Madison noted: "An old system of finance, discarded as incompetent to our necessities, an untried and precarious one substituted, and a total stagnation in prospect between the former and the operation of the latter" (letter to Jefferson, March 27, 1780, quoted in ibid., V, 97).

Settled several days before Madison took his seat, the Congress had tossed out an old form of financing and moved to a system that depended on the whims of the individual states. Neither the old form of financing nor the new were optimal. Both introduced serious problems for collective action in which state contributions resembled a voluntary contribution game. Several months later, he reiterated this point to Jefferson, noting:

> It is to be observed that the situation of Congress has undergone a total change from what it originally was. Whilst they exercised the indefinite power of emitting money on the credit of their constituents they had the whole wealth & resources of the continent within their command, and could go on with their affairs independently and as they pleased. Since the resolution passed for shutting the press, this power has been entirely given up and they are now as dependent on the States as the King of England is on the parliament. They can neither enlist pay nor feed a single soldier, nor execute any other pu[r]pose but as the means are first put into their hands. Unless the legislatures are sufficiently attentive to this change of circumstances and act in conformity to it, every thing must necessarily go wrong or rather must come to a total stop. (May 6, 1780, quoted in *The Papers of James Madison* [hereafter MP] 2, 20)

Madison's concerns with problems of collective action were only a piece of the puzzle. The Continental Congress was also racked with collective choice and coordination problems. As to the latter, finding experienced individuals willing to carry out the daily workload of Congress was difficult. Madison was not too far off the mark when noting that Congress by 1780 held a "defect of adequate statesmen." Even worse, the internal structure of Congress was such as to make it nearly impossible to generate consistent, coherent legislation. The Congress was racked by factions, but of a sort that prevented coalition-building. The rules not only permitted, but seemingly guaranteed, a setting in which almost anything could happen.

The institutional design of the Continental Congress, as Madison found it in 1780, was little different from the institution at the outset of the Revolutionary War. For purposes of this discussion, I focus on three components of the Continental Congress: the actors constituting the institution, the position rules embedded in the Congress, and the aggregation rules.[3] For more extensive details about the design of the institution, the interested reader should consult Jillson and Wilson (1994).

The Actors. Central to any decision-making body is the question of who is represented and who has voice. From the outset of the Continental Congress it was clear that the state delegations were merely bringing instructions from their state assemblies to Philadelphia. While the size of those delegations varied, no matter the size, each state had an equal voice. It quickly became apparent that carrying instructions from the various states was nearly impossible. Events presented to Congress quickly surpassed any instructions held by delegates. Moreover, delegates within a state were often at odds, with little agreement about the state's position.

Prior to the adoption of the Articles of Confederation in 1781, a single delegate could represent a state. This was to ensure that no state was denied a voice when balloting. Following ratification of the Articles at least two delegates were required to be present for a state's vote to be considered (see Jillson and Wilson 1994, 157–59). While a state with only a single delegate could continue to have a voice on the floor during debate and could have that delegate appointed to a committee, its vote could not count.

This definition of a state's voice presented a serious problem for the Congress in conducting day-to-day business. As part of its internal rules, members had implemented a quorum rule of nine states in July 1776. Frequent absences, however, led members to quickly lower the quorum to seven states. But even that failed to solve quorum problems. Throughout the 1780s attendance was erratic, with many delegates who were appointed to represent their state failing to show up. The Congress was powerless to compel attendance, even though it continuously sent letters to the various states urging that they take the responsibility to force their delegates to attend. On April 19, 1774, the Congress adopted a resolution prodding the states. The resolution tried to detail the consequences for lax attendance:

> *Resolved.* That the legislatures of the several states be informed, that whilst they are respectively represented in Congress by two delegates only, such an unanimity for conducting the most important public concerns is necessary as can be rarely expected. That if each of the thirteen states should be represented by two members, five out of twenty-six, being only a fifth of the whole may negative any measure requiring the voice of nine states: that of eleven states now on the floor of Congress, nine being represented by only two member from each, it is in the

power of three out of twenty-five, making only one-eighth of the whole, to negative such a measure, . . . that therefore Congress conceive it to be indispensably
necessary, and earnestly recommended, that each State, at all times when Congress
are sitting, be hereafter represented by three members at least; as the most injuri-
ous consequences may be expected from the want of such representations. (*Journals* 1774–89, 26, 245–46)

Aside from preventing Congress from tackling its business, the quorum rules
enhanced the capacity of a handful of members to obstruct action. To com-
plicate matters, in 1784 Congress appointed a committee to determine
which of its members, usually members in good standing and dutiful attendance, were now in violation of another feature of the Articles of Confederation. One of the articles mandated a form of term limits in which no member could serve longer than three years in any six-year period. James
Madison, although not reported by the committee, departed Congress as an
early victim of these limits on service. In short, states constituted the key actors in Congress. However, state interests were manifested through individual agents who often spoke with a mixed voice.

Positional Rules. The Continental Congress was an institution of equals
in which no delegate enjoyed any positional advantage. The only position
defined by the Congress was its president. However, that position was
toothless. A series of precedents, norms, and expectations were developed
in the first Congress, and then maintained through the history of the institution, that gave the president no assignment powers, no power to appoint
members to standing or ad hoc committees, and no power to control the
flow of business out of committees and back to the floor. Assignment and
committee appointment powers were exercised on the floor of Congress.
Resolutions, bills, and reports coming out of committee and returning to
the floor were taken up in the order in which they were delivered to the
secretary. Any questions arising over the priority among items lying on the
table were settled by a majority vote of the states. Once the floor decided
what it would consider, the president monitored the conduct of the debate
and little more (Sanders 1930, 39). The office of president was largely cer-
emonial, and it was sufficiently innocuous that through most of its history
it passed in yearly rotation among the states. Indeed, the office had so little
importance that John Hancock, re-elected as president in November 1785,
declined to attend. He took seven months to finally resign the post, and the
post was filled by an interim chairman, David Ramsay (Jillson and Wilson
1994, 87–88).

While most activity took place on the floor, committees were om-
nipresent and created a potential position of privilege. In the modern Con-

gress, committees enjoy clear property rights over issues, hold considerable expertise, and can exercise important forms of agenda control. Such a system, however, never developed in the Continental Congress. The Congress continually relied upon an extensive network of ad hoc committees to handle its workload. At various stages in its history the committee system was supplemented by standing committees, boards, and executive departments. These variations on the committee system proved to be less successful than hoped, largely because myriad ad hoc committees were created to oversee and investigate them. In addition, ad hoc committees invariably were charged to reconsider and often recast the reports and recommendations that the standing committees, boards, and departments sent to the Congress. As a result, ad hoc committees always remained the standard mechanism employed by the Congress to prepare issues for final deliberation on the floor.

The open nature of the committee system is demonstrated by the method for calling new committees into existence and selecting members to them. Committees were appointed when a majority of the states voted in favor of a motion to appoint a committee. When passed, nominations to fill positions on the committee were offered from the floor (*Journals* 1774–89, 2, 79; 3, 266; Burnett 1921–36, 2, 74; 2, 83–84). Once nominations closed each delegate cast a secret ballot for one of the nominees. The secretary of Congress tabulated the ballots and the president announced the names of the members elected. The individuals receiving the most votes were elected to the committee, with the top vote-getter serving as committee chair. "Grand Committees," composed of one member from each state, were occasionally selected to consider critical issues. In these instances, each delegation was allowed to nominate its own member, and then the slate was approved by a ballot of all members. These procedures guaranteed that the members on the floor controlled the committees of the Congress and that any significant divisions on the floor would be reproduced in each committee. Jillson and Wilson (1994, 124–27) provide evidence suggesting that over much of the life of the Continental Congress, committees were a reflection of the floor. This is a direct result of the process of selection and election.

Delegates to the Continental Congress were relentless in ensuring that specialized positions of power did not evolve. This is partly demonstrated by the pervasiveness of committees. Jillson and Wilson (1994) note that 3,249 separate committees were *elected* between 1774 and 1788. The vast majority of the committees employed each year were small ad hoc committees. More than three-quarters (76.8 percent) had only three members, and another 17.7 percent had five members. For a body that rarely had more than thirty-five members present, this proliferation of ad hoc committees generated an enor-

mous and varied workload for most delegates. At the extreme, delegates like
Abraham Clark (NJ), Hugh Williams (NC), and James Duane (NY) served
on more than three hundred committees during their time in Congress.

As early as 1776 the delegates experimented with standing committees,
and later with boards, commissions, and even executive departments. However, none of these innovations brought relief to delegates who continued to
be appointed to ad hoc committees (this point is detailed in ibid., ch. 4).
There was such concern with long-standing boards and departments that
Congress formalized oversight, resolving "that on the first Monday in July
and the first Monday in January in every year, five committees composed
each of five members, shall be appointed; which committees shall have in
charge to enquire fully, . . . and to report the result of their enquiries to Congress" (*Journals* 1774–89, 22, 334). The lesson here is that delegates jealously
guarded their prerogative to handle work on the floor.

Aggregation Rules. The Continental Congress was the quintessential egalitarian institution. Most of its work took place in the Committee of the
Whole, and its procedures guaranteed open discussion on the floor, ensured
that no faction gained monopoly agenda setting powers, and provided delegates with ample opportunity for discussion, amendment, obstruction, and
delay. Instead of adopting rules that awarded subsets of delegates special
agenda powers (the leadership or an equivalent of the modern Rules Committee), rules that narrowly prescribed when motions and amendments were
in order (closed or modified rules), or rules that allowed the formulation of
complex legislative packages (omnibus bills), the Continental Congress's
rules were minimal.

Minimal rules meant that the process could oftentimes be maddening. On
September 5, 1777, less than two months before he was elected president of
Congress, Henry Laurens wrote to fellow South Carolinian John Gervais
that he had "been witness to a Report made by a Committee of the Whole,
which had been entered upon the Journal, superseded by a new Resolution
even without reference to the Report. A Resolution carried almost *Nem
Con*—entered, and half an hour after reconsidered and expunged. When I
add that such irregularity is the work of almost every day, you will not wonder that I wish to be any where but in Congress" (Smith 1976–, 2, 482).

Seven months later, while serving as president, Laurens complained to
James Duane (NY) that "[l]ong and warm debates for many a day had led us
to the threshold of the Report from the Committee of the Whole. We had
Entered fairly the Door, by reading the whole for information, the first
Clause for debate, and received an amendment which was read by the Chair
and the question half put, when we were turned out by a New Motion—

debates arose upon the point of order" (Burnett 1921–36, 3, 170; see also 6, 21). Debates upon points of order were frequent in the Congress precisely because so little order existed. As Thomas Burke (NC) noted in an August 1779 letter to the North Carolina Assembly: "[C]ircumstances make rules of order . . . very arbitrary and uncertain, hence frequent disputes arise thereon . . . and the decisions at length depend upon the Integrity of the Majority. Thus Rules of order cease to be, what they ought, common checks upon excesses" (ibid., 4, 367–68). Rules could not constrain willful majorities.

The cyclic nature of majority rule processes under an open agenda procedure characterized the Congress prior to the adoption of the Articles of Confederation. Once ratified, however, the rules under which Congress operated were decisively altered. The new rules changed the dynamics of the institution from pervasive fluidity to an equally pervasive rigidity.

Following the adoption of the Articles of Confederation in 1781 the problems facing delegates to the Continental Congress were compounded by several changes in floor procedures. From the outset the Continental Congress operated under the "unit rule," in which each state was accorded a single vote that was a function of a simple majority of each state's delegation. Each member of the state delegation cast a separate ballot. The secretary tallied the ballots and the state's vote was announced. The Articles changed the number of positive votes needed to decide issues in Congress. Before the Articles were approved a simple majority of the states present and voting could decide matters. After the Articles were ratified, seven positive votes were required to conclude regular business, and nine positive votes were required to decide important business. While the latter included the ratification of treaties and all matters of great financial concern, in practice almost any issue could be declared "important."

This change in the Articles had a dramatic effect on the capacity for delegates to build legislation. The status quo was now privileged because requiring a seven- or nine-state majority effectively meant imposing a near unanimity rule. Even though simple majority rule was all that was required for minor matters, that meant a simple majority of thirteen states. When only nine states were in attendance, simple majority rule demanded that seven-ninths of the states vote for passage. While technically requiring a simple majority, in practice this led to the imposition of near unanimity rule as attendance fell. Jillson and Wilson (1994, 141) calculate that prior to March 1, 1781, 60 percent of the motions offered in Congress passed. Following the change in rules only 30 percent of the motions offered in Congress passed. Delegates turned almost immediately from complaining about instability to complaining just as vociferously about deadlock.

In early March 1784, Thomas Jefferson explained to a correspondent what the rules embedded in the Articles meant for the conduct of business in the Congress. Jefferson wrote that "a ninth state appeared today, but eight of the nine being represented by two delegates each, all important questions will require not only an unanimity of states, but of members, for which we have no reason to hope. I very much apprehend we shall be unable to get through even those [questions] which seem indispensable" (Burnett 1921–36, 7, 458). Fixed supermajority requirements, in the face of low attendance, pushed what would have been a stiff supermajority requirement (nine of thirteen states, or 69 percent), toward a requirement of virtual unanimity both of states and individuals. The result, not unexpectedly, was a perverse form of stalemate.

Madison in Philadelphia

To this point the institution has been discussed independently of Madison's involvement. However, it is important to note the context within which he entered in 1780. At the outset, Madison arrived as a relative unknown. While he held legislative credentials, his competence in the Virginia House was not carried with him to Philadelphia. Once he took his seat at the Continental Congress he became known as a dependable legislator. A number of scholars have debated the content of Madison's activities in the Continental Congress. Debates have centered on whether Madison became a nationalist, striving to build a strong national government (see the traditional view by Brant [1948]), or whether Madison sought to maintain state sovereignty (see the challenge posed by Banning [1995]). The interest here is less with Madison's accomplishments within the Continental Congress and more with his experiences. My argument is that those experiences shaped the way he viewed institutional design.

Madison quickly became an important member of the Congress. While his first year was spent learning the ropes, by 1781 Madison was in the thick of the major disputes in Congress. It is possible to objectively see his involvement grow. Figure 10.1 shows the number of committees to which Madison was assigned by congressional year.[4] As can be seen, Madison quickly surpassed the average number of committee assignments. As noted above, his assignments were not so much a function of his expertise as a function of his competence. Members were elected to committee assignments, and Madison's continual election was a sign that others valued his abilities.

Madison's voting record usually was in line with his counterparts, both in the South and in Virginia. However, on some issues Madison became prominent in building coalitions, particularly with delegates from the Middle At-

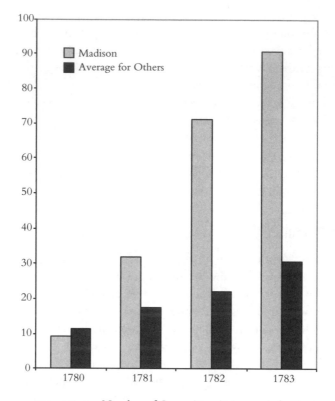

FIG. 10.1. Number of Committee Assignments by Year

lantic states. The most useful way of viewing Madison's voting behavior within Congress is to consider how he voted relative to others. This is easily accomplished by using a multidimensional scaling technique across all votes in order to uncover common dimensions that capture the voting patterns of delegates. This technique is detailed in Jillson and Wilson (1994) and resembles the more ubiquitous Nominate scores developed by Poole and Rosenthal (2000). Throughout the period examined here, a two-dimensional scaling structure does quite well in capturing the relative positions of delegate votes. The scaling technique used here allows delegates to be compared with one another. The resulting scale can be considered a proximity measure, with delegates who are closer to one another typically voting with one another. Delegates further apart in the two-dimensional space are least likely to have voted together.

Figures 10.2 through 10.5 produce delegate positions for each congressional year from 1780 through 1783. In each instance Madison's position is labeled, as is a sampling of other notable members of Congress. The diamond-shaped marks on the figure represent delegates from the Northern states; the rectangles represent delegates from Middle Atlantic states; and the circles represent delegates from Southern states. In Figure 10.2 (1780) it is clear that Madison is voting at variance with the Southern delegation. His position is most closely aligned with that of the Northern delegates. In 1781 his general voting pattern had moved toward the Southern delegation—at least along dimension 1 (which nominally is a North/South basis for cleavage), although Madison continues to stand out with respect to the Southern delegation. By 1782, Madison is tightly clustered with the Southern block. In 1783, Madison is again at odds with the Southern delegates and more closely aligned with delegates from the Middle Atlantic. Of course, throughout this period the regional divisions are not as strong as they would be in the mid and later 1780s. Madison, then, while often in line with his fellow Southern delegates, was not closely tied to all of them. In large part this was because he quickly became adept at using the Continental Congress's institutional mechanisms to build coalitions around new legislative policies. Two examples, the funding of federal debt and the western lands question, are briefly treated below.

FINANCING PUBLIC DEBT

From the outset of his service, Madison was concerned with the problems of financing the country's debt. While interested in finding some mechanism for funding debt, Madison was deeply concerned with expanding federal powers. Because of the logic of collective action, Madison had a difficult time thinking of any way out except to invoke a central state. His early thinking on this came in a letter to Jefferson in which he argued as follows:

> The necessity of arming Congress with coercive powers arises from the shameful deficiency of some of the states which are most capable of yielding their apportioned supplies, and the military extractions to which others already exhausted by the enemy and our own troops are in consequence exposed. Without such powers too in the general government, the whole confederacy may be insulted and the most salutary measures frustrated by the most inconsiderable State in the Union. (April 16, 1781, in MP 3, 72)

Taxation handed to the central government, of course, would concentrate both the power of the sword and the purse. This was a major expansion of national power and one with which Madison struggled. But Madison also understood that the states were unlikely to voluntarily provide contributions

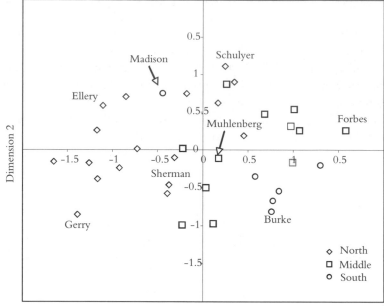

FIG. 10.2. Delegate Voting Positions—1780

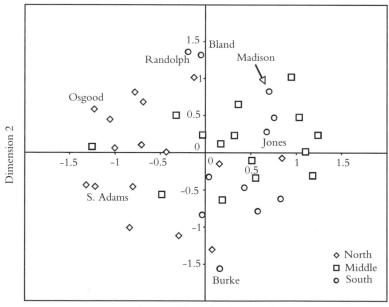

FIG. 10.3. Delegate Voting Positions—1781

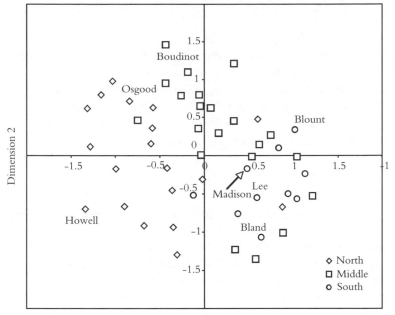

FIG. 10.4. Delegate Voting Positions—1782

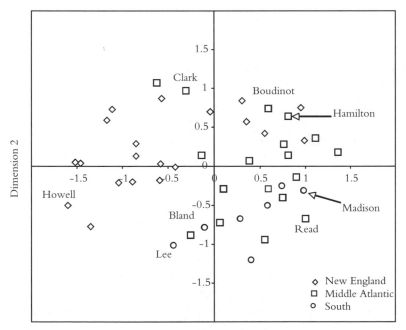

FIG. 10.5. Delegate Voting Positions—1783

to the public good. Although Madison did not articulate the "logic of collective action," he had a clear understanding that the existing system, dependent on voluntary contributions, was not going to succeed.

Madison, from 1781 through 1783, undertook a number of actions to resolve the problems he saw facing the country. While voting against a 5 percent impost on foreign trade, levied by the Congress, he proposed an amendment that would have the states impose a 5 percent impost, with collections made by agents of Congress. In the summer following ratification of the Articles, he wrote a committee report recommending that the Congress turn the army loose on states to compel them to pay their delinquent requisitions. Throughout 1781 and 1782, Madison routinely backed the efforts by Secretary of Finance Robert Morris (if not advocating those efforts). In 1783, Morris threatened resignation if something was not done to provide a steady income to the Congress. Again Madison recognized that none of the states, individually, were likely to contribute to the central treasury. As Madison noted to Edmund Randolph: "If there are not revenue laws which operate at the same time through all the states and are exempt from the control of each, the mutual jealousies which already begin to appear among them will assuredly defraud both our domestic and foreign creditors" (January 22, 1783, in ibid. 6, 55). Following a famous dinner with Hamilton, among others, on February 20, 1783 (which foreshadowed another famous dinner seven years later that cemented a deal fixing the location of the capital and finally resolved the problem of retiring the debt), Madison took a direct lead in fighting for a national impost. It appeared to be the only solution to ensuring a steady source of funding.[5]

Scholars have since debated whether the logic of collective action led Madison to advocate centralization in the form of a strong national government. The important point is that Madison understood the implications behind provisioning public goods.[6] Whether he was an unreconstructed nationalist or sought to preserve state sovereignty remains open to interpretation.

MADISON AND WESTERN LANDS

Several issues occupied Madison and the Congress during the early 1780s. Dougherty (this volume) pays some attention to the problem of resolving the national debt and provides some sense of the frustrations experienced by Madison. Madison also keenly understood the benefits of low attendance and what amounted to a supermajority rule. Madison was sufficiently clever to understand the strategic value of such rules in preventing legislation that was harmful to his state's interests. Throughout late 1781 and into 1783,

Madison worked to protect Virginia's claims to western lands. Here I digress a bit to visit the problem of western lands and the efforts by Virginia (and Madison) to cede claims to parts of the western lands, while protecting their own interests. As a number of authors have noted, the issues were terribly convoluted (see, for example, Abernethy 1937). Each of the states—particularly New York, Connecticut, and Virginia—had differing interpretations of what was granted them by their Colonial charters. At the same time a number of land companies had long been engaged in a brisk business of selling lands in the west and wanted to make certain that state claims did not intrude on their own flimsy claims to the lands. Congress cast an eye toward the western lands as an asset that could be used to help pay off debts from the war. Finally there was a question whether the states could define their boundaries and make room for additional states. Into this fray Madison was given the responsibility to ensure that Virginia's claims were not undermined.

By 1781 the major claimants to the western lands had proposed cessions in their claims. In part this was to encourage Maryland to ratify the Articles of Confederation and in part each state was jockeying for a favorable status. Virginia, for example, gave up claims to lands that lay to the northwest of its borders, but wished to preserve claims to its immediate west that would preserve land titles that had been issued by the state. As Jensen (1936) notes, however, New York's cession, which gained that state a very favorable western boundary, abandoned claims that overlapped with those by Virginia. Many states, particularly those in the Northeast, felt that the New York cessions trumped those offered by Virginia and consequently voided claims to territory that Virginia insisted on preserving. This set the stage for a showdown in Congress that most delegates thought could be resolved, though perhaps not easily.

Madison was part of a group that fought, following the adoption of the Articles, to insist that a bare majority of five states (a majority of a quorum), rather than seven states, was all that was needed in order to pass legislation. This was not to be, and Madison, among others, was defeated in his efforts. But, by late October 1781, Madison was pleased by the need for an oversized majority. The initial battle over the cessions of western lands was beginning to heat up at this point. In a letter to Edmund Pendleton, Madison noted:

> Since the close of the Confederation however, it has been understood that seven votes are necessary to carry every question. This rule in proportion to the thinness of Congress opposes a difficulty to those who attack. It will therefore I believe be impossible for the Enemys of Virginia to obtain any positive injury to her rights. (MP 3, 297)

Madison felt reasonably confident that Virginia's interests would be saved by the fact that there were not enough votes to meet the oversized coalition required by low attendance and the rule mandated under the Articles.

The opening salvo took place in November 1781, when a committee report came to the floor, weighing off the various claims (for a good, general, discussion of the chronology of events, see Jensen 1939; also, the discussion in Onuf 1977 is useful). The report, led by a group hostile to the interests of Virginia, indicated that Congress should accept the New York cessions and reject those by Virginia. This would constrain Virginia to land east of the Alleghenies and open up the west to claims made by a number of Middle State and Northern land speculators. The committee report was quickly tabled, and it became clear that no quick resolution was in the offing. Madison, however, immediately began to construct a defense that would mute the worst features of the committee report. In a letter to Jefferson dated November 18, 1781, Madison admitted that it was likely that the Virginia cessions would be rejected when a vote came to the floor. However, he asked Jefferson to get very clear instructions from the Virginia Assembly about the nature and legality of the state's claims. Madison thought it possible to delay and blunt some of the effects. As he noted: "[It] is a rule observed since the Confederation was completed, that seven votes are requisite in every question, and there are seldom more than 7, 8, 9 or 10 States presented, even the opinion of a Majority of Congress is a very different thing from a constitutional vote" (Burnett 1921–36, 6: 265). Madison was accounting for the rules in play, anticipating how easy it would be to block efforts to impose the committee report.

By April 1782 the Virginia delegation brought up its cession. Although no one expected it to pass, Madison and others thought this would prod the Virginia Assembly to advance its claims more forcefully. By this time the issue of western lands became entangled with the possibility that a new state, Vermont, would be added to the Confederation. In a letter to Jefferson on April 16, Madison was upbeat that the issue would not soon be resolved. He wrote: "It is in the first place very uncertain when a determination will take place, even if it takes place at all; and in the next it will assuredly not be a final one, unless Virg[in]a means to be passive and silent under aggression on her rights" (ibid., 330). He implored Jefferson to provide any documentation that would help vindicate the claims. At the same time Madison worked with Arthur Lee to antagonize proponents of the committee report. In a series of motions, Lee asked that on each vote on the committee report (or consideration of the Virginia cessions) each member, before voting, stand and affirm that he had no financial stake in the western lands. While the series of motions never passed, they did demonstrate to all the members the extent to which it would be impossible to resolve the committee report. In a private letter to Samuel Adams dated April 21, Arthur Lee (never shy in his opinions) wrote that he was returning to Virginia to serve in the legislature and that he did not think he could do much more in Congress on the issue. He noted: "I can only lament what I cannot prevent and make vain efforts to redeem an infatuated Majority from the bondage of folly and private interest. For what can be expected from an Assembly in which a Member is allowed to sit, who is avowedly an Agent for the Enemies to our cause and Country, an Insolvent, and a profligate Adventurer" (ibid., 331).

Lee was referring to Samuel Wharton of Delaware, but his ire was directed at a large number of people. Madison was much more circumspect, working diligently to ensure that the issue would remain focused on the Virginia cessions or that the committee report would remain blocked. Finally, on May 6, 1782, after numerous votes, the report was postponed *sine die*. This was what Madison was seeking, because it meant that the Virginia Assembly would now have the time to develop a case for its cessions (or try another angle of attack).

The point to this digression is to illustrate the fact that complex issues could be easily sidetracked under the rules. Madison was fully willing to use those rules to the advantage of Virginia, and Madison's efforts proved to be useful. Although the issue was revisited again in the fall of 1782 and the New York cessions were accepted, this led to questions about the status of cessions from the other states. Madison continued to press for Virginia to revisit its earlier cessions, and ultimately the Virginia Assembly brought forward a new set of cessions for consideration by the Congress. The issue was not resolved until March 1, 1784.

DISCUSSION

The basic point to take away from this discussion is that Madison had plenty of experience within the Continental Congress. He became a well-respected legislator, he was at the forefront on all the major issues driving Congress, and he was instrumental in building coalitions to pass (and sometimes obstruct) major pieces of legislation. Madison also experienced all of the turmoil that followed ratification of the Articles, the end of the war with Britain, and the rapid inflation that made the Congress's money worthless. His experiences, once he departed Congress in 1783, prepared him for considering an alternative institutional arrangement, one that better fit his vision of a functioning legislative body.

Madison and Postcongressional Concerns

Both during and following his service in the Continental Congress, Madison was concerned with several general problems that have commanded the
attention of the new institutionalists. Foremost was Madison's running concern with the collective action problem inherent in requisitions from the
states. A second class of problems concerned supermajoritarianism. This took
two forms: concerns with achieving an oversized majority and concerns
with minority blocking coalitions that prevented majorities from implementing their will. This was intimately tied to considering social choice
rules and what would encourage shifting majorities (preventing permanent
factions), while at the same time yielding coherent outcomes.

In 1786, Madison undertook a lengthy study of confederated systems. His
notes detailed what was positive and what was disastrous for the different
confederacies he studied. In April 1787, Madison then collected his thoughts
on the "Vices of the Political System of the United States," in which he reflected on the problems attendant with the Continental Congress. Madison's
ruminations are important not only because of his encyclopedic study of
other confederacies but also because of his experiences in the Continental
Congress and because this sketch of ideas foreshadowed his participation in
the Constitutional Convention.

Madison's first point concerned the recurring problem of funding the
fledgling government. The impost was never agreed to by all the states, and
the collective action problem of getting voluntary contributions was never
going to succeed (for an excellent discussion of the problems of funding the
Continental Congress, see Dougherty 2001). Madison stated the point in a
straightforward manner:

> 1. Failure of the States to Comply with the Constitutional Requisitions. This
> evil has been so fully experienced both during the war and since the peace, re-
> sults so naturally from the number and independent authority of the States and
> has been so uniformly exemplified in every similar Confederacy, that it may be
> considered as not less radically and permanently inherent in than it is fatal to the
> object of the present system. (Meyers 1973, 83)

He well understood that the failure to comply was not simply a matter
unique to the Continental Congress. Rather it was endemic in any confederacy. Voluntary contributions simply would not work and would inex-
orably lead to the demise of the institution.

How such an institution might fail was also very clear. His seventh point
turned to the inability of the Continental Congress to sanction and coerce
the various states. Instead, the Continental Congress depended on unanim-

ity—especially when it came to making fundamental changes to the process of funding a government. Madison's statement on the unanimity principle is not surprising to anyone who has read Buchanan and Tullock (1962)—where bargains across states could not be guaranteed, the possibility of getting everyone to agree was nearly impossible.

> It is no longer doubted that a unanimous and punctual obedience of 13 independent bodies, to the acts of the federal Government ought not to be calculated on.... How indeed could it be otherwise? In the first place, Every general act of the Union must necessarily bear unequally hard on some particular member or members of it, secondly the partiality of the members to their own interests and rights, a partiality which will be fostered by the courtiers of popularity, will naturally exaggerate the inequality, where it exists, and even suspect it where it has no existence, thirdly a distrust of the voluntary compliance of each other may prevent the compliance of any, although it should be the latent disposition of all. here are causes & pretexts which will never fail to render federal measures abortive. (Meyers 1973, 86)

Here Madison offers a statement about self-interest and its sources. He expresses no doubt that the various states will always have different interests and that those differences will always allow any state to object to carefully constructed legislation by the Continental Congress. Even if unanimity could be achieved in the Continental Congress (a nearly impossible task), when sent forward to the states for consideration, careful deliberation would likely give way to incautious expressions of self-interest. The sources, in his mind, were obvious.

Madison was uncomfortable in pressing for a national government that could possibly be taken over by a unified majority faction. Banning (1995) is quite right when painting Madison as a less than enthusiastic nationalist. Madison had spent too much time in the Continental Congress not to have learned the possibilities for faction in a purely majoritarian institution. In his eleventh and final point on the "Vices" Madison turned to the problem of factionalism. In the prior points Madison detailed the problems of a multiplicity of laws in the various states—many of which covered the same legal point, but led to confusion. Even worse, coupled with a multiplicity of laws was the fact that such laws were in a constant state of flux. The various state courts constantly changed their rulings, and this was viewed as a threat to trade. Madison's eleventh point concerned the "Injustice of the Laws of the States." This section anticipates *Federalist* Number 10 (in fact segments were lifted directly and inserted into *Federalist* Number 10). He argues that there are two sources to unjust laws: representative bodies and people themselves. His first point fixes on the interests of representatives.

Representative appointments are sought from 3 motives. 1. ambition. 2. personal interest. 3. public good. Unhappily the two first are proved by experience to be the most prevalent. Hence the candidates who feel them, particularly, the second, are most industrious, and most successful in pursuing their object: and forming often a majority in the legislative Councils, with interested views, contrary to the interest and views of their constituents, join in a perfidious sacrifice of the latter to the former. (Meyers 1973, 88–89)

On this score Madison is not optimistic that representative bodies will constrain themselves. Certainly the capacity to build majority factions with no concern for other constraints is most likely to undermine the common interest.

However, the most likely cause of unjust laws stems from human nature. In a now familiar argument, Madison contends:

A still more fatal if not more frequent cause, lies among the people themselves. All civilized societies are divided into different interests and factions . . . In republican Government the majority however composed, ultimately give the law. Whenever therefore an apparent interest or common passion unites a majority what is to restrain them from unjust violations of the rights and interests of the minority, or of individuals? Three motives only 1. a prudent regard to their own good as involved in the general and permanent good of the community. This consideration although of decisive weight in itself, is found by experience to be too often unheeded. . . . 2dly. respect for character. however strong this motive may be in individuals, it is considered as very insufficient to restrain them from injustice. In a multitude its efficacy is diminished in proportion to the number which is to share the praise or the blame. Besides, as it has reference to public opinion, which within a particular Society, is the opinion of the majority, the standard is fixed by those whose conduct is to be measured by it. . . . 3dly. will Religion the only remaining motive be a sufficient restraint? It is not pretended to be such on men individually considered. (Ibid., 89–90)

Obviously, in Madison's mind, men are not angels. An institution that little constrains the behavior of individuals is likely to give rise to narrow self-interest. This in turn will give rise to permanent factions through individuals joining together to pursue their private interests, unchecked by other institutions. Madison picked up on this theme by arguing: "The great desideratum in Government is such a modification of the sovereignty as will render it sufficiently neutral between the different interests and factions, to controul one part of the society from invading the rights of another, and at the same time sufficiently controuled itself, from setting up an interest adverse to that of the whole Society" (ibid., 91). The trick, he understood, is the appropriate design of an institution.

Conclusion

The Continental Congress was an institution that lacked the capacity to pit interests against one another and to prevent free-riding. By the time Madison re-entered the Continental Congress that body was severely split by a North/South line of cleavage. When coupled with supermajority rules and low attendance it was virtually impossible to accomplish anything of substance. Madison's earlier experiences had attuned him to the importance of institutional mechanisms for ameliorating private passions. The hodgepodge mechanism of the Continental Congress was inadequate for the task. Moreover, encouraging voluntary contributions to retire public debt was a certain disaster. The Continental Congress was an inadequate mechanism for retiring the debt. As such it was no wonder that Madison pressed so hard to have it replaced in the Convention and worked so diligently to see the new Constitution ratified.

Notes

Thanks go to Laura Delgado, Carmen Huerta, and Martin Johnson for their assistance in tracking down sources. Thanks also go to Rod Kiewiet, Gary Cox, and Sam Kernell for their thoughtful comments. All of the above are absolved from errors I've persisted in committing by ignoring their good advice.

1. At the time that Madison arrived, the delegates were still operating under the guise of the Second Continental Congress. During his tenure the Articles of Confederation were finally adopted. Relying on a convention that I (and many others before me) have used before, I will refer to both congresses as the Continental Congress.

2. For a delightful and thorough discussion of this, see Dougherty, this volume.

3. This manner of thinking of institutions is influenced by Ostrom, Gardner, and Walker 1994, esp. ch. 2.

4. A congressional year ran from November of the preceding year through October. So, the congressional year 1780 began in November 1779 and ran through October 1780. Madison, by arriving in March 1780, had already missed a portion of the year.

5. For discussions of this period, see Banning 1995; Rakove 1990a. In addition, Dougherty (2001) gives an excellent overview of the general issues at stake.

6. See Dougherty 2002 for an excellent discussion of this point.

Chapter 11

Vote Trading in the First Federal Congress?
James Madison and the Compromise of 1790

D. RODERICK KIEWIET

Introduction

It is fitting that the men who designed the Constitution of the United States in 1787 are known as "the Framers," for that document is skeletal indeed. This is not to say that these individuals chose to engage in an abstract exercise in implementation theory. Advocates of particular policies, eager to have their preferences graven into constitutional bedrock, compelled delegates to the Constitutional Convention to consider all the major issues of the day. With a few exceptions, however, specific policies were not embedded into the Constitution, as doing so would have precluded adoption or stymied ratification. It was thus left to the First Federal Congress, elected in the first federal election of 1788, to address the many thorny questions that the Convention had left unresolved.

The achievements of this Congress—drafting the Bill of Rights, the creation of the first federal revenue system, and the establishment of the federal executive and judiciary branches—are impressive to this day. But perhaps its most famous product is the Compromise of 1790. On June 20 of that year, Thomas Jefferson, then secretary of state, hosted a dinner attended by Virginia congressman James Madison and Secretary of the Treasury Alexander Hamilton. Here, according to Jefferson, he and his guests struck a deal to resolve two crucial issues—referred to at the time as the residence and the assumption—with which Congress had been struggling. Hamilton promised that he and his supporters in Congress would facilitate the removal of the nation's seat of government from New York to a site along the Potomac, allowing initially for a long, temporary stay in Philadelphia. In exchange, Madison and/or Jefferson agreed to round up the votes needed to secure passage of a key element of Hamilton's funding plan—federal assumption of outstanding debts incurred by the states during the Revolutionary War.[1] In the days following the dinner at Jefferson's, Congress duly adopted both measures. In the eyes of political historians, this compromise was crucial to the survival of the embryonic union, and presaged other celebrated pacts struck between the North and the South in the antebellum era—the Missouri Compromise and the Compromise of 1850 (Bowling 1968, 1991; Cooke 1970; Elkins and McKitrick 1993; Ellis 2000).

The Compromise of 1790 is of great historical significance, but it holds continuing fascination for political scientists for another reason: it is generally regarded as the product of some sort of vote trade, wherein proponents of one measure agree to support another that they would otherwise oppose, while the latter measure's backers agree to do likewise (Aldrich 1995). Through such reciprocity is achieved the passage of two pieces of legislation that would both fail if considered on their own. The arrangement that Jefferson reports having brokered would appear to be a very early instance of a mode of legislative politics that has come to seem so quintessentially congressional.

But what actually happened in 1790? Some historians accept, at least in large measure, Jefferson's telling of the tale. Others find his version of events wanting, either incomplete, inaccurate on specific matters, or generally erroneous. In this paper, I seek to resolve some of the many controversies that have swirled around historical studies of the Compromise of 1790. In seeking to do so, I analyze the politics of the First Federal Congress from James Madison's vantage point. Adopting the approach that for better or worse has come to be known as the "rational choice" perspective, I assume that Madison sought to maximize his prospects for re-election.[2] In light of the re-election motive, I specify the legislative goals Madison sought to achieve, the obstacles that stood in his path, and the strategies that he pursued to overcome them.

The account that I construct of this intriguing chapter of legislative history leaves a number of loose ends. At many junctures, it is long on inference and short on hard evidence. I conclude, though, that what has been characterized as the Compromise of 1790 was not the product of a vote trade between Hamilton and Madison. Indeed, the distribution of preferences in Congress would have made a deal of this nature extremely problematic if not impossible. What I do find is that in the First Federal Congress, James Madison became a master of the game he had been so instrumental in devising.

The Dinner–Table Bargain

Jefferson probably jotted down his first notes on his famous dinner with Madison and Hamilton some two years after the event, his second memo nearly thirty years later (see the Appendix at the end of this chapter for the actual texts). Neither Madison nor Hamilton left any written record of their version of events. Memory—even Jefferson's—is fallible, and often readily altered by intervening events. In this particular instance, much of Jefferson's motivation for writing these memoranda was to explain how it was that he had come to deal with the treacherous monarchist Hamilton—not to leave a precise narrative for future historians. Both versions are vague in many places, and as Bowling (1991, 269) puts it, "self-serving and sometimes inaccurate."

Still, there are many reasons to accept the basic features of Jefferson's account of the Compromise. There had long been talk of such a bargain involving the residence and the assumption being fashioned, particularly among Madison's fellow Virginians. In a letter written to Madison on September 9, 1789, several months before the dinner at Jefferson's, Edward Carrington clearly sketched out the rough outline of the Compromise. After alluding to the difficulties of fixing a permanent site, he wrote: "Pensylva. might perhaps agree to take a temporary position—if the Southern states would unite with her for this object, several considerations of a commercial kind might some short day hence induce the Eastern states to join the southern in coming further" (*The Papers of James Madison* [hereafter MP], 12, 393). Another Virginian, Henry Lee, writing to Madison on March 30, 1790, asserted that only the placement of the capital on the Potomac could assuage Virginia's supreme unhappiness with assumption: "This govt. which we both admired so much, will I fear prove ruinous in its operation to our native state. Nothing as I said in my letr. the other day can alleviate our sufferings but the establishment of the permanent seat near the center of territory" (MP 13, 102–3).

Furthermore, soon after the dinner rumors circulated that the deal had been cut (Bowling 1991, 188). When Congress subsequently approved both the Philadelphia-Potomac residence measure and assumption, politicians, political observers, and polemicists all agreed that a vote trade had occurred. A letter from "B.K." to the *New-York Journal* charged that the federal government was leaving New York because "the Pennsylvania and Potomac interests have been purchased with *twenty-one and an half millions of dollars*" [the total amount of state debt that was assumed] (quoted in ibid., 196). Another piece in the same newspaper charged that "Miss Assumption" had been seduced by "Mr. Residence," and had given birth to two illegitimate children, "Philadelphia" and "Potowmacus" (quoted in Malone 1951, 303). In a letter written to Madison on the last day of the year, George Nicholas (from the Kentucky District of Virginia) vented his unhappiness over assumption and with the vote trade that he believed had produced it: "The Assumption of the State debts was I think unjust and also exceeded your powers; but I do not dislike the measure as much as I do the mode of carrying it. As a separate question there was certainly a majority against it, and nothing could have carried it but the local interests of some States in other questions then depending" (MP 13, 337–38).

In addition to this and other documentary evidence, there are social scientific considerations that point to the necessity of a vote trade in this situation. First, even though the nation's population at the time was strung out along a narrow band running from Massachusetts to Georgia, Black's Theorem—which would presumably point to the choice of a median location somewhere in the Middle States of Pennsylvania or New Jersey—clearly did not hold. The Confederation Congress, predecessor of the First Federal Congress, had cycled over dozens of proposals for siting the capital (Jillson and Wilson 1994; Aldrich, Jillson, and Wilson 2002). The First Federal Congress had been similarly stymied in its first session (Bowling 1991). Secondly, Hamilton's proposal that the federal government assume outstanding state war debts had all the earmarks of "divide the dollar," a well-known coreless game form wherein any alternative can be defeated by some other majority-preferred alternative. Some sort of grand bargain would appear to have been necessary to break the logjam on these two measures.

Other theoretical considerations, however, suggest caution in accepting this version of events. It is, at best, incomplete. Assume that there was in fact a vote trade involving the residence and the assumption. In light of the well-known instability results regarding vote trades, why was it that this particular vote trade prevailed and not some other? It is not as if members of the First Federal Congress were unable to conceive of or contemplate alternative bargains. As Representative William L. Smith from South Carolina observed in early June of 1790: "Negotiations, cabals, plots, and counterplots have prevailed for months past without yet ripening to any decision" (quoted ibid., 180).

The historiography on the Compromise of 1790 also reveals sources of doubt surrounding crucial features of Jefferson's account. It is clear from both the 1792 and 1818 texts that Madison had agreed to induce his fellow Virginians White and Lee, who had previously voted against assumption, to switch their votes and thus effect passage of the measure. Exactly what Hamilton was supposed to do in return is the subject of considerable controversy. Jefferson's notes from 1792 indicate that Hamilton had promised to work with Robert Morris to persuade the Pennsylvania delegation to support the Philadelphia-Potomac residence agreement: "This Hamilton took on himself, and chiefly, as I understood, through the agency of Robert Morris, obtained the vote of that state, on agreeing to an intermediate residence at

Philadelphia" (Boyd 1965 [hereafter JP], 17, 206–7). The 1818 *Anas* version is similar:"Hamilton undertook to carry the other point. In doing this, the influence he had established over the eastern members, with the agency of Robert Morris with those of the middle States, effected his side of the engagement" (Jefferson 1818, 276).

Malone (1951) and Cooke (1970) infer from these passages that Hamilton promised to round up votes from Morris and the Pennsylvanians for passage of the Residence Bill. Bowling (1991) and Ellis (2000) disagree. There certainly is an asymmetry here—while explicitly providing the names of the Virginians who were to switch their votes on assumption, Jefferson is much more vague as to exactly what Hamilton was to do. According to Bowling (1991, 185), moreover, Madison did not need votes to achieve passage of the Philadelphia-Potomac measure. A vote trade in which only one party to the bargain supplies votes seems remarkably asymmetric, to say the least.

Bowling and other scholars infer that what Hamilton must have promised instead was to intercede with proassumption New Englanders to persuade them not to make counterproposals that would derail the Philadelphia-Potomac arrangement for the seat of government. If so, the Compromise of 1790 would actually consist of an agreement by Madison to supply votes for assumption in return for an agreement by Hamilton to break a voting cycle on siting the capital. As we shall see, however, in the days following the dinner at Jefferson's, New Englanders and New Yorkers continued their attempts to derail the Philadelphia-Potomac Bill. If this was the arrangement, then, it does not seem to me that Hamilton was able to deliver on any such promise. That being the case, I also doubt that Madison would have believed that Hamilton was even capable of delivering, and would therefore not have agreed to terms such as these.

Other historians note that the dinner at Jefferson's was merely one of several meetings held in June of 1790 to consider various means of jointly resolving the residence and assumption questions. According to Ellis (2000, 51), Jefferson's account is "essentially true," but "it vastly oversimplifies the history that was happening at that propitious moment. Which is to say that several secret meetings were occurring at the same time; and the political corridors were even more labyrinthine than Jefferson's imperfect memory of events." More specifically, Bowling (1991, 182–83) describes a series of fateful meetings in the week prior to the dinner at Jefferson's that appear to have cemented key features of the Compromise, particularly the Philadelphia-Potomac bargain on the residence. Elkins and McKitrick (1993, 160) also find a number of holes in Jefferson's account of the dinner and the Compromise, but conclude that "a bargain at this level is not to be judged on simple mechanical criteria, so many votes this way or that."

Cooke (1970, 524), by far the most skeptical of the assumption-in-return-for-residence scenario, argues that "one has only to read the debates of Congress and examine congressional roll call votes to doubt that the agreement was responsible for the passage of the residence bill or assumption." By his account, essential agreements on residence had been reached before the dinner at Jefferson's, and assumption was approved because Congress had first made significant changes in Hamilton's original proposal. He also argues that "[t]he dinner table bargain, finally, involved votes in the House, whereas the crucial battle for both assumption and the residence took place in the Senate" (525). In light of these and other difficulties, Cooke concludes that "the bargain worked out by Jefferson, Madison, and Hamilton was not consummated.... Each [bill] was treated separately and its passage was owing to sub rosa congressional negotiations and compromises relating only to that measure" (ibid.). In a recent econometric analysis of roll call data from the First Federal Congress, Clinton and Meirowitz (2002) reach a similar conclusion.

The editors of Madison's papers, Hobson and Rutland, even doubt that Madison either promised or attempted to persuade anyone to change his vote on assumption (MP 13, 246). For the most part they choose not to speculate as to exactly what happened in 1790. As they put it: "A paucity of documentation makes it impossible to reconstruct the tangled web of political maneuvering that ended so happily in compromise" (MP 13, 243). More specifically, they report that "JM's letters during June and July provide neither sufficient evidence for coupling the assumption and residence bills nor any clues to his role in bringing about the compromise. In fact, JM leaves the impression that he was an observer rather than manipulator of events" (ibid., 245).

An observer rather than manipulator of events? If that was in fact the impression Madison sought to create, it should immediately raise our suspicions that he did so in order to best serve his purposes. If nothing else, the utter improbability of this characterization of Madison implies that it could be very instructive to re-examine the Compromise of 1790 in light of Madison's legislative goals and the strategies he undertook to achieve them.

Madison of Virginia

The central role he played at the Constitutional Convention and his coauthorship of the *Federalist Papers* identified Madison as the chief architect of the new federal government. These efforts, however, played better in the country as a whole than they did back home in Virginia. Leader of the Federalist forces at the Virginia Ratification Convention, Madison prevailed by only a slim margin of votes (89–79) after a tough, rancorous fight. After the ensuing state elections, his nemesis Patrick Henry and the Anti-Federalists

controlled the Virginia legislature. Madison knew he had no chance of being named to the Senate. Seeking instead a seat in the House in the election
of 1788, Madison also found that he had been gerrymandered into a district
with strong Anti-Federalist leanings (Rakove 1991).

Running against James Monroe—his friend, neighbor, and business associate—Madison was forced to campaign hard, at least by the standards of the
time. Finding that his opposition to amending the new Constitution was politically untenable, Madison changed course, promising the voters in his district that if elected, he would work tirelessly for the adoption of amendments
they favored (Bowling 1988). Although many remained skeptical of his conversion, Madison managed to defeat Monroe by a vote of 1,308 to 972. The
father of the Constitution was now a freshman congressman from Virginia
whose prospects for re-election were far from certain.

Madison was a brilliant man, but even a person of modest intellect could
have identified the objectives that, if realized, would guarantee his re-election and political future. As we have just noted, his constituents strongly favored several amendments to the Constitution. The key role he played in obtaining passage of what ultimately became known as the Bill of Rights not
only bolstered his re-election prospects, but also secured for him a special
place in the history of democratic government.

But there were other, more tangible issues that Madison would seek to resolve to his and to his constituents' advantage. The first was the location of
the seat of government, or what we call the residence—a vexing problem
that Madison had been working on since 1783. Placement of the capital on
the Potomac River would reduce dramatically the conflict that his Virginia
constituents increasingly sensed between the interests of their state and the
interests of the new United States. The Potomac, furthermore, had become
George Washington's chief priority, if not an obsession. According to Bowling (1991), Washington evinced "almost fanatic attention" to the issue of the
new capital. Madison worked closely with the president, keeping him well
informed as to what was going on in Congress. Madison could imagine few
things that would give him more satisfaction than delivering the Potomac
site to Washington.

Secondly, Madison needed to see that Virginia fared as well as possible in
the ongoing reconciliation of state and federal debt and expenditure accounts from the Revolutionary War. Some states, particularly Massachusetts
and South Carolina, had paid off little of their war debts. Other states, notably Virginia, had retired much of the debt accumulated during the war. If
the federal government were to adopt Hamilton's funding plan of assuming
outstanding state debts and apportion taxes accordingly, Virginia would come

out a net loser unless otherwise compensated. Letters Madison received from leading citizens of Virginia were unanimous in condemning the injustice that they perceived in this proposal. Speaking before Congress in opposition to the assumption proposal, Madison nicely summarized these objections: "The citizens of a state will be burthened, in proportion as their state has made exertions to discharge its obligations" (MP 13, 63).

In addition to the possibility of debt assumption, there was also the issue of "settlement." In 1787 the Confederation Congress had established a Board of Commissioners to review states' claims of expenditures incurred during the war for the "common cause." Unfortunately for Virginia and other Southern states, the board had been taking a tough, legalistic line in accepting claims for expenses. As Ferguson (1961, 207) observes: "With the exception of South Carolina, whose accounts were in fairly good condition, there was never the slightest possibility that claims of the southern states could be supported by documents." As in the case of assumption, then, the settlement of expenditure claims threatened to go badly for Virginia, giving rise to increasing anxiety and anger among Madison's constituents. If Virginia were to have any future in the union and he any future in politics, Madison would need to turn this situation around.

The Residence

It is not hard to understand why members of the First Federal Congress desired to have the nation's seat of government reside in their own region, state, or city. Proximity is a crucial advantage in acquiring information about new legislation, contracts, or government jobs. This was especially true in an era in which traveling even twenty miles overland was an arduous undertaking. Building a federal city would likely produce a real estate boom as well, yielding windfall gains to landowners. Not surprisingly, between 1783 and 1790, the Confederation and Federal Congress entertained proposals for more than thirty different sites for the "Federal City."

Madison faced a seemingly insurmountable obstacle in gaining a Potomac site. It was too far south. In the First Federal Congress there were twenty-three representatives from New York and New England, twenty-eight from the Southern states (counting Maryland and Delaware), and eleven from the Middle States of Pennsylvania and New Jersey. The situation in the Senate was similar, with five Northern states, six Southern states, and two Middle States.[3] It seemed obvious to most people at the time that the seat of government would surely end up somewhere in the middle—that is, in either Pennsylvania or New Jersey. Indeed, Anti-Federalists charged that the desire to gain the capital had unfairly facilitated ratification of the Constitution in both these states.

The record of the Confederation Congress in choosing a seat of government further bolstered expectations of a median location. In 1783 the arrival of large numbers of unpaid and seriously disgruntled Continental soldiers (the so-called Philadelphia Mutiny) induced the Confederation Congress, which had been meeting in Philadelphia, to move to Princeton, New Jersey. Accommodations there were spartan. Sharing a narrow bed with a fellow delegate from Virginia, Madison reported that the room in his boarding house was so small that one person had to stay in bed while the other dressed (Bowling 1991, 50). In October of that year, the Confederation Congress adopted a proposal offered by Elbridge Gerry and Arthur Lee to rotate the seat of government between two permanent sites—one on the Delaware, the other on the Potomac. In December 1784, however, Congress rescinded this decision and adopted a proposal to situate the "Federal Town" (an appropriately modest title, given the prevailing view that the powers of the federal government should be very limited) at the falls of the Delaware, just south of Trenton, New Jersey. The proposal also called for Congress to meet temporarily in New York. This detour was necessary to permit construction of a meeting site and boarding houses in the new town, and also to meet the demands of John Jay, who avowed that he would serve as secretary of foreign affairs only if Congress agreed to go to New York. The nine state delegations in attendance at that time unanimously approved a subsequent resolution to appropriate $100,000 for the new federal town (ibid., 65).[4] Madison opposed the move to New York. He feared that moving farther north would make it even more difficult to eventually achieve a Potomac site (ibid., 42).

When the First Federal Congress took up a Seat of Government Bill in September 1789, Madison knew that if the Potomac site were to be selected, he would first need to defeat its many competitors.[5] Above all, Madison knew that it would be difficult to prevent selection of a more northerly and thus more central location. An obvious choice was Philadelphia, by far the largest and most important city in the middle of the country. It had hosted both the Continental and Confederation Congresses, as well as the Constitutional Convention. Furthermore, in the 1788 election, Pennsylvania had elected eight representatives at large, guaranteeing that Philadelphians would dominate the state delegation to Congress.

Proponents of Philadelphia were actually seeking a site in the environs of Philadelphia, Germantown being the most likely. Philadelphia was already the state capital, and in 1788 the Pennsylvania Ratification Convention had resolved that the federal capital could be placed anywhere in the state except in the city of Philadelphia per se. They did so because they were desirous to retain state jurisdiction over the state's only port and the revenues it generated, and to thwart ongoing efforts to move the state capital westward. Robert Morris, international merchant, former superintendent of finance under the Confederation, preeminent Federalist, and newly chosen senator from Pennsylvania, had also acquired a considerable amount of real estate in Germantown.

Another major Pennsylvania contender for the federal capital was a location along the banks of the Susquehanna River, near present-day Columbia. Being near the mouth of the Susquehanna in Chesapeake Bay also put Baltimore in contention, as it would be favored by some Pennsylvanians and, presumably, by at least two Marylanders in the House and one in the Senate. Another leading possibility was the lower falls of the Delaware, which would put the capital at or near the Trenton, New Jersey, site that the Confederation Congress had chosen earlier. By 1787, Robert Morris had acquired property in this area as well.

Several features of the choice over residence, however, gave Madison room to maneuver. During this era, as now, the ease and rapidity of moving between two points (which is presumably where the utility in minimizing spatial distance comes from) was not a simple function of linear distance. Representatives traveling from the Southern states, for example, could reach New York (an ice-free, deep-sea port) faster and more dependably than locations on either the Delaware, up the Chesapeake, or still farther up the Susquehanna. Questions about the removal of obstacles to navigation on the Susquehanna, and at what and whose expense, plagued those who supported that site.

Nonspatial features of each site also militated against their selection. Philadelphia, home of Benjamin Franklin, Benjamin Rush, and other ardent opponents of slavery, was particularly objectionable to many Southerners. Pennsylvania law mandated that any slave residing in the state continuously for six months would become free. This created a major inconvenience for Southern congressmen (as well as for George Washington), who were thereby forced to take the slaves in their entourage out of the state for at least a few hours every six months (ibid., 212). Philadelphia encountered opposition from the North as well. Representatives from New York and eastern (i.e., northern) New Jersey were determined that if the federal government was not to remain in New York, then at least it would not end up with their arch-rival Philadelphia. Indeed, much of the attractiveness of the Susquehanna and Delaware sites owed simply to the fact that they were not Philadelphia. Robert Morris and those congressmen in his sway, conversely, saw the Susquehanna as the major threat to the sites they favored—that is, Germantown, or failing that, the falls of the Delaware.

A final source of complication lay in the fact that in addition to a permanent site, Congress needed to select a site to serve as a temporary capital until new facilities for the federal government were constructed. In short, the issue of space was fully multidimensional. Maclay, in his notes on the battle over the residence, calculated that "the Mariners compass has 32 points the political one perhaps as many hundreds, and the Schemers an indefinite number" (Bowling and Veit 1988 [hereafter MD], 145).

A flurry of proposals and counterproposals concerning the residence surfaced during the first session of the new Congress. New Yorkers had sought to make the members of the First Federal Congress as comfortable as possible, and most members had enjoyed their stay there. Still, they knew their city had no chance of becoming the permanent capital, and so their representatives sought to make any deal that would prolong Congress's stay in New York for as long as possible. Madison was fully aware of their strategy. In a letter to Virginia representative Alexander White, he wrote: "This I believe is the ultimate [aim?] of the N.Y. party, and will not do for us. I suspect they begin to despair of a long possession of Congs. and consequently mix the permanent with the temporary considerations" (MP 12, 353).

The overture the New Yorkers made to the pivotal Pennsylvanians was to support a permanent site in Pennsylvania (as long as it was not Philadelphia) in return for a long, temporary residence in New York. New Englanders made the proposal more specific—a permanent site on the Susquehanna in return for temporary residence in New York. Besides gaining the support of most Pennsylvanians, the two Marylanders (Smith and Seney) whose districts were on that river would presumably also be in favor (Bowling 1991).

In his subsequent meeting with the Pennsylvanians, Madison countered with a proposal—a permanent capital on the Potomac, preceded by a long, temporary residence in Philadelphia. Maclay, a staunch supporter of the Susquehanna, was horrified, as revealed in his diary entry of August 29: "a moment after I met Mr. Smith of Maryland. He had a Terrible Story, *and from the most undoubted authority.* A contract was entered into by the Virginians and Pennsylvanians. to fix the permanent Residence on the Potowmac, right or Wrong. And the temporary residence was to be in Philada. and Clymer and Fitzsimons were gone to Philadelphia to reconcile the Citizens of that place to it" (MD, 140). When Maclay checked out the rumor with House members from Pennsylvania, they all denied it.

Faced with this threat, some New Englanders thought it best to counter with Baltimore, believing this would win the support of Marylanders and

Pennsylvanians who favored the Upper Chesapeake. Morris, meanwhile, lobbied members from New Jersey and New England to switch their support from the Susquehanna to the Delaware.

On September 3, the Goodhue Resolution, precursor of a bill that would place the capital on the Susquehanna, came to the House floor. Madison pulled out all the stops in opposing it. He intimated darkly that Virginia's loyalty to the union would be shaken if Congress chose the Susquehanna instead of the Potomac: "[G]ive me now leave to say that if a prophet had risen in that body [the Virginia ratification convention] and brought the declarations and proceedings of this day into their view, that I as firmly believe, Virginia might not have been a part of the union at this moment" (MP 12, 372). His speech to the House the following day was, for the most part, a long discourse on the merits of the Potomac relative to the Susquehanna. He allowed that the Susquehanna was currently closer to the population center of the country, but predicted that the Potomac soon would be, as new settlers moved to the South and West. In any case, the Potomac was *geographically* more central than the Susquehanna, and allowed for easier access to the emerging West. What caught attention, however, were Madison's opening remarks. Incredibly, the man who had recently authored many of the *Federalist Papers* described the new nation as a "confederacy of states" and asserted that "local governments will ever possess a keener sense and capacity, to take advantage of those powers, on which the protection of local rights depend" (ibid., 373). If Madison sounded desperate, he probably was and should have been, as we shall see.

It is doubtful that Madison's speeches changed anyone's mind. A direct challenge to the Goodhue Resolution showed the Potomac a clear loser, as Lee's motion to replace the Susquehanna with the Potomac failed 29–21. Madison's own amendment to add the words "or Potomac" similarly failed. After other challenges failed, the House approved a motion to replace the "east bank of the Susquehanna" with the "banks of the Susquehanna." A centrist outcome appeared to be locked in, and prospects for the Potomac looked bleak. In a letter to Edmund Pendleton written on September 14, Madison reports the failure of his overture to the Pennsylvanians. He promised to fight on, but seemed resigned to the Susquehanna:

> On the side of Penna. who was full of distrust and animosity agst. N. Engd. & N. York, the Potowmac was presented as the reward for the temporary advantages if given by the S. States. Some progress was made on this ground, and the prospect became flattering, when a reunion was produced among the original parties by circumstances which it wd be tedious to explain. The Susquehanah has in consequence been voted. The bill is not yet brought in and many things may yet hap-

pen. We shall parry any decision if we can, tho' I see little hope of attaining our own object, the Eastern states being inflexibly opposed to the Potomwac & for some reasons which are more likely to grow stronger than weaker—and if we are to be placed on the Susquehanah, the sooner the better. (Ibid. 12, 402–3)

The first hint that the Potomac site might still have a chance came with the approval of an amendment offered by Gale of Maryland. This Proviso, as it came to be called, stipulated that before any land could be purchased by the federal government for a new capital, Maryland and Pennsylvania must demonstrate to the president that the river (i.e., the Susquehanna) had been made navigable from that site all the way to the Chesapeake Bay. This favored the interests of Baltimore over Philadelphia, but, more important, gave President Washington the ability to postpone movement to that site. After failing initially, the Proviso passed when the speaker (Frederick Muhlenberg of Pennsylvania) broke a tie and voted for it. Many of the Pennsylvanians apparently decided to go along with it in the belief that the Proviso would be dropped in the Senate and thus in conference as well.

Madison continued his fight against the bill. He argued that it was unconstitutional: Congress alone had the power to choose its residence, whereas this bill, after adoption of the Proviso, delegated such power to the president. He also asserted that describing the site chosen as the "permanent" seat of government was at odds with the Constitution, which made no mention of any decision being permanent. Both challenges failed, and on September 17 the Susquehanna Bill passed 31–17.

Despite the seemingly overwhelming support in the House for the Susquehanna site, Madison knew that the battle was not yet lost. In a September 23 letter to Edmund Pendleton, he expressed hope that a coalition of minorities would form in the Senate to thwart the bill:

> The bill however is by no means sure of passing the Senate in its present form. It is even possible that it may fall altogether. Those who wish to do nothing at this time, added to those who disapprove of the Susquehannah, either as too far South, or too far North, or not susceptible of early conveniences for the fiscal administration, may form a majority who will directly or indirectly frustrate the measure. In case of an indirect mode, some other place, will be substituted for Susquehannah, as Trenton, or Germantown, neither of which can I conceive be effectively established, and either of which might get a majority, composed of sincere and insidious votes. (Ibid., 419)

Madison's sense that bicameralism would come to his rescue was no doubt enhanced by his knowledge that when the Senate took up the bill, floor management would by convention be assumed by a senator from the state in question—in this case, none other than Robert Morris, a greater foe of the Susquehanna than Madison himself.[6] Morris first sought to amend the bill by deleting the Gale Proviso. Failing that, he moved to substitute Germantown for the Susquehanna, and personally guaranteed to spend $100,000 to develop the new site if the Pennsylvania legislature were unwilling to do so! Morris had also promised the New York senators that the capital would remain temporarily in New York until at least January 1793. After losing initially, Morris won when a Delaware senator who claimed not to have understood the nature of the bill changed his vote and supported Morris's amendment. Vice president Adams broke the 9–9 tie in favor of Morris's motion for Germantown, and the bill returned once more to the House (Bowling 1991, 157–58). The Philadelphians' expectations that Adams would favor them appeared to have been borne out.[7]

Madison sought unsuccessfully to postpone consideration of the bill until the next session, but did manage to carry a motion for a one-day adjournment. Then, seemingly resigned to defeat, on September 28 he proposed one last amendment. He pointed out that once Congress assumed jurisdiction of the territory at the Germantown site, it would be without benefit of law. He therefore urged the House to "provide against one inconvenience," and moved that the laws of Pennsylvania remain in effect until Congress specified otherwise (MP 12, 424). Madison's housekeeping amendment was adopted, and the bill as a whole carried 31–24. This sent the bill back to the Senate. Bowling (1991, 158) reports that Madison "spent all weekend in a desperate attempt to kill the bill." He succeeded. The Senate voted to postpone consideration of the bill until next session, effectively killing it.

Expectations of the bill's ultimate failure may also have influenced the behavior of many congressmen at prior stages of consideration. Most notably, some members of the House may have decided not to oppose the Susquehanna bill in the belief that it would eventually be derailed. Fisher Ames of Massachusetts, for example, asserted that he and other New Englanders much preferred seeing the measure fail than end up in Germantown (Bowling 1991, 160). Whatever the case, the first session ended with no decision made on the residence. Madison, if not the creator of it, at the very least was able to exploit a voting cycle induced by the bicameral structure of the new Congress to defeat both Germantown and the Susquehanna. As the first session adjourned, Madison had so far won nothing on the residence. However, he had managed to live to fight another day

In assessing Madison's successful defense against contenders to the Potomac, historians have been impressed not by his shrewd legislative strategy but by his apparent break with Hamilton and the Federalists. According to

Bowling (1991, 143), "Madison's long and widely reported speech [on the location of the capital] marked the public debut of a fundamental shift in his political stance from architect of a strong federal government to a defender of states' rights and from a leader of the Federalists to a spokesman for a new opposition party built on a foundation of decentralism." The historical record is certainly consistent with Bowling's assessment. As we know, in the next session of Congress Madison became the chief opponent of Hamilton's proposal for federal assumption of state debts. In Washington's second term the schism that had developed between Hamilton and the Jefferson-Madison faction flared into a bitter partisan divide.

It is my belief, however, that this interpretation of Madison's speech is too heavily colored by these highly salient subsequent developments, and overstates the extent of the breach between Hamilton and Madison (as well as Jefferson) that was present at this time. In response to a letter from Tench Coxe, who informed Madison that he (Coxe) had found his speech quite disturbing, Madison claims that he had not meant his remarks about Virginia and its dissatisfaction with the union to be as ominous as they sounded. According to Madison, the newspaper article reporting his speech "discoloured much the remarks which it puts in my mouth," as it had failed to place his comments in the context of a rebuttal to John Laurance of New York (MP 12, 409). The editor of the *Daily Advertiser* published the same clarification of Madison's speech—most likely due to a complaint from Madison (ibid., 396). In actuality, Madison remained perfectly willing to bargain with Hamilton. The deal he would eventually seek, however, was not, as conventional accounts of the Compromise of 1790 would have it, the residence in return for assumption.

Assumption

The second session of the First Federal Congress, which opened in January of 1790, soon took up consideration of the financial plan Hamilton had formulated in his celebrated *Report on the Public Credit*. Most features of the plan had broad congressional support, but the proposal that the federal government assume the existing debts of the state did not. Disagreement over assumption was not particularly ideological. Many states, particularly the hard-money state of Massachusetts, felt that assumption of their debts was necessary for their financial survival. Even leading Anti-Federalist Elbridge Gerry supported assumption, as did the erstwhile states' rights champions of South Carolina, who had been specifically instructed by their state legislature to support assumption. Other states, notably Virginia, had extinguished large amounts of their war debts by following the standard Colonial practice of "currency finance" and accepting state loan certificates (and in some cases federal certificates) in payment for taxes owed (Ferguson 1961). Finally, it should be noted that by 1790 the vast bulk of state debt, from both the North and the South, was held by a few thousand merchants and financiers in New York and New England.

Madison quickly emerged as leader of the opposition to assumption. Hamilton was baffled by Madison's stance, and felt blindsided as well. Madison was the other half of Publius. He and Madison had seen eye to eye on financial matters during the entirety of the Confederation Congress—including agreement on the desirability of federal assumption of state debts. Actually there was little in the plan that had not been present in Morris's plan of 1783, which both had supported. In preparing to write the *Report on the Public Credit* in September of 1789, Madison was one of the first persons Hamilton had consulted for advice. Madison's reply—that he was too busy and otherwise lacked the expertise to respond with useful comment—should probably have tipped Hamilton off that something was amiss.

According to Bowling (1991, 169), Madison's opposition to assumption "publicly confirmed the change of mind which he had first intimated during the seat of government debate in September: he would act more consciously as a decentralist, a southerner, and a Virginian." Indeed, by this time Sedgwick of Massachusetts regarded Madison as "an apostate from all his former principles. Whether he is really a convert to antifederalism . . . or whether he means to put himself at the head of the discontented in America time will discover" (quoted in Bickford and Bowling 1989, 95). Ellis (2000, 55) concurs: "During the six months prior to the dinner at Jefferson's quarters, Madison went through a conversion process, or perhaps a reconversion, from the religious faith of nationalism to the old revolutionary faith of Virginia." Elkins and McKitrick (1993, 146), finally, speak of "the divided mind of James Madison." Although "he had never doubted that the national honor required an unassailable national credit," it was also true that "Madison did what he did because of a spreading repugnance within himself to the entire system of which assumption was a part, that the more he saw of it the less he liked it."[8]

As indicated earlier, in my view these historians have overestimated the extent to which Madison had broken with Hamilton at this time. I also think that Hamilton was naive in failing to anticipate Madison's opposition to assumption. Both misunderstandings spring from the same source, and that is in not appreciating that at this time Madison was first and foremost a re-election-seeking congressman from rural Virginia. How could Madison effectively represent his constituents and *not* oppose assumption? Virginia, as noted above, had relatively few debts to assume, and would be a net loser under Hamilton's plan.

Virginia was also faring badly in the settlement of expenditures made during the war. The state's inability to provide documentation for its claims, combined with looming and lapsed deadlines, portended significant financial losses. The Virginians' worst fear, however, was that the passage of assumption, which would add approximately $25 million to the debt of the federal government, would guarantee that their claims for expenditures would continue to be given short shrift. During the First Federal Congress, Madison received several letters from leading citizens of Virginia, including Henry Lee, Edward Carrington, Edmund Randolph, and Edmund Pendleton, all expressing fervent opposition to assumption.

It is also important to note that Madison's opposition to assumption was not grounded in principle, and was not absolute. At several junctures he indicated that he would countenance assumption if certain conditions could be met. His chief demand was that assumption be linked to adequate provision for Virginia's large (though undocumented) claims in the settlement of wartime expenditures. As Banning (1995, 318) argues: "All the surviving evidence suggests that Madison was concerned, at the beginning, with the equity of Hamilton's proposal, that he might indeed have voted for it if he had been able to amend it to assure fair treatment of Virginia."

In late February 1790 the House began debate on the assumption resolution—specifically, "That the debts of the respective states ought, with the consent of the creditors, to be assumed and provided for by the United States" (MP 13, 60). Speaking against the resolution on February 24, Madison first argued that making the taxing power of the federal government the sole means of raising revenue to manage debt would be counterproductive; federal, state, and local taxing authorities, working independently and thus allowing for variation in the types of taxes that citizens of different states were willing to tolerate, would raise more revenue (ibid., 61). He also argued that Virginia was being penalized for having paid off debt:

> One great objection to the original proposition is, that by taking up the debts of the several states, as you find them now, you do great injustice to those states, who have, by their exertions, discharged the greatest part of the equal debts contracted during the late war: By this means compelling them, after having done their duty, to contribute to those states who have not equally done their duty. Now, my idea is, that instead of considering the debts as they are found at this moment, we contemplate them as in the state they existed at the close of the late war. (Ibid., 72)

His most serious objection to Hamilton's plan, however, is that it failed to address Virginia's ongoing concern that its claims for expenditures were not being honored. He therefore proposed that the assumption resolution include the following amendment: "that effectual provision be, at the same time, made for liquidating and crediting, to the states, the whole of their expenditures during the war, as the same hath been or may be stated for the purpose; and, in such liquidation, the best evidence shall be received that the nature of the case will permit" (ibid., 61). Assumption, in short, must be linked to settlement. Defending his amendment on the floor, he dismissed those who argued that Virginia should simply trust in the good faith of the Board of Commissioners charged with settling state accounts:

> It may be said that this is a superfluous condition; because there is a board in existence charged with the trust: But, sir, their power does not reach the great object contemplated. The limitation act has already barred a great number of equitable claims of one state; perhaps there are other states in the same predicament. . . . [If] adequate provision is not made on this head, a great deal more injustice will be done than by a refusal to assume the state debts.
>
> I hope I shall be excused for connecting these provisions; because I think it is impossible to separate them, in justice or propriety. (Ibid., 61 62)

On February 26, Madison came back to the same point. As the *Congressional Register* (IV, 67) summarized his remarks: "Mr. Madison . . . believed there was but one ground upon which the assumption of the state debts could be justified; and that was, securing, at the same time, a speedy and effectual provision for the liquidation and apportionment of the expenditures of the late war" (MP 13, 65). On March 1 he said it again: "There is no other way to obviate these objections, than by making our measures subservient to the ultimate settlement of the accounts between the United States and individual states, as in this alone can equality be found: So far then, as this object is kept in view, it [assumption of state debts] may have my approbation; but on no other condition" (ibid., 73–74).

Madison did not succeed in getting the House to adopt his amendment.[9] However, when the critical vote on assumption itself occurred on April 12, the proposal failed, 31–29. Proassumption New Englanders were devastated, and it was they who now intimated that maybe it would be better that the union be dissolved.[10] Well into the second session, then, the First Federal Congress had not only failed to resolve the questions of residence and assumption, but had endangered the future of the union in the process.

Madison's Strategic Problem: The Linkage between the Residence and Assumption

The ill will and disappointment that the defeat of assumption engendered among the measure's advocates led many to question whether the still fragile union would survive. Madison's unflagging efforts to defeat assumption would seem to parallel the tenacity of his fight against contenders to the Potomac in the battle over the residence in the first session. Here his opposition had been so strenuous and so strident that many inferred he had abruptly shifted his fundamental political beliefs. Why was Madison willing to play such serious political hardball to defeat Hamilton's proposal, and to risk so much?

I believe that at this point it is important to understand the absolute necessity, from Madison's point of view, of turning back assumption, and why he had been so determined to defeat the Susquehanna. True, in both cases these were the positions his constituents strongly supported. But there is more to it than that. Although assumption was reasonably popular in Congress and many had expected it to pass, in reality Hamilton and his allies, as we have just seen, were a few votes short. In return for these last few crucial votes, Hamilton calculated, he could in return supply support for a proposal on the residence. This is precisely the deal, of course, that has been seen to constitute the Compromise of 1790. The most promising prospect in this regard was the Pennsylvania delegation. Hartley, Fitzsimons, Clymer, and Wynkoop favored assumption. Both Muhlenbergs, Hiester, and Scott were opposed, but reportedly not adamantly so. On a number of occasions, then, Hamilton proposed that the latter four members provide the votes for assumption in return for the residence—on the Susquehanna, in Germantown, the falls of the Delaware, or wherever.

The extreme danger that a bargain of this nature posed to Madison is due to the fact that the Pennsylvania delegation was at the same time the source of the votes that Madison needed to obtain the residence for the Potomac! His proposal to them, as indicated earlier, was for a permanent capital on the Potomac, preceded by a long, temporary residence in Philadelphia.

But the Pennsylvanians could not go both ways. If they agreed to a deal with Hamilton involving the permanent residence in Pennsylvania in return for assumption, Madison's proposal to the Pennsylvanians—a permanent site on the Potomac in exchange for a temporary stay in Philadelphia—would be trumped. For Madison, losing on the residence would mean losing on assumption. Losing on assumption would mean losing on the residence. To win the capital for the Potomac, Madison not only needed to defeat the Susquehanna. He also needed to defeat assumption.

The Residence, Again

The failure of the assumption bill, following the deadlock in the previous session over the residence, sets the stage nicely for the fateful dinner at Jefferson's house and the compromise. Many historians believe, however, that Jefferson had succumbed to what social psychologists refer to as "fundamental attribution error"—the all-too-human tendency to overestimate the importance of one's own role in the course of events. Hobson and Rutland (MP 13), Bowling (1991), and Elkins and McKitrick (1993) all conclude that the Virginia and Pennsylvania delegations in Congress had arrived at the Philadelphia-Potomac bargain on the residence in the week prior to the dinner at Jefferson's.

As indicated previously, Madison had first made the Philadelphia-Potomac proposal to the Pennsylvanians in the first session, but had gotten nowhere with it. While still in New York following the end of the first session, however, he received a letter dated October 7 from William Grayson, senator from Virginia, who was in Philadelphia at that time. Grayson had recently met and dined with Robert Morris, who remained "very much irritated with his disappointment" over the last-minute loss of Germantown, and blamed the New Englanders and New Yorkers for his defeat. Morris, furthermore, had agreed with Grayson's assessment of the situation:

> [If] any place in Pensylvy. was proposed except Susquehannah, that N.York would be agt. them, & that if Susquehannah was made the happy spot we should have the assistance of Jersey; that I even doubted N.York & the Eastern people of possessing any *real* sentiments than those that were *frustatory* that we should be cautious about stirring the subject again unless upon sure grounds & thereby [bring] them to form combinations against us. (MP 12, 431)

A subsequent meeting with Thomas Scott, a member of the Pennsylvania delegation in the House, had gone even better:

> . . . & Scott thinks that a majority of the delegation are so irrietated [sic] as to go unconditionally to the Potowmack by way of spiting N.York. It is clear to me that our contest about the Potowmack has been of infinite consequence; she is gaining friends daily, by being brought into view; & I agree with you that we played a great game & staked nothing. I would now (though never sanguine before) bett her agt. the field. (Ibid., 432)

Sensing real opportunity in the air, Madison immediately set off for Philadelphia. As Risjord (1976, 311) reports, he too met with Morris, and "the two reaffirmed the Pennsylvania-Virginia alliance and mapped strategy for the 1790 session." By November 20, Madison informed George Washington that the Philadelphia-Potomac deal was looking up: "He [Morris] broke the subject of the residence of Congs, and made observations which betrayed his dislike of the upshot of the business at N.York, and his desire to keep alive the Southern project of an arrangement with Pennsylvania" (MP 12, 452).

In short, Morris and Madison cemented an agreement on the Philadelphia-Potomac proposal that had been in the works for some time. Believing that Hamilton and his forces in Congress had acted in bad faith to defeat his ideal point (Germantown), Morris decided that a long temporary residence (previous proposals involving the temporary residence had been for three to four years) was the best he could get. He also shared the entirely reasonable belief, indeed the prevailing belief at the time, that once the federal government opened for business at the "temporary" site in Philadelphia, it would never leave. Maclay certainly felt that even a few years would allow the Philadelphians "to fortify and entrench themselves with such systematic arrangements that we should never get away" (quoted by Risjord 1976, 313). The fact that Washington had nearly died in May no doubt strengthened his belief that temporary possession of the capital could be parlayed into a permanent one.

A comparison of House and Senate roll calls on the residence between the first and second sessions of the First Congress shows clearly that the inter-session meetings between Madison and Morris had borne fruit. The Virginia-Pennsylvania alliance was clearly in place by the time the House returned to the residence question in late May of 1790—well in advance of the dinner at Jefferson's, and well in advance of the meetings of a week earlier. These data are presented in Table 11.1. During the first session, dominated by consideration of the Susquehanna and Germantown, the Virginia and Pennsylvania delegations were in total disagreement on virtually every vote. During the second session, however, they were solidly aligned with each other on virtually every vote. This was true on the nine votes in the House *prior* to the June 20 dinner at Jefferson's, as well as on the thirteen that followed the dinner. In a letter to James Monroe written on the day of the dinner, Thomas Jefferson made note of the alliance: "The Pennsylvania and Virginia delegations have conducted themselves honorably and unexceptionally on the question of residence.... [T]hey have seen that their true interests lay in not listening to insidious propositions made to divide and defeat them" (JP 16, 538).

This is not to say that all went swimmingly for Madison and the Philadelphia-Potomac deal. After voting on May 31 to go to Philadelphia for the next session by a whopping 38–22 margin, on June 11 the House voted to instead go to Baltimore, 31–28. The absence of two New Jersey votes and the defections of the Marylanders from the Chesapeake were responsible for this reversal.

At this point, however, I think Madison was aware that he had several things working in his favor. The alliance with Pennsylvania was intact, and would hopefully continue to withstand Hamilton's efforts to pull it apart. All

TABLE 11.1. Roll Call Votes on the Residence:
Pennsylvania and Virginia Delegations

	Total Agreement	Strong Agreement	Strong Disagreement	Total Disagreement
House				
1st Session	1	2	0	9
2nd Session	19	3	0	0
Senate				
1st Session	0	1	1	2
2nd Session	24	2	0	0

Note: The two state delegations were classified as being in total agreement when all members of both delegations voted the same way on a bill, in total disagreement when all members of one delegation voted one way and all members of the other delegation voted the other way. Strong agreement occurred when all but one member in each delegation voted the same way. The case of strong disagreement that is recorded (Senate, 1st Session) occurred when one senator from each state voted one way while the other senator from each state voted the other way.

the Marylanders had voted with him on the May 31 vote, and the Baltimore proposal had no chance in the Senate. He also knew by this time that the Senate was strongly inclined to support the Potomac as the permanent site. Certain problems remained, and Madison continued to soft-pedal the Potomac's chances in his letters to Virginia. I think he was confident, however, that as far as the residence was concerned, victory was within sight.

Assumption, Again

While Madison was closing the deal with Morris and the Pennsylvanians on the residence, Hamilton continued to pursue the votes that would deliver him assumption. As we have seen, however, Hamilton's strategy for obtaining them involved a bargain with Pennsylvania on the residence, and Madison, as revealed in letters to Washington, Monroe, and others, was ever mindful of the threat this posed to the Potomac. Jefferson expressed similar fears in a letter to George Gilmer, warning of "A bargain between the Eastern members who have it [assumption] so much at heart, and the middle members who are indifferent about it, to adopt those debts without any modification on condition of removing the seat of government to Philadelphia or Baltimore" (ibid., 575).

After the House had rejected assumption in April, the Senate took up consideration of Hamilton's financial plan in early June—shortly after postponing action on the Residence Act. During debate, Morris, ever willing to consider a better offer, suggested that he would favor assumption pending favorable resolution of the residence issue. Hamilton soon approached him with a new offer: Hamilton's allies in the House would support either Germantown or the Falls of the Delaware (i.e., Trenton) for the permanent site if Morris could obtain one vote for assumption in the Senate and five in the House. As indicated earlier, it seemed to Hamilton that at least four of the House votes that were needed to pass assumption could be obtained from the Pennsylvanians who strongly desired the residence but were not strongly opposed to assumption (the delegation had split on the April 12 vote, three in favor, four against).

As noted above, however, reaching an agreement with Hamilton would require that Morris renege on his arrangement with Madison. Morris, probably figuring that he could always fall back on his agreement with Madison and thereby win at least the temporary residence, demanded the temporary residence in Philadelphia as well. Bowling speculates that Hamilton might have been able to muster a majority for assumption in both houses, but not at Morris's price—that is, both the temporary and permanent residences in Pennsylvania. New York and New England, which is presumably where Hamilton would have gone for the votes on residence in return for Morris's on assumption, would not go this far (Bowling 1991, 179). I am more in agreement with Risjord's (1976) assessment that the major reason this deal did not prevail was the fact that Hamilton was actually not able to produce votes for Morris on the Residence Bill, nor Morris for Hamilton on assumption (see also Cooke 1970 and Aldrich 1995). Contrary to Hamilton's expectations, the four antiassumptionist Pennsylvanians were not open to a bargain. Described by Hobson and Rutland (MP 13, 243) as "the only surviving evidence in JM's papers that explicitly links location of the national capital with the proposal to assume the state debts," a note sent to Madison from Virginia congressman Josiah Parker clearly indicates that Pennsylvanians were not going to go along:

> A Charte Blanche is offered to the Pennsilvania Delegation respecting the permanent & temporare Seat of Congress if they consent to the Assumption of the State debts as reported by the Secy. of the Treasury. A meeting has been on the Subject. Gen'l M. [Peter Muhlenberg] Genl. H. [Daniel Hiester] & Mr. S. [Thomas Scott] would not consent—this is from indubitable Authority. (MP 13, 246)

Dinner at Jefferson's

When Jefferson encountered him in front of the President's Mansion on Broadway on the morning of June 20, Hamilton was not his normal, cocky self. He was instead, Jefferson remembered, "sombre, haggard, and dejected beyond description. Even his dress uncouth and neglected" (JP 17, 205). It is now easy to understand why. Hamilton was beaten. His many efforts to trade votes on the residence in return for assumption had failed. Now, with the Philadelphia-Potomac bargain looking increasingly like a done deal, the means to achieve assumption (vote switches by the four Pennsylvanians) had slipped away as well. He told Jefferson that he feared New England would desert the union, and felt that the failure to carry assumption meant he should resign as secretary of the Treasury.

This leads us, then, to the central problem with the traditional "dinner table" account of the Compromise of 1790. As indicated at the beginning of this paper, Madison, feeling the Potomac within his grasp, did not need any votes from Hamilton to sew up the Philadelphia-Potomac Residence Bill. But if it were the case that Madison had put together an unstoppable coalition on the residence, what was it that Hamilton could provide that would justify Madison not only acquiescing to assumption, but actually rounding up the votes needed to achieve its passage? What Jefferson had written in his 1792 notes on the dinner-table bargain was that Hamilton was to obtain the support of Morris and the Pennsylvanians for the Philadelphia-Potomac Residence Bill. But as we have seen, the historical record makes it quite clear that Morris and the Pennsylvanians had already concluded an agreement with Madison on this very measure. Indeed, it was this very agreement that Hamilton had been striving to unravel. As we have also seen, Jefferson's letter to Monroe of June 20 reveals that he was fully aware of both the Virginia-Pennsylvania alliance and of Hamilton's efforts to break it.

Bowling (1968) and other historians put more credence in the 1818 *Anas* account, in which Jefferson refers to Hamilton agreeing to exert the "influence he had established over the eastern members" (Jefferson 1818). They infer that what Madison had asked from Hamilton was that he [Hamilton] persuade his New England allies to cease their efforts to unravel the Philadelphia-Potomac deal. There is some evidence that suggests this may have occurred. When the Senate returned to consideration of the Residence Bill in late June, Rufus King of New York sought to keep the capital temporarily in New York in return for a permanent site in Baltimore. This measure was supported by the six senators from the states south of Virginia (much to the chagrin of Madison) as well as by those from New York, Connecticut, and Rhode Island. The Massachusetts senators voted against the proposal, however, thus defeating King's challenge.

There is also reason to doubt, however, that the Massachusetts senators were doing Hamilton's bidding. In the votes leading up to King's motion they had consistently supported measures to remain in New York, but consistently opposed measures that would put the capital in Baltimore. According to Bowling, they feared the development of Baltimore as a commercial rival; the only port on the Potomac—Alexandria—was far too modest to pose a similar threat. Moreover, as noted above by Risjord (1976), the failure of Hamilton to cut a deal with Morris on assumption was due to Hamilton's inability to move votes on the Residence Bill, combined with Morris's inability to move votes on assumption. Why would Madison ask Hamilton to intervene with the New Englanders, then, when he knew this was something Hamilton could not deliver, or, perhaps more accurately, something that would occur of its own accord—that is, the Massachusetts opposition to Baltimore? Just as Hamilton knew he had lost, then, Madison knew he had won. The April 12 vote had shown that he could block assumption. He also knew that the Philadelphia-Potomac measure deprived Hamilton of all his residence-based bargaining chips.

This brings us to the real business transacted that night at Jefferson's dinner table: Madison was now in a position to dictate terms to Hamilton, and thus to extract the best terms possible for Virginia on assumption and the settlement. Madison had sought throughout the 1790 session of Congress to pursue Virginia's interests in these areas, but all his efforts—the amendment to link assumption and settlement, his proposal to add two additional members to the Board of Commissioners, and his attempt to persuade Washington to replace the current commissioners—had come to naught.

As the author of assumption and secretary of the Treasury, Hamilton was in a position to see to it that Virginia received "adequate provision" for her "equitable claims," as Madison had demanded in his speech before the House. As he had stated on several occasions, Madison was prepared to support assumption if his conditions could be met. On this score he was far more willing to negotiate than was the median voter back in Virginia. Indeed, in correspondence following the April 12 vote against assumption, Madison began spinning hard to prepare his constituents for the eventual passage of the measure. He knew that no matter how good a deal he was able to obtain on assumption, he would still have to sell it. In letters to James Monroe (MP 13, 150), Edmund Pendleton (ibid., 148–49, 184), and Edmund Randolph (ibid., 189), he sought to convince them of both some bad news—some form of assumption was bound to pass—and some good news—it might work out not to be such a bad deal for Virginia after all.

In this regard many historians have commented on the intemperate letter of April 3 that Madison received from Henry Lee. Characterizing assumption as a "mad policy," Lee opined that

> To disunite is dreadful to my mind, but dreadful as it is, I consider it a lesser evil than union on the present conditions.

> I had rather myself submit to all the hazards of war & risk the loss of every thing dear to me in life, than to live under the rule of a fixed insolent northern majority. . . . No policy will be adopted by Congress which does not more or less tend to depress the south & exalt the north. . . . How do you feel, what do you think, is your love for the constitution so ardent, as to induce you to adhere to it tho it should produce ruin to your native country? (Ibid., 137)

Writing back to Lee on April 13, Madison informed him that the House had rejected assumption the previous day. He predicted the issue would resurface, however, but that Virginia would not necessarily fare badly: "The minority do not abandon however their object, and 'tis impossible to foretell the final destiny of the measure. It has some good aspects, and under some modifications would be favorable to the pecuniary interests of Virginia—and not inconsistent with the general principle of justice" (ibid., 147).

In the days following the dinner at Jefferson's, the assumption bill did receive, to borrow Madison's language, "some modifications that were favorable to the pecuniary interests of Virginia." By the time the Senate approved the debt-funding bill on July 21, the total amount of state debt to be assumed had dropped from $25 million to $21.5 million. Virginia's allotment for the loan taken out to underwrite assumption was pegged at $3.5 million. By my calculations, this made Virginia, with 17.8 percent of the population (all free persons plus 60 percent of the total number of slaves), responsible for 16.3 percent of the loan. This amount was virtually identical to the whole of her remaining state debt. For Virginia, assumption had become a wash. As Madison explained later that month in a letter to his father:

> The truth is that in a pecuniary light, the assumption is no longer of much consequence to Virginia, the sum allotted to her being about her proportion of the whole, & rather exceeding her present debt. She will consequently pay no more to the general Treasury than she now pays to the State Treasy. and perhaps in a mode that will be less disagreeable to the people, tho' not more favorable to their true interests. (Ibid., 285)

Madison's chief demand, however, was that assumption be linked to adequate provision for Virginia's large (though undocumented) claims in the settlement of wartime expenditures. Actually, as Risjord (1976, 311) reports, Hamilton had already signaled a willingness to satisfy Madison on this score. On April 16, four days after the defeat of assumption in the House, Fitzsimons (Hamilton's associate) moved to appoint a committee to draft a bill for the "speedy settlement of state accounts." Things soon began to look up for Virginia: "Toward the end of May, when the substance of the settlement bill became known, Madison and William Davies, Virginia's commissioner of accounts, spent several days re-examining their state's claims, and they were 'happy to find' that Virginia would be as well off as 'her more immediate antagonists, Massachusetts and South Carolina, should the business of assumption be brought up again' " (ibid., 312).

As the implementation of the settlement of accounts transpired, Virginia continued to fare well. According to Ferguson (1961, 323): "If one can judge by Virginia's experience after 1790, the General Board freely accepted and approved claims of every description." The board permitted Virginia's commissioner of accounts, William Davies, to sit in on every meeting. Davies concluded that Virginia's lack of expense vouchers had actually become quite an advantage, as by August of 1791 the board had rejected not a single claim, save one submitted by mistake. Virginia ultimately emerged with a credit of $19,085,981. The other Southern states also fared extremely well in the settlement (Ferguson 1961).

Hamilton's end of the bargain, in short, was to accept modifications to the assumption bill that were friendly to the interests of Virginia, and to continue to see that the expenditure claims of Virginia (and other states in similar circumstances) were settled on generous terms. There is, of course, nothing in either of Jefferson's accounts of the dinner to support this conclusion. On the other hand, letters that Jefferson wrote to James Monroe and to Thomas Randolph on June 20, 1790, clearly sketch out the general outline of a bargain for making assumption palatable to Virginia and the other states in its position:

> Congress are much embarrassed by the two questions of assumption, and residence. All proceedings seem to be arrested till these can be gotten over. And for the peace and continuance of the union, a mutual sacrifice of opinion and interest is become the duty of everyone: . . . In this situation of things, the only choice is among disagreeable things. The assumption must be admitted, but in so qualified a form as to divest it of it's injustice. This may be done by assuming to the creditors of every state a sum exactly proportioned to the contributions of the state: so that the state will on the whole neither gain nor lose. . . . On the question of residence, the compromise proposed is to give it to Philadelphia for 15. Years and then permanently to George town by the same act. This is the best arrangement we have now any prospect of, and therefore the one to which all our wishes are at present pointed. If this does not take place, something much worse will; to wit an unqualified assumption and the permanent seat on the Delaware. (JP 16, 540–41)

The passage above is from the letter to Randolph, but the letter to Monroe is virtually identical. Jefferson's description of the modifications to be made to the assumption bill are fuzzy, and he indicates that Philadelphia was to have the temporary residence for fifteen years instead of ten (suggesting the letters were written prior to the dinner instead of after). Still, these contemporaneous letters present a much more accurate account of the bargain struck over dinner at Jefferson's house than the notes he made in 1792 and in 1818.

As several historians have noted, Jefferson subsequently came to regret the role he had played in arranging the Compromise of 1790. In a September 9, 1792, letter to George Washington, he describes the affair as something "I was duped into by the Secretary of the treasury, and made a tool for forwarding his schemes, not then sufficiently understood by me; and of all the errors of my political life, this has occasioned me the deepest regret" (ibid. 24, 352). In his 1792 notes he describes assumption as unjust, and, in the *Anas* (Jefferson 1818, 276), as a "pabulum to the stock-jobbing herd." However, I think by far the greater source of his regret lay in the fact that the bargain had allowed Hamilton to survive politically. In the months and years that followed, of course, a massive rift developed between Jefferson/Madison and Hamilton, whom they came to view as an avowed monarchist presenting a clear and present danger to the republic. In Jefferson's view, they had been induced to rescue assumption by the exaggerated threat of disunion. He and Madison had also been much too disposed to assist Hamilton in extracting himself from his political predicament. Had they instead discounted Hamilton's dire warnings and let the April 12 vote against assumption stand, they might thereby have knocked Hamilton out of national politics when they had had the chance.

Nailing Down the Residence

When Madison left Jefferson's house on June 20, he had presumably extracted all from Hamilton that he could. Remaining, however, were the still dicey tasks of winning passage of the Philadelphia-Potomac Bill and, to keep his promise to Hamilton, of shepherding the modified assumption bill through as well. As noted earlier, efforts on the former had initially gone well in the second session, but things had become stuck again when opponents of the temporary capital in Philadelphia won a vote to go to Baltimore instead. The House then decided to postpone action until after the Senate had taken up the bill. Whether this was an intentional piece of strategy on Madison's part I do not know, but it turned out to be a shrewd move.

Madison's expectations that the Senate would look favorably upon the Potomac were soon realized. After decisively rejecting a move to Baltimore, on June 28 the Senate voted by a 16–9 margin to accept the Potomac as the permanent seat of government. The Pennsylvania-Virginia alliance had picked up the votes of all other senators from the Middle States and all but one from the South to overcome nearly unanimous opposition from New York and New England.

Also as expected, opponents of the plan attempted to overturn it by knocking out Philadelphia as the temporary site. The most serious challenge appears to have been a 13–12 vote in favor of Rufus King's motions to make New York the temporary capital until 1800, but I think this was not the case. The bill under consideration, authored by Pierce Butler of South Carolina, had left a blank in the clause specifying the location and duration of the temporary site. King's motions simply filled in the blanks, thereby putting New York into consideration. When the Senate actually voted on the measure the next day, it failed, 9–16. The votes cast on this measure were virtually identical to those cast on the Potomac roll call. In my view, the more serious challenges were the motions to remain in New York a bit longer—first, until the end of 1794, then until the end of 1792. In both cases Vice President Adams cast no votes to break 13–13 ties. In any case, these turned out to be rear guard actions, as the Senate approved the Philadelphia-Potomac Bill on June 30.

The beauty of letting the Senate move first is that the House would now decide the fate of the residence by acting upon the Senate bill. Madison, who in the previous session had used a housekeeping amendment to send the ill-fated Germantown Bill back to a cruel fate in the Senate, now urged his colleagues in the House to eschew amendments and adopt the Senate bill as it was written. He warned that if it were returned to the Senate it could come back to them once again proposing the Delaware or Susquehanna sites! Elbridge Gerry provided clear refutation of any notion that Hamilton could have stifled New Englanders opposed to the Philadelphia-Potomac Bill. Resurrecting a combination of counteroffers that had been made in the Senate, he proposed to remain in New York temporarily and then move to Baltimore for the permanent site. Among other things, Gerry asserted that New York had been promised the temporary residence if it supported ratification of the Constitution without amendment. His motion lost 37–23.

After turning back several amendments proposing the familiar list of alternative locations (Germantown, Baltimore, Delaware, between the Susquehanna and Potomac), the House approved the Philadelphia-Potomac Bill on July 9 by a vote of 32–29. Recalling the debate months later, Smith of South Carolina described Madison as "a general who marshalled his troops so well that not a single change was made to the Senate bill" (quoted in Bowling 1991, 193). By this point, however, the clock was in Madison's favor. Opponents of the Philadelphia-Potomac Bill, of whom many were anxious to return to the business of assumption, were simply willing to give up. As Fisher Ames put it: "I would not find fault with Fort Pitt, if we could assume the debts, and proceed in peace and quietness. But this despicable grog-shop contest, whether the taverns of New York or Philadelphia shall get the custom of Congress keeps us in discord, and covers us all with disgrace" (quoted in ibid., 178).

Delivering Assumption

Madison now needed to persuade enough erstwhile opponents of assumption to switch their votes to ensure passage of the bill. Unfortunately the senators and representative from Rhode Island had finally arrived during the last few days of June, and they were all antiassumptionist. He thus needed to find four votes in the House and likely one in the Senate, not just the two in the House that Jefferson claims he had promised to Hamilton. There is no doubt that he found them. After the House defeated a motion, 29–32, to delete assumption from the bill, the New York newspapers reported the names of the vote switchers (ibid., 199). In addition to Alexander White and Richard Bland Lee from Virginia, he found two more in the Maryland delegation—Daniel Carroll and George Gale, author of the Proviso that had so muddied the waters in debate over the Susquehanna site in the first session. Maryland senator Charles Carroll also provided a vote for assumption in the Senate, although he had not previously gone on the record opposing it.

What all five shared in common, of course, was their proximity to the Potomac. This, more than anything else, is the prima facie evidence that has persuaded so many for so long that despite their inaccuracies, Jefferson's 1792 and 1818 accounts of the Compromise of 1790 were essentially correct. We have concluded, however, that Madison and Hamilton did not have a quid pro quo agreement involving the residence and assumption. By this time, moreover, the five vote switchers were all perfectly aware that the Potomac residence had been won as a consequence of the alliance with Pennsylvania. Why, then, did Madison choose the Potomac Five to be the ones to switch their votes on assumption? And how did he persuade them to do it?

I can envision Madison making a series of interlaced arguments to them. For the most part I think they were the same arguments that he himself had found persuasive. The first was simply that Hamilton's concessions on assumption and intervention in the settlement had actually made the bill a reasonable proposition from Virginia's standpoint. Most likely he also pointed out that the measure had George Washington's blessing (Malone 1951, 297).

In order to make it more palatable to the people back home, however, it would not hurt at all to foster the impression that the residence had come in a bargain involving assumption. The impression of linkage between the two matters would similarly allow Hamilton's supporters to conclude that the loss of the residence was a necessary price for the overall success of his funding plan.

Secondly and more important, I think Madison was able to convince them that they should back assumption, not in exchange for the residence, but precisely because they had succeeded in winning the residence. What good would a national capital on the Potomac be if the nation itself was not strong and viable? Most likely the New England states would not actually follow through on their threats of dissolution were assumption to be rejected, but doubts about their loyalty and commitment would have a stifling effect on the growth and progress of the United States. Winning the residence, in short, had significantly increased Virginia's stake in the success of the new nation. It thus made sense for the Virginians to deliver on assumption. It was no longer a bad deal for Virginia and, by assuaging New England, would go far in strengthening the ties of union.

Finally, according to Bowling (1991), Madison added some inducements. He promised Lee that he would back legislation in the next session to specify that Lee's hometown of Alexandria would be in the federal district. Daniel Carroll of Georgetown was assured that the federal buildings would be built on the Maryland side. I suspect he would have gotten these votes anyway, but it does mean that at this point something of a quid pro quo involving the residence and assumption did take place. The irony is that Madison was in a position to sweeten the deal in this manner because his overall strategy of *not* commingling the issue of assumption in his pursuit of the residence had prevailed, while Hamilton, who had proffered any number of bargains involving the residence and assumption, had failed.

The record is mixed on the question of whether Madison was ever able to sell assumption to the people of Virginia. He himself, of course, continued to vote against it. In a letter to Madison dated August 1, 1790, John Dawson told him that he still found assumption objectionable, but that the final measure was "in a less exceptionable shape than it first appear'd" (MP 13, 290–91). In an August 10 letter, Governor Beverly Randolph of Virginia expressed disappointment that Madison's proposal to add two new members to the Board of Commissioners had failed, but added: "The Assumption Business as it is now modified will I believe be more favorably received than it would have been in it's original Dress, but never will become a favorite in Virginia" (292). In late 1790 the Virginia state legislature sent a memorial to

Congress condemning the funding bill (Bowling 1991, 204). Still, the acid test here is that of re-election, and in 1790 all Virginia incumbents were returned to Congress.

Discussion

The Compromise of 1790 was not the product of a quid pro quo vote trade between Madison and Hamilton, whereby Madison would win the residence for the Potomac and Hamilton would gain approval of assumption. A deal of this nature would actually have been highly problematic. In seeking to win over the final few votes needed for assumption, Hamilton had repeatedly offered the Pennsylvania delegation his allies' support for the residence of a permanent capital in their state. The Pennsylvania delegation, however, was also the source of the votes that Madison needed to obtain the residence for the Potomac. In return, Madison had agreed to a long temporary stay for the government in Philadelphia. The Pennsylvanians could not go both ways. If they agreed to a deal with Hamilton involving the residence in return for assumption, Madison's proposal to the Pennsylvanians—a permanent site on the Potomac in exchange for a temporary stay in Philadelphia—would necessarily be rejected. For both Hamilton and Madison, losing on the residence would mean losing on assumption, and losing on assumption would mean losing on the residence.

In the end, the Pennsylvanians cast their lot with Madison, who thereby achieved the residence for the Potomac. Madison could now deal with Hamilton from a position of strength, and he exploited this position fully. In return for supplying the votes Hamilton needed for assumption, Madison won important concessions in the plan itself. Just as important, Virginia (and other states) received extremely favorable consideration in the settlement of large (though undocumented) claims for wartime expenditures. Although this interpretation of the Compromise diverges from Jefferson's 1792 and 1818 accounts of the dinner-table bargain, it adheres closely to the proposals he sketched out in letters written to James Monroe and to Thomas Randolph on the same day as the dinner.

My hope is that this chapter has arrived at a clearer and more compelling account of what actually took place in 1790. However, it also raises several questions for which there are no easy answers. The first involves the point we have just addressed—namely, Jefferson's documents. Why did his 1792 and 1818 accounts of the dinner-party bargain, particularly with respect to Hamilton's role in the piece, differ from the contemporaneous and, in my view, more accurate and veridical letters written to Monroe and Randolph?

The subsequent accounts frequently sought to put Hamilton in the worst possible light. However, reporting that Hamilton agreed to seek votes from Morris and the Pennsylvanians on the Residence Bill (1792) or to persuade his congressional allies to cease and desist (1818) hardly seems to put him in a worse light than indicating his willingness to accept amendments to the assumption bill and to ensure generous treatment for Virginia in the settlement.

This leads directly to another question. Why was Hamilton apparently unwilling to alter his proposal for the assumption of state debts in order to satisfy Madison at the very beginning of House action? Why did he and his allies in Congress march straight into the April 12 defeat, which could easily have derailed his entire funding plan? Perhaps he feared that acquiescing to Madison would trigger a bidding war among the states, thereby leading to a total debt too large to be serviced by the taxes that Congress was willing to put in place. It is also possible that he acted out of a combination of hubris and irrational exuberance when it came to forecasting votes, but one should generally prefer explanations that do not posit the actors in question making bad mistakes.

Another question, also involving Hamilton, is why was the vote trade he proposed to the pivotal Pennsylvania delegation—votes for assumption in return for the permanent residence in their state—rejected? According to Bowling, as many as four of them were only weakly opposed to assumption. Part of the answer, of course, is that there was considerable disagreement among them as to where in Pennsylvania the permanent residence should be sited. By accepting Madison's proposal over Hamilton's, however, they were essentially revealing that they were more anxious to win a long temporary residence than the permanent one. As indicated previously, many at the time believed that in the case of the residence, as in property law, possession was worth a great deal. They predicted that once the government had moved to Philadelphia, the move to the Potomac would never occur. Correspondingly, Philadelphia supporters feared that if the government remained in New York much longer it would never leave there. I am reluctant to characterize Morris and the other backers of the temporary residence as having inappropriately high discount rates; in 1790 the survival of the United States for ten years was hardly a sure thing. Nevertheless, I must say that I am left with the sense that they were engaging in wishful thinking to think that in 1800 the government would not move to the Potomac.

Finally, why did Robert Morris not blame Madison, at least to some degree, for the defeat of Germantown at the end of the first session? He certainly knew Madison was the author of the seemingly innocuous amendment that sent the bill back to the Senate. Nor does the intent of Madison's amendment seem to have been open to interpretation. As Maclay noted in his diary on Monday, September 28, the day Madison's amendment was approved:

> just as I was leaving the Hall. Izard took me aside asked me to stay. said a Trifling amendment will be made in the lower house just enough to bring it up here & we will throw it out, I told him I wished nothing so much as to see an End of the Business. I was not able to attend, but if I was I could not be with him on this question. Well then You must not tell Morris, of this I was just going away and said I will not. (MD, 169)

In my view, Morris was perfectly aware that Madison was the author of this last-ditch effort to derail Germantown. I think the conclusion he drew from this episode, however, was that it would be very difficult to get anything through Congress that Madison opposed. Morris therefore decided that it would be far more fruitful to work with Madison than against him. Soon after returning to Philadelphia, he thus made the overture to Grayson that led the way to the ultimately successful Virginia-Pennsylvania alliance.

Conclusion

The second session of Congress ended on August 12, 1790, but Madison decided to stay in New York a few weeks longer. Doing so would be better for his health, and would allow him to travel back to Virginia with Jefferson. He thus wrote to his father, asking him to pass on to the appropriate people a letter announcing his willingness to return to Congress if his constituents so desired. In this letter he outlined, in an understated sort of way, what had been accomplished in the First Federal Congress:

> The Sessions of Congs. was closed yesterday. The list of Acts inclosed will give you a general idea of what has been done. The subjects which conduced most to the length of the Session are the assumption of the State-debts, and the Seat of Government. The latter has been decided in a manner more favorable to Virginia than was hoped. The former will be less acceptable to that State. It has however been purged of some of its objections and particularly of its gross injustice to Virginia, which in a pecuniary view is now little affected one way or the other. (MP 13, 293)

Ellis (2000, 74) is more straightforward in describing what Madison had accomplished: "It was a three-sided deal—residence, revised assumption, and settlement—and Virginia won on each score." I would put it this way: it is far more accurate to characterize the Compromise of 1790 as Madison's Triumph of 1790.

Appendix

Jefferson's first account of the dinner-table bargain, most likely written in late 1792, is as follows:

> On considering the situation of things I thought the first step towards some conciliation of views would be to bring Mr. Madison and Colo. Hamilton to a friendly discussion of the subject. I immediately wrote to each to come and dine with me the next day, mentioning that we should be alone, that the object was to find some temperament for the present fever, and that I was persuaded that men of sound heads and honest views needed nothing more than explanation and mutual understanding to enable them to unite in some measures which might enable us to get along. They came. I opened the subject to them, acknowledged that my situation had not permitted me to understand it sufficiently but encouraged them to consider the thing together. They did so. It ended in Mr. Madison's acquiescence in a proposition that the question should be again brought before the house by way of amendment from the Senate, that tho' he would not vote for it, nor entirely withdraw his opposition, yet he should not be strenuous, but leave it to it's fate. It was observed, I forget by which of them, that as the pill would be a bitter one to the Southern states, something should be done to soothe them; that the removal of the seat of government to the Patowmac was a just measure, and would probably be a popular one with them, and would be a proper one to follow the assumption. It was agreed to speak to Mr. White and Mr. Lee, whose districts lay on the Patowmac and to refer to them to consider how far the interests of their particular districts might be a sufficient inducement to them to yield to the assumption. This was done. Lee came into it without hesitation. Mr. White had some qualms, but finally agreed. The measure came down by way of amendment from the Senate and was finally carried by the change of White's and Lee's votes. But the removal to Patowmac could not be carried unless Pennsylvania could be engaged in it. This Hamilton took on himself, and chiefly, as I understood, through the agency of Robert Morris, obtained the vote of that state, on agreeing to an intermediate residence at Philadelphia. This is the real history of the assumption, about which many erroneous conjectures have been published. (JP 17, 206–7)

The second account, written in 1818 and published originally in the *Anas*, is very consistent with the first. It is assumed that Jefferson consulted his original 1792 notes in writing it:

> I proposed to him [Hamilton], however, to dine with me the next day, and I would invite another friend or two, bring them into conference together, and I thought it was impossible that reasonable men, consulting together coolly, could fail, by some mutual sacrifices of opinion, to form a compromise which was to save the Union.
>
> The discussion took place. I could take no part in it but an exhortatory one,

because I was a stranger to the circumstances which should govern it. But it was finally agreed, that whatever importance had been attached to the rejection of this proposition, the preservation of the Union and of concord among the States was more important, and that therefore it would be better that the vote of rejection should be rescinded, to effect which, some members should change their votes. But it was observed that this pill would be peculiarly bitter to the southern States, and that some concomitant measure should be adopted, to sweeten it a little to them. There had before been propositions to fix the seat of government either at Philadelphia, or at Georgetown on the Potomac; and it was thought that by giving it to Philadelphia for ten years, and to Georgetown permanently afterwards, this might, as an anodyne, calm in some degree the ferment which might be excited by the other measure alone. So two of the Potomac members (White and Lee, but White with a revulsion of stomach almost convulsive,) agreed to change their votes, and Hamilton undertook to carry the other point. In doing this, the influence he had established over the eastern members, with the agency of Robert Morris with those of the middle States, effected. his side of the engagement. (Jefferson 1818, 275–76)

Notes

I would like to thank Jenna Bednar, Andrea Campbell, Brandice Canes-Wrone, Liz Gerber, Gary Jacobson, Jonathan Katz, William Keech, Sam Kernell, Lorraine Kiewiet, Richard McKelvey, and Rick Wilson for their comments and criticism, and Iljie Kim for her valuable research assistance. I am particularly indebted to Kenneth Bowling of the First Federal Congress Project for identifying numerous errors in the previous draft, ranging from minor and annoying to major and serious.

1. It is not clear whether it was Madison or Jefferson who actually accepted the task of persuading a sufficient number of erstwhile opponents of assumption to change their votes. Malone (1951) believes that because Madison continued to vote against assumption it must have been Jefferson. Most scholars agree with Bowling (1971, 1991) that it was Madison. A strong hint that it was Madison comes from the 1792 manuscript describing the bargain; the first three words of the sentence, "It was agreed to speak to Mr. White and Mr. Lee ..." [about changing their votes] originally began "Mr. Madison undertook," but Jefferson crossed them out (JP 17, 208). Given Madison's leadership of the Virginia delegation and my sense that Jefferson would have considered this too tawdry a business to actually carry out himself, and, as we shall see later, that there were many other aspects of the resurrection of assumption that Jefferson does not touch upon, I concur with the conventional wisdom that it was Madison who brokered the delivery of the votes promised for assumption.

2. The assumption of re-election maximization may seem anachronistic, given the typically short and desultory nature of service in Congress before the

twentieth century (Polsby 1968; Kernell 1977). In the case of Madison, however, I think it is not. He was without question a career politician. Even if one confines attention to the context of Congress, the assumption of re-election maximization is reasonable. More specifically, Madison, along with seventeen others from the group of sixty-six who served in the First Federal Congress, continued to serve through the Fourth—a reasonably long congressional career even by today's standards.

3. Maryland and Delaware also might be classified as Middle States, but this of course does not change the political geography of the battle over the residence. Also, the problem for Madison and the Potomac in the first session of 1789 was actually worse, because the five representatives from North Carolina did not arrive until well into the second session. The lone representative from Rhode Island arrived shortly after the North Carolinians.

4. Contrary to Aldrich, Jillson, and Wilson (2002), it was not necessarily the voting rules of the Confederation Congress that impeded selection of a site for the capital. The problem here was that the $100,000 for the federal town was never actually appropriated, and the commission to oversee construction was never appointed. The chief obstacle to siting was thus the lack of revenue-raising power under the Articles of Confederation. For their part, the citizens of New Jersey did not believe it was worth putting up their own money to acquire the necessary land or to begin the construction of governmental buildings.

5. This section of the chapter draws heavily upon Bowling's (1991) comprehensive and authoritative study of the creation of Washington, D.C. To avoid making countless citations to this work I do so only when reference to a particular page number is particularly helpful or necessary.

6. Things might conceivably have gone differently had the bill gone to William Maclay, the other senator from Pennsylvania and a strong backer of the Susquehanna site. Maclay, however, was far less prominent than Morris, having been elected to the two-year term and Morris to the six-year term. The prickly Maclay was also quite ill during much of his time in New York, and, in my judgment, exhibited symptoms of clinical depression.

7. Benjamin Rush had strongly lobbied Adams in behalf of Philadelphia as soon as Adams had been elected vice president. In what was ostensibly a letter of congratulations, Rush nonetheless informed his old friend that "[t]here is an expectation here which I have humored that your influence will be exerted immediately in favor of a motion to bring Congress to Philadelphia." He also warned that "[by] delaying the removal of Congress to Philadelphia, you will probably be dragged in a few years to the Potomac, where Negro slaves will be your servants by day, mosquitoes your sentinels by night, and bilious fevers your companions every summer and fall, and pleurisies every spring" (quoted in Bowling 1991, 103).

8. In contrast to studies that point to important changes in Madison's views regarding the Constitution, the Bill of Rights, and the nature of the most seri-

ous threats facing the new republic, Banning (1995, 7) argues that his political thought remained fundamentally consistent throughout his long career. For what it is worth, late in his life Madison agreed with Banning.

9. The Committee of the Whole approved Madison's amendment linking assumption to settlement, but the measure ultimately failed when the entire bill was taken up by the House.

10. An ardent foe of assumption, a gleeful William Maclay describes the dismay of assumption advocates:

> When he [Sedgwick] returned his Visage to me bore the visible marks of Weeping. Fitzsimons reddened like Scarlet his Eyes were full. Clymer's color always pale now verged to a deadly White. his lips quavered, and his neither Jaw shook with convulsive Motions. His head neck & Breast consented to Gesticulations resembling those of a Turkey or Goose, nearly strangled in the Act of deglutition. Benson bungled like a Shoemaker who had lost his End. Ames's Aspect was truly hippocratic, a total change of face & feature. he sat torpid as if his faculties had been benumbed. Gerry exhibited the advantages of a cadaverous appearance. at all times pallid, and far from pleasing, he ran no risk of deterioration. . . . Thro' an interruption of Hectic hems and consumptive coughs. he delivered himself of a declaration, That the Delegates of Massachusetts. would proceed no further, but write to their State for instructions. happy Impudence sat enthroned on Lawrence's brow. he rose in puffing pomp, and moved that the Committee should rise. And Assigned the agitation of the House as a Reason. Wadsworth hid his Grief Under the rim of a round hat. Boudinot's wrinkles rose in ridges. And the Angles of his mouth were depressed, and their apperture assumed a curve resembling an horse Shoe. (MD, 242)

Yet Maclay himself realized the game was still afoot:

> Fizsimons first discovered recollection. and endeavoured to rally the discomfited & disheartened heroes. He hoped the good Sense of the House would still predominate and lead them to reconsider the Vote which had now been taken. and he doubted not but it would yet be adopted. Under proper Modifications. The Secretary's Group pricked up their Ears and Speculation wiped the Tear from either Eye. (Ibid.)

Chapter 12

Madison and the Founding of the Two-Party System

NORMAN SCHOFIELD

1. Introduction

During the Federal Convention in the summer of 1787, and later during their collaboration over the *Federalist*, James Madison and Alexander Hamilton were allies in their support of the union. By early 1791, Madison had come to view Hamilton's fiscal scheme for the republic with alarm. As the decade of the 1790s progressed, the two-party system came into being. In essence, the commercial interests cohered into a Federalist Party, including Washington, John Adams, and Hamilton, while agrarian interests came together as a Republican Party under Thomas Jefferson and Madison.

This early schism among the Federalist supporters of 1787 can be interpreted as an illustration of the notion of "partisan realignment" used by writers such as Sundquist (1983) to characterize political transformations in the late 1890s and mid-1930s. I shall argue that the partisan realignment of the 1790s and the critical election of Jefferson in 1800 created a two-party political equilibrium that persisted until 1852.

Many historians (and economic historians) have discussed the gestation of the two-party system in the 1790s. My purpose in adding to the discussion is to use ideas from modern social choice theory and political economy to throw light on the social beliefs held by Hamilton, on the one hand, and Madison and Jefferson, on the other. Although it is clearly anachronistic to use modern technical theories to interpret the beliefs of agents long dead, I shall argue that the theories that I shall describe were well understood, though possibly in rudimentary form, by these protagonists.

Although the technical structures of these two theories are well understood today, the applicability of the theories in understanding modern polities is quite contentious. I shall argue that the developing conflict between the Federalists and the Republicans in the 1790s grew out of differing beliefs over the significance and meaning of these theories for the "design" of the U.S. political economy.

Modern social choice theory has a number of somewhat irreconcilable subthemes. One theme can be interpreted as a version of Montesquieu's constitutional theory. For Montesquieu, monarchy, aristocracy, and democracy all possessed different virtues that could be combined to advantage in a single constitutional system. Democracy, while dangerous because of its likely "turbulence," was necessary to prevent the potential tyranny of monarchy. Aristocracy was required to temper the arrogance of monarchy with wisdom. As I suggest below in the next section, one theme of social choice theory is that democracy is indeed turbulent, but this feature can be controlled by the concentration of power implied by aristocracy or, more generally, autocracy. Obviously, the Framers of the Constitution held to a version of this theory, but varied in their emphasis on the dangers of turbulence, and the costs of autocracy. Hamilton's bold version of a powerful U.S. commercial empire inclined him to a preference for autocracy.

In contrast, Madison, in *Federalist* 10, offered the entirely different theory of the extended republic. Acknowledging that democracies tend to be turbulent, Madison then proposed that a republic "in which the scheme of representation takes place" provides the cure for turbulence. The "large" republic will "present a . . . greater probability of a fit choice" (Rakove 1999, 164–65). Present-day pluralist democratic theorists interpret Madison's argument to mean that "competing interests cancel one another out" (Williams 1998, 39).[1] I argue below, in Section 6, that Madison had an entirely different logic in mind. Although the extended republic argument is usually traced to Hume's "Idea of a Perfect Commonwealth" (Adair 1943; 2000), there is a deeper connection to Condorcet's *Essai sur l'application de l'analyse* (Condorcet, 1785). I offer evidence that Madison, in late 1787, had received elements of Condorcet's *Essai* from Jefferson in Paris. The *Essai* was concerned with the *probability* of a jury, or committee, making a "true" choice. If we interpret "true" to mean "valid" or "virtuous," then Madison's argument can be seen as an application or extension of the Condorcet theorem to the election of the chief magistrate.

I contend that this Condorcetian aspect is a key feature of the constitutional thought of both Madison and Jefferson in the 1790s. In his writing up to the *Federalist Papers*, Madison obviously viewed faction, party, and interest as inimical to the stability of the republic and likely to generate mutability or turbulence. Madison's view changed during the 1790s.

In 1790 and 1791, Hamilton, as secretary of the Treasury, prepared his *Report on the Public Credit, Report on the National Bank*, and *A Report on the Subject of Manufactures*. All three reports made it clear that Hamilton had in mind the creation of a commerce-based American empire "able to dictate the terms of connection between the old and the new world," to quote from Hamilton's *Federalist* 11 (Freeman 2001, 208).

It is well known that Hamilton's scheme owed much for its inspiration to the economic and fiscal structures devised in Britain, during the period of Whig supremacy under Walpole's leadership in the period from 1720 to 1740. What has been less examined is how, precisely, the Walpole scheme led to the creation of Britain's maritime empire. In Section 3, below, I argue that Walpole's scheme can be seen to be consistent with a political economic theory relating to the role of the state in balancing the economic factors of land, capital, and labor, and avoiding turbulence. Elements of this theory are present in Hume's *Essay on Commerce,* where he comments, with approval, that commercial advancement "augments the *power of the state*" (Hume 1985, 265).

I argue that Madison and Jefferson were well aware of the probable consequences of the success of Hamilton's scheme. This knowledge presented them (and, in their view, the entire society) with a dilemma.

Although what I call the "Walpole Equilibrium" was crucial for Britain's growth to hegemony, it had deleterious consequences for that century's agricultural laborers. Modern research in economic history (discussed in Section 4) has shown how Britain's use of tariffs and excise protected land, drove up the price of land, and stimulated increased agricultural productivity. However, capital substituted for labor, and consequently real wages for both farm and skilled labor remained flat, or even declined. Although the precise economic details of Britain's growth in the eighteenth century may not have been known to Madison and Jefferson, its overall consequences were. For example, as Porter (2000, 317) has recently observed, Oliver Goldsmith's *The Deserted Village* of 1770 "damned the depopulating effects of enclosure."

Because of the differing economic structure of Britain and the United States, Hamilton's commercial scheme would necessarily have advantaged capital over both the landed interests *and* agrarian labor. I argue in Section 6 that Jefferson, during his residence in Paris in the 1780s, had been much influenced by Condorcet's theories of political economy. Condorcet's later *Es-*

quisse of 1794 summed up these ideas and presented an optimistic view of economic development. This thesis was later contested by Malthus's *Essay on the Principle of Population* published in 1798 (Malthus, 1970).

One coherent vision of the future development of the United States consistent with Condorcet's view would emphasize the growth of an agrarian empire. By focusing on free trade, and by increasing total agricultural output through expansion, both the landed interest *and* free agricultural labor would be advantaged. The choice between these two development paths, one commercial and one agrarian, was the point of the election of 1800. To implement this vision held by both Jefferson and Madison, it was necessary to destroy the commercial agrarian coalition that had supported union in 1787, and to create an agrarian Republican Party. In so doing, I believe, Madison and Jefferson both accepted the underlying logic implicit in Condorcet's *Essai*, and, in essence, created a stable two-party system.

What I mean by this requires some elaboration. Firstly, the fact that in 1800 there were available two entirely different development paths, one agrarian and one commercial, meant that a compromise between the two was impossible. Contrary to the pluralist notion of democracy, in which various interests cancel each other out, the society in 1800 faced a dilemma over which choice to pursue. From the Condorcetian perspective, only one of the choices could be "true." Of course, in 1800, which one of the choices was "true" was hidden behind the veil of the future. Madison and Jefferson clearly believed that their agrarian vision was superior. The more information available about the consequences of the two choices, the better would be the decision of the society. As a result, the 1790s saw vigorous and intense argument about the policy choices available: about alliance with France or Britain, about the probable growth and structure of the U.S. economy, about government debt, trade protection, and so forth. These debates could not simply be reduced to interests, but were based on the *beliefs* of the protagonists.

This distinction between interests and beliefs is implicit in Madison's *Federalist* 10, but I shall offer some further clarification, based on modern social choice theory. This theory assumes individual action is based on "rational" preferences of individuals. Such preferences can be derived from "interests," the holding of property or the exercise of factor power, such as labor or capital. As the theory suggests, and as Madison feared, such interests can collide to induce instability. Indeed, Madison expressed such fears later in life over the question of slavery and states' rights (McCoy 1989). If interests dominate among the representatives of the people, then the legislature will itself be turbulent.

However, when the republic faces a dilemma, as it did in 1800, over the choice between two competing and incompatible visions for society, then these two visions may be represented by two presidential contenders. In such a case, interest plays less of a role than belief. Since no individual can see the future with certainty, each one can only guess (with some subjective probability) which alternative is likely to be the better. While interest may affect such a choice, it does not determine it. However, to create a winning coalition, it is necessary to create faction, mobilize interest, and indeed, bring into existence a party. Madison and Jefferson came to understand this logic during the 1790s. Just as in jury decision-making, the selection of a president, and of a choice for the future, depends on persuasion, rhetoric, and contest.

The division of society in 1800 into two parties, one Republican and one Federalist, was, as Beard (1915) has argued, partly based on the opposing interests of land and agrarian labor on the one hand, and capital and industrial labor on the other. However, this division in the United States was very different from the division between Court and Country parties in Britain in the 1700s. One obvious difference was that the Republican coalition had to dampen the possible conflict between free labor and the slave-owning land interest. The optimistic agrarian vision presented by Madison and Jefferson was important in creating and maintaining this coalition.

What I call the Madison-Jefferson Equilibrium, created after the election of 1800, was remarkably stable and dominated U.S. politics until it began to fracture in the 1840s over this issue of slavery. However, it is even more remarkable that the U.S. polity has retained a two-party system throughout two hundred years, even though the party coalitions comprise can be dramatically transformed at critical elections (Miller and Schofield 2003; Schofield 2003). At each such critical election (whether 1860, 1896, 1932, or 1960), the contest between the parties has involved a choice between two competing visions of the future. The resolution of the conflict turns on the creation of a new coalition or partisan alignment among the various interests of land, labor, and capital. The comments made here on the election of 1800, and on the beliefs of Madison and Jefferson, are offered in the hope of extending social choice theory and political economy in order to understand the phenomenon of long-run dynamic equilibrium.

2. Social Choice and Constitutional Theory

Figure 12.1 gives a diagrammatic exposition of social choice theory. The first axis describes the degree to which a polity is democratic. A "veto group" is a group of individuals all of whom must agree to any policy choice in some

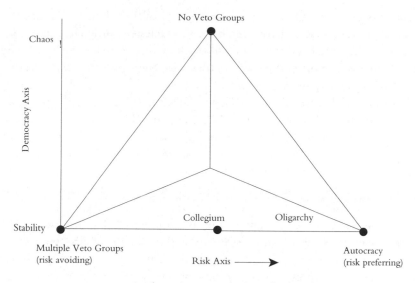

FIG. 12.1. A schematic representation of political power

domain of political decision-making. A "collegium" is a group that has veto power in every political domain, while an oligarchy is a group that not only holds veto power in every domain but also (if they all agree) can determine policy on any domain. An autocrat, or dictator, is a single individual with oligarchic power. A pure democracy obviously cannot have veto groups, collegia, oligarchies, or dictators. The U.S. Constitution, as Dahl (2002) has recently argued, is not "democratic" precisely because the balance of power among executive, legislative, and judicial branches allows for veto. (For example, Southern Democrats in the Senate used the filibuster, and the difficulty of creating a countercoalition to effect cloture, in order to block civil rights legislation from the period of Reconstruction until 1964.)

The purest form of democracy is simple majority rule—every enfranchised individual has an equal vote, and the coalition of the largest wins. Modern social choice theory suggests that pure democracy can lead to "chaos" (McKelvey 1976; Schofield 1978; McKelvey and Schofield 1986; Saari 1997; Austen-Smith and Banks 1999).

In its most general form, chaos means that politics is intrinsically unpredictable. As Riker (1980, 444) argued: "[N]early anything can happen in politics."

Political theorists of the eighteenth century also believed that democracy was fundamentally chaotic. As Madison wrote in *Federalist* 10: "A pure Democracy . . . can admit of no cure for the mischiefs of faction. A common passion or interest will . . . be felt by a majority of the whole. . . . Hence it is that such Democracies have ever been spectacles of turbulence and contention; have ever been found incompatible with personal security . . . and have . . . been as short in their lives as they have been violent in their deaths" (Rakove 1999, 164: see appendix).

What we call chaos, Madison called turbulence, or "mutability"—the incoherence of the law. In *Federalist* 62, Madison discussed the "mischievous effects of mutable government": "It will be of little avail to the people that the laws are made by men of their own choice, if laws be so . . . incoherent that they cannot be understood; if they be repealed or revised before they are promulgated, or undergo such incessant changes that no man who knows what the law is today can guess what it will be tomorrow" (ibid., 343: see appendix).

In contrast to chaos is equilibrium, or rationality, what Madison called "stability in government" in *Federalist* 37 (ibid., 196). Twentieth-century political pluralists have taken Madison's argument about the extended republic from *Federalist* 10 to mean that factional or "competing interests cancel one another out" (Williams 1998, 39). This inference, however, is at odds with social choice theory on the operation of democratic rule. I shall return, below, to Madison's extended republic argument. Before this, however, I shall comment on two theoretical methods of avoiding chaos. The first is by restricting, in some fashion, the domain of political choice. However, if we follow Madison in acknowledging the heterogeneity of interests in the extended republic, then it would seem impossible to restrict the domain of political choice sufficiently to avoid chaos.

The second method is to concentrate power either in dictatorship, oligarchy, collegium, or through some related veto principle. As Figure 12.1 suggests, concentrating power in this fashion can induce stability (Arrow 1951), but there will be effects on the "risk posture" of the society.

The constitutional theorists of the eighteenth century were well aware that autocracy could induce stability, but at the cost of tyranny. However, tyrants wish to extend their power, and are likely to engage in war. Indeed, the Declaration of Independence, penned by Thomas Jefferson, accused George III of precisely such risk-taking, tyrannical behavior. A common understanding of British political history is that autocracy did indeed lead to risk-taking and war. Oliver Cromwell had, in large degree, taken on dictatorial powers precisely in order to prosecute war against France, and in Ireland. As Madison put it, in his "Vices of the Political System of the United States," while a great desideratum of the prince is a sufficient neutrality between the different interests and factions, "[in] absolute Monarchies, the prince is sufficiently, neutral towards his subjects, but frequently sacrifices their happiness to his ambition" (Rakove 1999, 79).

Weaker veto power can also induce stability, as in oligarchy or collegium. If we identify collegium with aristocracy, then as Adair observed, there will be an "inveterate and incorrigible" tendency to use the apparatus of government to serve the special interests of the aristocratic few (Adair 1974a, 173). If the rule in the "aristocratic" Senate permits many veto groups, then the outcome may be the opposite of risk preferring autocracy or monarchy. With many such groups, it will be impossible to make decisions. Such a situation may be termed risk avoiding.

Figure 12.1 may be interpreted in terms of Montesquieu's constitutional theory of balance between democracy, aristocracy, and monarchy (Adair 1974a). It was evident in 1787 that Madison and Hamilton differed in how the balance was to be obtained. To judge from Hamilton's essays in the *Federalist*, he clearly had in mind the creation of a commercial empire. As he wrote in *Federalist* 11:

> The superiority [Europe] has long maintained, has tempted her to plume herself as the Mistress of the World, . . . It belongs to us . . . to teach that assuming brother moderation. . . . Let the thirteen States, band together in a strict and indissoluble Union, concur in erecting one great American system . . . to control all trans-atlantic force . . . and able to dictate to the terms of the connection between the old and the new world! (Freeman 2001, 208)

As Adair observed, the constitutional theory of Montesquieu suggested that only monarchy possessed the necessary *energy, secrecy, and dispatch* to order an empire.

While the Federal Convention would not, of course, accept a monarchy, Hamilton pressed for almost autocratic power for the executive: first, on June 4, 1787, for an absolute veto and second, on June 18, for appointment for life.

On June 4, Madison had responded that "[to] give such a prerogative would certainly be obnoxious to the temper of the Country; its present temper at least" (*The Papers of James Madison* [hereafter MP] 10, 24). Later, in developing his balance theory in *Federalist* 51, Madison noted that "[An] absolute negative, on the legislative appears at first view to be the natural defence with which the executive magistrate should be armed. But perhaps it would be neither altogether safe, nor alone sufficient." Although Madison and Hamilton seem from their written and spoken remarks to agree on the political logic inherent in Figure 12.1, they disagreed about how to create the constitutional apparatus of the republic so as to avoid the costs both of democratic chaos and of risk accepting autocracy. As I have intimated in the introduction, Britain's experience in the eighteenth century was relevant to this disagreement.

3. The Political Economy of Britain in the Eighteenth Century

The critical requirement facing any government in an era of war was to raise revenue for defense. Taxes could never cover costs in time of war, so it was necessary to devise methods to deal with debt. In the United States, the eventual financial costs of the War of Independence were, by Hamilton's account, foreign debt of $11.7 million, with an additional domestic debt of $40 million, plus $25 million state and $2 million unliquidated Continental paper (McDonald 1979, 168). A classic account of the move to union in 1787 emphasized the conflicts between creditors and debtors in the Confederated States (Beard 1913). With a free population of 3.2 million in 1789, debt per capita in the United States was about $25. British per capita debt about this time was £7.5 sterling, or approximately $30. (As a basis for comparison, real wages for agricultural laborers in Britain were of the order of $80 per annum.)

However, Britain had devised a sophisticated and "responsible" fiscal system that allowed her to increase her burden of government debt without excessive costs. In contrast, France had doubled her level of debt to approximately $400 million during the conflict with Britain from 1779 to 1783. This unmanageable level of debt contributed to the onset of the French Revolution (Norberg 1994).

For Hamilton and Madison, war and debt were problems that any successful government had to face. How Britain had dealt with them was particularly relevant for Hamilton.

Although the extravagance of the Stuart monarchs (and also that of the Protector Cromwell) had been something of a problem, government debt at the time of the Glorious Revolution of 1688 had been negligible. However, British debt rose to £36 million sterling in the period from the beginning of the Nine Years War in 1689 to the end of the War of Spanish Succession in 1713. In the same period, government income had risen from £3.6 million to £5.4 million sterling.

The contract implicit in the Glorious Revolution had been that Parliament would effectively order the fisc through the operation of the Bank of England, and commit itself to a level of taxation to cover interest on the growing debt (North and Weingast 1989). However, when war weariness had brought in a Tory government in 1710, the fear grew that the Tories would renege on this fiscal responsibility by repudiating some of the debt. The consequence was a jump in the long-term interest rates from 6 percent to 10 percent (Stasavage 2003). The reason for this market fear was that the proportion of government income raised from the land tax was about 35 percent (Brewer 1988, 31). Indeed, O'Brien (1988) estimates that the proportion of direct taxes derived from what he calls "manifestations of wealth and income" was 40 percent in 1710. The quandary facing the government was that Parliament consisted mostly of the agrarian interest. What political logic would require landowners to commit themselves to cover the costs of debt? Just as later in the U.S. Ratification period of 1787–88, there had appeared in Britain in 1710–20 a conflict between the agrarian and commercial interests. Commercial interests obviously benefited from the existence of the Bank of England, and from the presumed guarantee that their loans to government would be honored. This guarantee seemingly depended on the willingness of the Parliament to tax itself, to force or persuade its own members to pay something of the order of 15 percent per annum on their land holdings. To some degree this conflict overlapped with the antagonism between Tories and Whigs after the death of Queen Anne in 1714. Tories, such as Viscount Bolingbroke, previously minister to Anne, had a preference for the continuation of the Stuart line (through James Edward, son of James II) and peace with France. Whigs supported the Hanoverian George I and the probability of war with France.

Given the rise in government debt to £50 million sterling by 1720, coupled with the problems associated with the land tax, Sunderland, the First Lord of the Treasury, accepted a proposal from the South Sea Company to fund £20 million sterling. The company expected to make huge profits under the Asiento agreement with Spain, involving the slave trade in the Spanish colonies. Share prices rose tenfold and then collapsed. In an atmosphere of desperation, Robert Walpole restored confidence by a transfer of £18 million sterling of South Sea stock to the Bank of England. In April 1721, Walpole became "first . . . prime minister in fact if not in name" (Williams 1960, 179) and set about reorganizing government debt and its funding. Debt remained stable, falling to £46 million by 1739, and interest on the debt was only £2 million sterling. It is significant that about 50 percent of the government revenue of approximately £5 million came from excise and stamp duty, with an additional 24 percent from customs (O'Brien 1988, 9).

The reliance on customs and excise persisted in large degree through the eighteenth century, and even until the repeal of the Corn Laws in 1846 (McLean 2001). This fiscal strategy provided Britain with the revenue to fight France and eventually vanquish her in 1815. Kennedy (1987, 81) has estimated that British government expenditure during the Napoleonic War was well in excess of £1 billion sterling.

The theoretical point was that, by building up an extensive bureaucratic apparatus to collect the growing customs and excise revenues, Britain managed to avoid political conflict. Indeed, this entire period from 1720 to 1815 was one of Whig dominance. For this fiscal solution to Britain's debt quandary, I shall use the term "Walpole Equilibrium." To see why it was so successful, we need to consider the notion of factor coalitions and the underlying mercantilist trade theory.

In the early seventeenth century, Britain had been no match for the more populous and much richer France. Under Cromwell's autocratic rule, the first Navigation Act was passed (1651) followed by the "massive [naval] build up of the First Dutch War" (Baugh 1994). In 1655, Jamaica was captured and became the core of the rich commercial maritime empire that grew rapidly in the eighteenth century. The military quandary for the British was that the cost of maintaining both navy and army was too high to be sustainable. In fact, Cromwell's risky strategy of building up both navy and army contributed to the conflicts between him and Parliament, and led to his dissolution of the latter in 1654.

The solution to this military situation was to extend the navy, while maintaining a relatively small army except in time of war. The consequence of the British naval predominance was the growth of its empire. The mercantilist theory associated with this growth of empire was that the state, by controlling trade through the Navigation Acts and by customs and excise, would accumulate specie and maintain its access to resources to fund both the navy and any necessary military adventures.

This mercantilist strategy had a number of consequences, perhaps unintended, which became increasingly obvious during the eighteenth century.

In the early eighteenth century, British imports were approximately equally balanced between manufactures, foodstuffs, and raw materials. While there were customs duties on manufactures (such as linen, silk, etc.), the highest duties were on foodstuffs (tea, sugar, salt) with very high levels of customs and excise on wine, beer, tobacco, and so forth. The restrictions on wine imports were possibly directed against France (Nye 1992), but the more general effect of these trade restrictions was to "artificially" increase the price of land. Modern trade theory (Rogowski 1989) suggests the reason for this effect. British imports that were subject to these tariffs were "intense" in the factor of land. Land in Britain can be regarded as less abundant, in some general sense, in comparison with the availability of land in North America, for example. Thus, artificially restricting demand for land-intensive imports raised the relative price of this factor against the relative prices of both capital and labor. Allen (1988) has examined the apparent contradiction (noticed by economic historians) that the rate of return on investment in land appeared to be below that provided by investment in government debt. He argues, however, that the long-term increase in the price of land meant that "free hold land was *not* trading at a price that exceeded its economic value" (ibid., 48).

If this inference is correct, then the nature of the "Walpole Equilibrium" becomes clear. The landed interest was placated by the use of customs and excise to maintain or increase the price of the principal asset, land, held by the majority of the members of Parliament. The quid pro quo was the commitment of the landed interest to accept the land tax, to cover interest on government debt. Commercial interests and creditors were also advantaged, since this fiscal mechanism provided the means of honoring the debt. It is hardly surprising that the implementation of this Walpole Equilibrium led to a "hundred years of stable single party Whig government" (Plumb 1967, 158).

Walpole's principal constitutional opponent in the creation of this fiscal equilibrium was Henry St. John, Viscount Bolingbroke. In exile in France, he wrote against the perversion of the English constitution by the corruption attending the Whig dominance, against the "placemen" and "stockjobbers" who maintained this equilibrium (Krammick 1990,165; see also Krammick 1992).

Thomas Jefferson was much persuaded by Bolingbroke's rhetoric. In a letter to Francis Eppes (January 19, 1821), Jefferson wrote of Bolingbroke's style as being "lofty, rhythmical . . . ," with the "eloquence of Cicero" and "conceptions . . . bold and strong" (Peterson 1984, 1451). As a consequence, perhaps, historians have explored the relationship between Bolingbroke's constitutional conceptions and the ideas of the Republicans in the United States in the 1790s (Krammick 1990).

If my inferences about the nature of Walpole Equilibrium in the eighteenth century are correct, then Bolingbroke's arguments missed the crucial feature of the Whig capital-land coalition in Britain. However, Britain and the United States differed completely in their economic structure in 1790. I shall argue that Hamilton's efforts to implement a version of the Walpole Equilibrium in the United States in 1790–1800 necessarily brought the opposing interests of land and capital into conflict. In the following sections I shall attempt to indicate how the social choice and political economy theories just presented give us some insight into this conflict.

4. A Commercial or an Agrarian Empire for the United States

It is evident that Hamilton believed, from 1787 on, that it was necessary for the United States to construct a stable fiscal apparatus parallel to the British device. It was an obvious inference that this device had been crucial to Britain's economic growth. The fact that land prices were maintained and capital available would have suggested to any economically astute observer that increasing investment in British agriculture was rational. In fact, both land utilization and crop yields in Britain increased from 1700 to 1790 (Allen 1994, 112) while there was a fall in the proportion of the population engaged in agriculture (Crafts 1994, 46). Although Britain's imports of land-intensive foodstuffs increased in this period, the high agricultural productivity also meant that agricultural exports increased as a proportion of total exports in the period from 1700 to 1750 (Engermann 1994, 188). Meanwhile, real wages both for farm laborers and skilled workers were basically flat for this half-century (Lindert 1994, 370). Increased agricultural output facilitated rapid population growth (from about 5 million in England in 1700 to 7.7 million in 1790) and increased urbanization (Schofield 1994, 64, 88).

These changes in Britain in the eighteenth century were all well understood in a general fashion, though not perhaps in as much detail as economic historians now know. It was also apparent that the political mechanism that I have called the Walpole Equilibrium benefited the land and capital interests at the cost of labor. While increased manufacturing output led to the relative abundance of capital, the increased demand for capital maintained the share of domestic product accruing to the commercial interest. An important element of the Walpole Equilibrium was the limited enfranchisement of the population. Brewer (1976, 6) comments that the extension of the enfranchised population in Britain in the first half of the eighteenth century was about half that of the rate of population growth.

To put in place a fiscal apparatus in the United States in the 1790s parallel to Britain's would plausibly have the following effects: Firstly, to raise government revenue to cover interest on debt would necessitate either a land tax or a system of tariffs. Since the tariffs affect imports, these would have consequences for the relative price of the factor in which imports were most intensive. American imports included a very large proportion of manufactures, and thus can be viewed as relatively capital intensive. Since capital was relatively scarce in the United States, in comparison with abundant land, trade restriction would necessarily maintain or raise the relative price of capital. Manufacturers, the commercial interest, would thus be advantaged.

Secondly, since landowners are generally capital short, being dependent on debt, the implication was that the agrarian interest would suffer. Thirdly, since U.S. manufactured imports originated in Britain, the consequence of raising tariffs would inevitably be retaliation by higher British protection against U.S. land-intensive exports. The agrarian interest would be affected in all three ways. Whether or not labor would be affected by a Hamiltonian scheme would depend on its dependence on capital or land. The large proportion of the population engaged in agriculture would suffer a decline in real wages. For industrial labor, principally in the Northeast engaged in the infant manufacturing sector, protection would increase their real wage. The origins of the two-party system lay in this conflict between capital and industrial labor on the one hand, and the agrarian interest on the other. However, the agrarian interest was divided between free labor, particularly in the western states, and Southern slave-owning agricultural producers. The use of slave labor could indirectly affect the real wage of free labor, if slave-produced products were substitutes in some sense for the product of free agrarian labor. However, Southern cotton was intended for export to the manufacturers of Britain, and this would tend to have little impact on the foodstuffs or timber produced by Northern labor. In brief, the Republican party (and later the Democracy) depended on the coalition among the agrarian interests made possible by suppressing the issue of slavery. The Federalist Party, later the Whigs, had their principal strength among the commercial interests, and industrial labor. It is obvious that the electoral strength of these parties would not reside solely in the North or the South. Northern states, such as Pennsylvania, would have a mix of commerce and agriculture. Even Southern states such as Virginia would have commercial interests. The intersectional feature of this two-party system was stable until the interests of free labor and slave owners began to diverge later in the nineteenth century.

I suggest that the party system that came into being in the 1790s was based on stable factor coalitions of land and agrarian labor against capital and industrial labor. To emphasize the parallel with the Walpole Equilibrium in Britain, based on a coalition of land and capital, I shall use the term "Madison-Jefferson Equilibrium" for the basis of the Republican coalition of land and agrarian labor.

To better understand the nature of this equilibrium it is useful to briefly refer to the period of conflict between Britain and the Colonies, starting in 1756, and to the creation of a land-capital coalition in the United States in the 1780s, during ratification of the Constitution.

5. Land and Capital in North America, 1756–90

Historians have emphasized many points of conflict between the metropole and the Colonies, including religion, hatred of tyranny, taxation, and so forth. My view is that land was the fundamental source of this conflict.

In the 1750s, the American Colonies were hemmed in by the French domains of Louisiana and Quebec. Although the Colonies claimed land to the Mississippi, they had no resources to wrest it from the French. Whether by accident or intent, George Washington's expedition into the Ohio Valley and the killing of a young French ensign, Joseph Coulon de Villiers de Jumonville, and some of his troops, set in motion the military machines of Britain and France (Anderson 2000, 52). During the Seven Years War of 1756–63, Britain took Havana, Manila, Quebec, and Guadalupe in the Caribbean. After France's defeat, Britain kept Cape Breton, Canada, and Louisiana, east of the Mississippi, but returned Guadalupe to France. Possibly to prevent Louisiana, west of the Mississippi from falling to Britain, France ceded this domain to Spain, its ally against Britain.

For the landed interests in the Colonies, the close of the Seven Years War gave them hope that the vast region of the Ohio Valley would be available for land speculation and settlement. However, the peace had also brought war with the Native American tribes under Pontiac, a chief of the Ottawa, opposed to colonial settlement. To appease Pontiac, the British government issued a proclamation closing the Ohio Valley to settlement, but it was forced to maintain a series of forts on the line, at a cost of nearly £400,000 sterling. In an attempt to cover some of the costs, the British government passed the Stamp Act and Sugar Act. These, together with the proclamation, infuriated the agrarian elite. Benjamin Franklin, in London in 1764, argued that the acts were without justification, since the conflict with the French and Indians was of no concern to the Colonies. The Quebec Act of 1774 tried to close the Ohio Valley to settlement by including it in the jurisdiction of the Quebec authorities. It was this threat by the British to the expansion of the Colonies that exasperated the agrarian elite. The costs of taxation may have angered the people, but the burden of taxation could not be considered sufficient to induce war. Chown (1994, 218), for example, estimates that the taxes were intended to raise about £16,000 sterling, excluding collection costs. The risk of losing the war against the formidable British naval and military power meant that the Continental Congress delayed declaring independence until there was reasonable cause to believe that France would aid them. Schofield (2002a) argues that the Committee of Secret Correspondence, chaired by Franklin, heard news of the promise of aid from Louis XVI in late June 1776. With this aid, combined with the French military and naval assistance, the Colonies were successful, and in the final peace treaty, they obtained the entire territory east of the Mississippi.

Spain, however, never recognized the United States, and during the War of Independence it laid claim to the northern territory of what is now Michigan, as well as the region bordering the Floridas. It was this threat that

John Jay, secretary of foreign affairs, tried to allay by a treaty with Spain's agent, Diego de Gardoqui. Seven of the thirteen states agreed in principle to the proposed treaty, and it was this fact that caused Madison to fear that the weak confederation of states would fragment (J. Madison to T. Jefferson, August 20, 1784, in Smith 1995, 337–42; J. Madison to G. Washington, December 7, 1786, in Rakove 1999, 60; J. Madison to T. Jefferson, March 19, 1787, in Smith 1995, 472). Supporters of the Jay-Gardoqui treaty believed that the increased trade offered by Spain would benefit their particular commercial interests. Those opposed tended to be states dominated by the members of the agrarian interest who saw the opportunity of expansion into the Louisiana territory. This threat by Spain, and the resulting disagreement between the states, made it clear that there was a conflict of interest between what Hume called the "landed and trading" parts of the nation (Hume 1985). Although conflict between these interests may indeed have been muted in Britain, this was because of the nature of the Walpole Equilibrium. In the United States, the potential conflict between land and capital was temporarily overcome in the period of ratification of the Constitution, 1787–88.

In his classic statement, Beard (1913) argued that the supporters of union in 1787 were adherents of a hard money principle—namely, "merchants, money lenders, security holders, manufacturers, shippers, capitalists, and financiers" (ibid., 17). Opponents of union were those who favored soft money—"non-slaveholding farmers and the debtors." The threat from Spain, however, was real, and as the essays by Jay and Hamilton in the *Federalist* made clear, union was the obvious way to overcome this threat (Riker 1964, 13). For agrarian interests, the choice between union and the confederation was determined by whether the subjective costs associated with hard money or the Spanish threat were predominant (Schofield 2002b).

Although the decision was close in many of the states, the new Constitution was eventually ratified. Obviously enough, the Constitution involved a complex balance among a number of political objectives. However, it would seem from the above observations that Beard's argument concerning the Federalist coalition of 1787 was not entirely valid. The pro-union coalition consisted not just of the commercial interest but of landed interests as well. In general, the landed interest will tend to be opposed to capital, because, as Beard implied, the former tend to be indebted, and therefore, in favor of soft money. The threat from Spain, and the response in creating a federal apparatus, temporarily overcame these conflicts. However, with the threat diminished and the union completed, the Federalist coalition of commercial and agrarian interests became unstable. Although it was necessary to devise a fiscal apparatus to deal with debt, it became obvious by 1790 that Hamilton's scheme would set the country on a course of commercial, rather than agrarian, expansion. Hamilton's writings suggest that he believed that his scheme would resemble the Walpole Equilibrium of Britain in the earlier part of the century, and be compatible with the interests of both land and capital. As I have argued in Section 4, economic theory suggests he was incorrect in this inference. His protagonists, Madison and Jefferson, were well aware of the consequences and costs of Hamilton's scheme. Moreover, they had a shared vision of the future of the United States, which, I shall argue, derived in large part from the constitutional writings of Condorcet. The conflict of the 1790s, and thus the creation of the two-party system, arose out of the incompatibility of these two contrasting theories associated with Hamilton on the one hand, and Madison and Jefferson on the other.

6. The Influence of Condorcet on Madison and Jefferson

The intellectual influence of the English and Scottish constitutional theorists on the Founders, and particularly on Madison and Jefferson, has long been studied. Adair (1943; 2000), for example, in his argument against Beard (1913), relied on Hume's assertion that there was no conflict in principle, between the "landed and trading parts of the nation." In accepting Hume's logic, Adair asserted that Hamilton's belief about the disequilibrium between democracy and aristocracy was also invalid. However, Hume also contended that the election of the chief magistrate would necessarily be attended by tumult. As Hume says: "The filling of the [position of elective magistrate] is a point of too great and too general interest, not to divide the whole people into factions. Whence a civil war, the greatest of ills, may be apprehended almost with certainty, upon every vacancy" (Hume 1985, 18).

A similar theme is apparent in the work of Bolingbroke, and even in Gibbon's *History of the Decline and Fall of the Roman Empire* (Gibbon 1994; see Womersley 2002). In a later essay, Hume goes on to refer to "the common opinion that no large state, such as FRANCE or GREAT BRITAIN could ever be modelled into a commonwealth, but that such a form of government can only take place in a city or small territory" (Hume 1985, 527). Hume attempts his refutation of this small-republic argument of Montesquieu by proposing that in "a large government, which is modelled with masterly skill, there is compass and room enough to refine the democracy, from the lower people . . . to the higher magistrates. . . . [T]he parts are so distant that it is very difficult . . . to hurry them into any measures against the public interest" (ibid., 528). Adair is clearly correct to see in Hume's argument the essence of Madison's extended republic thesis. I concur with Adair that

Hume's logic was absorbed into Madison's essay on the "Vices of the Political System of the United States," written in April 1787 (Rakove 1999, 69–80; see appendix). However, there are important differences between Madison's essay of April 1787 and the clearer thesis of *Federalist* 10 of November 22, 1787.

I contend that Madison's later logic suggests the influence of the work of the Marquis de Condorcet (1743–94). Indeed, I shall argue further that Condorcet's work in constitutional theory, fiscal theory, trade theory, and economic growth were utilized by Madison and Jefferson to provide a coherent logic to what I have called the Madison-Jefferson equilibrium. In this argument, I enlarge on the points made by McLean (Chapter 2, this volume).

As is well known, Jefferson arrived in Paris as minister plenipotentiary in August 1784, to take over from Franklin. As Jefferson's biographer Randall notes, Condorcet, Lafayette and other *philosophes* joined Jefferson's intimate circle of friends (Randall 1993, 431). Condorcet had been elected permanent secretary of the French Academy of Science, and certainly knew Franklin as both a colleague and a friend.[2] Condorcet's work on social choice theory (surveyed in McLean and Hewitt 1994) is still relevant today. Condorcet's fame, at least in social choice theory, rests on his *Essai sur l'application de l'analyse a la probabilite des voix* (Condorcet 1785).[3] He is more widely known for his *Esquisse d'un tableau historique* (Condorcet 1794). This latter stimulated Malthus to write his famous essay (Malthus 1970).

Condorcet's "jury theorem" proposed that each voter, i, say, could be characterized by some probability, p_i, say, of voting for the truth. The theorem showed that in a binary choice (yea or nay), majority rule maximized the probability P, say, that the jury (or committee) selected the truth. Moreover, as the jury size increased without bound, then this probability P approached 1. When Condorcet attempted to extend this result to one with multiple choices, he found an incoherence theorem, similar in kind to what I have termed chaos. Condorcet's results were presented in the French Academy of Science in 1785, and given Franklin's interest in the topic, I conjecture that Franklin would have understood them, and possibly discussed them in the context of the Society for Political Enquiry that Franklin created in 1787 after he returned to Philadelphia. It has been suggested by McGrath (1983) that Madison was aware of Condorcet's "incoherence" theorem and had it in mind when arguing for the separation of powers implicit in *Federalist* 51. The analyses by Urken (1991) and McLean and Urken (1992) suggest otherwise. Their arguments turn on Madison's rejection of unicameralism.

It is known that Madison did receive a sketch of Condorcet's work, sent by Jefferson, and included in a book by the Italian Philip Mazzei. The volume was entitled *Recherches historiques sur les Etats-Unis* (see McLean and Hewitt 1994, 64. Also see Marchione,1975, for the collected works of Mazzei). Madison mentions receipt of the volume in a letter to Jefferson, dated September 6, 1787 (Smith 1995, 492). In his contribution, Condorcet asserts that it can be proven rigorously "that increasing the number of legislative bodies could never increase the probability of obtaining true decisions" (McLean and Hewitt 1994, 325). Obviously, this can be taken as an argument for unicameralism. Since Madison seemingly rejected this principle, in *Federalist* 51, that would seem to be the end of it.

Although Condorcet believed his jury theorem applied to legislative decision-making, it is not evident that it does. As Madison's remarks on "mutability" imply, a legislative body makes laws, and these may be incoherent. In contrast, when an electorate chooses a representative, or a chief magistrate, it picks a person. A person may not be "true" in Condorcet's sense, but can be "pre-eminent for ability and virtue," to use Hamilton's phrase (in *Federalist* 68; Rossiter 1961, 414).

Thus, if we interpret Madison's term "a fit choice" to mean a virtuous representative or chief magistrate, then there is a clear similarity between the extended republic argument of *Federalist* 10 and Condorcet's Jury Theorem. As in Condorcet's result, the larger, or more heterogeneous and populous the republic, the greater will be "the probability of a fit choice" (Rakove 1999, 165; see also the appendix). Madison's term "the probability of a fit choice" does not appear in the essay on "Vices" in April 1787, but it *does* occur in the *Federalist* 10 essay of November. Notice that this logic only applies formally to binary choice, as in situations in which there are two candidates, Federalist or Republican, say. Moreover, Condorcet's theorem, and its apparent application by Madison in *Federalist* 10, is only valid when the electorate is knowledgeable. I have suggested in the Introduction that this fundamental proposition is important in understanding the actions of Madison and Jefferson in the constitutional disagreement with the Federalists in the 1790s.

Before Jefferson left France in October 1789, he had witnessed the opening ceremony of the Estates General in Versailles in May, and collaborated with Lafayette and Condorcet on a draft of what was eventually to be the *Declaration of the Rights of Man and the Citizen* in August 1789 (McLean and Hewitt 1994, 55). Implicit in Jefferson's thought at this time was what Randall calls the "explosive doctrine of perpetual revolution" (Randall 1993, 486). In Jefferson's letter to Madison of September 6, 1789, he asks the question "[w]hether one generation of men has a right to bind another" and answers that "no man can by *natural right* oblige the lands he occupied . . . or the persons who succeed him, to the paiment [*sic*] of debts contracted by him." Thus "*the earth belongs in usufruct to the living*" (Peterson 1984, 959).[4]

As Sloan (1995, 242) observes, on the same day, Condorcet's letter to Comte de Montmorency computes, mathematically, the length of time of a generation, about twenty years (in fact, this term is the half-life of a population). Jefferson, using an identical calculation, estimates the half-life at eighteen years and eight months. Then Jefferson makes the following point: the French debt of "ten thousand milliard of livres" had impoverished the nation. Limiting debt to whatever could be paid within the half-life of a generation would have avoided this unjust imposition on later generations.

This parallel between the calculations of Condorcet and Jefferson merely reflects their mutual engagement and friendship (Sloan records that Condorcet was present at a farewell dinner for Jefferson on September 17, 1789). There are deeper connections. Debt was the prime concern of Anne Robert Turgot, chosen by Louis XVI as controller general of finances in 1774, to reorganize France's debt. Turgot's refusal to agree to Vergenne's scheme to aid the American colonies in 1776 led to his dismissal. Indeed, the increase of debt as a result of this decision forced Louis XVI to call the estates general in 1789. Condorcet was Turgot's protégé and wrote Turgot's biography in 1787, as well as editing his work.

Appleby (1992) also indicates that Jefferson accepted the arguments of Turgot and Condorcet on the utility of free trade. Moreover, "Jefferson was an early advocate of the commercial exploitation of American agriculture" (ibid.). In a letter to Jefferson on June 19, 1786, Madison assumed that the agricultural surplus of the new lands would increase without bound, and that the "equal partition of property must result in a greater simplicity of manners, consequently, a less consumption of manufactured superfluities, and a less proportion of idle proprietors and domestics" (Smith 1995, 422).

McCoy has further argued that Jefferson kept to his "vision of a predominantly agricultural America that would continue to export its bountiful surpluses of food abroad" (McCoy 1980a, 268). Indeed, Jefferson later consistently rejected the Malthusian thesis that population would outstrip food production. In 1818 he arranged the translation of an essay, Treatise of Political Economy, by Destutt de Tracy to that effect (McCoy 1980b; Mayer 1994, 352).[5] Jefferson's belief in this regard parallels Condorcet's opinion, as set out in the Esquisse d'un tableau historique des Progres de l'esprit humain. The Esquisse was written while Condorcet was in hiding in 1794 from the Jacobins, and only published after his death by the efforts of his wife Sophie de Grouchy. Clearly, Condorcet's beliefs about the development of the human spirit could not have been read by Jefferson in the early 1790s; however, there is clear evidence that the optimism that Jefferson and Madison expressed in the late 1790s did owe a considerable debt to Condorcet.[6]

7. Origins of the Two-Party System in the 1790s

The conflict between Federalists and Republicans has been described many times (e.g., Weisberger 2000), so I shall comment only on those features that seem to reflect the coherent political economic philosophies of Madison and Jefferson, on the one hand, and Hamilton on the other.

Madison was defeated in Virginia's Senate election in November 1788, but elected to the House of Representatives in February 1789. Almost immediately, he moved

> that Congress establish a revenue system to enable the nation to pay its debts. . . . He proposed high import duties on . . . luxuries (rum, liquors, wine, molasses, tea, sugar, spices, coffee and cocoa). . . . Madison asserted that though he was a "friend to a very free system of commerce" . . . and regarded "commercial shackles as unjust, oppressive, and impolitic," tariffs were nevertheless justifiable in some cases: to protect temporarily new industries . . . , to discourage luxury spending . . . and to retaliate against unfair commercial regulations by other countries. (Ketcham 1971, 280)

Madison also argued for discrimination against Britain, to use America's importation of manufactures and export of food as a device to open further trade with Europe so as to oppose Britain's dominance. Madison would return to this theme later, particularly in a number of long speeches in January and February 1794 (MP 15, 167, 180, 182, 205, 206, 247). It is pertinent to the agrarian thesis that, on April 9, 1789, Madison argued in Congress for the encouragement of

> the great staple of the United States; I mean agriculture, which may justly be stiled [sic] the staple of the United States. . . . If we compare the cheapness of our land with that of other nations, we see so decided an advantage in that cheapness, as to have full confidence of being unrivaled; with respect to the object of manufacture, other countries may and do rival us; but we may be said to have a monopoly in agriculture. . . . If my general principle is a good one . . . commerce ought to be free, and labour and industry left at large to find its object. (MP 12, 73)

This speech, together with Madison's earlier letters to Jefferson, make it clear that by 1789, Madison had a well-articulated theory based on free trade and agrarian expansion for the United States. While there was mutual advantage for Britain and the United States to exploit their comparative advantages, nonetheless, the United States had to defend itself against commercial exploitation by Britain.

On January 9, 1790, Hamilton, as secretary of the Treasury, brought out his *Report on Public Credit* (Freeman 2001, 531–74). Madison, in Congress, argued against the assumption of debts that had been pressed by Hamilton. The defeat of the proposal by a logroll in Congress may have reinforced Hamilton's belief in the inherent incoherence of the legislature. The *Report on Credit* was followed by further long reports on a *National Bank* (February 23, 1791) and on *The subject of manufactures* (December 5, 1791).

Madison tried to halt the national bank by asking "if the power [to establish] an incorporated bank was among the powers vested by the constitution in the legislature of the United States" (Rakove 1999, 481–82). The bank scheme went ahead. "When subscriptions were opened on July 4, 1791, they were filled within one hour" (Elkins and McKitrick 1993, 242).

These three reports were indicative of Hamilton's earnest wish to put in place an American analogue of Walpole's British Equilibrium. As I have indicated, since the United States *exported* land-intensive goods, the only logically feasible path to creating a commercial economy was to sustain manufactures either by tariff or by direct government assistance. It is interesting that Hamilton deals immediately with what I have intimated was an underlying component of the Madison-Jefferson vision—that the future of the U.S. economy lay principally in the cultivation of the land. Indeed, in the *Report on Manufactures*, Hamilton takes up the argument of Adam Smith (1984):

> The labour of Artificers being capable of greater subdivision and simplicity of operation than that of Cultivators, it is susceptible, in a proportionably [*sic*] greater degree, of improvement in its *productive* powers, whether to be derived from an accession of Skill, or from the application of ingenious machinery, . . . That with regard to an augmentation of the quantity of useful labour, must depend essentially upon an increase of capital. (Freeman 2001, 651)

Hamilton's argument clearly sets out his view of the necessary evolution of the U.S. economy: By the creation of a national bank to generate capital, by protection of industry, and by tariff to cover government debt, the United States would grow rapidly.

On September 9, 1792, Jefferson wrote to George Washington

> That I have utterly disapproved of the system of the Secretary of Treasury, I acknolege [*sic*] and avow: and this is not merely a speculative difference. This system flowed from principles averse to liberty [and] was calculated to undermine and demolish the republic, by creating an influence of his department over the members of the legislature. (Peterson 1984, 994)

By denying that his rejection was speculative, Jefferson meant that he had good reasons (both empirical and theoretical) to believe that the Hamiltonian system would induce corruption and undermine liberty. From Jefferson's own reading of Bolingbroke, he believed that the creation of a capitalist system in the United States would make it possible for a Hamilton, in the guise of Walpole, to bribe and maneuver among the factions of the legislature, to act as autocrat.

In addition to the allegations of corruption, I contend that Madison and Jefferson believed that Hamilton's commercial empire in the United States would generate precisely the same phenomenon of immiseration as in Britain. Were agriculture to be diminished, then agrarian labor would experience a diminution of real income. Indeed, ascendant capital would eventually control land, as in Britain, in the form of great estates.[7] This would necessarily require the further disenfranchisement of labor. Beard (1915) in his analysis of Jeffersonian America quotes from the *Treatise* of John Taylor, of Caroline County (published in 1814): "The policy of protecting duties to force manufacturing . . . will produce the same consequences as that of enriching . . . a paper interest . . . and the wealth of the majority will continually be diminished" (Beard, 1915, 341).

Indeed, this view of the conflict of land and capital, of the agrarian against the commercial interest, is one that pervades debate in the United States until the Civil War. While Taylor's essay postdates the election of 1800, it is clear that the views expressed by Taylor in 1814 reflected the opinions of Madison and Jefferson in the 1790s.

8. Conclusion

I shall conclude with some brief remarks about the consequences of this conflict. Although I have posed the conflict in terms of an agrarian interest against a commercial interest, I have also suggested that Madison and Jefferson viewed it in terms of how best to organize the economic development of the United States. Consistent with my interpretation of Condorcet's optimism, the two Republicans believed that agricultural expansion could lead to increased economic power for the United States. However, Hamilton appeared correct in his view that only manufacturing was capable of rapid productivity increase. Thus, for the growth of the agrarian empire, it was necessary for the United States to expand its boundaries. This makes Jefferson's appetite for the western territory of Louisiana perfectly intelligible. If this expanded agrarian empire was made available to free labor, then the immiseration of labor would not occur. However, this would depend on maintaining the productivity of free agrarian labor against that of slave labor in the plantation economy.

Secondly, it is clear from Madison's polemics in Congress in 1794 that he understood that Britain's commercial empire could dominate an agrarian economy such as that of the United States through Britain's control of both capital and trade. The basis of his argument for a trade war against Britain was that Britain's fundamental need for food exceeded America's need for manufactures. In Madison's view, manufactures were superfluities. In actual fact (if I understood nineteenth-century British-U.S. trade correctly), Britain maintained a persistent trade deficit with the United States that it covered by a large trade surplus with the rest of the world. Madison appears to have been correct in his long-term view.

For Madison and Jefferson, the issue of reconstructing the political economic configuration in the period leading up to the 1800 election was of paramount importance. From the Condorcetian perspective, such an election involves collective decision-making under risk. The more debate and information about possible futures, the more likely would the election lead to the attainment of a superior alternative. I have suggested that Madison considered that a heterogeneous electorate may choose representatives "preeminent for ability and virtue." This suggests that the election of Jefferson, and later Madison, justified their particular perspectives on the future.

There is one final point relevant to current political theory. The particular restructuring of political support that occurred between 1787 and 1800 has elements of what is called partisan realignment. Current theories suggest that these occur at the onset of critical elections (as in 1896, 1932, 1960). Miller and Schofield (2003) argue that these critical elections are associated with relatively rapid transformations of coalition structure among the three factors discussed in this essay—namely, land, labor, and capital. Between such elections there are relatively stable equilibria, based on the competition between two parties. In the presidential election of 1800, while there may have nominally been two parties, there were four candidates: Adams, Pinckney, Burr, and Jefferson. How this factional competition cohered into the relatively stable two-party system of the next fifty years is worth further study. Indeed, a close examination of the flow of argument, and the consequent change of electoral beliefs around 1800, could give some insight into the general validity of Madison's argument concerning the "probability of a fit choice" in the Republic.

Notes

I thank Sam Kernell, Jonathan Dull, and the anonymous reviewers of Stanford University Press for their comments, particularly with regard to various inaccuracies in an earlier version of this chapter. I am also grateful to seminar participants at Tulane University, New York University, Washington University in St. Louis, and the University of Michigan for their remarks on my attempt to understand the Founding of the Republic. Conversations with Iain McLean, Andrew Rehfeld, and Andrew Rutten were also very helpful. Claude-Anne Lopez and Nicolas Rieucau very kindly provided me with information on Condorcet, Franklin, and Jefferson.

1. It is unclear precisely what such a phrase means. One possible interpretation is that political competition leads to a "centrist" balance between competing interests (Downs 1957). This implies that all political parties become identical. There is empirical evidence to suggest that this is an invalid conclusion (Miller and Schofield 2003).

2. Condorcet was elected permanent secretary of the French Academy of Science in August 1776. See Baker 1975, 47. During the nearly nine years that Franklin resided in Paris, he and Condorcet became well known to each other. On Franklin's return to Philadelphia in 1785 he proposed Condorcet as a member of the American Philosophical Society. After Franklin's death in 1790, Condorcet published a *Eulogy* to his friend.

3. Condorcet's work in his *Essai* can be seen as an extension of Hume's idea of "probable belief," set out in Hume's *Treatise* (Hume 1985). Indeed, Condorcet's biographer, Baker (1975, 13), notes the line of thought from Hume through Condorcet to the twentieth century (Keynes 1921; Popper 1959). Condorcet's work may be seen as an early but important contribution to the theory of "collective decision-making under risk."

4. Mayer (1994, ch. 10) discusses the further correspondence between Madison and Jefferson in 1790 over the issue of debt, and the possibility of constitutional change.

5. Baker (1975, 393) observes that Jefferson seemed to approve of Destutt de Tracy's idea of social science, the notion that society can be understood in scientific terms.

There is another intriguing indirect connection between Jefferson, Destutt, and Condorcet. The *Commentaire sur l'esprit des lois de Montesquieu* by Destutt de Tracy (1798) was published in Paris in 1798, after Condorcet's death in prison four years before. This volume contained an essay by Condorcet on the twenty-ninth book of *L'Esprit*. The essay seems to deny the relevance of Montesquieu's notion about the necessary balance between monarchy, aristocracy, and democracy. Mayer (1994, 136) points out that Jefferson himself (after retiring from the presidency) translated Destutt's *Commentaire* and arranged for its publication. The close relationship that Jefferson and Condorcet developed in Paris prior to Jefferson's departure (Darnton, 1997) leads me to infer that Jefferson would have obtained copies of Condorcet's *Esquisse* and of his *Essai* on Montesquieu as soon as they were available in Paris. There is still much to be learnt about the complex intellectual connections between the Scottish Enlightenment thinkers (Smith and Hume), the writers Condorcet, Destutt and their colleagues in France, and Jefferson and Madison. For example, Rothschild (2001) provides an excellent discussion of Adam Smith and Condorcet, and mentions Jefferson's "course of reading "of 1799 that included both Smith and Condorcet.

6. As Mayer notes, Jefferson wrote in his letter in 1799, that, like Condorcet, he believed that the mind of man was "perfectible to a degree of which we cannot as yet form any conception" (Mayer 1994, 306).

7. There is one consequence of the Hamilton scheme that I have not discussed, though it is consistent with the view presented by Madison and Jefferson. If the United States focused on manufacturing development, then it would be dependent on British capital, and thus become a satellite of the metropole. It is possible that the defeat of Hamilton was necessary for the creation of what Jefferson later called the "Empire for Liberty."

James Madison, "Vices of the Political System of the United States" (April 1787; MP 9, 348–57)

1. Failure of the States to comply with the Constitutional requisitions.

This evil has been so fully experienced both during the war and since the peace, results so naturally from the number and independent authority of the States and has been so uniformly examplified in every similar Confederacy, that it may be considered as not less radically and permanently inherent in, than it is fatal to the object of, the present System.

2. Encroachments by the States on the federal authority.

Examples of this are numerous and repetitions may be foreseen in almost every case where any favorite object of a State shall present a temptation. Among these examples are the wars and Treaties of Georgia with the Indians—The unlicensed compacts between Virginia and Maryland, and between Pena. & N. Jersey—the troops raised and to be kept up by Massts.

3. Violations of the law of nations and of treaties.

From the number of Legislatures, the sphere of life from which most of their members are taken, and the circumstances under which their legislative business is carried on, irregularities of this kind must frequently happen. Accordingly not a year has passed without instances of them in some one or other of the States. The Treaty of peace—the treaty with France—the treaty with Holland have each been violated. The causes of these irregularities must necessarily produce frequent violations of the law of nations in other respects.

As yet foreign powers have not been rigorous in animadverting on us. This moderation however cannot be mistaken for a permanent partiality to our faults, or a permanent security agst. those disputes with other nations, which being among the greatest of public calamities, it ought to be least in the power of any part of the Community to bring on the whole.

4. Trespasses of the States on the rights of each other.

These are alarming symptoms, and may be daily apprehended as we are admonished by daily experience. See the law of Virginia restricting foreign vessels to certain ports—of Maryland in favor of vessels belonging to her own citizens—of N. York in favor of the same.

Paper money, instalments of debts, occlusion of Courts, making property a legal tender, may likewise be deemed aggressions on the rights of other States. As the Citizens of every State aggregately taken stand more or less in the relation of Creditors or debtors, to the Citizens of every other State, Acts of the debtor State in favor of debtors, affect the Creditor State, in the same manner, as they do its own citizens who are relatively creditors towards other citizens. This remark may be extended to foreign nations. If the exclusive regulation of the value and alloy of coin was properly delegated to the federal authority, the policy of it equally requires a controul on the States in the cases above mentioned. It must have been meant 1. to preserve uniformity in the circulating medium throughout the nation. 2. to prevent those frauds on the citizens of other States, and the subjects of foreign powers, which might disturb the tranquility at home, or involve the Union in foreign contests.

The practice of many States in restricting the commercial intercourse with other States, and putting their productions and manufactures on the same footing with those of foreign nations, though not contrary to the federal articles, is certainly adverse to the spirit of the Union, and tends to beget retaliating regulations, not less expensive & vexatious in themselves, than they are destructive of the general harmony.

5. want of concert in matters where common interest requires it.

This defect is strongly illustrated in the state of our commercial affairs. How much has the national dignity, interest, and revenue suffered from this cause? Instances of inferior moment are the want of uniformity in the laws concerning naturalization & literary property; of provision for national seminaries, for grants of incorporation for national purposes, for canals and other works of general utility, wch. may at present be defeated by the perverseness of particular States whose concurrence is necessary.

6. want of guaranty to the States of their Constitutions & laws against internal violence.

The confederation is silent on this point and therefore by the second article the hands of the federal authority are tied. According to Republican Theory, Right and power being both vested in the majority, are held to be synonimous. According to fact and experience a minority may in an appeal to force, be an overmatch for the majority. 1. If the minority happen to include all such as possess the skill and habits of military life, & such as possess the great pecuniary resources, one third only may conquer the remaining two thirds. 2. One third of those who participate in the choice of the rulers, may be rendered a majority by the accession of those whose poverty excludes them from a right of suffrage, and who for obvious reasons will be more likely to join the standard of sedition than that of the established Government. 3. Where slavery exists the republican Theory becomes still more fallacious.

7. want of sanction to the laws, and of coercion in the Government of the Confederacy.

A sanction is essential to the idea of law, as coercion is to that of Government. The federal system being destitute of both, wants the great vital principles of a Political Cons[ti]tution. Under the form of such a Constitution, it is in fact nothing more than a treaty of amity of commerce and of alliance, between so many independent and Sovereign States. From what cause could so fatal an omission have happened in the articles of Confederation? from a mistaken confidence that the justice, the good faith, the honor, the sound policy, of the several legislative assemblies would render superfluous any appeal to the ordinary motives by which the laws secure the obedience of individuals: a confidence which does honor to the enthusiastic virtue of the compilers, as much as the inexperience of the crisis apologizes for their errors. The time which has since elapsed has had the double effect, of increasing the light, and tempering the warmth, with which the arduous work may be revised. It is no longer doubted that a unanimous and punctual obedience of 13 independent bodies, to the acts of the federal Government, ought not be calculated on. Even during the war, when external danger supplied in some degree the defect of legal & coercive sanctions, how imperfectly did the States fulfil their obligations to the Union? In time of peace, we see already what is to be expected. How indeed could it be otherwise? In the first place, Every general act of the Union must necessarily bear unequally hard on some particular member or members of it. Secondly the partiality of the members to their own interests and rights, a partiality which will be fostered by the Courtiers of popularity, will naturally exaggerate the inequality where it exists, and even suspect it where it has no existence. Thirdly a distrust of the voluntary compliance of each other may prevent the compliance of any, although it should be the latent disposition of all. Here are causes & pretexts which will never fail to render federal measures abortive. If the laws of the States, were merely recommendatory to their citizens, or if they were to be rejudged by County authorities, what security, what probability would exist, that they would be carried into execution? Is the security or probability greater in favor of the acts of Congs. which depending for their execution on the will of the state legislatures, wch. are tho' nominally authoritative, in fact recommendatory only.

8. Want of ratification by the people of the articles of Confederation.

In some of the States the Confederation is recognized by, and forms a part of the constitution. In others however it has received no other sanction than that of the Legislative authority. From this defect two evils result: 1. Whenever a law of a State happens to be repugnant to an act of Congress, particularly when the latter is of posterior date to the former, it will be at least questionable whether the latter must not prevail; and as the question must be decided by the Tribunals of the State, they will be most likely to lean on the side of the State. 2. As far as the Union of the States is to be regarded as a league of sovereign powers, and not as a political Constitution by virtue of which they are become one sovereign power, so far it seems to follow from the doctrine of compacts, that a breach of any of the articles of the confederation by any of the parties to it, absolves the other parties from their respective obligations, and gives them a right if they chuse to exert it, of dissolving the Union altogether.

9. Multiplicity of laws in the several States.

In developing the evils which viciate the political system of the U. S. it is proper to include those which are found within the States individually, as well as those which directly affect the States collectively, since the former class have an indirect influence on the general malady and must not be overlooked in forming a compleat remedy. Among the evils then of our situation may well be ranked the multiplicity of laws from which no State is exempt. As far as laws are necessary, to mark with precision the duties of those who are to obey them, and to take from those who are to administer them a discretion, which might be abused, their number is the price of liberty. As far as the laws exceed this limit, they are a nusance: a nusance of the most pestilent kind. Try the Codes of the several States by this test, and what a luxuriancy of legislation do they present. The short period of independency has filled as many pages as the century which preceded it. Every year, almost every session, adds a new volume. This may be the effect in part, but it can only be in part, of the situation in which the revolution has placed us. A review of the several codes will shew that every necessary and useful part of the least voluminous of them might be compressed into one tenth of the compass, and at the same time be rendered tenfold as perspicuous.

10. mutability of the laws of the States.

This evil is intimately connected with the former yet deserves a distinct notice as it emphatically denotes a vicious legislation. We daily see laws repealed or superseded, before any trial can have been made of their merits: and even before a knowledge of them can have reached the remoter districts within which they were to operate. In the regulations of trade this instability becomes a snare not only to our citizens but to foreigners also.

11. Injustice of the laws of States.

If the multiplicity and mutability of laws prove a want of wisdom, their injustice betrays a defect still more alarming: more alarming not merely because it is a greater evil in itself, but because it brings more into question the fundamental principle of republican Government, that the majority who rule in such Governments, are the safest Guardians both of public Good and of private rights. To what causes is this evil to be ascribed?

These causes lie 1. in the Representative bodies. 2. in the people themselves.

1. Representative appointments are sought from 3 motives. 1. ambition 2. personal interest. 3. public good. Unhappily the two first are proved by experience to be most prevalent. Hence the candidates who feel them, particularly, the second, are most industrious, and most successful in pursuing their object: and forming often a majority in the legislative Councils, with interested views, contrary to the interest, and views, of their Constituents, join in a perfidious sacrifice of the latter to the former. A succeeding election it might be supposed,

would displace the offenders, and repair the mischief. But how easily are base and selfish measures, masked by pretexts of public good and apparent expediency? How frequently will a repetition of the same arts and industry which succeeded in the first instance, again prevail on the unwary to misplace their confidence?

How frequently too will the honest but unenlightened representative be the dupe of a favorite leader, veiling his selfish views under the professions of public good, and varnishing his sophistical arguments with the glowing colours of popular eloquence?

2. A still more fatal if not more frequent cause lies among the people themselves. All civilized societies are divided into different interests and factions, as they happen to be creditors or debtors—Rich or poor—husbandmen, merchants or manufacturers—members of different religious sects—followers of different political leaders—inhabitants of different districts—owners of different kinds of property &c &c. In republican Government the majority however composed, ultimately give the law. Whenever therefore an apparent interest or common passion unites a majority what is to restrain them from unjust violations of the rights and interests of the minority, or of individuals? Three motives only 1. a prudent regard to their own good as involved in the general and permanent good of the Community. This consideration although of decisive weight in itself, is found by experience to be too often unheeded. It is too often forgotten, by nations as well as by individuals that honesty is the best policy. 2dly. respect for character. However strong this motive may be in individuals, it is considered as very insufficient to restrain them from injustice. In a multitude its efficacy is diminished in proportion to the number which is to share the praise or the blame. Besides, as it has reference to public opinion, which within a particular Society, is the opinion of the majority, the standard is fixed by those whose conduct is to be measured by it. The public opinion without the Society, will be little respected by the people at large of any Country. Individuals of extended views, and of national pride, may bring the public proceedings to this standard, but the example will never be followed by the multitude. Is it to be imagined that an ordinary citizen or even an assemblyman of R. Island in estimating the policy of paper money, ever considered or cared in what light the measure would be viewed in France or Holland; or even in Massts or Connect.? It was a sufficient temptation to both that it was for their interest: it was a sufficient sanction to the latter that it was popular in the State; to the former that it was so in the neighbourhood. 3dly. will Religion the only remaining motive be a sufficient restraint? It is not pretended to be such on men individually considered. Will its effect be greater on them considered in an aggregate view? quite the reverse. The conduct of every popular assembly acting on oath, the strongest of religious Ties, proves that individuals join without remorse in acts, against which their consciences would revolt if proposed to them under the like sanction, separately in their closets. When indeed Religion is kindled into enthusiasm, its force like that of other passions, is increased by the sympathy of a multitude. But enthusi-

asm is only a temporary state of religion, and while it lasts will hardly be seen with pleasure at the helm of Government. Besides as religion in its coolest state, is not infallible, it may become a motive to oppression as well as a restraint from injustice. Place three individuals in a situation wherein the interest of each depends on the voice of the others, and give to two of them an interest opposed to the rights of the third? Will the latter be secure? The prudence of every man would shun the danger. The rules & forms of justice suppose & guard against it. Will two thousand in a like situation be less likely to encroach on the rights of one thousand? The contrary is witnessed by the notorious factions & oppressions which take place in corporate towns limited as the opportunities are, and in little republics when uncontrouled by apprehensions of external danger. If an enlargement of the sphere is found to lessen the insecurity of private rights, it is not because the impulse of a common interest or passion is less predominant in this case with the majority; but because a common interest or passion is less apt to be felt and the requisite combinations less easy to be formed by a great than by a small number. The Society becomes broken into a greater variety of interests, of pursuits, of passions, which check each other, whilst those who may feel a common sentiment have less opportunity of communication and concert. It may be inferred that the inconveniences of popular States contrary to the prevailing Theory, are in proportion not to the extent, but to the narrowness of their limits.

The great desideratum in Government is such a modification of the Sovereignty as will render it sufficiently neutral between the different interests and factions, to controul one part of the Society from invading the rights of another, and at the same time sufficiently controuled itself, from setting up an interest adverse to that of the whole Society. In absolute Monarchies, the prince is sufficiently, neutral towards his subjects, but frequently sacrifices their happiness to his ambition or his avarice. In small Republics, the sovereign will is sufficiently controuled from such a Sacrifice of the entire Society, but is not sufficiently neutral towards the parts composing it. As a limited Monarchy tempers the evils of an absolute one; so an extensive Republic meliorates the administration of a small Republic.

An auxiliary desideratum for the melioration of the Republican form is such a process of elections as will most certainly extract from the mass of the Society the purest and noblest characters which it contains; such as will at once feel most strongly the proper motives to pursue the end of their appointment, and be most capable to devise the proper means of attaining it.

12. Impotence of the laws of the States

James Madison, *Federalist* 10 (November 22, 1787)

Among the numerous advantages promised by a well constructed Union, none deserves to be more accurately developed than its tendency to break and control the violence of faction. The friend of popular governments, never finds himself so much alarmed for their character and fate, as when he contemplates their propensity to this dangerous vice. He will not fail therefore to set a due value on any plan which, without violating the principles to which he is attached, provides a proper cure for it. The instability, injustice and confusion introduced into the public councils, have in truth been the mortal diseases under which popular governments have every where perished; as they continue to be the favorite and fruitful topics from which the adversaries to liberty derive their most specious declamations. The valuable improvements made by the American Constitutions on the popular models, both ancient and modern, cannot certainly be too much admired; but it would be an unwarrantable partiality, to contend that they have as effectually obviated the danger on this side as was wished and expected. Complaints are every where heard from our most considerate and virtuous citizens, equally the friends of public and private faith, and of public and personal liberty; that our governments are too unstable; that the public good is disregarded in the conflicts of rival parties; and that measures are too often decided, not according to the rules of justice, and the rights of the minor party; but by the superior force of an interested and over-bearing majority. However anxiously we may wish that these complaints had no foundation, the evidence of known facts will not permit us to deny that they are in some degree true. It will be found indeed, on a candid review of our situation, that some of the distresses under which we labor, have been erroneously charged on the operation of our governments; but it will be found, at the same time, that other causes will not alone account for many of our heaviest misfortunes; and particularly, for that prevailing and increasing distrust of public engagements, and alarm for private rights, which are echoed from one end of the continent to the other. These must be chiefly, if not wholly, effects of the unsteadiness and injustice, with which a factious spirit has tainted our public administrations.

By a faction I understand a number of citizens, whether amounting to a majority or minority of the whole, who are united and actuated by some common impulse of passion, or of interest, adverse to the rights of other citizens, or to the permanent and aggregate interests of the community.

There are two methods of curing the mischiefs of faction: the one, by removing its causes; the other, by controling its effects.

There are again two methods of removing the causes of faction: the one by destroying the liberty which is essential to its existence; the other, by giving to every citizen the same opinions, the same passions, and the same interests.

It could never be more truly said than of the first remedy, that it is worse than the disease. Liberty is to faction, what air is to fire, an aliment without which it instantly expires. But it could not be a less folly to abolish liberty, which is essential to political life, because it nourishes faction, than it would be to wish the annihilation of air, which is essential to animal life, because it imparts to fire its destructive agency.

The second expedient is as impracticable, as the first would be unwise. As long as the reason of man continues fallible, and he is at liberty to exercise it, different opinions will be formed. As long as the connection subsists between his reason and his self-love, his opinions and his passions will have a reciprocal influence on each other; and the former will be objects to which the latter will attach themselves. The diversity in the faculties of men from which the rights of property originate, is not less an insuperable obstacle to a uniformity of interests. The protection of these faculties is the first object of Government. From the protection of different and unequal faculties of acquiring property, the possession of different degrees and kinds of property immediately results: and from the influence of these on the sentiments and views of the respective proprietors, ensues a division of the society into different interests and parties.

The latent causes of faction are thus sown in the nature of man; and we see them every where brought into different degrees of activity, according to the different circumstances of civil society. A zeal for different opinions concerning religion, concerning Government and many other points, as well of speculation as of practice; an attachment to different leaders ambitiously contending for preeminence and power; or to persons of other descriptions whose fortunes have been interesting to the human passions, have in turn divided mankind into parties, inflamed them with mutual animosity, and rendered them much more disposed to vex and oppress each other, than to cooperate for their common good. So strong is this propensity of mankind to fall into mutual animosities, that where no substantial occasion presents itself, the most frivolous and fanciful distinctions have been sufficient to kindle their unfriendly passions, and excite their most violent conflicts. But the most common and durable source of factions, has been the various and unequal distribution of property. Those who hold, and those who are without property, have ever formed distinct interests in society. Those who are creditors, and those who are debtors, fall under a like discrimination. A landed interest, a manufacturing interest, a mercantile interest, a monied interest, with many lesser interests, grow up of necessity in civilized nations, and divide them into different classes, actuated by different sentiments and views. The regulation of these various and interfering interests forms the principal task of modern Legislation, and involves the spirit of party and faction in the necessary and ordinary operations of Government.

No man is allowed to be a judge in his own cause; because his interest would certainly bias his judgment, and, not improbably, corrupt his integrity. With equal, nay with greater reason, a body of men, are unfit to be both judges and parties, at the same time; yet, what are many of the most important acts of legislation, but so many judicial determinations, not indeed concerning the rights of single persons, but concerning the rights of large bodies of citizens; and what are the different classes of legislators, but advocates and parties to the causes which they determine? Is a law proposed concerning private debts? It is a question to which the creditors are parties on one side, and the debtors on the other. Justice

ought to hold the balance between them. Yet the parties are and must be themselves the judges; and the most numerous party, or, in other words, the most powerful faction must be expected to prevail. Shall domestic manufactures be encouraged, and in what degree, by restrictions on foreign manufacturers? are
questions which would be differently decided by the landed and the manufacturing classes; and probably by neither, with a sole regard to justice and the public good. The apportionment of taxes on the various descriptions of property, is
an act which seems to require the most exact impartiality; yet, there is perhaps
no legislative act in which greater opportunity and temptation are given to a
predominant party, to trample on the rules of justice. Every shilling with which
they over-burden the inferior number, is a shilling saved to their own pockets.

It is in vain to say, that enlightened statesmen will be able to adjust these clashing interests, and render them all subservient to the public good. Enlightened
statesmen will not always be at the helm: Nor, in many cases, can such an adjustment be made at all, without taking into view indirect and remote considerations, which will rarely prevail over the immediate interest which one party
may find in disregarding the rights of another, or the good of the whole.

The inference to which we are brought, is, that the *causes* of faction cannot
be removed; and that relief is only to be sought in the means of controling its *effects*.

If a faction consists of less than a majority, relief is supplied by the republican
principle, which enables the majority to defeat its sinister views by regular vote:
It may clog the administration, it may convulse the society; but it will be unable
to execute and mask its violence under the forms of the Constitution. When a
majority is included in a faction, the form of popular government on the other
hand enables it to sacrifice to its ruling passion or interest, both the public good
and the rights of other citizens. To secure the public good, and private rights,
against the danger of such a faction, and at the same time to preserve the spirit
and the form of popular government, is then the great object to which our enquiries are directed: Let me add that it is the great desideratum, by which alone
this form of government can be rescued from the opprobrium under which it
has so long labored, and be recommended to the esteem and adoption of mankind.

By what means is this object attainable? Evidently by one of two only. Either
the existence of the same passion or interest in a majority at the same time, must
be prevented; or the majority, having such co-existent passion or interest, must
be rendered, by their number and local situation, unable to concert and carry
into effect schemes of oppression. If the impulse and the opportunity be suffered
to coincide, we well know that neither moral nor religious motives can be relied
on as an adequate control. They are not found to be such on the injustice and
violence of individuals, and lose their efficacy in proportion to the number combined together; that is, in proportion as their efficacy becomes needful.

From this view of the subject, it may be concluded, that a pure Democracy, by which I mean, a Society, consisting of a small number of citizens, who assemble and administer the Government in person, can admit of no cure for the mischiefs of faction. A common passion or interest will, in almost every case, be felt by a majority of the whole; a communication and concert results from the form of Government itself; and there is nothing to check the inducements to sacrifice the weaker party, or an obnoxious individual. Hence it is, that such Democracies have ever been spectacles of turbulence and contention; have ever been found incompatible with personal security, or the rights of property; and have in general been as short in their lives, as they have been violent in their deaths. Theoretic politicans, who have patronized this species of Government, have erroneously supposed, that by reducing mankind to a perfect equality in their political rights, they would, at the same time, be perfectly equalized and assimilated in their possessions, their opinions, and their passions.

A Republic, by which I mean a Government in which the scheme of representation takes place, opens a different prospect, and promises the cure for which we are seeking. Let us examine the points in which it varies from pure Democracy, and we shall comprehend both the nature of the cure, and the efficacy which it must derive from the Union.

The two great points of difference between a Democracy and a Republic are, first, the delegation of the Government, in the latter, to a small number of citizens elected by the rest: secondly, the greater number of citizens, and greater sphere of country, over which the latter may be extended.

The effect of the first difference is, on the one hand to refine and enlarge the public views, by passing them through the medium of a chosen body of citizens, whose wisdom may best discern the true interest of their country, and whose patriotism and love of justice, will be least likely to sacrifice it to temporary or partial considerations. Under such a regulation, it may well happen that the public voice pronounced by the representatives of the people, will be more consonant to the public good, than if pronounced by the people themselves convened for the purpose. On the other hand, the effect may be inverted. Men of factious tempers, of local prejudices, or of sinister designs, may by intrigue, by corruption or by other means, first obtain the suffrages, and then betray the interests of the people. The question resulting is, whether small or extensive Republics are most favorable to the election of proper guardians of the public weal: and it is clearly decided in favor of the latter by two obvious considerations.

In the first place it is to be remarked that however small the Republic may be, the Representatives must be raised to a certain number, in order to guard against the cabals of a few; and that however large it may be, they must be limited to a certain number, in order to guard against the confusion of a multitude. Hence the number of Representatives in the two cases, not being in proportion to that of the Constituents, and being proportionally greatest in the small Republic, it follows, that if the proportion of fit characters, be not less, in the large than in the small Republic, the former will present a greater option, and consequently a greater probability of a fit choice.

In the next place, as each Representative will be chosen by a greater number of citizens in the large than in the small Republic, it will be more difficult for unworthy candidates to practise with success the vicious arts, by which elections are too often carried; and the suffrages of the people being more free, will be more likely to centre on men who possess the most attractive merit, and the most diffusive and established characters.

It must be confessed, that in this, as in most other cases, there is a mean, on both sides of which inconveniencies will be found to lie. By enlarging too much the number of electors, you render the representative too little acquainted with all their local circumstances and lesser interests; as by reducing it too much, you render him unduly attached to these, and too little fit to comprehend and pursue great and national objects. The Federal Constitution forms a happy combination in this respect; the great and aggregate interests being referred to the national, the local and particular, to the state legislatures.

The other point of difference is, the greater number of citizens and extent of territory which may be brought within the compass of Republican, than of Democratic Government; and it is this circumstance principally which renders factious combinations less to be dreaded in the former, than in the latter. The smaller the society, the fewer probably will be the distinct parties and interests composing it; the fewer the distinct parties and interests, the more frequently will a majority be found of the same party; and the smaller the number of individuals composing a majority, and the smaller the compass within which they are placed, the more easily will they concert and execute their plans of oppression. Extend the sphere, and you take in a greater variety of parties and interests; you make it less probable that a majority of the whole will have a common motive to invade the rights of other citizens; or if such a common motive exists, it will be more difficult for all who feel it to discover their own strength, and to act in unison with each other. Besides other impediments, it may be remarked, that where there is a consciousness of unjust or dishonorable purposes, communication is always checked by distrust, in proportion to the number whose concurrence is necessary.

Hence it clearly appears, that the same advantage, which a Republic has over a Democracy, in controling the effects of faction, is enjoyed by a large over a small Republic—is enjoyed by the Union over the States composing it. Does this advantage consist in the substitution of Representatives, whose enlightened views and virtuous sentiments render them superior to local prejudices, and to schemes of injustice? It will not be denied, that the Representation of the Union will be most likely to possess these requisite endowments. Does it consist in the greater security afforded by a greater variety of parties, against the event of any one party being able to outnumber and oppress the rest? In an equal degree does the encreased variety of parties, comprised within the Union, encrease this security. Does it, in fine, consist in the greater obstacles opposed to the concert and accomplishment of the secret wishes of an unjust and interested majority? Here, again, the extent of the Union gives it the most palpable advantage.

The influence of factious leaders may kindle a flame within their particular States, but will be unable to spread a general conflagration through the other States: a religious sect, may degenerate into a political faction in a part of the Confederacy: but the variety of sects dispersed over the entire face of it, must secure the national Councils against any danger from that source: a rage for paper money, for an abolition of debts, for an equal division of property, or for any other improper or wicked project, will be less apt to pervade the whole body of the Union, than a particular member of it; in the same proportion as such a malady is more likely to taint a particular county or district, than an entire State.

In the extent and proper structure of the Union, therefore, we behold a Republican remedy for the diseases most incident to Republican Government. And according to the degree of pleasure and pride, we feel in being Republicans, ought to be our zeal in cherishing the spirit, and supporting the character of Federalists.

James Madison, *Federalist* 51 (February 6, 1788)

To what expedient then shall we finally resort for maintaining in practice the necessary partition of power among the several departments, as laid down in the constitution? The only answer that can be given is, that as all these exterior provisions are found to be inadequate, the defect must be supplied, by so contriving the interior structure of the government, as that its several constituent parts may, by their mutual relations, be the means of keeping each other in their proper places. Without presuming to under-take a full developement of this important idea, I will hazard a few general observations, which may perhaps place it in a clearer light, and enable us to form a more correct judgment of the principles and structure of the government planned by the convention.

In order to lay a due foundation for that separate and distinct exercise of the different powers of government, which to a certain extent, is admitted on all hands to be essential to the preservation of liberty, it is evident that each department should have a will of its own; and consequently should be so constituted, that the members of each should have as little agency as possible in the appointment of the members of the others. Were this principle rigorously adhered to, it would require that all the appointments for the supreme executive, legislative, and judiciary magistracies, should be drawn from the same fountain of authority, the people, through channels, having no communication whatever with one another. Perhaps such a plan of constructing the several departments would be less difficult in practice than it may in contemplation appear. Some difficulties however, and some additional expence, would attend the execution of it. Some deviations therefore from the principle must be admitted. In the constitution of the judiciary department in particular, it might be inexpedient to insist rigorously on the principle; first, because peculiar qualifications being essential in the members, the primary consideration ought to be to select that mode of choice, which best secures these qualifications; secondly, because the permanent tenure by which the appointments are held in that department, must soon destroy all sense of dependence on the authority conferring them.

It is equally evident that the members of each department should be as little dependent as possible on those of the others, for the emoluments annexed to their offices. Were the executive magistrate, or the judges, not independent of the legislature in this particular, their independence in every other would be merely nominal.

But the great security against a gradual concentration of the several powers in the same department, consists in giving to those who administer each department, the necessary constitutional means, and personal motives, to resist encroachments of the others. The provision for defence must in this, as in all other cases, be made commensurate to the danger of attack. Ambition must be made to counteract ambition. The interest of the man must be connected with the constitutional rights of the place. It may be a reflection on human nature, that such devices should be necessary to controul the abuses of government. But what is government itself but the greatest of all reflections on human nature? If men were angels, no government would be necessary. If angels were to govern men, neither external nor internal controuls on government would be necessary. In framing a government which is to be administered by men over men, the great difficulty lies in this: You must first enable the government to controul the governed; and in the next place, oblige it to controul itself. A dependence on the people is no doubt the primary controul on the government; but experience has taught mankind the necessity of auxiliary precautions.

This policy of supplying by opposite and rival interests, the defect of better motives, might be traced through the whole system of human affairs, private as well as public. We see it particularly displayed in all the subordinate distributions of power; where the constant aim is to divide and arrange the several offices in such a manner as that each may be a check on the other; that the private interest of every individual, may be a centinel over the public rights. These inventions of prudence cannot be less requisite in the distribution of the supreme powers of the state.

But it is not possible to give to each department an equal power of self defence. In republican government the legislative authority, necessarily, predominates. The remedy for this inconveniency is, to divide the legislature into different branches; and to render them by different modes of election, and different principles of action, as little connected with each other, as the nature of their common functions, and their common dependence on the society, will admit. It may even be necessary to guard against dangerous encroachments by still further precautions. As the weight of the legislative authority requires that it should be thus divided, the weakness of the executive may require, on the other hand, that it should be fortified. An absolute negative, on the legislature, appears at first view to be the natural defence with which the executive magistrate should be armed.

But perhaps it would be neither altogether safe, nor alone sufficient. On ordinary occasions, it might not be exerted with the requisite firmness; and on extraordinary occasions, it might be perfidiously abused. May not this defect of an absolute negative be supplied, by some qualified connection between this weaker department, and the weaker branch of the stronger department, by which the latter may be led to support the constitutional rights of the former, without being too much detached from the rights of its own department?

If the principles on which these observations are founded be just, as I persuade myself they are, and they be applied as a criterion, to the several state constitutions, and to the federal constitution, it will be found, that if the latter does not perfectly correspond with them, the former are infinitely less able to bear such a test.

There are moreover two considerations particularly applicable to the federal system of America, which place that system in a very interesting point of view.

First. In a single republic, all the power surrendered by the people, is submitted to the administration of a single government; and usurpations are guarded against by a division of the government into distinct and separate departments. In the compound republic of America, the power surrendered by the people, is first divided between two distinct governments, and then the portion allotted to each, subdivided among distinct and separate departments. Hence a double security arises to the rights of the people. The different governments will controul each other; at the same time that each will be controuled by itself.

Second. It is of great importance in a republic, not only to guard the society against the oppression of its rulers; but to guard one part of the society against the injustice of the other part. Different interests necessarily exist in different classes of citizens. If a majority be united by a common interest, the rights of the minority will be insecure. There are but two methods of providing against this evil: The one by creating a will in the community independent of the majority, that is, of the society itself; the other by comprehending in the society so many separate descriptions of citizens, as will render an unjust combination of a majority of the whole, very improbable, if not impracticable. The first method prevails in all governments possessing an hereditary or self appointed authority. This at best is but a precarious security; because a power independent of the society may as well espouse the unjust views of the major, as the rightful interests, of the minor party, and may possibly be turned against both parties. The second method will be exemplified in the federal republic of the United States. Whilst all authority in it will be derived from and dependent on the society, the society itself will be broken into so many parts, interests and classes of citizens, that the rights of individuals or of the minority, will be in little danger from interested combinations of the majority. In a free government, the security for civil rights must be the same as for religious rights. It consists in the one case in the multiplicity of interests, and in the other, in the multiplicity of sects. The degree of security in both cases will depend on the number of interests and sects; and this may be presumed to depend on the extent of country and number of people comprehended under the same government. This view of the subject must particularly recommend a proper federal system to all the sincere and considerate friends of republican government: Since it shews that in exact proportion as the territory of the union may be formed into more circumscribed confederacies or states, oppressive combinations of a majority will be facilitated, the best security under the republican form, for the rights of every class of citizens, will be diminished; and consequently, the stability and independence of some member of the government, the only other security, must be proportionally increased. Justice is the end of government. It is the end of civil society. It ever has been, and ever will be pursued, until it be obtained, or until liberty be lost in the pursuit. In a society under the forms of which the stronger faction can readily unite and oppress the weaker, anarchy may as truly be said to reign, as in a state of nature where the weaker individual is not secured against the violence of the stronger: And as in the latter state even the stronger individuals are prompted by the uncertainty of their condition, to submit to a government which may protect the weak as well as themselves: So in the former state, will the more powerful factions or parties be gradually induced by a like motive, to wish for a government which will protect all parties, the weaker as well as the more powerful. It can be little doubted, that if the state of Rhode Island was separated from the confederacy, and left to itself, the insecurity of rights under the popular form of government within such narrow limits, would be displayed by such reiterated oppressions of factious majorities, that some power altogether independent of the people would soon be called for by the voice of the very factions whose misrule had proved the necessity of it. In the extended republic of the United States, and among the great variety of interests, parties and sects which it embraces, a coalition of a majority of the whole society could seldom take place on any other principles than those of justice and the general good; and there being thus less danger to a minor from the will of the major party, there must be less pretext also, to provide for the security of the former, by introducing into the government a will not dependent on the latter; or in other words, a will independent of the society itself. It is no less certain than it is important, notwithstanding the contrary opinions which have been entertained, that the larger the society, provided it lie within a practicable sphere, the more duly capable it will be of self government. And happily for the *republican cause,* the practicable sphere may be carried to a very great extent, by a judicious modification and mixture of the *federal principle.*

James Madison to Thomas Jefferson (October 24, 1787; MP 10, 207–15)

You will herewith receive the result of the Convention, which continued its Session till the 17th. of September. I take the liberty of making some observations on the subject which will help to make up a letter, if they should answer no other purpose.

It appeared to be the sincere and unanimous wish of the Convention to cherish and preserve the Union of the States. No proposition was made, no suggestion was thrown out, in favor of a partition of the Empire into two or more Confederacies.

It was generally agreed that the objects of the Union could not be secured by any system founded on the principle of a confederation of sovereign States. A *voluntary* observance of the federal law by all the members, could never be hoped for. A *compulsive* one could evidently never be reduced to practice, and if it could, involved equal calamities to the innocent & the guilty, the necessity of a military force both obnoxious & dangerous, and in general, a scene resembling much more a civil war, than the administration of a regular Government.

Hence was embraced the alternative of a Government which instead of operating, on the States, should operate without their intervention on the individuals composing them; and hence the change in the principle and proportion of representation.

This ground-work being laid, the great objects which presented themselves were 1. to unite a proper energy in the Executive and a proper stability in the Legislative departments, with the essential characters of Republican Government. 2. to draw a line of demarkation which would give to the General Government every power requisite for general purposes, and leave to the States every power which might be most beneficially administered by them. 3. to provide for the different interests of different parts of the Union. 4. to adjust the clashing pretensions of the large and small States. Each of these objects was pregnant with difficulties. The whole of them together formed a task more difficult than can be well concieved by those who were not concerned in the execution of it. Adding to these considerations the natural diversity of human opinions on all new and complicated subjects, it is impossible to consider the degree of concord which ultimately prevailed as less than a miracle.

The first of these objects as it respects the Executive, was peculiarly embarrassing. On the question whether it should consist of a single person, or a plurality of coordinate members, on the mode of appointment, on the duration in office, on the degree of power, on the re-eligibility, tedious and reiterated discussions took place. The plurality of co-ordinate members had finally but few advocates. Governour Randolph was at the head of them. The modes of appointment proposed were various, as by the people at large—by electors chosen by the people—by the Executives of the States—by the Congress, some preferring a joint ballot of the two Houses—some a separate concurrent ballot allowing to each a negative on the other house—some a nomination of several canditates by one House, out of whom a choice should be made by the other. Several other modifications were started. The expedient at length adopted seemed to give pretty general satisfaction to the members. As to the duration in office, a few would have preferred a tenure during good behaviour—a considerable number would have done so, in case an easy & effectual removal by impeachment could be settled. It was much agitated whether a long term, seven years for example, with a subsequent & perpetual ineligibility, or a short term with a capacity to be re-elected, should be fixed. In favor of the first opinion were urged the danger of a gradual degeneracy of re-elections from time to time, into first a life and then a heriditary tenure, and the favorable effect of an incapacity to be reappointed, on the independent exercise of the Executive authority. On the other side it was contended that the prospect of necessary degradation, would discourage the most dignified characters from aspiring to the office, would take away the principal motive to the faithful discharge of its duties—the hope of being rewarded with a reappointment, would stimulate ambition to violent efforts for holding over the constitutional term—and instead of producing an independent administration, and a firmer defence of the constitutional rights of the department, would render the officer more indifferent to the importance of a place which he would soon be obliged to quit for ever, and more ready to yield to the incroachmts. of the Legislature of which he might again be a member. The questions concerning the degree of power turned chiefly on the appointment to offices, and the controul on the Legislature. An *absolute* appointment to all offices—to some offices—to no offices, formed the scale of opinions on the first point. On the second, some contended for an absolute negative, as the only possible mean of reducing to practice, the theory of a free Government which forbids a mixture of the Legislative & Executive powers. Others would be content with a revisionary power to be overruled by three fourths of both Houses. It was warmly urged that the judiciary department should be associated in the revision. The idea of some was that a separate revision should be given to the two departments —that if either objected two thirds; if both three fourths, should be necessary to overrule.

In forming the Senate, the great anchor of the Government, the questions as they came within the first object turned mostly on the mode of appointment, and the duration of it. The different modes proposed were, 1. by the House of Representatives 2. by the Executive, 3. by electors chosen by the people for the purpose. 4. by the State Legislatures. On the point of duration, the propositions descended from good-behavior to four years, through the intermediate terms of nine, seven, six, & five years. The election of the other branch was first determined to be triennial, and afterwards reduced to biennial.

The second object, the due partition of power, between the General & local Governments, was perhaps of all, the most nice and difficult. A few contended for an entire abolition of the States; some for indefinite power of Legislation in the Congress, with a negative on the laws of the States: some for such a power without a negative: some for a limited power of legislation, with such a negative: the majority finally for a limited power without the negative. The question with regard to the Negative underwent repeated discussions, and was finally rejected by a bare majority. As I formerly intimated to you my opinion in favor of this ingredient, I will take this occasion of explaining myself on the subject. Such a check on the States appears to me necessary 1. to prevent encroachments on the

General authority. 2. to prevent instability and injustice in the legislation of the States.

　1. Without such a check in the whole over the parts, our system involves the evil of imperia in imperio. If a compleat supremacy some where is not necessary in every Society, a controuling power at least is so, by which the general authority may be defended against encroachments of the subordinate authorities, and by which the latter may be restrained from encroachments on each other. If the supremacy of the British Parliament is not necessary as has been contended, for the harmony of that Empire; it is evident I think that without the royal negative or some equivalent controul, the unity of the system would be destroyed. The want of some such provision seems to have been mortal to the antient Confederacies, and to be the disease of the modern. Of the Lycian Confederacy little is known. That of the Amphyctions is well known to have been rendered of little use whilst it lasted, and in the end to have been destroyed by the predominance of the local over the federal authority. The same observation may be made, on the authority of Polybius, with regard to the Achaean League. The Helvetic System scarcely amounts to a Confederacy, and is distinguished by too many peculiarities, to be a ground of comparison. The case of the United Netherlands is in point. The authority of a Statholder, the influence of a Standing army, the common interest in the conquered possessions, the pressure of surrounding danger, the guarantee of foreign powers, are not sufficient to secure the authority and interests of the generality, agst. the antifederal tendency of the provincial sovereignties. The German Empire is another example. A Hereditary chief with vast independent resources of wealth and power, a federal Diet, with ample parchment authority, a regular Judiciary establishment, the influence of the neighbourhood of great & formidable Nations, have been found unable either to maintain the subordination of the members, or to prevent their mutual contests & encroachments. Still more to the purpose is our own experience both during the war and since the peace. Encroachments of the States on the general authority, sacrifices of national to local interests, interferences of the measures of different States, form a great part of the history of our political system. It may be said that the new Constitution is founded on different principles, and will have a different operation. I admit the difference to be material. It presents the aspect rather of a feudal system of republics, if such a phrase may be used, than of a Confederacy of independent States. And what has been the progress and event of the feudal Constitutions? In all of them a continual struggle between the head and the inferior members, until a final victory has been gained in some instances by one, in others, by the other of them. In one respect indeed there is a remarkable variance between the two cases. In the feudal system the sovereign, though limited, was independent; and having no particular sympathy of interests with the great Barons, his ambition had as full play as theirs in the mutual projects of usurpation. In the American Constitution The general authority will be derived entirely from the subordinate authorities. The Senate will represent the States in

their political capacity; the other House will represent the people of the States in their individual capac[it]y. The former will be accountable to their constituents at moderate, the latter at short periods. The President also derives his appointment from the States, and is periodically accountable to them. This dependence of the General, on the local authorities, seems effectually to guard the latter against any dangerous encroachments of the former: Whilst the latter, within their respective limits, will be continually sensible of the abridgment of their power, and be stimulated by ambition to resume the surrendered portion of it. We find the representatives of Counties and corporations in the Legislatures of the States, much more disposed to sacrifice the aggregate interest, and even authority, to the local views of their Constituents: than the latter to the former. I mean not by these remarks to insinuate that an esprit de corps will not exist in the national Goverment or that opportunities may not occur, of extending its jurisdiction in some points. I mean only that the danger of encroachments is much greater from the other side, and that the impossibility of dividing powers of legislation, in such a manner, as to be free from different constructions by different interests, or even from ambiguity in the judgment of the impartial, requires some such expedient as I contend for. Many illustrations might be given of this impossibility. How long has it taken to fix, and how imperfectly is yet fixed the legislative power of corporations, though that power is subordinate in the most compleat manner? The line of distinction between the power of regulating trade and that of drawing revenue from it, which was once considered as the barrier of our liberties, was found on fair discussion, to be absolutely undefinable. No distinction seems to be more obvious than that between spiritual and temporal matters. Yet wherever they have been made objects of Legislation, they have clashed and contended with each other, till one or the other has gained the supremacy. Even the Boundaries between the Executive, Legislative & Judiciary powers, though in general so strongly marked in themselves, consist in many instances of mere shades of difference. It may be said that the Judicial authority under our new system will keep the States within their proper limits, and supply the place of a negative on their laws. The answer is, that it is more convenient to prevent the passage of a law, than to declare it void after it is passed; that this will be particularly the case, where the law aggrieves individuals, who may be unable to support an appeal agst. a State to the supreme Judiciary; that a State which would violate the Legislative rights of the Union, would not be very ready to obey a Judicial decree in support of them, and that a recurrence to force, which in the event of disobedience would be necessary, is an evil which the new Constitution meant to exclude as far as possible.

2. A constitutional negative on the laws of the States seems equally necessary to secure individuals agst. encroachments on their rights. The mutability of the laws of the States is found to be a serious evil. The injustice of them has been so frequent and so flagrant as to alarm the most stedfast friends of Republicanism. I am persuaded I do not err in saying that the evils issuing from these sources

contributed more to that uneasiness which produced the Convention, and prepared the public mind for a general reform, than those which accrued to our national character and interest from the inadequacy of the Confederation to its immediate objects. A reform therefore which does not make provision for private rights, must be materially defective. The restraints agst. paper emissions, and violations of contracts are not sufficient. Supposing them to be effectual as far as they go, they are short of the mark. Injustice may be effected by such an infinitude of legislative expedients, that where the disposition exists it can only be controuled by some provision which reaches all cases whatsoever. The partial provision made, supposes the disposition which will evade it. It may be asked how private rights will be more secure under the Guardianship of the General Government than under the State Governments, since they are both founded on the republican principle which refers the ultimate decision to the will of the majority, and are distinguished rather by the extent within which they will operate, than by any material difference in their structure. A full discussion of this question would, if I mistake not, unfold the true principles of Republican Government, and prove in contradiction to the concurrent opinions of theoretical writers, that this form of Goverment, in order to effect its purposes, must operate not within a small but an extensive sphere. I will state some of the ideas which have occurred to me on this subject. Those who contend for a simple Democracy, or a pure republic, actuated by the sense of the majority, and operating within narrow limits, assume or suppose a case which is altogether fictitious. They found their reasoning on the idea, that the people composing the Society, enjoy not only an equality of political rights; but that they have all precisely the same interests, and the same feelings in every respect. Were this in reality the case, their reasoning would be conclusive. The interest of the majority would be that of the minority also; the decisions could only turn on mere opinion concerning the good of the whole, of which the major voice would be the safest criterion; and within a small sphere, this voice could be most easily collected, and the public affairs most accurately managed. We know however that no Society ever did or can consist of so homogeneous a mass of Citizens. In the savage State indeed, an approach is made towards it; but in that State little or no Government is necessary. In all civilized Societies, distinctions are various and unavoidable. A distinction of property results from that very protection which a free Government gives to unequal faculties of acquiring it. There will be rich and poor; creditors and debtors; a landed interest, a monied interest, a mercantile interest, a manufacturing interest. These classes may again be subdivided according to the different productions of different situations & soils, & according to different branches of commerce, and of manufactures. In addition to these natural distinctions, artificial ones will be founded, on accidental differences in political, religious or other opinions, or an attachment to the persons of leading individuals. However erroneous or ridiculous these grounds of dissention and faction, may appear to the enlightened Statesman, or the benevolent philosopher, the bulk of mankind who are neither Statesmen nor Philosophers, will continue to view them in a different light. It remains then to be enquired whether a majority having any common interest, or feeling any common passion, will find sufficient motives to restrain them from oppressing the minority. An individual is never allowed to be a judge or even a witness in his own cause. If two individuals are under the biass of interest or enmity agst. a third, the rights of the latter could never be safely referred to the majority of the three. Will two thousand individuals be less apt to oppress one thousand, or two hundred thousand, one hundred thousand? Three motives only can restrain in such cases. 1. a prudent regard to private or partial good, as essentially involved in the general and permanent good of the whole. This ought no doubt to be sufficient of itself. Experience however shews that it has little effect on individuals, and perhaps still less on a collection of individuals, and least of all on a majority with the public authority in their hands. If the former are ready to forget that honesty is the best policy; the last do more. They often proceed on the converse of the maxim: that whatever is politic is honest. 2. respect for character. This motive is not found sufficient to restrain individuals from injustice, and loses its efficacy in proportion to the number which is to divide the praise or the blame. Besides as it has reference to public opinion, which is that of the majority, the Standard is fixed by those whose conduct is to be measured by it. 3. Religion. The inefficacy of this restraint on individuals is well known. The conduct of every popular Assembly, acting on oath, the strongest of religious ties, shews that individuals join without remorse in acts agst which their consciences would revolt, if proposed to them separately in their closets. When Indeed Religion is kindled into enthusiasm, its force like that of other passions is increased by the sympathy of a multitude. But enthusiasm is only a temporary state of Religion, and whilst it lasts will hardly be seen with pleasure at the helm. Even in its coolest state, it has been much oftener a motive to oppression than a restraint from it. If then there must be different interests and parties in Society; and a majority when united by a common interest or passion can not be restrained from oppressing the minority, what remedy can be found in a republican Government, where the majority must ultimately decide, but that of giving such an extent to its sphere, that no common interest or passion will be likely to unite a majority of the whole number in an unjust pursuit. In a large Society, the people are broken into so many interests and parties, that a common sentiment is less likely to be felt, and the requisite concert less likely to be formed, by a majority of the whole. The same security seems requisite for the civil as for the religious rights of individuals. If the same sect form a majority and have the power, other sects will be sure to be depressed. Divide et impera, the reprobated axiom of tyranny, is under certain qualifications, the only policy, by which a republic can be administered on just principles. It must be observed however that this doctrine can only hold within a sphere of a mean extent. As in too small a sphere oppressive combinations may be too easily formed agst. the weaker party; so in too extensive a one, a defensive concert may be rendered too difficult against the oppression of those entrusted with the administration. The great desideratum in Government is, so to modify the sovereignty as that it may be sufficiently neutral between different parts of the Society to controul one part from invading the rights of another, and at the same time sufficiently controuled itself, from setting up an interest adverse to that of the entire Society. In absolute monarchies, the Prince may be tolerably neutral towards different classes of his subjects, but may sacrifice the happiness of all to his personal ambition or avarice. In small republics, the sovereign will is controuled from such a sacrifice of the entire Society, but is not sufficiently neutral towards the parts composing it. In the extended Republic of the United States, The General Government would hold a pretty even balance between the parties of particular States, and be at the same time sufficiently restrained by its dependence on the community, from betraying its general interests.

Begging pardon for this immoderate digression I return to the third object abovementioned, the adjustment of the different interests of different parts of the Continent. Some contended for an unlimited power over trade including exports as well as imports, and over slaves as well as other imports; some for such a power, provided the concurrence of two thirds of both House were required; Some for such a qualification of the power, with an exemption of exports and slaves, others for an exemption of exports only. The result is seen in the Constitution. S. Carolina & Georgia were inflexible on the point of the slaves.

The remaining object created more embarrassment, and a greater alarm for the issue of the Convention than all the rest put together. The little States insisted on retaining their equality in both branches, unless a compleat abolition of the State Governments should take place; and made an equality in the Senate a sine qua non. The large States on the other hand urged that as the new Government was to be drawn principally from the people immediately and was to operate directly on them, not on the States; and consequently as the States wd. lose that importance which is now proportioned to the importance of their voluntary compliances with the requisitions of Congress, it was necessary that the representation in both Houses should be in proportion to their size. It ended in the compromise which you will see, but very much to the dissatisfaction of several members from the large States.

Abernethy, Thomas P. 1937. "Western Lands and the American Revolution." Vol. 25 in *University of Virginia Institute for Research in the Social Sciences*. New York: D. Appleton-Century.

Adair, Douglass G. 1943. "The Intellectual Origins of Jeffersonian Democracy: Republicanism, the Class Struggle, and the Virtuous Farmer." Ph. D. dissertation, Yale University.

———. 1974a. *Fame and the Founding Fathers*. Ed. Trevor Colbourn. New York: W. W. Norton.

———. 1974b. " 'That Politics May Be Reduced to a Science': David Hume, James Madison and the Tenth Federalist," in *Fame and the Founding Fathers*, 93–106. New York: W. W. Norton.

———. 1974c. "The Tenth Federalist Revisited," in *Fame and the Founding Fathers*, ed. Trevor Colbourn. New York: W. W. Norton.

———. 2000. *The Intellectual Origins of Jeffersonian Democracy*. Lanham, MD: Lexington.

Aldrich, John. 1995. *Why Parties? The Origin and Transformation of Party Politics in America*. Chicago: University of Chicago Press.

Aldrich, J. H., C. C. Jillson, and R. K. Wilson. 2002. "Why Congress?: What the Failure of the Continental and the Survival of the Federal Congress Tell Us About the New Institutionalism," in *Party, Process, and Political Change in Congress: New Perspectives on the History of Congress*, ed. D. W. Brady and M. D. McCubbins. Stanford, CA: Stanford University Press.

Allen, Robert. 1988. "The Price of Freehold Land and the Interest Rate in the Seventeenth and Eighteenth Centuries." *Economic History Review* 41 (Feb.): 33–50.

American Reference Library (CD-ROM). 1998. Western Standard Publishing.

Anderson, Fred. 2000. *Crucible of War*. New York: Random House.

Appleby, Joyce. 1992. *Liberalism and Republicanism in the Historical Imagination*. Cambridge, MA: Harvard University Press.

Appleby, J., and T. Ball, eds. 1999. *Jefferson: Political Writings*. Cambridge: Cambridge University Press.

Arago, F. X., and A. O'Connor. 1847–49. *Condorcet: Oeuvres de Condorcet*. 12 vols. Paris: Firmin Didot.

Arrow, Kenneth. 1951. *Social Choice and Individual Values*. New York: Wiley.

Ashley, W. J. 1903. *The Tariff Problem*. London: P. S. King.

——, ed. 1911. *The Federalist*. London: Dent (Everyman).

Austen-Smith, David, and Jeffrey Banks. 1999. *Positive Political Theory*. Ann Arbor: Michigan University Press.

Axelrod, Robert M. 1984. *The Evolution of Cooperation*. New York: Basic.

Bailyn, Bernard. 1967. *The Ideological Origins of the American Revolution*. Cambridge, MA: Belknap.

——, ed. 1993. *The Debate on the Constitution*. 2 vols. New York: Library of America.

Baker, Keith M. 1975. *Condorcet: From Natural Philosophy to Social Mathematics*. Chicago: University of Chicago Press.

Baker, Lynn A., and Samuel H. Dinkin. 1997. "The Senate: An Institution Whose Time Has Gone?" *Journal of Law and Politics* 13: 21–103.

Baker, Ross K. 1995. *House and Senate*. 2d ed. New York: W. W. Norton.

Ball, Terence. 1988. " 'A Republic—If You Can Keep It,' " in *Conceptual Change and the Constitution,* ed. Terence Ball and J. G. A. Pocock, 137–64. Lawrence: University of Kansas Press.

Banning, Lance. 1987. "The Practicable Sphere of a Republic: James Madison, the Constitutional Convention, and the Emergence of Revolutionary Federalism," in *Beyond Confederation: Origins of the Constitution and American National Identity*, ed. Richard Beeman, Stephan Botein, and Edward C. Carter II, 162–87. Chapel Hill: University of North Carolina Press.

——. 1995. *The Sacred Fire of Liberty: James Madison and the Founding of the Federal Republic*. Ithaca, NY: Cornell University Press.

Baugh, Daniel. 1994. "Maritime Strength and Atlantic Commerce: The Uses of a 'Grand Marine Empire,' " in *An Imperial State at War,* ed. Lawrence Stone, 185–223. London: Routledge.

Beard, Charles. 1913. *An Economic Interpretation of the Constitution of the United States*. New York: Macmillan.

——. 1915. *Economic Consequences of Jeffersonian Democracy*. New York: Macmillan.

Beeman, Richard, Stephen Botein, and Edward C. Carter II, eds. 1992. "The Justification of Bicameralism." *International Political Science Review* 13: 101–16.

Bentley, Arthur. 1908. *The Process of Government*. Chicago: University of Chicago Press.

Benton, Wilbourn E., ed. 1986. *1787: Drafting the U. S. Constitution*. 2 vols. College Station: Texas A&M University Press.

Bessette, Joseph M. 1994. *The Mild Voice of Reason: Deliberative Democracy and American National Government*. Chicago: University of Chicago Press.

Bickel, Alexander. 1962. *The Least Dangerous Branch: The Supreme Court at the Bar of Politics*. Indianapolis, IN: Bobbs-Merrill.

Bickford, Charlene, and Kenneth Bowling. 1989. *Birth of the Nation: The First Federal Congress, 1789–91*. Madison, WI: Madison House.

Birch, A. H. 1971. *Representation*. New York: Praeger.

Bourke, Paul. 1975. "The Pluralist Reading of James Madison's Tenth Federalist." *Perspectives in American History* 9: 271–95.

Bowling, Kenneth. 1968. "Politics in the First Federal Congress, 1789–1791." Ph. D. dissertation, University of Wisconsin. Subsequently published by Garland Publishing, New York, 1990.

————. 1971. "Dinner at Jefferson's: A Note on Jacob E. Cooke's 'The Compromise of 1790.'" *William and Mary Quarterly* 28: 629–48.

————. 1988. "A 'Tub to the Whale': The Founding Fathers and the Adoption of the Federal Bill of Rights." *Journal of the Early Republic* 8: 223–51.

————. 1991. *The Creation of Washington, D.C.: The Idea and Location of the American Capitol*. Fairfax, VA: George Mason University Press.

Bowling, Kenneth, and Helen Veit, eds. 1988. *The Diary of William Maclay*. Vol. IX, *Documentary History of the First Federal Congress, 1789–1791*. Baltimore: Johns Hopkins University Press.

Boyd, Julian, ed. 1961. *The Papers of Thomas Jefferson*. Princeton: Princeton University Press.

Brand, Donald R. 1983. "Corporatism, the NRA, and the Oil Industry." *Political Science Quarterly* 98, no. 1: 99–118.

Brant, Irving. 1948. *James Madison: The Nationalist, 1780–1787*. Indianapolis, IN: Bobbs-Merrill.

————. 1950. *James Madison: Father of the Constitution, 1787–1800*. Indianapolis, IN: Bobbs-Merrill.

Brewer, John. 1976. *Party Ideology and Popular Politics at the Accession of George III*. Cambridge: Cambridge University Press.

————. 1988. *The Sinews of Power*. Cambridge: Harvard University Press.

Brock, R. W. 1930. *The Simon Report on India: An Abridgement*. London: Dent.

Brown, Roger H. 1993. *Redeeming the Republic: Federalists, Taxation, and the Origins of the Constitution*. Baltimore: Johns Hopkins University Press.

Bryce, J. 1911 [1888]. *The American Commonwealth*. 2 vols. 4th ed. New York: Macmillan.

Buchanan, J., and G. Tullock. 1962. *Calculus of Consent*. Ann Arbor, University of Michigan Press.

Burnett, Edmund C., ed. 1921–36. *Letters of the Members of the Continental Congress*. 8 vols. Washington, DC: Carnegie Institution.

Burns, James MacGregor. 1963. *The Deadlock of Democracy*. Englewood Cliffs, NJ: Prentice-Hall.

Cain, Bruce E., and W. T. Jones. 1989. "Madison's Theory of Representation," in *The Federalist Papers and the New Institutionalism,* ed. Bernard Grofman and Donald Wittman. New York: Agathon.

Cain, Michael J. G., and Keith L. Dougherty. 1999. "Suppressing Shays' Rebellion: Collective Action and Constitutional Design under the Articles of Confederation." *Journal of Theoretical Politics* 11 (2): 233–60.

Calomiris, Charles W. 1988. "Institutional Failure, Monetary Scarcity, and the

Depreciation of the Continental." *Journal of Economic History* 48, no. 1 (Mar.): 47–68.

Cappon, L. J. 1959. *The Adams-Jefferson Letters.* Chapel Hill: University of North Carolina Press.

Carey, George W. 1978. "Separation of Powers and the Madisonian Model: A Reply to Critics." *American Political Science Review* 72 (Mar.): 151–64.

———. 1989. *The Federalist: Design for a Constitutional Republic.* Urbana: University of Illinois Press.

Ceaser, James W. 1979. *Presidential Selection: Theory and Development.* Princeton: Princeton University Press.

Chandler, Alfred D., Jr. 1977. *The Visible Hand: The Managerial Revolution in American Business.* Cambridge, MA: Harvard University Press.

———. 1990. *The Scale and Scope: The Dynamics of Industrial Capitalism.* Cambridge, MA: Belknap.

Chappell, Henry W., Jr., and William R. Keech. 1989. "Electoral Institutions in *The Federalist Papers*: A Contemporary Perspective," in *The Federalist Papers and the New Institutionalism,* ed. Bernard Grofman and Donald Wittman. New York: Agathon.

Choper, Jesse. 1977. "The Scope of National Power vis-a-vis the States: The Dispensability of Judicial Review." *Yale Law Journal* 86: 1552–1621.

———. 1980. *Judicial Review and the National Political Process: A Functional Reconsideration of the Role of the Supreme Court.* Chicago: University of Chicago Press.

Chown, John F. 1994. *The History of Money.* London: Routledge.

Clinton, Joshua, and Adam Meirowitz. 2002. "The Fruit of Jefferson's Dinner Party: Roll Call Analysis of the Compromise of 1790 with Substantive and Relational Constraints." Manuscript, Princeton University.

Clough, A. H., ed. 1899. *Plutarch's Lives.* Boston: Little, Brown.

Cochran, Thomas C. 1932. *New York in the Confederation: An Economic Study.* Philadelphia: University of Pennsylvania Press.

Collier, Christopher. 1971. *Roger Sherman's Connecticut: Yankee Politics and the American Revolution.* Middletown, CT: Wesleyan University Press.

Condorcet, M. J. A. N. de Caritat, Marquis de. 1785. *Essai sur l'application de l'analyse à la probabilité des décisions rendues à la pluralité des voix.* Paris: Imprimerie Royale.

———. 1794. *Esquisse d'un tableau historique des Progres de l'esprit humain.* Paris: Gravier.

Cooke, Jacob. 1970. "The Compromise of 1790." *William and Mary Quarterly* 27: 523–45.

Corwin, Edward S. 1925. "The Progress of Constitutional Theory between the Declaration of Independence and the Meeting of the Philadelphia Convention." *American Historical Review* 30 (Apr.): 511–36.

Coutel, C. 1988. "Décembre 1792: Les objections au *Rapport sur l'instruction publique*: Réponses de Condorcet," in *Condorcet: mathématicien, économiste, philosophe, homme politique,* ed. P. Crépel and C. Gilain, 251–61. Paris: Minerve.

Cox, Gary W., and Mathew D. McCubbins. 1993. *Legislative Leviathan: Party Government in the U. S. House.* Berkeley: University of California Press.

Crafts, Nick. 1994. "The Industrial Revolution," in *The Economic History of Britain since 1700,* vol. 1, ed. Roderick Floud and Deirde McCloskey, 44–59. Cambridge: Cambridge University Press.

Dahl, Robert A. 1956. *A Preface to Democratic Theory.* New Haven: Yale University Press.

———. 2002. *How Democratic Is the American Constitution?* New Haven: Yale University Press.

Darnton, Robert. 1997. "Condorcet and the Craze for America in France," in *Franklin and Condorcet,* ed. Jonathan Brown, 27–39. Philadelphia: American Philosophical Society.

Davis, Joseph L. 1977. *Sectionalism in American Politics, 1774–1787.* Madison: University of Wisconsin Press.

The Debate on the Constitution: Federalist and Antifederalist Speeches, Articles, and Letters during the Struggle over Ratification. 1993. 2 vols. New York: Library of America.

De Pauw, Linda Grant. 1966. *The Eleventh Pillar: New York State and the Federal Constitution.* Ithaca, NY: Cornell University Press.

Destutt de Tracy, Antoine-Louis-Claude. 1798. *Commentaire sur l'esprit des lois de Montesquieu.* Paris: Desoer.

Diamond, Martin. 1959. "Democracy and the Federalist: A Reconsideration of the Framers' Intent." *American Political Science Review,* 53: 52–68.

Dicey, A.V. 1939 [1885]. *Introduction to the Study of the Law of the Constitution.* 9th ed. London: Macmillan.

Dodd, Lawrence C., and Calvin Jillson, eds. 1994. *The Dynamics of American Politics: Approaches and Interpretations.* Boulder: Westview.

Dougherty, Keith L. 1999. "Public Goods and Private Interests: An Explanation for State Compliance with Federal Requisitions, 1775–1789," in *Public Choice Interpretations of American Economic History,* ed. Jac Heckelman et al. Dordrecht: Kluwer Academic.

———. 2001. *Collective Action under the Articles of Confederation.* New York: Cambridge University Press.

Dougherty, Keith L., and Michael J. G. Cain. 1997. "Marginal Cost Sharing and the Articles of Confederation." *Public Choice* 90: 201–13.

Downs, Anthony. 1957. *An Economic Theory of Democracy.* New York: Harper and Row.

Duer, William Alexander. 1833. *Outlines of the Constitutional Jurisprudence of the United States.* New York: Collins and Hannay.

Eidelberg, Paul. 1968. *The Philosophy of the American Constitution.* New York: Free Press.

Elkins, Stanley, and Eric McKitrick. 1993. *The Age of Federalism: The Early American Republic, 1788–1800*. Oxford: Oxford University Press.

Ellis, Joseph. 2000. *Founding Brothers*. New York: Alfred A. Knopf.

Ely, John Hart. 1980. *Democracy and Distrust: A Theory of Judicial Review*. Cambridge, MA: Harvard University Press.

Engeman, Thomas S., Edward J. Erler, and Thomas B. Hofeller. 1988. *The Federalist Concordance*. Chicago: University of Chicago Press.

Engermann, Stanley. 1994. "Mercantilism and Overseas Trade," in *The Economic History of Britain since 1700*, vol. 1., ed. Roderick Floud and Deirde McCloskey, 182–204. Cambridge: Cambridge University Press.

Epstein, David. 1984. *The Political Theory of the Federalist*. Chicago: University of Chicago Press.

Epstein, Richard A. 1993. "*The Federalist Papers*: From Practical Politics to High Principle." *Harvard Journal of Law and Public Policy* 16, no. 1: 13–21.

Eubanks, Cecil L. 1989. "New York: Federalism and the Political Economy of Union," in *Ratifying the Constitution*, ed. Michael Allen Gillespie and Michael Lienesch. Lawrence: University of Kansas Press.

Fabbrini, S. 1999. "American Democracy from a European Perspective." *Annual Review of Political Science* 2: 465–91.

Farrand, Max, ed. 1966. *The Records of the Federal Convention of 1787*. 4 vols. New Haven: Yale University Press.

Ferguson, E. James. 1961. *The Power of the Purse: A History of American Public Finance, 1776–1790*. Chapel Hill: University of North Carolina Press.

———. 1969. "The Nationalists of 1781–1783 and the Economic Interpretation of the Constitution," *Journal of American History* 56, no. 2 (September): 241–61.

Finer, S. E. 1997. *A History of Government*. 3 vols. Oxford: Oxford University Press.

Fiorina, Morris P. 1989. *Congress: Keystone of the Washington Establishment*. 2d ed. New Haven: Yale University Press.

Fiorina, Morris P., and Kenneth A. Shepsle. 1989. "Formal Theories of Leadership: Agents, Agenda-Setters, and Entrepreneurs." In *Leadership and Politics*, ed. Bryan D. Jones. Lawrence: University Press of Kansas.

Ford, Henry Jones. 1898. *The Rise and Growth of American Politics*. New York: Macmillan.

Ford, Worthington Chauncey. 1904. "Alexander Hamilton's Notes in the Federal Convention of 1787." *American Historical Review*. 10: 97–101.

Freeman, E. A. 1863. *History of Federal Government from the Foundation of the Achaian League to the Disruption of the United States*. Vol. 1, *General Introduction and History of Greek Federations*. London: Macmillan.

Freeman, Joanne, ed. 2001. *Hamilton: Writings*. New York: Library of America.

Friedman, Barry. 1993. "Dialogue and Judicial Review." *Michigan Law Review* 91: 577–682.

Galligan, Brian. 1995. *A Federal Republic: Australia's Constitutional System of Government*. Melbourne: Cambridge University Press.

Galloway, Joseph. 1972 [1780]. *Historical and Political Reflections on the Rise and Progress of the American Rebellion.* Ed. Merrill Jensen. New York: Johnson Reprint.

Gay, Sidney Howard. 1884. *James Madison.* Boston and New York: Houghton, Mifflin.

Gibbon, Edward. 1994 [1781]. *The History of the Decline and Fall of the Roman Empire.* Ed. D. Womersley. Harmondsworth, UK: Penguin.

Giesecke, Albert Anthony. 1970 [1910]. *American Commercial Legislation before 1789.* New York: Burt Franklin.

Gillespie, Michael Allen, and Michael Lienesch, eds. 1989. *Ratifying the Constitution.* Lawrence: University of Kansas Press.

Gladstone, W. E. 1878. "Kin beyond Sea." *North American Review* 127, no. 264: 179–212.

Grofman, Bernard, and Donald Wittman, eds. 1989. *The Federalist Papers and the New Institutionalism.* New York: Agathon.

Gross, Donald R. 1982. "Bicameralism and the Theory of Voting." *Western Political Quarterly* 35: 511–26.

Gwyn, William B. 1965. *The Meaning of the Separation of Powers.* New Orleans: Tulane University Press.

Hamilton, Alexander. 1962–. *The Papers of Alexander Hamilton.* Ed. Harold C. Syrett. New York: Columbia University Press.

Hamilton, Alexander, James Madison, and John Jay. 1961 [1788]. *The Federalist Papers.* Ed. Clinton Rossiter. New York: Mentor.

———. 1961b. *The Federalist.* Ed. Jacob E. Cooke. Middletown, CT: Wesleyan University Press.

Hammond, Thomas H., and Gary J. Miller. 1987. "The Core of the Constitution." *American Political Science Review* 72: 472–82.

Handlin, Oscar, and Mary Flug Handlin. 1969. *Commonwealth: A Study of the Role of Government in the American Economy: Massachusetts, 1774–1861.* Cambridge, MA: Belknap.

Hardin, Russell. 1982. *Collective Action.* Baltimore: Johns Hopkins University Press.

Haynes, George H. 1960 [1938]. *The Senate of the United States: Its History and Practice.* New York: Russell and Russell.

Henry, Patrick. 1969 [1891]. *Patrick Henry: Life Correspondence and Speeches.* Ed. William Wirt Henry. New York: Burt Franklin.

Herring, Edward Pendleton. 1929. *Group Representation before Congress.* Baltimore: Johns Hopkins University Press.

Hobson, Charles F. 1979. "The Negative on State Laws: James Madison, the Constitution, and the Crisis of Republican Government." *William and Mary Quarterly* 36, no. 2: 215–35.

Holmes, Stephen. 1990. "The Secret History of Self-Interest," in *Beyond Self-Interest,* ed. Jane J. Mansbridge. Chicago: University of Chicago Press.

Höwe, Daniel W. 1987. "The Political Psychology of The Federalist." *William and Mary Quarterly* 44 (July): 485–509.

Hume, David. 1978 [1739–40]. *A Treatise of Human Nature.* Ed. L. A. Selby Biggs. Oxford: Clarendon.

———. 1985 [1777]. *Essays, Moral, Political, and Literary.* Indianapolis: Liberty Classics.

———. 1994 [1741–42]. *Political Essays.* Ed. K. Haakonssen. Cambridge: Cambridge University Press. (Madison is believed to have used the edition of 1758.)

Hunt, Galliard. 1900. *The Writings of James Madison.* New York: G.P. Putnam's Sons.

Hutcheson, F. 1993. *On Human Nature.* Ed. T. Mautner. Cambridge: Cambridge University Press.

Hutson, James H. 1987. "Riddles of the Federal Constitution." *William and Mary Quarterly* 44, no. 3 (July): 411–23.

Jackson, Robert J., and Doreen Jackson. 1998. *Politics in Canada.* 4th ed. Scarborough, Ont.: Prentice Hall Allyn and Bacon Canada.

Jardin, Andre. 1988. *Tocqueville: A Biography.* New York: Farrar, Straus and Giroux.

Jefferson, Thomas. 1781. "Notes on the State of Virginia." Query XIII in *The Portable Thomas Jefferson,* ed. Merrill D. Peterson, 153–176. New York: Penguin, 1975.

———. 1789. "Letter to James Madison," in *Jefferson: Political Writings,* ed. J. Appleby and T. Ball, 593–98. Cambridge: Cambridge University Press, 1999.

———. 1818. *Anas.* The text of the *Anas* is available at the Electronic Text Center, University of Virginia Library (http://etext.lib.virginia.edu/toc/modeng/public/JefBvo12.html)

———. 1950–. *The Papers of Thomas Jefferson.* Ed. Julian P. Boyd. Princeton: Princeton University Press.

Jensen, Merrill. 1936. "The Cession of the Old Northwest." *Mississippi Valley Historical Review* 23: 27–48.

———. 1939. "The Creation of the National Domain." *Journal of American History* 26: 323–42.

———. 1950. *The New Nation: A History of the United States during the Confederation, 1781–89.* New York: Alfred A. Knopf.

———. 1959. *Notes on the State of Virginia The Articles of Confederation: An Interpretation of the Social-Constitutional History of the American Revolution, 1774–1781.* Madison: University of Wisconsin Press.

———, ed. 1976–. *The Documentary History of the Ratification of the Constitution.* Madison: State Historical Society of Wisconsin.

Jillson, Calvin C. 1988. *Constitution Making: Conflict and Consensus in the Federal Convention of 1787.* New York: Agathon.

Jillson, Calvin C., and Thornton Anderson. 1978. "Voting Bloc Analysis in the Constitutional Convention: Implications for an Interpretation of the Connecticut Compromise." *Western Political Quarterly* 31 (Dec.): 535–47.

Jillson, Calvin C., and Cecil L. Eubanks. 1984. "The Political Structure of Constitution Making: The Federal Convention of 1787." *American Journal of Political Science* 28 (Aug.): 435–58.

Jillson, Calvin, and Rick K. Wilson. 1994. *Congressional Dynamics: Structure, Coordination, and Choice in the First American Congress, 1774–1789.* Stanford: Stanford University Press.

Jones, Alice Hanson. 1980. *Wealth of a Nation to Be: The American Colonies on the Eve of the Revolution.* New York: Columbia University Press.

Jones, Tom. 1971. *Whitehall Diary.* Vol. III, *Ireland 1918–1925.* Ed. K. Middlemas. London: Oxford University Press.

Journals of the Continental Congress [JCC]. 1774–89. Ed. Worthington C. Ford et al. Washington, DC. <http://memory.loc.gov/ammem/amlaw/lwjc.html>.

Kaminski, John, and Gaspare Saladino. 1988. *Commentaries on the Constitution: Public and Private.* 5 vols. Madison: State Historical Society of Wisconsin.

Kelly, Alfred H., Winfred A. Harbison, and Herman Belz. 1983. *The American Constitution.* New York: Norton.

Kennedy, Paul. 1987. *The Rise and Fall of the Great Powers.* New York: Random House.

Kenyon, Cecilia. 1955. "Men of Little Faith: The Antifederalists on the Nature of Representative Government." *William and Mary Quarterly,* third ser., 12: 3–43.

Kernell, Samuel. 1977. "Toward Understanding 19th Century Congressional Careers: Ambition, Competition, and Rotation." *American Journal of Political Science* 21: 669–93.

Kerr, Clara H. 1895. *The Origin and Development of the United States Senate.* Ithaca, NY: Andrus and Church.

Ketcham, Ralph. 1971. *James Madison: A Biography.* Charlottesville: University Press of Virginia.

Keynes, John Maynard. 1921. *A Treatise on Probability.* Vol. 8 of *Collected Writings.* London: Macmillan.

Keyssar, Alexander. 2000. *The Right to Vote: The Contested History of Democracy in the United States.* New York: Basic.

Kiewiet, D. Roderick, and Mathew D. McCubbins. 1991. *The Logic of Delegation.* Chicago: University of Chicago Press.

Kingdon, John W. 1995. *Agendas, Alternatives, and Public Policies.* 2d ed. New York: HarperCollins.

Kramer, Larry D. 2000. "Putting the Politics Back into the Political Safeguards of Federalism." *Columbia Law Review* 100: 215–93.

———. 2001. "The Supreme Court 2000 Term: Foreword: We the Court." *Harvard Law Review* 115: 4–168.

Krammick, Isaac. 1990 [1968]. *Republicanism and Bourgeois Radicalism.* Ithaca, NY: Cornell University Press.

———. 1992. *Bolingbroke and His Circle.* Ithaca, NY: Cornell University Press.

Kurland, Philip B., and Ralph Lerner, eds. *The Founders' Constitution.* Chicago: University of Chicago Press, 1987.

Latham, Earl. 1952. *The Group Basis of Politics*. New York: Octagon.

Latham, Sir John. 1952. "Interpretation of the Constitution," in *Essays on the Australian Constitution,* ed. R. Else-Mitchell, 1–50. Sydney: Law Book Co. of Australasia.

Lee, Frances E., and Bruce I. Oppenheimer. 1999. *Sizing up the Senate: The Unequal Consequences of Equal Representation.* Chicago: University of Chicago Press.

Levmore, Saul. 1992. "Bicameralism: When Are Two Decisions Better than One?" *International Review of Law and Economics* 12: 145–62.

Lichbach, Mark Irving. 1996. *The Cooperators' Dilemma.* Ann Arbor: University of Michigan Press.

Lindert, Peter. 1994. "Unequal Living Standards," in *The Economic History of Britain since 1700.* Vol. 1. Ed. Roderick Floud and Deirde McCloskey, 357–386. Cambridge: Cambridge University Press.

Lippmann, Walter. 1922. *Public Opinion.* New York: Harcourt, Brace.

Lipset, S. M., and S. Rokkan. 1967. *Party Systems and Voter Alignments.* New York: Free Press.

List, C., I. McLean, J. Fishkin, and R. Luskin. 2000. "Can Deliberation Induce Greater Preference Structuration? Evidence from Deliberative Opinion Polls." Paper to APSA Conference 2000. Available online at *http: //pro. harvard. edu/abstracts/008/008003McLeanIain. htm.*

Lutz, Donald S. 1984. "The Relative Influence of European Writers on Late Eighteenth-Century American Political Thought." *American Political Science Review* 78 (Mar.): 189–97.

Madison, James. 1969–85. *The Papers of James Madison.* 15 vols. Various eds. (William M. E. Rachel, Robert A. Rutland, Charles F. Hobson, and others). Chicago: University of Chicago Press; Charlottesville: University Press of Virginia.

———. 1966. *Notes of debates in the Federal Convention of 1787, reported by James Madison.* (Originally published in 1840 in *The Papers of James Madison.*) Athens, Ohio: Ohio University Press.

Mahoney, Dennis J. 1987. "The Newer Science of Politics: *The Federalist* and American Political Science in the Progressive Era," in *Saving the Revolution: The Federalist Papers and the American Founding,* ed. Charles R. Kessler, 250–64. New York: Free Press.

Main, Jackson Turner. 1973. *The Sovereign States, 1775–1783.* New York: New Viewpoints.

Malone, Dumas. 1951. *Jefferson and the Rights of Man.* Boston: Little, Brown.

Malthus, Thomas. 1970 [1798]. *An Essay on the Principle of Population.* London: Penguin.

Marchione, Margherita. 1975. *Philip Mazzei: Jefferson's 'zealous Whig.'* New York: American Institute of Italian Studies.

Matson, Cathy D. 1996. "The Revolution, The Constitution, and the New Nation," in *The Cambridge Economic History of the United States.* Vol. 1, *The Colo-*

nial Era, ed. Stanley L. Engerman and Robert E. Gallman. New York: Cambridge University Press.

Matthews, Richard K. 1995. *If Men Were Angels: James Madison and the Heartless Empire of Reason*. Lawrence: University Press of Kansas.

Mayer, David. 1994. *The Constitutional Thought of Thomas Jefferson*. Charlottesville: University Press of Virginia.

McCormick, Richard P. 1964. *New Jersey from Colony to State*. New Brunswick: Rutgers University Press.

McCoy, Drew R. 1980a. "Jefferson and Madison on Malthus: Population Growth in Jeffersonian Political Economy." *Virginia Magazine of History and Biography* 88 (June): 259–76.

———. 1980b. *The Elusive Republic*. Williamsburg, VA: University of North Carolina Press.

———. 1989. *The Last of the Fathers: James Madison and the Republican Legacy*. Cambridge: Cambridge University Press.

McCusker, John J., and Russell Menard. 1985. *The Economy of British America, 1607–1789*. Chapel Hill: University of North Carolina Press.

McDonald, Forrest. 1958. *We the People: The Economic Origins of the Constitution*. Chicago: University of Chicago Press.

———. 1979. *Alexander Hamilton: A Biography*. New York: Norton.

———. 1985. *Novus Ordo Seculorum: The Intellectual Origins of the Constitution*. Lawrence: University Press of Kansas.

———. 2000. *States' Rights and the Union: Imperium in Imperio, 1789–1876*. Lawrence: University Press of Kansas.

McGrath, David. 1983. "James Madison and Social Choice Theory. The Possibility of Republicanism." Unpublished Ph.D. dissertation, University of Maryland.

McGuire, Robert A., and Robert L. Ohsfeldt. 1986. "An Economic Model of Voting Behavior over Specific Issues at the Constitutional Convention of 1787." *Journal of Economic History* 46, no. 1 (Mar.): 79–111.

McKelvey, Richard D. 1976. "Intransitivities in Multi-dimensional Voting Models and Some Implications for Agenda Control." *Journal of Economic Theory* 12: 472–82.

McKelvey, Richard D., and Norman Schofield. 1986. "Structural Instability of the Core." *Journal of Mathematical Economics* 15 (Dec.): 267–84.

McLean, Iain. 2001. *Rational Choice and British Politics*. Oxford: Oxford University Press.

McLean, Iain, and Fiona Hewitt. 1994. *Condorcet: Foundations of Social Choice and Political Theory*. Aldershot, UK: Edward Elgar.

McLean, Iain, and Arnold Urken. 1992. "Did Jefferson or Madison Understand Condorcet's Theory of Social Choice?" *Public Choice* 73 (Dec.): 445–57.

McSweeney, Edward F. 1917. "New England's Opportunities and Needs." *American Industries* 17, no. 7 (Feb.): 27.

Merriam, Charles. 1931. *New Aspects of Politics*. Chicago: University of Chicago Press.

Meyers, Marvin, ed. 1973. *The Mind of the Founder: Sources of the Political Thought of James Madison*. Ed. L. W. Levy and A. F. Young. The American Heritage Series. Indianapolis: Bobbs-Merrill.

Miller, Eugene F., ed. 1987 [1741–77]. *David Hume: Essays Moral, Political, and Literary*. Indianapolis, IN: Liberty Classics.

Miller, Gary J., Thomas H. Hammond, and Charles Kile. 1996. "Bicameralism and the Core: An Experimental Test." *Legislative Studies Quarterly* 2 (Feb.): 83–103.

Miller, Gary, and Norman Schofield. 2003. "Activists and Partisan Realignment." *American Political Science Review* 97 (May): in press.

Miller, William Lee. 1992. *The Business of May Next: James Madison and the Founding*. Charlottesville: University Press of Virginia.

Moe, Terry M. 1981. "Toward a Broader View of Interest Groups." *Journal of Politics* 43, no. 2: 531–43.

———. 1984. "The New Economics of Organization." *American Journal of Political Science* 28, no. 4: 739–77.

Monroe, James. 1898. *The Writings of James Monroe*. Ed. Stanislaus Hamilton. New York: G. P. Putnam's Sons.

Montesquieu, Charles-Louis de Secondat, baron de La Brède et de. 1989. *The Spirit of the Laws*. Ed. Anne Cohler, Basia Miller, and Harold Stone. Cambridge: Cambridge University Press.

Monypenny, W. F., and G. E. Buckle. 1910–20. *The Life of Benjamin Disraeli, Earl of Beaconsfield*. 6 vols. London: John Murray.

Morgan, Robert J. 1974. "Madison's Theory of Representation in the Tenth Federalist." *Journal of Politics* 36: 852–85.

Morris, Richard B. 1987. *The Forging of the Union: 1781–1789*. New York: Harper and Row.

Morris, Robert. 1973–. *Papers of Robert Morris*. Ed. E. James Ferguson. Pittsburgh: University of Pittsburgh Press.

Mosteller, F., and D. Wallace. 1984. *Applied Bayesian and Classical Inference: The Case of the Federalist Papers*. New York: Springer-Verlag. (Originally published in 1964 as *Inference and Disputed Authorship: The Federalist*.)

Mouw, Calvin, and Michael MacKuen. 1992. "The Strategic Agenda in Legislative Politics." *American Political Science Review* 86, no. 1 (Mar.): 67–105.

Mueller, Dennis C., ed. 1997. *Perspectives on Public Choice: A Handbook*. New York: Cambridge University Press.

Murrin, Mary R. 1969. "The Nationalists of 1781–1783 and the Economic Interpretation of the Constitution." *Journal of American History* 56: 241–61.

———. 1987. *To Save This State from Ruin: New Jersey and the Creation of the United States Constitution, 1776–1789*. Trenton: New Jersey Historical Commission.

Nelson, William E. 1987. "Reason and Compromise in the Establishment of the Federal Constitution, 1787–1801." *William and Mary Quarterly* 44, no. 2 (Apr.): 458–84.

Nettels, Curtis P. 1962. *The Emergence of a National Economy, 1775–1815.* New York: Holt, Rinehart, and Winston.

Nevins, Allan. 1924. *The American States during and after the Revolution, 1775–1789.* New York: Macmillan.

Newell, Margaret Ellen. 2000. "The Birth of New England in the Atlantic Economy: From Its Beginning to 1770," in *Engines of Enterprise: An Economic History of New England,* ed. Peter Temin, 11–68. Cambridge, MA: Harvard University Press.

Norberg, Kathryn. 1994. "The French Fiscal Crisis of 1788 and the Financial Origins of the Revolution of 1789," in *Fiscal Crisis, Liberty, and Representative Government 1450–1789,* ed. Philip Hoffman and Kathryn Norberg, 253–98. Stanford, CA: Stanford University Press.

North, Douglass, and Barry Weingast. 1989. "Constitutions and Commitment: The Evolution of Institutions Governing Public Choice in Seventeenth Century England." *Journal of Economic History* 49 (Dec.): 803–32.

Nozick, Robert. 1974. *Anarchy, State, and Utopia.* Oxford: Blackwell.

Nye, John. 1992. "Guerre, Commerce, Guerre Commercial: L'economie politique des echanges franco-anglais." *Annales: Economies, Societes, Civilisations* 3 (May): 613–32.

O'Brien, Patrick. 1988. "The Political Economy of British Taxation 1660–1815." *The Economic History Review* 41 (Feb.): 1–32.

Odegard, Peter. 1928. *Pressure Politics: The Story of the Anti-Saloon League.* New York: Octagon.

Oliver, F. S. 1906. *Alexander Hamilton: An Essay on American Union.* London: Nelson.

———. 1914. *What Federalism Is Not.* London: John Murray.

Olson, Mancur. 1965. *The Logic of Collective Action.* Cambridge, MA: Harvard University Press.

Onuf, Peter S. 1977. "Toward Federalism: Virginia, Congress, and the Western Lands." *William and Mary Quarterly* 34, no. 3: 353–74.

———. 1983. *The Origins of the Federal Republic: Jurisdictional Controversies in the United States, 1775–1787.* Philadelphia: University of Pennsylvania Press.

———. 1988. "State Sovereignty and the Making of the Constitution," in *Conceptual Change and the Constitution,* ed. Terence Ball and J. G. A. Pocock, 78–98. Lawrence: University Press of Kansas.

———. 1989. "Reflections on the Founding: Constitutional Historiography in Bicentennial Perspective." *William and Mary Quarterly* 46, no. 2 (Apr.): 341–75.

Ordeshook, Peter C. 1996. "Russia's Party System: Is Russian Federalism Viable?" *Post-Soviet Affairs* 12, no. 3: 145–217.

Ordeshook, Peter C., and Olga Shvetsova. 1995. "If Madison and Hamilton Were Merely Lucky, What Hope Is There for Russian Federalism?" *Constitutional Political Economy* 6, no. 2: 107–26.

Ostrogorski, M. 1964. *Democracy and the Organization of Political Parties*. Ed. Seymour Martin Lipset. Chicago: Quadrangle.

Ostrom, Elinor, Roy Gardner, and James Walker. 1994. *Rules, Games and Common-Pool Resources*. Ann Arbor: University of Michigan Press.

Ostrom, Vincent. 1987. *The Political Theory of a Compound Republic*. Lincoln: University of Nebraska Press.

Pangle, Thomas L. 1988. *The Spirit of Modern Republicanism*. Chicago: University of Chicago Press.

Peters, William. 1987. *A More Perfect Union*. New York: Crown.

Peterson, Merrill D., ed. 1975. *The Portable Thomas Jefferson*. New York: Penguin.

———. ed. 1984. *Thomas Jefferson: Writings*. New York: Library of America.

Petrocik, John. 1996. "Issue Ownership in Presidential Elections, with a 1980 Case Study." *American Journal of Political Science* 40 (Aug.): 825–51.

Pierson, Paul. 2000. "Increasing Returns, Path Dependence, and the Study of Politics." *American Political Science Review* 94, no. 2 (June): 251–67.

Pisani, Donald J. 1987. "Promotion and Regulation: Constitutionalism and the American Economy. *Journal of American History* 74, no. 3 (Dec.): 740–68.

Pitkin, Hanna Fenichel. 1967. *The Concept of Representation*. Berkeley: University of California Press.

Plumb, John H. 1967. *The Growth of Political Stability in England: 1675–1725*. London: Macmillan.

Polishook, Irwin H. 1969. *Rhode Island and the Union, 1774–1795*. Evanston: Northwestern University Press.

Polsby, Nelson. 1968. "The Institutionalization of the House of Representatives." *American Political Science Review* 62: 144–68.

Poole, Keith T., and Howard Rosenthal. 2000. *Congress: A Political-Economic History of Roll Call Voting*. Oxford: Oxford University Press.

Popper, Karl. 1959. *The Logic of Scientific Discovery*. London: Hutchinson.

Porter, Roy. 2000. *Enlightenment: Britain and the Creation of the Modern World*. London: Allen Lane.

Quick, J., and R. Garran. 1901. *The Annotated Constitution of the Australian Commonwealth*. Sydney: Legal.

Rakove, Jack. 1990. *James Madison and the Creation of the American Republic*. Glenview, IL: Harper Collins.

———. 1996. *Original Meanings: Politics and Ideas in the Making of the Constitution*. New York: Alfred A. Knopf.

———. 2000. "Madison Theorizing." Unpublished MS, Stanford University.

———. 2002. "Judicial Power in the Constitutional Theory of James Madison." *William and Mary Law Review* 43, no. 4: 1513–47.

———, ed. 1990b. *Interpreting the Constitution: The Debate over Original Intent*. Boston: Northeastern University Press.

———, ed. 1999. *James Madison: Writings*. New York: Library of America.

Randall, Willard S. 1993. *Thomas Jefferson: A Life*. New York: Holt Rinehart.

Rice, Stuart Arthur. 1924. *Farmers and Workers in American Politics*. New York: Columbia University Studies in the Social Sciences.

Riesman, Janet A. 1987. "Money, Credit, and Federalist Political Economy," in *Beyond Confederation: Origins of the Constitution and American National Identity*, ed. Richard Beeman, Stephen Botein, and Edward Carter III, 128–61. Chapel Hill: University of North Carolina Press.

Riker, William H. 1964. *Federalism: Origin, Operation, Significance*. Boston: Little, Brown.

———. 1980. "Implications from the Disequilibrium of Majority Rule for the Study of Institutions." *American Political Science Review* 74 (Dec.): 432–46.

———. 1982. *Liberalism against Populism: A Confrontation between the Theory of Democracy and the Theory of Social Choice*. Prospect Heights, IL: Waveland.

———. 1987. *The Development of American Federalism*. Boston: Kluwer Academic.

———. 1991. "Why Negative Campaigning Is Rational: The Rhetoric of the Ratification Campaign of 1787–1788." *American Political Development* 5 (fall): 224–83.

———. 1992. "The Justification of Bicameralism." *International Political Science Review* 13, no. 1: 101–16.

———. 1996. *The Strategy of Rhetoric: Campaigning for the American Constitution*. New Haven: Yale University Press.

Riley, Johnathan. 2001. "Imagining Another Madisonian Republic." in John Ferejohn, Jack N. Rakove and Jonathan Riley, eds., *Constitutional Culture and Democratic Rule,* 170–204. Cambridge: Cambridge University Press.

Risjord, Norman. 1976. "The Compromise of 1790: New Evidence on the Dinner Table Bargain." *William and Mary Quarterly* 33: 309–14.

Robbins, Caroline. 1954. " 'When it is that Colonies may Rebel': An Analysis of the Environment and Politics of Francis Hutcheson." *William and Mary Quarterly*, 3d ser., 11: 214–51.

Robertson, David Brian. 1988. "Policy Entrepreneurs and Policy Divergence: John R. Commons and William Beveridge." *Social Service Review* 62, no. 3 (Sept.): 504–31.

———. 2000. *Capital, Labor, and State: The Battle for American Labor Markets from the Civil War to the New Deal*. Lanham, MD: Rowman and Littlefield.

Robertson, Ross M., and Gary M. Walton. 1977. *History of the American Economy*. 4th ed. New York: Harcourt Brace Jovanovich.

Rogers, Lindsay. 1926. *The American Senate*. New York: A. A. Knopf.

Rogowski, Ronald. 1989. *Commerce and Coalitions*. Princeton: Princeton University Press.

Rohde, David W. 1991. *Parties and Leaders in the Postreform House*. Chicago: University of Chicago Press.

Rosen, Gary. 1999. *American Compact: James Madison and the Problem of Founding*. Lawrence: University Press of Kansas.

Rossiter, Clinton, ed. 1961. *The Federalist Papers by Alexander Hamilton, James Madison, and John Jay*. New York: New American Library.

Rothschild, Emma. 2001. *Economic Sentiments.* Cambridge, MA: Harvard University Press.

Saari, Donald. 1997. "Generic Existence of a Core for q-rules." *Economic Theory* 9 (June): 219–60.

Sabatier, Paul A., ed. 1999. *Theories of the Policy Process.* Boulder, CO: Westview.

Sabl, Andrew. 2002. *Ruling Passions: Political Offices and Democratic Ethics.* Princeton: Princeton University Press.

Sanders, Jennings B. [1930] 1971. *The Presidency of the Continental Congress 1774–1789: A Study in American Institutional History.* Reprint. Gloucester, MA: Peter Smith.

Sandler, Todd. 1992. *Collective Action: Theory and Applications.* Ann Arbor: University of Michigan Press.

Schattschneider, E. E. 1942. *Party Government.* New York: Farrar and Rinehart.

Schofield, Norman. 1978. "Instability of Simple Dynamic Games." *Review of Economic Studies* 45 (Oct.): 475–94.

———. 2002a. "Evolution of the Constitution." *British Journal of Political Science* 32 (Jan.): 1–20.

———. 2002b. "Quandaries of War and Union." *Politics and Society* 30 (Mar.): 5–49.

———. 2003. "Consitutional Quandaries and Critical Elections." *Politics, Philosophy and Economics* 2 (Feb.): 5–36.

Schofield, Roger. 1994. "British Population Change, 1700–1871," in *The Economic History of Britain since 1700.* Vol. 1. Ed. Roderick Floud and Deirde McCloskey, 60–95. Cambridge: Cambridge University Press.

Schwartz, Thomas. 1989. "Publius and Public Choice," in *The Federalist Papers and the New Institutionalism,* ed. Bernard Grofman and Donald Wittman. New York: Agathon.

Shepsle, Kenneth A., and Mark S. Bonchek. 1997. *Analyzing Politics: Rationality, Behavior, and Institutions.* New York: Norton.

Sidgwick, H. 1996 [1891]. *The Elements of Politics.* 3d ed. Bristol: Thoemmes.

Sinclair, Barbara. 1995. *Legislators, Leaders, and Lawmaking.* Baltimore: Johns Hopkins University Press.

Sloan, Herbert E. 1995. *Principle and Interest: Thomas Jefferson and the Problem of Debt.* New York: Oxford University Press.

Slonim, Shlomo. 2000. "Securing States' Interests at the 1787 Constitutional Convention: A Reassessment." *Studies in American Political Development* 14, no. 1 (spring): 1–19.

Smith, Adam. 1981 [1776]. *An Inquiry into the Nature and Causes of the Wealth of Nations.* Indianapolis, IN: Liberty Fund.

Smith, James Allen. 1907. *The Spirit of American Government.* New York: Macmillan.

Smith, James M., ed. 1995. *The Republic of Letters, Vol. 1.* New York: Norton.

Smith, Paul, et al., eds. 1976–. *Letters of Delegates to Congress, 1774–1789.* 23 vols. Washington, DC: Library of Congress.

Sommerlad, Fiona, and Iain McLean. 1989. *The Political Theory of Condorcet*. Oxford University Social Studies Faculty Centre Working Paper 1/89, Oxford.

South Carolina House of Representatives. 1788. *Debates which arose in the House of Representatives of South Carolina on the Constitution Framed for the United States by a Convention of Delegates Assembled at Philadelphia*. Charleston: City Gazette Printing Office. Evans #21470.

Stasavage, David. 2003. "Credible Commitment in Early Modern Europe: North and Weingast Revisited." *Journal of Law, Economics and Organization*, 18 (1): 155–86.

Stone Sweet, Alec. 2000. *Governing with Judges: Constitutional Politics in Europe*. Oxford: Oxford University Press.

Storing, Herbert J. 1981. *What the Anti-Federalists Were For*. Chicago: University of Chicago Press.

Sundquist, James. 1983. *Dynamics of the Party System*. Washington, DC: Brookings Institution.

Swanstrom, Roy. 1985. *The United States Senate, 1787–1801*. Washington, DC: Government Printing Office.

Swift, Elaine K. 1996. *The Making of an American Senate: Reconstitutive Change in Congress, 1787–1841*. Ann Arbor: University of Michigan Press.

Truman, David. 1951. *The Governmental Process*. New York: A. Knopf.

Tsebelis, George, and Jeannette Money. 1997. *Bicameralism*. New York: Cambridge University Press.

United States. 1910–37. *Journals of the Continental Congress, 1774–1789*. Ed. Worthington Chauncey Ford et al. 34 vols. Washington, DC: Government Printing Office.

Urken, Arnold. 1991. "The Condorcet-Jefferson Connection and the Origins of Social Choice Theory." *Public Choice* 72 (June): 213–36.

U.S. Census Bureau. 1975. *Historical Statistics of the United States*. Washington, DC: Government Printing Office.

Vile, M. J. C. 1967. *Constitutionalism and the Separation of Powers*. Oxford: Clarendon.

Walton, Gary M., and Hugh Rockoff. 1998. *History of the American Economy*. 8th ed. Fort Worth: Dryden.

Walton, Gary M., and James F. Shepard. 1979. *The Economic Rise of Early America*. Cambridge: Cambridge University Press.

Washington, George. 1833–37. *The Writings of George Washington*. Ed. Jared Sparks. Boston: F. Andrews.

———. 1938. *The Writings of George Washington*. Ed. John Fitzpatrick. Washington, DC: Government Printing Office.

Weaver, David R. 1997. "Leadership, Locke, and the Federalist." *American Journal of Political Science*. 41 (Apr.): 420–46.

Wechsler, Herbert. 1954. "The Political Safeguards of Federalism: The Role of the States in the Composition and Selection of the National Government." *Columbia Law Review* 54: 543–60.

Weingast, Barry R. 1995. "The Economic Role of Political Institutions: Market-Preserving Federalism and Economic Development." *Journal of Law, Economics, and Organization* 7, no. 1: 1–31.

Weisberger, Bernard. 2000. *America Afire*. New York: Harper Collins.

Wilentz, Sean. 1992. "Property and Power: Suffrage Reform in the United States, 1787–1860," in *Voting and the Spirit of American Democracy: Essays on the History of Voting and Voting Rights in America,* ed. Donald W. Rogers. Urbana: University of Illinois Press.

Williams, Basil. 1960. *The Whig Supremacy, 1714–1760*. Oxford: Clarendon.

Williams, Melissa. 1998. *Voice, Trust and Money*. Princeton, NJ: Princeton University Press.

Williamson, Oliver. 1983. "Credible Commitments: Using Hostages to Support Exchange." *American Economic Review* 83, no. 4 (Sept.): 519–41.

Wilson, James Q. 1990. "Interests and Deliberation in the American Republic, or, Why James Madison Would Never Have Received the James Madison Award." *PS: Political Science and Politics* (Dec.): 558–62.

Wilson, Woodrow. 1885. *Congressional Government*. Boston: Houghton, Mifflin, and Company.

Witherspoon, John. 1778. *An Address to the Natives of Scotland residing in America*. London: Fielding and Walker.

————. 1982. *Lectures on Moral Philosophy*. Ed. J. Scott. Newark: University of Delaware Press.

Wolfe, Christopher. 1977. "On Understanding the Constitutional Convention of 1787." *Journal of Politics* 39, no. 1 (Feb.): 97–118.

Womersley, David. 2002. *Gibbon and the Watchmen of the Holy City*. Oxford: Oxford University Press.

Wood, Gordon S. 1969. *The Creation of the American Republic*. Chapel Hill: University of North Carolina Press.

————. 1987. "Interests and Disinterestness in the Making of the Constitution," in *Beyond Confederation: Origins of the Constitution and American National Identity*, ed. Richard Beeman, Stephan Botein, and Edward C. Carter II, 69–109. Chapel Hill: University of North Carolina Press.

Yarborough, Beth V., and Robert M. Yarborough. 1991. "Cooperation in the Liberalization of International Trade: After Hegemony, What?" in *International Political Economy: A Reader,* ed. Kendall W. Stiles and Tsuneo Akaha, 157–82. New York: HarperCollins.

Zagarri, Rosemarie. 1987. *The Politics of Size: Representation in the United States, 1776–1850*. Ithaca, NY: Cornell University Press.

Zuckert, Michael P. 1992. "The Virtuous Polity, the Accountable Polity: Liberty and Responsibility in the Federalist." *Publius: The Journal of Federalism* 22: 123–42.

In this index an "f" after a number indicates a separate reference on the next page, and an "ff" indicates separate references on the next two pages. A continuous discussion over two or more pages is indicated by a span of page numbers, e.g., "57–59." *Passim* is used for a cluster of references in close but not consecutive sequence.